WEEK I

SUNDAY, EVENING PRAYER 1

Ant. 1 Let my prayer rise as incense before you.

Psalm 141:1–9

I call upon you, O God; make haste
to help me!
Give ear to my voice, when I call to
you.
Let my prayer rise as incense before you,
and the lifting up of my hands as an
evening sacrifice!

Set a guard over my mouth, O God,
keep watch over the door of my lips!
Do not incline my heart to evil,
that I not busy myself with wicked
deeds
in company with those who work
iniquity;
let me not partake of their dainties!

Let a good person strike or rebuke me
in kindness,
but let the oil of wickedness never
anoint my head;
for my prayer is constantly against
wicked deeds.

When those who do evil are given over
to those who condemn them,
then they shall learn that your word is
true.
As a rock which one holds and shatters
on the ground,
so shall their bones be strewn at the
mouth of the grave.

But my eyes are turned toward you,
O God;
in you I seek refuge; leave me not
defenseless!
Keep me from the trap which evil lays
before me,
and from the snares of my own
wickedness.   Glory* . . .

---

*Glory to you, Source of all Being,
Eternal Word, and Holy Spirit . . .
As it was . . .

Ant. 2 You are my refuge, O God; my portion in the land of the living.

Psalm 142

I cry out with my voice to you, O God,
with my voice I make supplication to
you.
I pour out my complaints before you,
before you I place all my troubles.
When my spirit is faint, you, O God,
know my way!

In the path where I walk
hidden traps surround me.
I look to the right and watch,
but no one takes notice of me;
no human refuge remains for me,
no one cares for my soul.

I cry out to you, O God;
I say, you are my refuge,
my portion in the land of the living.
Give heed to my cry;
for I am brought low, indeed!

Deliver me from those who would
hurt me;
for they are too strong for me!
Bring me out of my distress,
that I may give thanks to your name!
Let your holy ones surround me;
for you will deal graciously with me.
Glory* . . .

Ant. 3 Every tongue will proclaim the glory of God.

Canticle: Philippians 2:6–11

Though he was in the form of God,
Jesus did not count equality with God
something to be grasped at.

But emptied himself
taking the form of a slave,
being born in human likeness.

Being found in human estate,
he humbled himself and became
obedient,
obediently accepting death,
even death on a cross!

Therefore God has highly exalted him
and bestowed on him the name
above every other name.

So that at the name of Jesus
every knee should bow, —

in heaven, on the earth,
and under the earth,
and every tongue proclaim
to the glory of God:
JESUS CHRIST IS LORD!   Glory* . . .

READING

RESPONSORY

In love and thanksgiving, we praise you, Holy God. —In love. . .
Your name is written in our hearts, —we praise. . .
Glory to you, Source of all Being, Eternal Word and Holy Spirit. —In love. . .

CANTICLE OF MARY

Ant.   Forever I will sing your praise.

INTERCESSIONS

PRAYER: Most loving God, you pursue creation with your love and
rescue us with your mercy. Look upon us, your people, this evening
with tenderness and compassion. Especially do we pray for all
world leaders. May they all find strength in your love and courage
in your wisdom. We ask this through the holy name of Jesus. Amen.

MORNING PRAYER

Ant. 1   As morning breaks I call upon
       your name, O God.

Psalm 63:1–9

O God, you are my God, I long for you;
my soul thirsts for you;
My body seeks for you
as in a dry and weary land without
     water.
So I have looked upon you in the
     sanctuary,
beholding your power and your glory.

For your constant love is better than
     life,
my lips will sing your praises.
So I will bless you as long as I live;
I will lift up my hands and call on your
     name.

My soul feasts on you and my mouth
     praises you,
as I think of you upon my bed,
and meditate on you in the watches
     of the night; ——

for you have been my help,
In the shadow of your wings I sing for
     joy.
My soul clings to you; your right hand
     upholds me.   Glory* . . .

Ant. 2   Not fearing the flames the three
       young men cried out with one voice:
       Blessed be God, alleluia.

Canticle   Daniel 3:57–88, 56

All you works of God, praise our God.
Praise and exalt God above all forever.
All you angels, sing God's praise,
you heavens and waters above.
Sun and moon, and stars of heaven,
sing praise with the heavenly hosts.

Every shower and dew, praise our God.
Give praise all you winds.
Praise our God, you fire and heat,
cold and chill—dew and rain.
Frost and chill, praise our God.
Praise God, ice and snow. —

Nights and days, sing hymns of praise,
light and darkness,
lightnings and clouds.

Let all the earth bless our God.
Praise and exalt God above all forever.
Let all that grows from the earth give
  praise
together with mountains and hills.
Give praise, you springs,
you seas and rivers,
dolphins and all water creatures.
Let birds of the air,
beasts, wild and tame,
together with all living peoples,
praise and exalt God above all forever.

O Israel, praise our God.
Praise and exalt God above all forever.
Give praise, you priests,
servants of the Most High,
spirits and souls of the just.
Holy ones of humble heart,
sing your hymns of praise.
Hananiah, Azariah, Mishael, praise
  our God.
Praise and exalt God above all forever.

Let us bless our God, Holy Mystery,
Source of All Being, Word and Spirit.
Let us praise and exalt God above all
  forever. —

Blessed are you, O God, in the
  firmament of heaven,
Praiseworthy and glorious and exalted
  above all forever.

**Ant. 3 Let the people of Zion rejoice,
alleluia.**

Psalm 149

Sing a new song to our God,
Give praise in the assembly of the
  faithful.
Let Israel be glad in its maker,
let Zion's heirs exult in the Most High.
Let them praise God's name with
  dancing,
and make music with timbrel and harp.

For you take delight in your people,
  O God.
You adorn the humble with victory.
Let the faithful exult in their glory,
in their rest, let them sing for joy.
Let the praises of God be on their lips
and two-edged swords in their hands,

to wreck vengeance on all that is
  wicked,
and chastisement on all injustice;
to bind what is evil in chains
and oppression in fetters of iron;
to carry out the sentence pre-ordained;
this is glory for all God's faithful
  ones.   Glory* . . .

READING

RESPONSORY

Christ, living word in our midst, hear our morning prayer. —**Christ**. . .
You are the light of the world, —**hear our**. . .
Glory to you, Source of all Being, Eternal Word and Holy Spirit. —**Christ**. . .

CANTICLE OF ZECHARIAH

Ant.   Most gracious God, may you bless us all our days.

INTERCESSIONS

PRAYER: O loving God, we take delight in your people and all of creation.
Together we unite our hearts and voices to sing your praise. Be with
us this day and help us to treat each other and all living creatures
with respect and appreciation. Grant this in the name of Jesus who
is our way, our truth and our life. Amen.

DAYTIME PRAYER

Ant. 1 O God, to whom shall we go? You alone are our refuge.

Psalm 118
I

We give thanks to you, for you are good,
and your steadfast love endures for
ever.

Let the descendants of Israel say:
"Your steadfast love endures for ever."
Let the descendants of Aaron say:
"Your steadfast love endures for ever."
Let those who fear you say:
"Your steadfast love endures for ever."

In my distress, I called to you;
you answered me and set me free.
With you at my side, I do not fear.
What can anyone do against me?
You are at my side to help me:
I shall withstand all evildoers.

It is better to take refuge in you,
than to trust in people:
it is better to take refuge in you
than to trust in our leaders.   Glory* . . .

Ant. 2 God's right hand has raised me up, alleluia.

II

All wickedness surrounded me;
in your name I crushed it.
It surrounded me, surrounded me
   on every side;
in your name I cut it off.
It surrounded me like bees;
it blazed like a fire among thorns.
In your name I crushed it.

I was pushed hard, and was falling
but you came to help me.
You are my strength and my song;
you are my salvation.

O God, your right hand has triumphed;
your right hand is exalted.
Your right hand has triumphed;
I shall not die, I shall live
and recount your wondrous deeds.
You have chastened me sorely,
but have not given me over to death.
   Glory* . . .

Ant. 3 Our God has let the light of the Most High to shine upon us, alleluia.

III

Open to me the gates of justice,
that I may enter and give thanks.
This is your gate, O God;
the just shall enter through it.
I thank you for you have answered me
you alone are my salvation.

The stone which the builders rejected
has become the corner stone.
This is your doing, O God,
it is marvelous in our eyes.
This is the day which you have made;
let us rejoice and be glad in it.

Save us, we beseech you, O God!
O God, grant us success.
Blessed are those who enter
in your holy name.
For you O God, are our God,
and you have given us light.

Let us go forward in procession with
   branches,
up to your holy altar.
You are my God, I thank you.
You are my God, I praise you.
We give thanks to you for you are good;
and your steadfast love endures for
   ever.   Glory* . . .

PRAYER: Most holy God, we rejoice in your gift of life as shared with us in
the paschal mystery. On this day of remembrance, help us to enter
more deeply into the mystery of life as lived among us, your people.
We ask this in the name of Jesus who lived as one of us and through
your Spirit who enlivens us. Amen.

SUNDAY, EVENING PRAYER II

Ant. 1 God's reign will last for ever, alleluia.

Psalm 110: 1–5, 7

God's revelation to the Anointed One:
"Sit at my side:
till I put injustice beneath your feet."

God will send forth from Zion
your scepter of power:
rule in the midst of your foes.

Your people will give themselves freely
on the day you lead your host
upon the holy mountains.
From the womb of the morning
your youth will come like dew.

God has sworn an oath that will not
be changed.
"You are a priest for ever,
after the order of Melchizedek."

The Anointed standing at your right
hand
will shatter rulers on the day of wrath.

Drinking from your streams by the
wayside
shall the Chosen One be refreshed.
Glory* . . .

**Ant. 2 Tremble, O earth, at the
presence of your God.**

Psalm 114

When Israel went forth from Egypt,
Jacob's heirs from an alien people,
Judah became God's sanctuary,
Israel, the dominion of the Most High.

The sea looked and fled,
Jordan turned back on its course.
The mountains skipped like rams,
the hills like yearling lambs.

What ails you, O sea, that you flee?
O Jordan, that you turn back?
Mountains, that you skip like rams,
hills, like yearling lambs?

Tremble, O earth, at the presence of
God,
at the presence of the God of your
ancestors,
who turns the rock into a pool,
the flint into a spring of water.
Glory* . . .

**Ant. 3 All power is yours, O God,
creator of all, alleluia.**

Canticle: Revelation 19:1, 5–7

Salvation, glory, and power
belong to you,
your judgments are honest and true.

All of us, your servants, sing praise to
you,
we worship you reverently, both great
and small.

You, our almighty God, are Creator
of heaven and earth.
Let us rejoice and exult, and give you
glory.

The wedding feast of the Lamb has
begun,
And the bride has made herself ready.
Glory* . . .

READING

RESPONSORY

Incline my heart to praise your goodness all the days of my life. —Incline . . .
For my prayer is always before you —all the . . .
Glory to you, Source of all Being, Eternal Word and Holy Spirit. —Incline . . .

CANTICLE OF MARY

Ant.   You fill us with goodness and mercy.

INTERCESSIONS

PRAYER: You, O God, are our place of refuge; you continue to call us forth to be your people in a world of division and distress. Help us to be people of faith, joy and love in the midst of chaos. This we ask through the intercession of Jesus, Mary and Joseph, who imaged community in a captive and oppressed land. Amen.

MONDAY

MORNING PRAYER

Ant. 1 Give heed to my words, O God, and listen to my morning prayer.

Psalm 5:1–9, 11–12

Give ear to my words, O God,
give heed to my groaning.
Attend to the sound of my cry,
O God, Most High.

For it is you to whom I pray.
In the morning you hear my voice;
I prepare a sacrifice for you,
watching and waiting.

You are not a God delighting in evil;
no sinner is your companion.
The boastful may not stand before you,
before your holy face.

You hate all that is evil;
you destroy all that is false.
The deceitful and the bloodthirsty
you chastise, O God.

But I through the abundance of your
    love
will enter your holy house.
I will worship at your holy temple,
filled with awe.

Lead me, O God, in your justice;
there are those who seek to seduce me,
make clear your way before me.

For there is no truth in their mouth,
their heart is destruction,
their throat a wide-open grave,
all flattery their speech.

Let all be glad who take refuge in
    you,
forever, sing out their joy.
Shelter those who love your name;
May they ever exult in you.

For you it is, who bless the just;
you cover them with favor,
    as with a shield.   Glory* . . .

Ant. 2 We sing your praises from generation to generation.

Canticle   1 Chronicles 29:10b–13

Blessed may you be,
O God of Israel,
from eternity to eternity.

Yours, O God, are grandeur and power,
majesty, splendor, and glory.

For all in heaven and on earth is yours;
yours, O God, is the sovereignty;
you are exalted as head over all.

Riches and honor are from you;
you have dominion over all.
In your hands are power and might;
it is yours to give grandeur and strength
    to all.

Therefore, our God, we give you thanks
and we praise the majesty of your name.
    Glory* . . .

Ant. 3 You are the Alpha and the Omega, the first and the last, the beginning and the end.

Psalm 29

O give to God, you heavenly beings,
give to God glory and power;
give glory to God's holy name.
Worship your God in holy array.

For God's voice is heard on the waters,
thundering on many waters;
the voice of God is powerful,
God's voice, full of splendor.

Your voice shatters the cedars,
it shatters the cedars of Lebanon;
you make Lebanon skip like a calf
and Sirion like a young wild-ox.

Your voice, O God, flashes flames of
    fire.

Your voice shakes the wilderness,
it shakes the wilderness of Kadesh;
it makes the oak trees whirl,
and strips the forests bare.

The God of glory thunders!
In your temple all cry: "Glory!"
You sit enthroned over the flood;
you sit, our sovereign for ever.

May you give strength to your people,
and bless your people with peace.
    Glory* . . .

READING

RESPONSORY

Shelter us, O God, in the safety of your dwelling place. —**Shelter**. . .
Your name is forever blessed, —**in the**. . .
Glory to you, Source of all Being, Eternal Word and Holy Spirit. —**Shelter**. . .

CANTICLE OF ZECHARIAH

Ant.   **You are faithful to your word, forever.**

INTERCESSIONS

PRAYER: O Holy God, you continue to bless us with your gifts of creation.
             May we give thanks to you for your kindness to your people and
             take delight in the gifts we share to bring about the fullness of
             your life in this our world. We pray this of you, Most Blessed
             Trinity, living in us and among us through all generations. Amen.

DAYTIME PRAYER

**Ant. 1 Teach us to love you and our
    neighbor, so as to fulfill your law.**

Psalm 19:7–14

Your law, O God, is perfect,
reviving the soul.
Your testimony is to be trusted,
making the simple wise.

Your precepts are right,
rejoicing the heart.
Your command is pure,
giving light to the eyes.

The fear of God is holy,
enduring for ever.
God's ordinances are true,
and all of them just.

More to be desired are they than gold,
more than the purest gold, —

and sweeter are they than honey,
than drippings from the comb.

By them your servant finds instruction;
great reward is in their keeping.
But who can detect all one's errors?
From hidden faults acquit me.

Restrain me from presumptuous sins,
let them not have rule over me!
Then shall I be blameless,
and clean from serious sin.

Let the words of my mouth,
the thoughts of my heart,
be acceptable in your sight,
O God, my rock and my redeemer.
    Glory* . . .

Ant. 2 Judge me, O God, according to your law.

Psalm 7

I

O God, in you I take refuge;
Save me from my pursuers and rescue
   me,
lest they tear me to pieces like a lion,
dragging me off with none to rescue me.

O God, if I have done this,
if my hands have done wrong,
if I have paid my friend with evil
or plundered without cause,
then let my foes pursue me and seize me,
let them trample my life to the ground
and lay my soul in the dust.

Let the assembly of nations gather
   round you,
taking your seat above them on high.
For you, O God, are judge of the
   peoples.

Judge me, O God, according to my
   justice,
and according to the integrity that is
   mine.
Put an end to the evil of the wicked;
and make the just stand firm, —

you who test the mind and heart,
you, our most just God!   Glory* . . .

Ant. 3 Search me, O God, and know my heart; cleanse me from all sin.

II

God is the shield that protects me,
who saves the upright of heart.
God is a just judge
slow to anger;
challenging the wicked every day,
those who are slow to repent.

God sharpens the sword,
bends the bow that is strung,
prepares deadly weapons for wickedness,
and barbs the arrows with fire.
Behold those who are pregnant with
   malice,
who conceive evil and bring forth lies.

They dig a pitfall, dig it deep;
and fall into the trap they have made.
Their malice will recoil on themselves;
on their own heads their violence will
   fall.

I will give thanks to you, God,
for your justice;
and will sing to your name,
   O Most High.   Glory* . . .

PRAYER: As we pause to remember your fidelity to us, O Source of Life,
continue to abide with us this day. Let us give thanks for all
people working for justice and peace. For you, O God, come in
power to give your people justice. We ask this through the
intercession of Jesus and all who have given their lives in the cause
of justice. Amen.

EVENING PRAYER

Ant. 1 Teach us how to act justly, and to walk humbly with one another.

Psalm 11

In God I have taken my refuge.
How can you say to my soul:
"Fly like a bird to the mountains.

See the wicked bending the bow;
they have fitted their arrows on the
   string
to shoot the upright in the dark.
If the foundations are destroyed,
what can the righteous do?"

But you are in your holy temple,
you, whose throne is in heaven.
Your eyes look down on the world;
your gaze tests mortal flesh.

God tests the just and the wicked,
scorned by the lovers of violence.
God will chastise those who do evil;
a scorching wind shall be their lot.

You are just and love justice;
the upright shall behold your face.
   Glory* . . .

Ant. 2 Create in me an upright spirit that I may serve you in others.

Psalm 15

Who shall visit in your tent,
and dwell on your holy mountain?

They who walk blamelessly,
and do what is right,
who speak the truth from their hearts;
and do not slander with their tongues;

they who do no wrong to each other,
nor cast reproaches on their neighbors,
who pray the godless to repent,
and honor those who fear the
    Most High;

they who keep their pledge, come
    what may;
who take no profit from injustice,
nor accept bribes against the innocent.
Such as these will stand firm for ever.
    Glory* . . .

Ant. 3 We are your people, chosen before the foundation of the world.

Canticle: Ephesians 1:3–10

Praised be the God
of our Lord Jesus Christ, —

who has blessed us in Christ
with every spiritual blessing
    in the heavens.

God chose us in him
before the foundation of the world,
that we should be holy
and blameless in God's sight.

We have been predestined
to be God's children through Jesus
    Christ,
such was the purpose of God's will,
that all might praise the glorious favor
bestowed on us in Christ.

In Christ and through his blood,
    we have redemption,
the forgiveness of our sins,
according to the riches of God's grace
    lavished upon us.

For God has made known to us
in all wisdom and insight,
the mystery of the plan set forth in
    Christ.

A plan to be carried out in Christ,
in the fullness of time,
to unite all things in Christ,
things in heaven and things on earth.
    Glory* . . .

READING

RESPONSORY

Look upon us graciously, O God, and have mercy on us. —**Look**. . .
For you are our source of love, —**have**. . .
Glory to you, Source of all Being, Eternal Word and Holy Spirit. —**Look**. . .

CANTICLE OF MARY

Ant.   I long for you, God of my life.

INTERCESSIONS

PRAYER: Most loving God, you love justice. Help us to be open to your ways
of mercy, compassion and truth that we may call forth in ourselves
and in one another your ways of wisdom and truth. We ask this
through the Holy Spirit of Wisdom living in you through all
eternity. Amen.

TUESDAY
MORNING PRAYER

Ant. 1 Blessed are the pure of heart, for they shall see God.

Psalm 24

Yours is the earth and its fullness,
the world and all who dwell there;
for you have founded it upon the seas,
and established it upon the rivers.

Who shall climb your mountain,
   O God?
Who shall stand in your holy place?
Those with clean hands and pure hearts,
who do not desire what is vain,
who have not sworn so as to deceive
   their neighbors.

They shall receive blessings from
   Yahweh
and reward from the God who saves
   them.
Such are those who seek after Yahweh;
who seek the face of the God of their
   ancestors.

O gates, lift up your heads;
grow higher, ancient doors.
Let enter the God of glory!

Who is this God of glory?
The One who is mighty and valiant,
valiant against all injustice.

O gates, lift up your heads;
grow higher, ancient doors.
Let enter the God of glory!

Who is this God of glory?
Yahweh, the God of hosts,
Yahweh is the God of glory.
   Glory* . . .

Ant. 2 Turn to me, O God, and show me your face.

Canticle   Tobit 13:1b–8

Blessed be God who lives forever,
whose realm lasts for all ages.

For you scourge, O God, and then
   have mercy;
you cast down to the depths of the
   nether world,
and bring up from the great abyss.
No one can escape your hand.

Praise God, you Israelites, before the
   Gentiles,
for though you are scattered among
   them,
you have seen God's greatness even
   there.

Exalt Yahweh before every living being,
because Yahweh is the Most High God,
our God for ever and ever.

God has scourged you for your
   iniquities,
but will again have mercy on you all.
Gathering you from all the Gentiles
among whom you have been scattered.

When you turn back to Yahweh with all
   your heart,
to do only what is right,
then Yahweh will turn back to you,
Yahweh's face will no longer be hidden.

So now consider what has been done
   for you,
and give praise with full voice.
Bless the God of righteousness,
and exalt the Ruler of the ages.

In the land of my exile I praise you,
   O God,
and show your power and majesty to
   a sinful nation.
"Turn back, you sinners! do what is
   right:
perhaps God may look with favor upon
   you
and show you mercy.

As for me, I exult in my God,
and my spirit rejoices.
Let all speak of God's majesty,
and sing God's praises in Jerusalem."
   Glory* . . .

Ant. 3 Blessed are those who hear your word and keep it.

Psalm 33

Rejoice in God, O you just;
praise is fitting for loyal hearts.

We give thanks to you with the lyre,
make melody with ten-stringed harps.
Let us sing a song that is new,
and play skillfully, full of gladness.

For your words, O God are faithful
and all your works to be trusted.
You love justice and righteousness,
and fill the earth with your steadfast
    love.

By your word the heavens were made,
by the breath of your mouth all the
    stars.
You gather the waters of the oceans;
you store up the depths of the seas.

Let all the earth fear you, O God,
all who live in the world, stand
    in wonder.
For you spoke; and it came to be.
You commanded; it sprang into being.

You frustrate the designs of the nations,
you upset the plans of the peoples.
Your own designs stand for ever,
the plans of your heart to all
    generations.

Happy are they, whose God you are,
the peoples you have chosen for
    your heritage.
From the heavens you look forth,
and see all the peoples of the earth.

From the place where you dwell you
    gaze
on all the dwellers of this earth,
you who fashion the hearts of them all
and observe all their deeds.

Rulers are not saved by their armies,
nor leaders preserved by their strength.
A vain hope for safety are our weapons;
despite their power they cannot save.

Look on those who reverence you,
on those who hope in your love,
to deliver their souls from death,
and keep them alive in famine.

Our souls are waiting for you;
you are our help and our shield.
In you do our hearts find joy;
we trust in your holy name.

Let your love be upon us, O God,
as we place all our hope in you.
    Glory* . . .

READING

RESPONSORY

You call us each by name, for we are blessed in you. —**You**. . .
Faithful to your promise, —**for we** . . .
Glory to you, Source of all Being, Eternal Word and Holy Spirit. —**You call**. . .

CANTICLE OF ZECHARIAH

Ant. **You are our God and holy is your name.**

INTERCESSIONS

PRAYER: Most compassionate God, touch our hearts this morning with your
mercy and love. Help us to be a source of love and light to those
who are suffering this day. May all who die today experience the
joy of being in your presence. Grant this through the intercession
of all who suffered persecution for the sake of justice. Amen.

DAYTIME PRAYER

**Ant. 1 The just shall praise you
    with upright hearts.**

Psalm 119:1–8

Blessed are they whose way is
    blameless,
who follow your law, O God!
Blessed are they who do your will,
who seek you with all their hearts, —

who never do anything wrong,
but walk in your ways.

You have laid down your precepts
to be diligently kept.
O that my ways may be firm
in obeying your statutes.
Then I shall not be put to shame
as I heed your commands.

I will praise you with an upright heart
as I learn your decrees.
I will obey your statutes;
do not forsake me.   Glory* . . .

**Ant. 2 My heart rejoices in your
saving grace, O God.**

Psalm 13

How long, O God? Will you forget me
   forever?
How long will you hide your face?
How long must I bear pain in my soul,
and sorrow in my heart day and night?
How long shall my oppressors prevail?

Look at me, answer me, my God!
Lighten my eyes lest I sleep the
   sleep of death,
lest my oppressors say: "I have
   overcome you";
lest they rejoice to see me shaken.

As for me, I trust in your merciful love.
My heart rejoices in your salvation;
I will sing to you for your goodness,
because you are gracious to me.
   Glory* . . .

**Ant. 3 Give us your wisdom that we
may follow your way.**

Psalm 14

Fools say in their hearts:
"There is no God!"
They are corrupt, their deeds, depraved;
there are none that do good.

But you look down from heaven,
upon the peoples of the earth,
to see if any are wise,
if any seek God.

All seem to have gone astray,
depraved, every one;
there are none that do good,
no, not even one.

Do evil-doers have no knowledge?
They eat up God's people
as though they were eating bread;
do they never call upon Yahweh?

There they shall be in great terror,
for God is with the just.
You may mock the hope of the poor,
but their refuge is the Most High God.

O that Israel's salvation might come
   from Zion!
When God delivers the people from
   bondage,
then Jacob shall rejoice and Israel
   be glad.   Glory* . . .

PRAYER: Gentle God, you remind us that you are our faithful friend, and
that you will deliver us from bondage. Look upon us, your people,
and deliver us from the chains that keep us from the fullness of
life. We pray this in love and confidence in Jesus' name. Amen.

EVENING PRAYER

**Ant. 1 Only in you, O God, will my soul
be at rest.**

Psalm 20

May God answer in time of trouble!
May the name of our God protect you.

Send your help, O God, from your
   sanctuary,
and give your support from Zion.
May you remember all our offerings
and receive our sacrifice with favor.

May you give us our heart's desire
and fulfill every one of our plans.
May we ring out our joy at your victory
and rejoice in your name, O God.
May you grant all our prayers.

Now I know that you, O God,
will give victory to your anointed;
you will reply from your holy heaven
with the help of your hand.

Some trust in chariots or horses,
but we trust in your holy name. —

They will collapse and fall,
but we shall rise and stand firm.

Give victory to your Anointed,
give answer on the day we call.
Glory* . . .

**Ant. 2 To know you, O God, is to
possess eternal life.**

Psalm 21:2–8, 14

O God, your strength gives joy to
your people;
how your saving help makes them glad!
You have granted them the desire of
their hearts;
you have not refused the prayer of
their lips.

You came to meet them with goodly
blessings,
you have set blessings on their heads.
They asked you for life and this you
have given,
length of days forever and ever.

Your saving help has given them glory.
Splendor you bestow upon them.
You grant your blessings to them
forever.
You gladden them with the joy of your
presence.

They put their trust in you;
through your steadfast love, they shall
stand firm
O God, we exult in your strength;
we shall sing and praise your goodness.
Glory* . . .

**Ant. 3 O God, you have made us
in your own image.**

Canticle: Revelation 4:11, 5:9, 10, 12

Worthy are you, O God, our God,
to receive glory and honor and power.

For you have created all things;
by your will they came to be and were
made.

Worthy are you to take the scroll
and to open its seals,

For you were slain, and by your blood,
you purchased for God
persons of every race and tongue,
of every people and nation.

You have made of them a kingdom,'
and priests to serve our God,
and they shall reign on the earth.

Worthy is the Lamb who was slain
to receive power and riches,
wisdom and strength,
honor and glory and praise.   Glory* . . .

READING

RESPONSORY

In you, Word of God, I place my trust and love. —**In you**...
For you are our redeemer, —**I place**...
Glory to you, Source of all Being, Eternal Word and Holy Spirit. —**In you**...

CANTICLE OF MARY

Ant.   My soul will sing your praises.

INTERCESSIONS

PRAYER: At the close of our day, we turn to you, our God, and with hearts
of gratitude, we ask you to remember our deeds of goodness and to
have mercy upon our shortcomings. May all who have died this
day find peace in you and may all the sorrowing find comfort in
those around them and in your compassionate heart. We ask this
mindful of your mercy and forgiveness. Amen.

WEDNESDAY

MORNING PRAYER

Ant. 1 You are the light of the world.

Psalm 36

Sin speaks to the wicked
in the depths of their hearts.
There is no fear of God
before their eyes.

They so flatter themselves in their
    own eyes
that they know not their own guilt.
In their mouths are mischief and deceit.
They no longer act wisely or good.

They plot the defeat of goodness
as they lie on their beds.
They set their feet on evil ways,
and do not spurn what is evil.

But your steadfast love extends to
    the heavens,
your faithfulness to the skies.
Your justice is like the mountain,
your judgments like the great deep.

To both human and beast you give
    salvation.
How precious is your love.
The children of this earth
take refuge in the shadow of your wings.

They feast on the riches of your house;
and drink from the stream of your
    delight.
In you is the fountain of life
and in your light we see light.

Keep on loving those who know you,
giving salvation to upright hearts.
Let the foot of the proud not crush me
nor the hand of the wicked drive me
    away.

There the evil-doers lie prostrate!
Thrust down, they are unable to rise.
    Glory* . . .

**Ant. 2 Let all creation bow down
    before you.**

Canticle   Judith 16:1, 13–15

Strike up the instruments,
a song to my God with timbrels, —

chant to the Most High with cymbals.
Sing a new song,
exalt and acclaim God's name.

A new hymn I will sing to you.
O God, great are you and glorious,
wonderful in power and unsurpassable.

Let your every creature serve you;
for you spoke, and they were made,
you sent forth your spirit, and they
    were created;
no one can resist your word.

The mountains to their bases, and the
    seas, are shaken;
the rocks, like wax, melt before your
    glance.
But to those who fear you,
you are very merciful.   Glory* . . .

**Ant. 3 We sing praise to you, Most
    High.**

Psalm 47

Clap your hands, all you peoples,
shout to God with songs of joy!
For the Most High we must fear,
great ruler over all the earth!

O God, you subdue evil oppression,
and challenge unjust nations.
You chose our heritage for us,
gave it to us out of love.

You go up with shouts of joy;
O God, with trumpet blast.
We sing praise to you, sing praise,
sing praise to you, Most High.

For your realm is all the earth.
We sing to you our hymns of praise!
Your reign is over all the nations;
Over all the peoples of this earth.

The leaders of the peoples gather
with the people of Abraham's God.
May all leaders of the earth pay heed,
to God who reigns over all.   Glory* . . .

READING

RESPONSORY

Living source of light and wisdom, be with us always. —**Living**...
In you we find new life, —**be with**...
Glory to you, Source of all Being, Eternal Word and Holy Spirit. —**Living**...

CANTICLE OF ZECHARIAH

Ant.   You are faithful to your promise, God of all the ages.

INTERCESSIONS

PRAYER: O God, source of our light, you are ever with us to reveal the way
of truth and justice. Be with us this day as we struggle to ease the
burdens of our sisters and brothers. We ask this in Jesus who is our
way, our truth and our life. Amen.

DAYTIME PRAYER

Ant. 1 Your law is written on my heart.

Psalm 119:9–16

How shall the young remain sinless?
By living according to your word.
I have sought you with all my heart:
let me not stray from your commands.

I carry your word in my heart
lest I sin against you.
Blessed are you, O God;
teach me your statutes.

With my lips I have recounted
all the decrees of your mouth.
I delight to do your will
as though all riches were mine.

I will meditate on your precepts
and fix my eyes on your ways.
I will delight in your statutes;
I will not forget your word.   Glory* . . .

**Ant. 2 You are a light to my eyes,
a lamp for my feet.**

Psalm 17

O God, hear a cause that is just,
attend to my cry.
Give ear to my prayer
from lips free of deceit.

If you should try my heart
or visit me by night;
if you should test me,
you will find no deceit in me;
my tongue has not deceived.

Because of the word of your mouth
I have avoided the ways of the violent.
My steps have held fast to your paths,
my feet have not slipped.

I call upon you, for you will hear me.
Turn your ear to me; hear my words.
Show your steadfast love,
to all who seek refuge
in the shelter of your hand.

Keep me as the apple of your eye.
Hide me in the shadow of your wings
from the wicked who seek to destroy.
    Glory* . . .

**Ant. 3 You are my portion, the God of
my life.**

II

They close their hearts to pity;
with their mouths they speak arrogantly.
They track me down, surrounding me;
setting their eyes to cast me to the
    ground
as though they were a lion eager to tear,
as a young lion lurking in ambush.

Arise, O God, confront them, strike
 them down!
Deliver my life from the wicked;
by your hand, O God, rescue me from
 evildoers,
from those whose portion is of this
 world.
May they be filled from the abundance
 of your storehouse; —

may their children have more than
 enough;
may their wealth extend to their
 offspring.

As for me, in my justice I shall see
 your face;
when I awake, I shall be filled with the
 sight of your glory.   Glory* . . .

PRAYER: God of wisdom, enlighten us with your spirit that we may work to
bring about your love and justice within our hearts and in the
hearts of all your people. Strengthen us with insight to be faithful
to your word revealed among us. Grant this through the
intercession of all those who faithfully heard your word and kept
it. Amen.

EVENING PRAYER

Ant. 1 **You are my dwelling place, in
you I take my rest.**

Psalm 27

O God, you are my light and my help;
whom shall I fear?
You are the stronghold of my life;
before whom shall I be afraid?

When evildoers assail me
uttering slanders against me,
it is they, my enemies and foes,
who shall stumble and fall.

Though an army encamp against me
my heart shall not fear.
Though war break out against me
yet will I trust.

One thing I have asked of you,
for this will I seek,
that I may dwell in your holy house
all the days of my life,
to behold the beauty of your
 countenance
and the holiness of your temple.

In your shelter you will hide me
in the day of trouble;
you will conceal me under the cover of
 your tent,
you will set me high upon a rock.

And now my head shall be raised
above my foes who surround me
and I will offer in your tent
sacrifices with songs of joy.

I will sing and make music to my God.
 Glory* . . .

Ant. 2 **It is you, O God that I seek.**

II

Hear my voice when I cry aloud,
be gracious to me and give answer!
You say to me: "Seek my face,
Seek the face of your God."

"Your face, O God, I do seek."
Hide not your face from me.
Do not dismiss me in anger;
you have been my help.

Do not cast me off or forsake me,
O God, my help!
Though father and mother forsake me,
You, O God, will receive me.

Teach me your way, O God;
lead me on a level path.
Give me not up to the will of evildoers;
who bear false witness and breathe
 out violence.

I believe I shall see your goodness
in the land of the living.
Hope in God, be strong and take heart.
Hope in God, the Most High!
 Glory* . . .

Ant. 3 Jesus is the image of the invisible God.

Canticle: Colossians 1:12–20

Let us give thanks to God
for having made us worthy
to share the inheritance of the
    saints in light.

God has delivered us
from the power of darkness
and transferred us
into the kingdom of God's beloved Son,
    Jesus,
in whom we have redemption,
the forgiveness of our sins.

Jesus is the image of the invisible God,
the first-born of all creation;
in him all things were created,
    in heaven and on earth,
things visible and invisible.

All things were created through him;
all were created for him.
He is before all else that is.
In him all things hold together.

He is the head of the body, the church!
He is the beginning,
the firstborn from the dead,
that in everything, he might be above
    all others.

In him all the fullness of God was
    pleased to dwell,
and, through him, to reconcile all
    things to himself,
whether on earth or in heaven,
making peace by the blood of his cross.
    Glory* . . .

READING

RESPONSORY

Hold me gently, O God, in the palm of your hand. —**Hold**. . .
In you I find my rest, —**in the**. . .
Glory to you, Source of all Being, Eternal Word and Holy Spirit. —**Hold me**. . .

CANTICLE OF MARY

Ant.   You have done great things for us and holy is your name.

INTERCESSIONS

PRAYER: In the evening we come to you, faithful friend, to thank you for
the blessings of this day. May we be ever mindful of your love in
the midst of life's joys and burdens and may all your people
experience your peace this night. This we ask placing ourselves in
your care, Most Blessed Trinity. Amen.

THURSDAY

MORNING PRAYER

**Ant. 1 In the early hours of the morning,
    my heart will sing your praise.**

Psalm 57

Have mercy on me, have mercy,
for in you my soul takes refuge.
In the shadow of your wings I take refuge
till the storms of destruction pass by.

I cry to God the Most High,
to God who has always been my help.
May you send from heaven and save me
and shame those who trample upon me.
O God, send your truth and your love.

My soul lies down among lions,
who greedily devour the peoples
    of the earth.—

Their teeth are spears and arrows,
their tongues a sharpened sword.

Be exalted, O God, above the heavens;
let your glory be over all the earth!

They laid a snare for my steps,
my soul was bowed down.
They dug a pit in my path
but they fell in it themselves.

My heart is steadfast, O God,
my heart is steadfast.
I will sing and make melody!
Awake, my soul,
awake, lyre and harp!
I will awake the dawn!

I will give thanks to you among the
    peoples,
I will praise you among the nations
for your love reaches to the heavens
your faithfulness to the skies.

Be exalted, O God, above the heavens!
let your glory be over all the earth!
    Glory* . . .

**Ant. 2 You are the bread of life; you
are the cup of salvation.**

Canticle   Jeremiah 31:10–14

Hear the word of God, O nations,
proclaim it on distant coasts, and say:
God who scattered Israel, now gathers
    them together,
and guards them as shepherds guard
    their flocks.

God will ransom the chosen people
and redeem them from the hands of
    their conquerors.

Shouting, they shall mount the heights
    of Zion,
they shall come streaming to Yahweh's
    blessings:
the grain, the wine, and the oil,
the sheep and the oxen;
they themselves shall be like watered
    gardens,
never again shall they languish.

Then the young shall make merry
    and dance,
old men and women as well.
I will turn their mourning into joy,
I will console and gladden them after
    their sorrows. —

I will lavish choice portions upon them,
and my people shall be filled with
    my blessings,
says our God.   Glory* . . .

Ant. 3 Let us build the city of God!

Psalm 48

O God, you are great and worthy to
    be praised
in your holy city.
Your holy mountain rising in beauty,
is the joy of all the earth.

Mount Zion, in the far north,
your holy city!
Within its citadels,
you show yourself its stronghold.

For invaders assembled together,
together they advanced.
As soon as they saw it,
    they were astounded;
in panic they took to flight.

Trembling took hold of them there,
like the anguish of a woman giving
    birth;
By the east wind you have shattered
the ships of Tarshish.

As we have heard, so we have seen
in the city of our God,
in the city of the Most High
which God establishes for ever.

O God, we ponder your love
in the midst of your temple.
Your praise, like your name
reaches to the ends of the earth.

With justice your hands are filled.
Let Mount Zion be glad!
The people of Judah rejoice
because of your judgments.

Walk through Zion, walk all round it;
number its towers.
Review its ramparts,
examine its citadels;

that you may tell the next generation
that this is our God,
our God for ever and ever.
You will always be our guide.
    Glory* . . .

READING

RESPONSORY

I have seen the glory of God, in the land of the living. —I...
You are with us always, —in the...
Glory to you, Source of all Being, Eternal Word and Holy Spirit. —I have...

CANTICLE OF ZECHARIAH

Ant.   In love let us ponder your word forever.

INTERCESSIONS

PRAYER: Most gracious God and Father, you are with us as we make our journey throughout this day. Help us to look lovingly upon all people and events that come into our lives today and to walk gently upon our land. Grant this through Jesus who lives and walks among us ever present at each moment. Amen.

DAYTIME PRAYER

Ant. 1 I am a sojourner on earth; teach me your ways.

Psalm 119:17–24

Bless your servant that I may live
and obey your word.
Open my eyes that I may behold
the wonders of your law.

I am a sojourner on earth;
hide not your commands from me!
My soul is consumed with longing
forever, for your decrees.

You rebuke the insolent,
who turn from your commands.
Relieve me of their scorn and contempt
for I have kept your word.

Though others sit plotting against me
I ponder on your statutes.
Your will is my delight;
your decrees are my counselors.
     Glory* . . .

Ant. 2 Lead me in your truth, and guide me in the path of salvation.

Psalm 25

To you, O God, I lift up my soul.
In you, I trust, let me not be
     put to shame; —

let not the wicked exult over me.
Those who wait on you shall not be
     put to shame;
but only those who wantonly break faith.

Make me know your ways, O God;
Teach me your paths.
Lead me in your truth, and teach me,
for you are God, my savior.
For you I wait all the day long.

Remember your mercy, O God,
and your steadfast love,
which you have given from of old.
Remember not the sins of my youth,
     or my transgressions;
But in your goodness, remember me
according to your steadfast love!

You, O God, are good and upright.
You instruct sinners in your way.
You lead the humble in the right path;
you teach your way to the poor.

All your ways are loving and constant
for those who keep your covenant
     and your decrees.
For your name's sake, O God,
pardon my guilt, for it is great.
     Glory* . . .

Ant. 3 Say but the word, and I shall be healed.

II

Those who fear you, O God,
you will instruct in the way they
    should choose.
They shall abide in prosperity,
and their children shall possess the land.
Your friendship is for those
    who revere you;
make known to them your covenant.

My eyes are ever turned toward you,
for you rescue my feet from the snare.
Turn to me and be gracious to me;
for I am lonely and afflicted.

Relieve the troubles of my heart
and bring me out of my distress.
See my affliction and my troubles,
and forgive all my sins.

See how many are my faults,
with what violence they pursue me.
Preserve my life and deliver me;
let me not be put to shame,
for I take refuge in you.
May integrity and uprightness
    preserve me:
for my hope is in you.

Redeem Israel, O God, from all its
    troubles.   Glory* . . .

PRAYER: To you, O God, we lift up our hearts at this midday prayer. We
ask you to remember us and all those who are troubled at this
time. Help us to reach out in justice and charity to those in need
among us. Grant this through the intercession of all who served
you in serving your poor. Amen.

EVENING PRAYER

Ant. 1 You heal my affliction; you restore my soul to life!

Psalm 30

I will praise you, O God, you have
    rescued me
and have not let evil triumph over me.

O God, I cried to you for help
and you have healed me.
You have raised my soul from the dead,
restored me to life from among those
    gone down to the grave.

We sing praises to you, we your people,
and give thanks to your holy name.
For your anger lasts but a moment,
    your favors for a lifetime.
At night there may be weeping,
but joy comes with the morning.

I said to myself in my prosperity,
"Nothing will ever disturb me."
By your favor, O God,
you have made me strong as a
    mountain;
when you hide your face, I am
    dismayed.

O God, to you I cried,
to you I make supplication:
"What profit is there in my death,
if I go down to the grave?
Can dust praise you, or tell of your
    faithfulness?"

Hear, O God, and be gracious to me!
O God be my help!
You have turned my mourning into
    dancing;
you have removed my sackcloth and
    clothed me with gladness,
that I may praise you with full voice,
and give thanks to you forever.
    Glory* . . .

Ant. 2 In the integrity of my heart, I lay my guilt before you.

Psalm 32

Happy are they whose faults are
    forgiven,
whose sins are covered.
Happy are they to whom our God
imputes no guilt,
in whose spirits there is no deceit.

When I declared not my sin,
my body wasted away
with groanings all the day long.
For day and night your hand
　　was heavy upon me;
my strength was dried up as by the
　　heat of summer.

When I acknowledged my sin to you,
and did not hide my guilt;
I said: "I will confess my sins
　　to you, O God."
Then you did forgive me the guilt
　　of my sin.

So let all who acclaim you offer
　　prayers;
in times of distress, the rush of the flood
waters will not reach them.
For you are a hiding place for me,
you preserve me from trouble;
you surround me with deliverance.

I will instruct you and teach you
the way you should go;
I will counsel you with my eye upon
　　you.
Be not like a horse or a mule,
　　without understanding,
which must be curbed with bit and
　　bridle else it will not keep you.

Many are the sorrows of the wicked;
but faithful love surrounds those who
　　trust in you.
We rejoice in you and are glad. —

Let all the upright in heart
rejoice and shout for you.　　Glory* . . .

**Ant. 3　Behold the Lamb of God, who
takes away the sins of the world.**

Canticle: Revelation 11:17–18;
12:10b–12a

We praise you, God Almighty,
who is and who was.
You have assumed your great power,
you have begun your reign.

The nations have raged in anger,
but then came your day of wrath
and the moment to judge the dead;
the time to reward your servants the
　　prophets
and the holy ones who revere you,
the great and the small alike.

Now have salvation and power come,
your reign, O God, and the authority
　　of your Anointed One.
For the accusers of our loved ones
　　have been cast out,
who night and day accused them.

By the blood of the Lamb have they
　　been defeated,
and by the testimony of your servants;
love for life did not deter them from
　　death.
So rejoice, you heavens,
and you that dwell therein!
　　Glory* . . .

READING

RESPONSORY

You gather us together in the bosom of your love. —**You**. . .
As a mother hen, —**in the**. . .
Glory to you, Source of all Being, Eternal Word and Holy Spirit. —**You**. . .

CANTICLE OF MARY

Ant.　In you I rejoice all the days of my life.

INTERCESSIONS

PRAYER:　You, Mother and God, are our safety in times of distress. Show us
　　　　　　your ways of peace that we may gather one another into your
　　　　　　loving embrace, into your dwelling place. May you be with us this
　　　　　　night and may all those in darkness walk in your light. Grant this,
　　　　　　Spirit of Comfort, through Jesus, our brother. Amen.

FRIDAY

MORNING PRAYER

Ant. 1 Create in me a clean heart, O God.

Psalm 51

Have mercy on me, O God,
according to your steadfast love;
in your abundant mercy blot out my
    sins.
Wash me thoroughly from my offenses,
and cleanse me from my sin!

For I know my offenses,
and my sin is ever before me.
Against you, you alone, have I sinned,
and done what is evil in your sight,
so you are justified in your sentence
and blameless in your judgment.
Behold, I was brought forth in a
    sinful world.

For you desire truth in my innermost
    being;
teach me wisdom in the depths of my
    heart.
O purify me, and I shall be clean;
O wash me, I shall be whiter than snow.
Fill me with joy and gladness;
let the bones you have broken rejoice.
Hide your face from my guilt,
and blot out all my offenses.

Create in me a clean heart,
put a steadfast spirit within me.
Cast me not from your presence,
take not your spirit from me.
Give me again the joy of your
    salvation,
with a willing spirit uphold me.

Then I will teach transgressors your
    ways
and sinners will return to you.
Deliver me from death,
O God of my salvation,
and my tongue will sing out your
    saving help.

Open my lips and my mouth will sing
    your praises.
For you take no delight in sacrifice;
were I to give a burnt offering, —

you would not be pleased.
A broken spirit you accept;
a contrite heart, you will not despise.

In your goodness, show favor to Zion;
rebuild the walls of Jerusalem.
Then will you delight in just sacrifices,
in gifts offered on your altar.
    Glory* . . .

**Ant. 2 You are our God, there is no
    other besides you.**

Canticle   Isaiah 45:15–25

Truly you are a God who is hidden,
the God of Israel, the savior!
They are put to shame and disgraced,
the makers of idols are put to confusion.

Israel, you are saved by Yahweh,
    with everlasting salvation!
You shall never be put to shame or
    disgraced for all eternity.

For thus says Yahweh,
the creator of the heavens,
who is God,
the designer and maker of the earth,
who established it,
not creating it as chaos,
but designing it to be lived in.

I am God, and there is no other.
I have not spoken in secret,
in a land of darkness;
I have not said to the descendants
    of my people,
"Look for me in chaos."
I, your God, speak the truth,
I declare what is right.

Come and assemble, gather together,
you survivors of the nations!
They are without knowledge who bear
    wooden idols
and pray to gods that cannot save.

Come here and declare
in counsel together!
Who declared this from the beginning

and foretold it from of old?
Was it not I, your God?
There is no other besides me,
a just and saving God!

Turn to me and be saved,
all you ends of the earth,
for I am God; there is no other!
By myself I have sworn,
uttering my just decree
and my word which cannot be changed.

To me every knee shall bend;
by me every tongue shall swear,
saying, "Only in Yahweh, our God,
are justice and righteousness.

You, O God, shall be the vindication
and the glory
of all the descendants of Israel."
Glory* . . .

READING

RESPONSORY

You are the good shepherd, have compassion upon us. —**You are**. . .
In you we find mercy, —**have**. . .
Glory to you, Source of all Being, Eternal Word and Holy Spirit. —**You**. . .

CANTICLE OF ZECHARIAH

Ant.   **You teach us the way of peace.**

INTERCESSIONS

PRAYER: Forgiving God, look not upon our sins this day but upon our desire
to serve you and one another. Dispel our darkness, and help us to
embrace our failings in loving union with your goodness. Heal us
this day, and may we be a source of strength and courage for
others. Grant this through the intercession of all those who fill up
what is wanting in the sufferings of Christ. Amen.

Ant. 3 **We are your people, the sheep
of your pasture.**

Psalm 100

All the earth cries out to you with
shouts of joy, O God,
Serving you with gladness;
coming before you, singing for joy.

You, Creator of all, are God.
You made us, we belong to you,
we are your people, the sheep of your
pasture.

We enter your gates with thanksgiving,
and your courts with songs of praise!
We give you thanks and bless your
name.

Indeed, how good you are,
enduring, your steadfast love.
You are faithful to all generations.
Glory* . . .

DAYTIME PRAYER

Ant. 1 **I cling to your will, O God.**

Psalm 119:25–32

My soul cleaves to the dust;
revive me according to your word!
I told of my ways and you answered
me;
teach me your statutes.

Make me understand the way of your
precepts
and I will ponder on your wonders.
My soul pines with sorrow;
strengthen me by your word.

Keep me from the way of falsehood;
and teach me your law!
I have chosen the way of faithfulness,
I set your decrees before me.

I cling to your will, O God;
let me not be put to shame!
I will run in the way of your commands;
when you enlighten my understanding.
    Glory* . . .

Ant. 2 I trust in God without wavering.

Psalm 26

Judge me, O God, for I walk in
    the way of integrity,
I trust in you without wavering.

Examine me, O God, and try me;
test my heart and my mind,
for your steadfast love is before me,
and I walk to you in faithfulness.

I do not sit with the wicked,
nor conspire with those who cause
    trouble;
I avoid the company of evildoers;
and those who speak falsehood.

I wash my hands in innocence,
and gather around your altar,
singing a song of thanksgiving,
and telling of all your wonders.

I love the house where you live,
the place where your glory dwells.
Do not sweep me away with sinners,
nor my life with those who oppress,
who plot evil deeds,
whose hands are full of bribes.

As for me, I walk the path of
    integrity.
Redeem me, and be gracious to me.
My foot stands on level ground;
I will bless you in the assembly.
    Glory* . . .

Ant. 3 I call to you, O God, hear the sound of my voice.

Psalm 28:1-3, 6-9

To you, O God, I call,
my rock, be not deaf to me.
If you turn your ear away from me,
I become like those in the grave.

Hear the voice of my pleading
as I cry to you for help,
as I lift up my hands in prayer
to your holy sanctuary.

Do not take me away with the wicked,
with those who are workers of evil,
who speak peace with their neighbors,
while evil is in their hearts.

I bless you, for you have heard
the voice of my supplication.
You are my strength and my shield;
in you my heart trusts.
I am helped, and my heart exults,
with my song I give you thanks.

You are the strength of your people,
you are the refuge of your anointed.
Save your people; and bless your
    heritage;
be their shepherd and carry them
    forever.   Glory* . . .

PRAYER: Jesus, our redeemer, you brought us into life by dying upon the
cross. May we search for new ways to alleviate suffering among all
creatures that your name be glorified and that peace may find a
home in us. We ask this in the name of all creation that groans for
your salvation to be realized within its being. Amen.

EVENING PRAYER

Ant. 1 Be gracious to me, O God, for I have sinned.

Psalm 41

Blessed are they who consider the poor!
O God, you deliver them in the day of
  trouble;
you guard them, and give them life;
they are called blessed in the land;
you do not give them up to temptation.
You sustain them on their sickbeds;
you heal them of all their infirmities.

As for me, I said: "O God, be gracious
  to me,
heal me, for I have sinned against you."
Some could say of me in malice:
"When will you die and your name
  perish?"
They come to see me, uttering empty
  words,
while their hearts gather mischief;
and spread it abroad.
They whisper about me, imagining the
  worst of me.

They say, "A deadly thing has come
  upon you;
you will not rise from where you lie."
Even my friend in whom I trusted,
who ate of my bread, has turned
  against me.

But you, O God, be gracious to me.
Raise me up in your great mercy.
By this I shall know that you are
  pleased with me,
that evildoers have not triumphed.
You have upheld me in my integrity,
and set me in your presence forever.

Blessed are you, God of Israel,
from everlasting to everlasting.
Amen. Amen.   Glory* . . .

Ant. 2 In the stillness we will hear your voice.

Psalm 46

God is our refuge and strength,
a helper in time of trouble. —

We shall not fear though the earth
  should rock,
though the mountains fall into the
  depths of the sea,
though its waters rage and foam,
though the mountains tremble with
  its tumult.

There is a river whose streams gladden
  the city of God,
the holy place of the Most High.
God is within, it shall not be moved;
God will help it at the dawning of the
  day.
Nations rage, sovereignties are shaken;
At the sound of God's voice, the earth
  melts away.

The God of hosts is with us;
the God of our ancestors is our refuge.

Come, behold the works of our God,
who has wrought wonders on the earth.
Making wars cease to the ends of the
  earth;
breaking the bow, snapping the spear,
burning the chariots with fire.
"Be still, and know that I am God,
I am exalted among the nations,
I am exalted on the earth!"

The God of hosts is with us;
the God of our ancestors is our refuge.
  Glory* . . .

Ant. 3 You are the ruler of all the ages, O God.

Canticle: Revelation 15:3–4

Great and wonderful are your works,
God, the Almighty One!
Just and true are your ways,
Ruler of all the ages!

Who shall refuse you honor,
or the glory due your name?

For you alone are holy,
all nations shall come and
  worship in your presence.
Your judgments are clearly seen.
  Glory* . . .

READING

RESPONSORY

In the spirit of Jesus, we give praise to our God. —**In the**...
For our sins are forgiven, —**we give**...
Glory to you, Source of all Being, Eternal Word and Holy Spirit. —**In the**...

CANTICLE OF MARY

Ant.   **Your covenant is one of mercy and forgiveness.**

INTERCESSIONS

PRAYER: Jesus, you heal the sick and brokenhearted. Let your mercy be
upon us so that we may be a sign of your mercy in our world. We
thank you for your forgiveness and for bringing us to this time of
our lives. May all those who died find rest in you. Grant this
through the intercession of all who died forgiving those who
oppressed them. Amen.

SATURDAY

MORNING PRAYER

Ant. 1 Before the dawn, O God, hear my call for help.

Psalm 119:145–152

With all my heart, I cry to you;
answer me, O God.
I cry to you; save me,
that I may observe your will.

I rise before dawn and cry for help;
I hope in your words.
My eyes watch throughout the night
meditating on your promises.

Hear my voice in your steadfast love;
in your justice preserve my life.
Those who persecute me draw near;
they are far from your law.

But you, O God, are near at hand,
all your commands are true.
Long have I known that your will
endures forever.   Glory* . . .

Ant. 2 Bring me to your holy mountain, the place of your dwelling.

Canticle   Exodus 15:1–4a, 8–13, 17–18

I will sing to you, O God, for you are
gloriously triumphant;
horse and rider you have cast into the
sea.

You are my strength and my courage,
you are my salvation.
You are my God, I praise you;
God of my ancestors, I extol you.

Pharaoh's chariots and army you cast
into the sea.
At a breath of your anger the waters
piled up,
the floods stood up in a heap;
the floods congealed in the midst of the
sea.

The enemy boasted, "I will pursue and
overtake them;
I will divide the spoils and have my fill
of them; —

I will draw my sword; my hand shall
destroy them!"
When your wind blew, the sea covered
them;
they sank as lead in the mighty waters.

Who is like you among the gods?
Who is like you, majestic in holiness,
terrible in glorious deeds, worker of
wonders?
You stretched out your hand,
the earth swallowed them!

In your love you led the people you
redeemed;
you guided them to your holy dwelling.

You bring them in and plant them on
your mountain,
the place you have made for your abode,
the sanctuary which your hands have
established.
You, O God, will reign forever and
ever. Glory* . . .

Ant. 3 O praise God, all you nations.

Psalm 117

Praise our God, all you nations!
Acclaim the Most High, all you peoples!

For great is your love for us;
and your faithfulness endures forever.
Glory* . . .

READING

RESPONSORY

Your love is round about me; in you I find my life. —**Your**. . .
Forever I will sing your praise, —**in you**. . .
Glory to you, Source of all Being, Eternal Word and Holy Spirit. —**Your**. . .

CANTICLE OF ZECHARIAH

Ant.   **You are the light of my salvation.**

INTERCESSIONS

PRAYER: You, O God, are a gift of life and in you we find our sanctuary.
May all displaced people find a place of sanctuary and safety in
our hearts and homes this day, and may all those who seek you
find you in the living word among us. Grant this through Jesus
who lives and reigns among us. Amen.

DAYTIME PRAYER

Ant. 1 Incline my heart to your decrees.

Psalm 119:33–40

Teach me the way of your precepts
and I will keep them to the end.
Give me understanding,
that I may keep your law
and observe it with all my heart.

Guide me in the path of your
commandments,
for there is my delight.
Incline my heart to your will
and not to love of profit.

Turn my eyes from what is vain;
by your ways, give me life.
Keep the promise you have made
to those who reverence you.

Turn away the reproach which I dread;
for your decrees are good.
Behold, I long for your precepts;
in your justice, give me life!
Glory* . . .

Ant. 2 O taste and see the goodness of our God!

Psalm 34

I will bless you, O God, at all times,
your praise always on my lips.
My soul makes its boast in you;
the afflicted shall hear and be glad.
Glorify our God with me.
Together let us praise God's name.

I sought you, and you answered me;
and delivered me from all my fears.
Look towards the Most High, and be
radiant;
let your faces not be ashamed.
These poor ones cried; you heard them,
and saved them from all their troubles.

Your angel, O God, is encamped
around those who revere you, to deliver
them.
Taste and see that God is good!
Happy are they who take refuge in you.

Revere the Most High, all you saints.
Those who revere you, have no want!
Young lions suffer want and hunger;
but those who seek you lack no blessing.
Glory* . . .

Ant. 3 Blessed are those who seek after peace.

II

Come children, listen to me,
I will teach you to reverence the
Most High.
Who among you longs for life
and many days to enjoy prosperity?

Keep your tongue from evil,
your lips from speaking deceit.
Turn aside from evil and do good;
seek peace and pursue it.

God's eyes are turned to the righteous,
God's ears toward their cry.
God's face turns away from evil,
that it not be remembered on earth.

When the just cry, the Most High hears,
and delivers them from their troubles.
God is close to the brokenhearted;
saving those whose spirits are crushed.

Many are the afflictions of the just;
they will be delivered from them all.
God will keep guard over all their bones,
not one of them shall be broken.

Evil shall be its own destruction;
oppression shall be condemned.
You redeem the lives of your servants;
those who take refuge in you shall
not be condemned.   Glory* . . .

PRAYER: Most provident God, you graciously give us all good gifts. Teach us to care for our earth: to till our soil responsibly, to keep our air pure, to free our waters from pollution, to harvest the warmth of our sun, and to respect the rights of all species. May we willingly share the gifts of your goodness with one another. We ask this of you, God of our universe. Amen.

WEEK II

SUNDAY EVENING PRAYER I

Ant. 1 Your word, O God, is a light for my path, alleluia.

Psalm 119:105–112

O God, your word is a lamp to my feet
and a light for my path.
I have sworn an oath and confirmed it
to observe your commandments.

I am sorely afflicted:
give me life according to your word!
Accept my offerings of praise,
and teach me your decrees.

Though I hold my life in my hands,
I do not forget your law.
Though the wicked try to ensnare me,
I do not stray from your precepts.

Your will is my heritage for ever,
the joy of my heart.
I incline my heart to carry out your will
forever, to endless ages.   Glory* . . .

Ant. 2 I have given you as a covenant to the people.

Psalm 16

Preserve me, O God, for in you I take refuge.
I say to you: "You are my God;
I have no good apart from you."
All my delight is in your saints;
the faithful who dwell in your land.

Those who choose other gods increase their sorrows;
their offerings of blood I will not pour out
or take their names upon my lips.

You are my portion and my cup;
you are my fortune, my prize.
The lines have fallen for me in pleasant places;
I have been given a welcome heritage.

I will bless you who gives me counsel;
in the night my heart instructs me.
I keep you always before me;
because you are near, I shall stand firm.

Therefore my heart is glad, and my soul rejoices;
even my body rests securely.
For you do not give me up to death,
or let your faithful see the grave.

You will show me the path of life;
in your presence there is fullness of joy,
in your hands, happiness for ever.
Glory* . . .

Ant. 3 For me to live is Christ and to die is gain.

Canticle: Philippians 2:6–11

Though he was in the form of God,
Jesus did not count equality with God
something to be grasped at.

But emptied himself,
taking the form of a slave,
being born in human likeness.

Being found in human estate,
he humbled himself and became
   obedient, obediently accepting death,
even death on a cross!

Therefore God has highly exalted him
and bestowed on him the name
above every other name,

So that at the name of Jesus
every knee should bow,
in heaven, on the earth,
and under the earth,
and every tongue proclaim
to the glory of God:
JESUS CHRIST IS LORD!   Glory* . . .

---

*Glory to you, Source of all Being,
Eternal Word, and Holy Spirit.
As it was . . .

READING

RESPONSORY

We call to you in our need, O God, for you hear the cry of the poor. —**We**...
You will not leave us orphans, —**for you**...
Glory to you, Source of all Being, Eternal Word and Holy Spirit. —**We call**...

CANTICLE OF MARY

Ant.   Be mindful of your mercy to us, O loving God.

INTERCESSIONS

PRAYER: O God, we long to love you with all our heart and mind and soul,
but we know we are divided. Give us a single heart. Make us one
as you are one with Jesus and your Holy Spirit. Amen.

MORNING PRAYER

**Ant. 1 You are members of the household
of God.**

Psalm 118

We give thanks to you, for you are good,
and your steadfast love endures for
ever.

Let the descendants of Israel say:
"Your steadfast love endures for ever."
Let the descendants of Aaron say:
"Your steadfast love endures for ever."
Let those who fear you say:
"Your steadfast love endures for ever."

In my distress, I called to you;
you answered me and set me free.
With you at my side, I do not fear.
What can anyone do against me?
You are at my side to help me:
I shall withstand all evildoers.

It is better to take refuge in you,
than to trust in people:
it is better to take refuge in you
than to trust in our leaders.

All wickedness surrounded me;
in your name I crushed it.
It surrounded me, surrounded me
on every side;
in your name I cut it off.
It surrounded me like bees;
it blazed like a fire among thorns.
In your name I crushed it.

I was pushed hard, and was falling
but you came to help me.
You are my strength and my song;
you are my salvation.

O God, your right hand has triumphed;
your right hand is exalted.
Your right hand has triumphed;
I shall not die, I shall live
and recount your wondrous deeds.
You have chastened me sorely,
but have not given me over to death.

Open to me the gates of justice,
that I may enter and give thanks.
This is your gate, O God;
the just shall enter through it.
I thank you for you have answered me
you alone are my salvation.

The stone which the builders rejected
has become the corner stone.
This is your doing, O God;
it is marvelous in our eyes.
This is the day which you have made;
let us rejoice and be glad in it.

Save us, we beseech you, O God!
O God, grant us success.
Blessed are those who enter
In your holy name.
For you O God, are our God,
and you have given us light.

Let us go forward in procession with
  branches,
up to your holy altar.
You are my God, I thank you.
You are my God, I praise you.
We give thanks to you for you are good;
and your steadfast love endures for
  ever.   Glory* . . .

**Ant. 2 How glorious is your name over
all the earth, alleluia.**

Canticle: Daniel 3:52–57

Blessed are you, God of our ancestors,
praiseworthy and exalted above all
  forever.
Blessed be your holy and glorious
  name,
praiseworthy and exalted above all for
  all ages.
Blessed are you in the temple of your
  glory,
praiseworthy and exalted above all
  forever.
Blessed are you on the throne of your
  kingdom,
praiseworthy and exalted above all
  forever.

Blessed are you who look into the depths
from your throne upon the cherubim,
praiseworthy and exalted above all
  forever.

Blessed are you in the firmament of
  heaven,
praiseworthy and glorious forever.

Blessed are you by all your works.
We praise and exalt you above all
  forever.   Glory* . . .

**Ant. 3 Let us praise God's infinite
greatness, alleluia.**

Psalm 150

We praise you, O God, in your holy
  sanctuary;
we praise you in your mighty heavens.
We praise you for your powerful deeds;
we praise you according to your
  greatness.

We praise you with trumpet sound;
We praise you with lute and harp!
We praise you with timbrel and dance,
We praise you with strings and pipe!

We praise you with sounding cymbals,
We praise you with clashing cymbals!
Let everything that breathes,
give praise to you, O God.   Glory* . . .

READING

RESPONSORY

Our hearts are restless, O God, till they rest in you. —**Our**. . .
Searching and waiting, —**till**. . .
Glory to you, Source of all Being, Eternal Word and Holy Spirit. —**Our hearts**. . .

CANTICLE OF ZECHARIAH

Ant.   May you give light to those who sit in darkness.

INTERCESSIONS

PRAYER: O God, on this first day of the week, we join all creation and
people of all ages in praising you. Your kindness and forgiveness
flow like a river through the centuries refreshing our faith, our
hope and our love. May you be forever praised throughout all the
ages. Amen.

DAYTIME PRAYER

**Ant. 1 You restore my soul in your
living waters, alleluia.**

Psalm 23

Yahweh, you are my shepherd;
I shall not want.
You make me to lie in green pastures.
You lead me to restful waters,
to restore my soul.
You guide me in paths of righteousness
for the sake of your name.
Even though I walk through the valley
  of the shadow of death,
I fear no evil;
for you are with me;
your crook and your staff
give me comfort.

You prepare a table before me
in the presence of my foes;
you anoint my head with oil,
my cup overflows.

Surely goodness and mercy shall follow
  me
all the days of my life.
and I shall dwell in your holy house
  for ever and ever.   Glory* . . .

**Ant. 2 Lead a life worthy of God,
who calls you to glory, alleluia.**

Psalm 76

In Judah you are made known, O God,
your name is great in Israel.
Your abode is established in Jerusalem,—

your dwelling place in Zion.
There you broke the flashing arrows,
the shield, the sword, the weapons of
  war.

You, O God, are glorious,
more majestic than the mountains.
The stouthearted were stripped of their
  spoil;
they sank into sleep;
all the provokers of war
were unable to use their hands.
At your rebuke, O God, our God,
both rider and horse lay stunned.
    Glory* . . .

**Ant. 3 Do not let the sun go down on
your anger, for God is a forgiving
God, alleluia.**

II

You, you alone, strike terror.
When your anger is aroused,
who can stand before you?
From heaven you utter judgment;
the earth feared and stood still,
when you arose to give judgment
to save the oppressed of the earth.

Our anger will serve to praise you;
its residue gird you round.
We fulfill the vows made before you;
  you whom we revere,
who cuts short the lives of leaders,
who strikes terror in unjust rulers.
    Glory* . . .

PRAYER: O God, you have created us to be free. Only through the power of
your love do you reign over us. Help us to be worthy of the gift of
freedom and teach us to respect all creation as the work of your
hands. We ask this, Creator God, giver of all good gifts, through
Jesus who taught us the way. Amen.

EVENING PRAYER II

Ant. 1 You are a priestly people according to the order of Melchizedeck, alleluia.

Psalm 110: 1-5, 7

God's revelation to the Anointed One:
"Sit at my side:
till I put injustice beneath your feet."

God will send forth from Zion
your scepter of power:
rule in the midst of your foes.

Your people will give themselves freely
on the day you lead your host
upon the holy mountains.
From the womb of the morning
your youth will come like dew.

God has sworn an oath that will not
    be changed.
"You are a priest for ever,
after the order of Melchizedek."

The Anointed standing at your right
    hand
will shatter rulers on the day of wrath.

Drinking from your streams by the
    wayside
shall the Chosen One be refreshed.
    Glory* . . .

Ant. 2 The heavens belong to you, but the earth has been given to us, alleluia.

Psalm 115

Not to us, Yahweh, not to us,
but to your name give glory
for the sake of your love and your truth!
Why should the nations say,
"Where is their God?"

But you are in the heavens;
you do whatever you please.
Their idols are silver and gold,
the work of human hands.

They have mouths, but cannot speak;
    eyes, but cannot see;
they have ears, but cannot hear;
    noses, but cannot smell.

They have hands, but cannot feel;
    feet, but cannot walk.
No sound comes from their throats.
Those who make them are like them;
    so are all who trust in them.

Descendants of Abraham, trust in God,
who is your help and your shield.
Descendants of Sarah, trust in God,
who is your help and your shield.
You who fear, trust in God,
who is your help and your shield.

Yahweh remembers us and will bless us,
blessing the descendants of Abraham,
blessing the descendants of Sarah.
God will bless those who fear,
the little no less than the great.

May God give you increase,
you and all your children.
May you be blessed by Yahweh,
who made heaven and earth!

The heavens belong to Yahweh
but the earth has been given to us.
The dead do not praise you,
nor those who go down into silence.
But we who live, bless you,
both now and for ever. Amen.
    Glory* . . .

Ant. 3 We come to join in your holy banquet, O God, alleluia.

Canticle: Revelation 19:1, 5-7

Salvation, glory, and power
    belong to you,
your judgments are honest and true.

All of us, your servants, sing praise to
    you.
We worship you reverently, both great
    and small.

You, our almighty God, are creator
    of heaven and earth.
Let us rejoice and exult, and give you
    glory.

The wedding feast of the Lamb has
    begun,
And the bride has made herself ready.
    Glory* . . .

READING

RESPONSORY

How can we repay you, O God, for your goodness to us? —**How**...
We will sing your praise, —**for your**...
Glory to you, Source of all Being, Eternal Word and Holy Spirit. —**How can**...

CANTICLE OF MARY

Ant.   **My spirit rejoices in God, my Savior.**

INTERCESSIONS

PRAYER: God of mystery, God of love, send your Spirit into our hearts with gifts of wisdom and peace, fortitude and charity. We long to love and serve you. Faithful God, make us faithful. This we ask through the intercession of all your saints. Amen.

MONDAY

MORNING PRAYER

Ant. 1 When from this exile shall we behold you face to face?

Psalm 42

Like the deer that yearns
for flowing streams,
so my soul is longing
for you, my God.

My soul is thirsting for God,
the living God.
When shall I come and see,
the face of God?

My tears have become my food,
by night and day,
while I hear it said all day,
"Where is your God?"

These things will I remember
as I pour out my soul:
how I led the throng,
to the house of God,
with shouts of gladness and
     songs of thanksgiving,
the multitude keeping festival.

Why are you cast down, my soul,
why disquieted within me?
Hope in God; I will again praise you,
my help and my God.

My soul is cast down within me,
therefore I think of you
from the land of Jordan and of Hermon,
     from Mount Mizar.

Deep calls to deep,
in the thunder of your waters;
all your waves and your billows
have swept over me.

By day you will send me
your steadfast love;
and at night your song is with me,
a prayer to the God of my life.

I will say to you, my rock:
"Why have you forgotten me?
Why do I go mourning
because of oppression?"

As with a deadly wound,
my adversaries taunt me,
saying to me all the day long:
"Where is your God?"

Why are you cast down, my soul,
why disquieted within me?
Hope in God; for I shall praise again,
my Savior and my God.   Glory*...

Ant. 2 Worker of wonders, show forth your splendor!

Canticle: Sirach 36:1–5, 10–13

Come to our aid, O God of the universe,
and put all the nations in dread of you!
Raise your hand toward the heathen,
that they may realize your power.

As you have used us to show them your
holiness,
so now use them to show us your glory.
Thus they will know, as we know,
that there is no God but you.

Give new signs and work new wonders;
show forth the splendor of your right
hand and arm.

Gather all the tribes of Jacob,
that they may inherit the land as of old.
Show mercy to the people called by
your name;
Israel, whom you named your first-born.

Take pity on your holy city,
Jerusalem, your dwelling place.
Fill Zion with your majesty,
your temple with your glory.
Glory* . . .

Ant. 3 The courts of heaven ring with the praise of our God.

Psalm 19a

The heavens tell of your glory, O
God,
and the firmament proclaims your
handiwork.
Day unto day pours forth the story
and night unto night reveals its
knowledge.

No speech, no word, no voice is heard;
yet their voice goes out to all the earth,
their words to the end of the world.

In them you set a tent for the sun;
it comes forth like a bridegroom leaving
his chamber,
rejoices like a champion running its
course.

Its rising is from the end of the heavens,
and its course to the end of them;
there is nothing concealed from its
heat. Glory* . . .

READING

RESPONSORY

You are present to us, O God, in all creation. —**You**. . .
Enriching our lives: —**in all**. . .
Glory to you, Source of all Being, Eternal Word and Holy Spirit. —**You are**. . .

CANTICLE OF ZECHARIAH

Ant. Blessed be God who has visited us and saved us.

INTERCESSIONS

PRAYER: O God, you have made us in your image and we long to see your
face. Quiet our minds and enkindle our hearts that walking the
way of your truth we may leave the imprint of your goodness
throughout the world. Grant this in the name of Jesus. Amen.

DAYTIME PRAYER

Ant. 1 Make love your aim, and desire every spiritual gift.

Psalm 119:41–48

Yahweh, let your love come upon me,
your salvation according to your
  promise;
Then I have answer for those who taunt
  me
for I trust in your word.

Take not truth from my mouth,
for my hope is in your decrees.
I shall always keep your law
for ever and ever.

I shall walk in the path of freedom
for I have sought your precepts.
I will speak of your will before rulers
and shall not be put to shame;

for my delight is in your
  commandments; these I have loved.
I revere your precepts,
and will ponder on your statutes.
  Glory* . . .

Ant. 2 My delight is to do your will, O God.

Psalm 40:2–14, 17–18

I waited patiently for you, O God
and you stooped down to me;
and heard my cry.

You drew me from the desolate pit,
out of the miry clay,
and set my feet upon a rock,
making my steps secure.

You put a new song in my mouth,
a song of praise to you.
Many shall see and fear
and place their trust in you.

Happy are we who have placed
  our trust in you, O God,
who do not turn to the proud,
to those who follow false gods!

For us you have multiplied,
  O God my Creator,
your wondrous deeds and plans;
none can compare with you!
Were I to proclaim and tell of them,
they are more than can be numbered.

Sacrifice and offering you do not desire;
but you have given me an open ear.
Burnt offering and sin offering
  you have not required.

Therefore, I said, "Here I am;
In the scroll of the book it is written
  of me:
my delight is to do your will;
your law is within my heart."
  Glory* . . .

Ant. 3 Your mercy is from age to age toward those who revere you.

II

Your deliverance I have proclaimed
in the great assembly.
I have not restrained my lips,
as you well know, O God.

I have not concealed your saving help
  within my heart;
but have spoken of your faithfulness,
  and your salvation;
I have not hidden your steadfast love
  nor your faithfulness
from the great assembly.

O God, you will not withhold
your mercy from me.
Your steadfast love and faithfulness
  always surround me.

For evils without number have
  encompassed me;
My sins have overtaken me,
till I cannot see.
They are more than the hairs of my
  head;
my heart fails me.

Be pleased, O God, to deliver me!
O God, make haste to help me!

May all who seek you
  rejoice and be glad;
May all who love your salvation
say evermore: "Great is our God!"

As for me, I am poor and needy;
but you take thought of me.
You are my help, my deliverer;
O God, do not delay.   Glory* . . .

PRAYER: God of justice, God of mercy, bless all those who are surprised with pain this day from suffering caused by their own weakness or that of others. Let what we suffer teach us to be merciful; let our sins teach us to forgive. This we ask through the intercession of Jesus and all who died forgiving those who oppressed them. Amen.

EVENING PRAYER

Ant. 1 O God, how great is your wisdom, so far beyond my understanding.

Psalm 139:1–18, 23–24

O God, you have searched me and
   you know me,
you know when I sit and when I stand;
you discern my thoughts from afar.
You mark when I walk or lie down,
with all my ways you are acquainted.

Before a word is on my tongue,
behold, O God, you know the whole
   of it.
Behind and before you besiege me,
You lay your hand upon me.
Such knowledge is too wonderful for me:
too high, beyond my reach.

O where can I go from your spirit,
or where can I flee from your presence?
If I climb to heaven, you are there!
If I lie in the grave, you are there!

If I take the wings of the morning
and dwell in the depths of the sea,
even there your hand shall lead me,
your hand shall hold me fast.

If I say: "Let darkness cover me,
and the light around me be night,"
even darkness is not dark to you
and the night is as bright as the day;
for darkness is as light to you.
   Glory* . . .

Ant. 2 You search the mind and probe the heart, giving to each as we deserve.

II

For it was you who formed my inmost
   parts,
knit me together in my mother's womb.
I praise you for the wonder of my being,
for the wonder of all your works.

Already you knew me well;
my body was not hidden from you,
when I was being made in secret
and molded in the depths of the earth.

Your eyes beheld my unformed
   substance;
in your book they all were written,
the days that you had formed for me
when none of them yet were.

How precious to me are your thoughts!
How vast the sum of them!
If I count them, they are more than the
   sand.
When I awake, I am still with you.

Search me, O God, and know my heart!
O test me and know my thoughts!
See that I follow not the wrong way
and lead me in the way of life eternal.
   Glory* . . .

Ant. 3 May Christ dwell in our hearts through faith that we may be rooted in love.

Canticle: Ephesians 1:3–10

Praised be the God
of our Lord Jesus Christ
who has blessed us in Christ
with every spiritual blessing
   in the heavens.

God chose us in him
before the foundation of the world,
that we should be holy
and blameless in God's sight.

We have been predestined
to be God's children through Jesus
   Christ,
such was the purpose of God's will,
that all might praise the glorious favor
bestowed on us in Christ.

In Christ and through his blood,
  we have redemption,
the forgiveness of our sins,
according to the riches of God's grace
  lavished upon us.
For God has made known to us
in all wisdom and insight,—

the mystery of the plan set forth in
  Christ.

A plan to be carried out in Christ,
in the fullness of time,
to unite all things in Christ,
things in heaven and things on earth.
  Glory* . . .

READING

RESPONSORY

You create us in your image, O God, we are co-creators with you. —**You**. . .
We are nothing without you: —**we are**. . .
Glory to you, Source of all Being, Eternal Word and Holy Spirit. —**You create**. . .

CANTICLE OF MARY

Ant.   I rejoice in your greatness, O God.

INTERCESSIONS

PRAYER: God of wisdom, God of our way, we have walked with you from
early morning. Renew our strength this night that we may rise to
serve you and one another with clear vision and strong hope. We
pray especially for all who will awake this night to the vision of
your glory. This we ask through Jesus who is the light of the
world. Amen.

TUESDAY

MORNING PRAYER

**Ant. 1 O God, let us walk as people of
light, that we may know what is
pleasing to you.**

Psalm 43

Defend me, O God, and plead my cause
against a godless nation.
From the deceitful and the unjust
rescue me, O God.

For in you I take refuge;
why have you cast me off?
Why do I go mourning
because of oppression?

O send out your light and your truth;
let these be my guide.
Let them bring me to your holy hill
and to your dwelling place.

Then I will go to the altar of God,
to God, my exceeding joy;
and I will praise you with the lyre,
O God, my God.

Why are you cast down, my soul,
why groan within me?
Hope in God; I shall again praise
  my savior and my God.   Glory* . . .

**Ant. 2 Seek first the reign of God,
and all things shall be yours as well.**

Canticle: Isaiah 38:10–14, 17b–20

Once I said,
"In the noontime of life I must depart!
I am consigned to the gates of death
  for the rest of my years."

I said, "I shall not see God
in the land of the living.
No longer shall I see my companions
among the dwellers of this world."

My dwelling is plucked up and removed
  from me
like a shepherd's tent;
like a weaver I have rolled up my life;
being cut off from the loom.

Day and night you give me over to
 torment;
I cry for help until daybreak;
like a lion you break all my bones;
day and night you give me over to
 torment.

Like a swallow or crane, I clamor,
I moan like a dove.
My eyes are weary gazing upward.
I am oppressed; be my security!

Restore me to health, make me live!
It was for my welfare that I had
 great bitterness;
you have held back my life from the
 pit of destruction,
you have cast all my sins behind your
 back.

For the nether world cannot thank you,
death cannot praise you;
those who go down to the pit
cannot hope for your faithfulness.

The living, the living give you thanks,
as I do this day;
Parents make known to their children,
O God, your faithfulness.

You, O God, will save us;
we will sing to stringed instruments
all the days of our life,
in your holy dwelling.   Glory* . . .

**Ant. 3 Consider the lilies of the field;
 they neither toil nor spin.**

Psalm 65

Praise is due to you,
O God, in Zion;
and to you shall vows be made,
to you who hear our prayer.

READING

RESPONSORY

You know our frailty, O God; give us your strength. —**You**...
You fill us with hope; —**give**...
Glory to you, Source of all Being, Eternal Word and Holy Spirit. —**You know**...

CANTICLE OF ZECHARIAH

Ant.   You, O God, have raised up a horn of salvation for us.

To you shall all flesh come
 because of its sins.
When our offenses bear us down,
you forgive them all.

Blessed are we whom you choose and
 draw near,
to dwell in your courts!
We are filled with the goodness of your
 house,
your holy temple!

With wonders you deliver us,
O God of our salvation.
You are the hope of all the earth
and of far distant seas.

By your strength, you established
 the mountains,
girded with might;
you still the roaring of the seas,
the roaring of their waves,
and the tumult of the peoples.

Those who dwell at earth's farthest
 bounds
stand in awe at your wonders;
you make the sunrise and sunset
 shout for joy.

You care for the earth, give it water,
you fill it with riches.
Your river in heaven brims over
to provide its grain.

You visit the earth and water it,
greatly enriching it;
you level it, soften it with showers,
blessing its growth.

You crown the year with your bounty;
Abundance flows in your path.
The pastures of the wilderness flow,
the hills gird themselves with joy,
the meadows clothe themselves with
 flocks,
the valleys deck themselves with grain,
they shout and sing together for joy.
 Glory* . . .

INTERCESSIONS

PRAYER: All loving God, let us know your presence as we begin this day. Guide us as we strive to choose what is good and just. Lift up our hearts to you when the demands of the day threaten to lead us astray. This we ask through Jesus who is our way, our truth and our life. Amen.

DAYTIME PRAYER

Ant. 1 Blessed are they who hear your word and keep it.

Psalm 119:49–56

Remember your word to your servant
by which you gave me hope.
This is my comfort in my affliction
that your promise gives me life.

Though the proud utterly deride me,
I do not turn from your law.
When I think of your precepts of old,
I take comfort, O God.

I am seized with indignation because
of the wicked
who forsake your law.
Your statutes have been my songs
in the house of my pilgrimage.

I remember your name in the night,
and keep your law.
This blessing has been given to me,
the keeping of your precepts.
Glory* . . .

Ant. 2 You free us from the bondage of sin and restore us to life.

Psalm 53

Fools say in their hearts:
"There is no God."
They are corrupt, doing wicked things;
there are none that do good.

God looks down from heaven
on the peoples of the earth,
to see if any are wise,
if any seek God.

They have all fallen away;
they are all alike depraved;
there are none that do good,
no, not even one.

Have the evildoers no understanding,
who eat up my people just as they eat
bread,
and do not call upon God?

There they are, in great terror,
such terror as has not been!
For God will chastise the oppressors;
they will be put to shame.

O that salvation might come from Zion!
When you restore the fortunes of your
people,
Jacob will rejoice and Israel be glad.
Glory* . . .

Ant. 3 O God, my eyes rejoice in your salvation.

Psalm 54:1–6, 8–9

Save me, O God, by your name;
deliver me by your might.
O God, hear my prayer;
give ear to the words of my mouth.

For the insolent have risen against me,
the ruthless seek my life;
they set themselves before you.
But I have you for my helper;
You uphold my life.

With a willing heart I make sacrifice;
and give thanks to your name.
You deliver me from all trouble,
my eyes rejoice in your salvation.
Glory* . . .

PRAYER: O God, you sent your son, Jesus, to call us to your realm of mercy and love. Let our memories of his words and deeds overflow into our lives, that following him, we may lead others to salvation. We ask this through the intercession of all those who lived as true disciples and now live eternally with you. Amen.

EVENING PRAYER

Ant. 1 Our riches lie in the glory of God.

Psalm 49

Hear this, all you peoples!
Give heed, all dwellers of the world,
you, both low and high,
rich and poor together!

My lips will speak words of wisdom;
my heart will ponder your ways.
I will incline my ear to a proverb;
I will solve my riddle on the lyre.

Why should I fear in times of trouble,
when the malice of my foes surrounds
  me,
those who trust in their wealth,
and boast of the vastness of their riches?

For we cannot buy our own ransom,
or give to God the price for our lives.
The ransom of our lives is beyond us.
It can never be enough,
to avoid going to the grave.

Both the wise and the foolish must
  perish
and leave their wealth to others.
Their graves are their homes for ever,
their dwelling places to all generations,
though their names spread wide
  through the land.
They are like the beasts that perish.
  Glory* . . .

Ant. 2 Be not afraid, I go before you.

II

This is the fate of those with foolish
  confidence,
the end of those who are pleased with
  their portion. —

Like sheep they are driven to the grave;
death shall be their shepherd;
straight to the grave they descend,
and their form shall waste away;
the grave shall be their home.

But you will ransom my soul
  from the power of the grave,
for you will receive me.

Be not afraid when people grow rich,
when the glory of their houses increases.
They carry nothing with them when
  they die,
their glory will not go down with them.

Though while they lived, they thought
  themselves happy,
and thought themselves praised for
  their success,
they will go to join their ancestors,
who will never more see the light.

People cannot abide in insolence;
they are like the beasts that perish.
  Glory* . . .

**Ant. 3 Worthy is the Lamb who was
  slain.**

Canticle: Revelation 4:11, 5:9, 10, 12

Worthy are you, O God, our God,
to receive glory and honor and power.

For you have created all things;
by your will they came to be and were
  made.

Worthy are you to take the scroll
  and to open its seals,

For you were slain, and by your blood,
you purchased for God
persons of every race and tongue,
of every people and nation.

You have made of them a kingdom,
and priests to serve our God,
and they shall reign on the earth.

Worthy is the Lamb who was slain
to receive power and riches,
wisdom and strength,
honor and glory and praise.   Glory* . . .

READING

RESPONSORY

Your compassion, O God, calls us to repentance. —**Your**. . .
Your love heals us, and —**calls**. . .
Glory to you, Source of all Being, Eternal Word and Holy Spirit. —**Your**
   compassion. . .

CANTICLE OF MARY

Ant.   My spirit rejoices in God, my Savior.

INTERCESSIONS

PRAYER: Spirit of God, promise of Jesus, come to our help at the close of
this day. Come with forgiveness and healing love. Come with light
and hope. Come with all that we need to continue in the way of
your truth. So may we praise you in the Trinity forever. Amen.

WEDNESDAY

MORNING PRAYER

**Ant. 1 You, O God are faithful; all
   your ways are holy.**

Psalm 77

I cry aloud to you, my God,
cry aloud that you may hear me.

In the day of my trouble I seek you,
in the night I stretch out my hand
   without tiring;
my soul refuses to be consoled.

I remember you and I moan;
I ponder, and my spirit faints.
You hold my eyelids from closing;
I am so troubled, I cannot speak.

I consider the days of old,
I remember the years long past.
I converse with my heart in the night;
I ponder and search my spirit:

"God, will you spurn us for ever,
and never again show us favor?
Has your love vanished for ever?
Are your promises at an end for all
   time? —

Have you forgotten to be gracious?
Has your anger withheld your
   compassion?"

I say: "This is the cause of my grief;
that the way of the Most High has
   changed."
I will call to mind your deeds;
I will remember your wonders of old,
I will meditate on all your works,
and ponder your mighty deeds.

Your ways, O God, are holy.
What god is great as our God?
You are the God who works wonders,
who shows your power among the
   peoples.
Your strong arm redeemed your people,
the descendants of Jacob and Rachel.

When the waters saw you, O God,
when the waters saw you, they were
   afraid,
the depths were moved with terror.
The clouds poured out water;
the skies gave forth thunder;
your arrows flashed to and fro.

Your thunder crashed in the whirlwind;
your flashes lighted up the world;
the earth trembled and shook.
Your way was through the sea,
your path through the great waters;
yet your footprints were not seen.

You led your people like a flock
by the hands of·Moses and Miriam.
  Glory* . . .

**Ant. 2 My heart exults in God, the
joy of my salvation.**

Canticle: 1 Samuel 2:1–10

My heart exults in Yahweh,
my strength is exalted in my God.
My lips renounce all that is evil,
because I rejoice in your salvation.

There is no Holy One like Yahweh;
there is no Rock like our God.
Speak no longer so boastfully,
nor let arrogance come from your
  mouth.
For God is a God of knowledge,
a God who weighs our deeds.

The bows of the mighty are broken,
but the feeble are circled with strength.
The full hire themselves out for bread,
while the hungry cease to hunger.
The barren have borne seven children,
but those who have many are forlorn.

O God, you put to death and give life;
you cast down to the grave and raise
  up.
You make poor and make rich;
you bring low, you also exalt.

You raise up the poor from the dust;
you lift the needy from the ash heap,
to seat them with those of renown
and inherit a seat of honor.

For the pillars of the earth are yours,
on them you set the world.
You will guard the steps of your
  faithful ones,
but wickedness shall perish in darkness.
For not by strength shall we prevail.

Against evil you will thunder on high.
You will judge the ends of the earth;
you will give strength to just leaders
and exalt the power of your anointed
  ones!   Glory* . . .

**Ant. 3 Rejoice, our God comes to save
us.**

Psalm 97

You reign over all; let the earth rejoice;
let the many coastlands be glad!
Clouds and thick darkness are round
  about you;
righteousness and justice, the foundation
  of your throne.

Fire goes before you,
burning up all that is evil.
Your lightnings lighten the world,
the earth sees and trembles.

Mountains melt like wax before you,
before you, Creator of all the earth.
The heavens proclaim your justice;
all peoples behold your glory.

All who pay homage to idols,
who boast in worthless gods,
are put to shame.
All gods bow down before you.

Zion hears and is glad;
the people of Judah rejoice,
because of your judgments, O God.
For you are most high over all the earth;
exalted far above all gods.

You love those who hate evil;
you preserve the lives of your saints;
you deliver them from wickedness.

Light dawns for the just
and joy for the upright of heart.
Rejoice in God, you that are just,
and give thanks to God's holy name.
  Glory* . . .

READING

RESPONSORY

O God, you are One; you love the singlehearted. —**O God**...
The pure of heart shall see you; —**you**...
Glory to you, Source of all Being, Eternal Word and Holy Spirit. —**O God,**...

CANTICLE OF ZECHARIAH

Ant.   Deliver us, O God, from all that is evil.

INTERCESSIONS

PRAYER: O God, our Creator, each morning we praise the wonder of your
love. Your tender care measures our strength and calls us to grow.
You give us courage before the challenge of the day. O Eternal
God, make us worthy of the time you have given us. This we ask
for ourselves and for all of creation through Jesus, our brother and
friend. Amen.

DAYTIME PRAYER

**Ant. 1 Be gracious to me according
to your promise.**

Psalm 119:57–64

You, O God, are my portion;
I promise to obey your words.
I entreat your favor with all my heart;
be gracious to me according to your
promise.

When I think of your ways,
I turn my feet to your will;
I hasten and do not delay
to keep your commandments.

Though the cords of the wicked
ensnare me
I do not forget your law.
At midnight I rise to praise you,
because of your just decrees.

I am a friend of all who revere you,
of those who obey your precepts.
The earth is full of your steadfast love;
teach me your statutes.   Glory* ...

**Ant. 2 Shelter me in the shadow of
your wings.**

Psalm 55:1–19, 22–24

O God, give ear to my prayer;
hide not from my supplication!
attend to me and answer me;
I am overcome by my troubles.

I am distraught by the lure of
corruption,
at oppression caused by wickedness.
The evil that brings trouble upon me,
and whose anger weighs on my soul.

My heart is in anguish within me,
the terrors of death fall upon me.
Fear and trembling come upon me,
and horror overwhelms me.

O that I had wings like a dove!
I would fly away and be at rest;
indeed, I would wander afar,
I would take refuge in the wilderness,
I would haste to find me a shelter
from the raging wind and tempest.

Overthrow this oppression, O God,
confuse all that seeks to destroy,
For I see violence and strife all around
me.
Day and night it patrols our cities;
They are full of wickedness and evil,
ruin is in their midst;
oppression and fraud do not depart
from their market places.   Glory* ...

**Ant. 3 Let us walk together in the ways
of our God.**

II

It is not our enemies who cause this;
then I might bear it; —

it is not our foes who oppress,
I might hide from them.

But it is ourselves, our companions,
    our familiar and intimate friends.
We used to speak together of justice;
We walked together in companionship
    in the ways of our God.

I will call out to you, O God,
and you will save me.
Evening, morning and at noon
I utter complaint and lament;
you will hear my voice.

You will deliver my soul in safety
in the attack waged all around;
for many things can bring me down,
but you will hear my cry.

You will give ear, and chastise us,
you, who reign from of old;
because we have not kept your law,
and have not revered you.

Cast your burdens on our God,
and you will be supported.
Never will God permit
the just ones to falter.

But you, O God, will bring down
to the pit of the grave,
all that is wicked and evil—
that oppresses the poor and the needy.

O God, we will trust in you.
    Glory* . . .

PRAYER: O God, our daily burdens weigh us down and fear for our future is
no stranger to us. Help us to remember the life and death of Jesus,
that strengthened by his hope, we too may become totally open to
your will. Grant this in Jesus' name. Amen.

EVENING PRAYER

**Ant. 1 In silence and stillness, my
    heart waits for you.**

Psalm 62

For God alone my soul waits in silence;
From God comes my salvation.
God alone is my rock and my
    stronghold,
my fortress; I shall not be moved.

How long will you set upon me
to break me down,
as though I were a leaning wall,
or a tottering fence?

They only plan to destroy.
They take pleasure in falsehood.
They bless with their mouths,
but inwardly they curse.

For God alone my soul waits in silence,
for my hope comes from the Most High.
God alone is my rock and my
    stronghold,
my fortress; I shall not be moved.

In you alone is my deliverance,
my mighty rock, my refuge.
We trust in you at all times
and pour out our hearts before you;
for you are our refuge.

Common folk are but a breath,
great persons are a delusion.
Placed on the scales, they go up;
together they are lighter than a breath.

Put no confidence in extortion,
set no vain hopes on robbery;
do not set your heart on riches,
even if they should increase.

Once God has spoken;
twice have I heard this:
that power belongs to God;
and to you, O God, steadfast love.
For you repay us according to our
    deeds.   Glory* . . .

Ant. 2 Your spirit, O God, moves upon the face of the earth.

Psalm 67

O God, be gracious to us and bless us
and make your face shine upon us.
That your ways be known upon earth,
your saving power among all nations.
Let the peoples praise you, O God;
let all the peoples praise you.

Let the nations be glad and sing for joy,
for you judge the peoples with equity
and guide the nations on earth.
Let the peoples praise you, O God;
let all the peoples praise you.

The earth has yielded its increase;
God, our God, has blessed us.
You, indeed, have blessed us;
let all the earth revere you!
     Glory* . . .

Ant. 3 You are God's temple; God's spirit dwells in you.

Canticle: Colossians 1:12–20

Let us give thanks to God
for having made us worthy
to share the inheritance of the
     saints in light.

God has delivered us
from the power of darkness
and transferred us
into the kingdom of God's beloved Son,
     Jesus,
in whom we have redemption,
the forgiveness of our sins.

Jesus is the image of the invisible God,
the first-born of all creation;
in him all things were created,
     in heaven and on earth,
things visible and invisible.

All things were created through him;
all were created for him.
He is before all else that is.
In him all things hold together.

He is the head of the body, the church!
He is the beginning,
the firstborn from the dead,
that in everything, he might be above
     all others.

In him all the fullness of God was
     pleased to dwell,
and, through him, to reconcile all
     things to himself,
whether on earth or in heaven,
making peace by the blood of his cross.
     Glory* . . .

READING

RESPONSORY

You love the poor, O God; you feed them with your word. —**You love**. . .
They call to you for life; —**you feed**. . .
Glory to you, Source of all Being, Eternal Word and Holy Spirit. —**You love**. . .

CANTICLE OF MARY

Ant.   Most holy be your name.

INTERCESSIONS

PRAYER: O God, we live in constant need. To whom shall we go but to
you? You are both father and mother to us, tending our days with
delicate care. We thank you for your love and mercy this day, and
we ask you to help us to forgive as we have been forgiven; to give
as we have received. This we, your children, ask of you in your
tender mercy. Amen.

THURSDAY
MORNING PRAYER

Ant. 1 I am the vine, you are the branches. The one who abides in me will bear much fruit.

Psalm 80

Give ear, O Shepherd of Israel,
you who lead Joseph like a flock!
You who are enthroned upon the
  cherubim,
shine forth before Ephraim, Benjamin
  and Manasseh!
Stir up your might and come to save us!

Restore us, God of hosts;
let your face shine, that we may
  be saved.

God of hosts, how long will you be
  angry
with your people's prayers?
You fed them with the bread of tears,
and gave them tears to drink in full
  measure.
You made us the scorn of our neighbors,
our enemies laugh among themselves.

Restore us, God of hosts;
let your face shine, that we may
  be saved.

You brought a vine out of Egypt;
you drove out the nations to plant it.
You cleared the ground before it;
it took root and filled the land.

The mountains were covered with its
  shade,
the mighty cedars with its branches;
it sent out its branches to the sea,
and its roots to the Great River.

Then why have you broken down its
  walls?
so that all who pass by pluck its fruit?
It is ravaged by the boar of the forest,
devoured by the beasts of the field.

Turn again, O God of hosts!
Look down from heaven, and see;
have regard for this vine,
the vine your right hand planted.
It has been burnt with fire and cut
  down.

Let your hand be on those you have
  chosen,
those you make strong for yourself!
Then we will never forsake you;
give us life, and we will call on your
  name.

Restore us, God of hosts!
let your face shine, that we may
  be saved.   Glory* . . .

Ant. 2 God is the joy of my salvation.

Canticle: Isaiah 12:1–6

I will give thanks to you, O God;
for though you were angry with me,
your anger turned away,
and you did comfort me.

Behold, you are my savior;
I will trust, and will not be afraid;
you are my strength and my song,
you have become my salvation.

With joy we will draw water
  from the wells of salvation.
We will say on that day:
"We give you thanks and call upon
  your name;
make known your deeds among the
  nations,
proclaim how exalted is your name.

"We sing our praise to you,
for all your glorious deeds;
let this be known in all the earth."
Shout, and sing for joy,
  O people of Zion,
for great in your midst
is the Holy One of Israel!   Glory* . . .

Ant. 3 Today if you should hear God's voice, harden not your heart.

Psalm 81

Sing aloud to God our strength;
shout for joy to the God of our people.

Raise a song and sound the timbrel,
the sweet-sounding harp and the lyre.
Blow the trumpet at the new moon,
when the moon is full, on our feast.

For this is a statute for Israel,
a command of our God.
Who made it a decree with Joseph,
when he went against the land of Egypt.

A voice I had not known said to me:
"I relieved your shoulder of the burden;
your hands were freed from the basket.
In distress you called, and I delivered
you;
I answered you, concealed in the storm
cloud,
I tested you at the waters of Meribah.

Hear, O my people, while I admonish
you!
O Israel, if only you would listen to me!
There shall be no strange god among
you;
you shall not worship an alien god.—

I am Yahweh your God,
who brought you up out of the land of
Egypt.
Open wide your mouth, and I will fill it.

But my people did not listen to my
voice;
Israel would have none of me.
So I gave them over to their stubborn
hearts,
to follow their own counsels.

O that my people would listen to me,
that Israel would walk in my ways!
I would soon subdue their enemies,
and turn my hand against their foes.

I would feed you with the finest wheat,
and with honey from the rock I would
fill you."   Glory* . . .

READING

RESPONSORY

O God, you promise life eternal, asking only that we love. —**O God,** . . .
You are kind to the brokenhearted; —**asking** . . .
Glory to you, Source of all Being, Eternal Word and Holy Spirit. —**O God,** . . .

CANTICLE OF ZECHARIAH

Ant.   Let us serve our God in holiness.

INTERCESSIONS

PRAYER: God of the universe, you speak to us in all of creation, but you call
to us most surely in the depths of our hearts. Help us to listen for
your voice today, gentling our work, our recreation, and our
relationships with others in ways that let us hear you. Deepen in
us our faith in your presence to us. Grant this through the
intercession of all your prophets who listened in sincerity and
truth. Amen.

DAYTIME PRAYER

**Ant. 1 Teach me discernment that I may
know your ways.**

Psalm 119:65–72

You have been good to your servant,
according to your word, O God.
Teach me discernment and knowledge,
for I trust in your commands.

Before I was afflicted I went astray;
but now I keep your word.
You are good and your deeds are good;
teach me your commandments.

The proud smear me with lies,
yet I keep your precepts.
Their hearts are closed to good
but I delight in your law.

It was good for me to be afflicted,
that I might learn your statutes.
The law of your mouth is better to me
than silver and gold.   Glory* . . .

**Ant. 2 Take heart, it is I; have
no fear.**

Psalm 56:1–7b, 9–14

Be gracious to me, O God,
some there are who crush me;
they trample upon me all day long,
for many fight proudly against me.

When I am afraid,
I put my trust in you.
In you, whose word I praise,
In you I trust without fear.
What can mortal flesh do to me?

All day long they injure my cause,
all their thoughts are for evil.
They band together, they lurk,
they watch my steps.

You have kept count of my wanderings;
you have kept a record of my tears!
Are they not written in your book?
Then my foes will be turned back
in the day when I call to you.

This I know, that God is with me.
In God, whose word I praise,
in the Holy One, whose word I praise,
in God I trust without a fear.
What can mortal flesh do to me?

My vows to you I will make, O God.
I will render you thanks.
For you delivered my soul from death,
my feet from falling,
that I may walk before you
in the light of life.   Glory* . . .

**Ant. 3 My heart is steadfast; I will
praise you all my days.**

Psalm 57

Have mercy on me, have mercy,
for in you my soul takes refuge.
In the shadow of your wings I take refuge
till the storms of destruction pass by.

I cry to God the Most High,
to God who has always been my help.
May you send from heaven and save me
and shame those who trample upon me.
O God, send your truth and your love.

My soul lies down among lions,
who greedily devour the peoples
   of the earth.
Their teeth are spears and arrows,
their tongue a sharpened sword.

Be exalted, O God, above the heavens;
let your glory be over all the earth!

They laid a snare for my steps,
my soul was bowed down.
They dug a pit in my path
but they fell in it themselves.

My heart is steadfast, O God,
my heart is steadfast.
I will sing and make melody!
Awake, my soul,
awake, lyre and harp!
I will awake the dawn!

I will give thanks to you among the
   peoples,
I will praise you among the nations,
for your love reaches to the heavens,
your faithfulness to the skies.

Be exalted, O God, above the heavens!
let your glory be over the earth!
   Glory* . . .

PRAYER: O God, you bless those who hunger and thirst for justice. We ask
for the gift of this desire. Imprint on our minds and in our hearts
the longings of your son, Jesus, that our labor this day may be
done justly and that we too may bless those who labor for the sake
of justice. This we ask through the intercession of all who died
working for justice and peace. Amen.

EVENING PRAYER

Ant. 1 You are the salt of the earth; you are the light of the world.

Psalm 72

Give justice to your Anointed, O God,
and righteousness to those Chosen!
That your people may be judged in
   righteousness,
and your poor with justice.

Let the mountains bring forth peace for
   the people,
and the hills, justice!
May your Anointed
defend the cause of the poor,
give deliverance to the needy,
and punish the oppressor!

May your Anointed endure like the sun,
and as long as the moon, through all
   ages,
like rain that falls on the mown grass,
like showers that water the earth.

In that day justice shall flourish
and peace till the moon be no more!
Your Anointed shall rule from sea to
   sea,
from the River to the ends of the earth!

May evil bow down before the Holy
   One,
and wickedness lick the dust!
The kings of Tarshish and of the isles
   shall render tribute.

May rulers of Sheba and Seba
   bring gifts.
All will fall down before the Anointed,
all nations serve and pay homage.
   Glory* . . .

Ant. 2 God will save the poor from oppression and violence.

II

The Anointed delivers the needy when
   they call,
the poor and those who are helpless.
Having pity on the weak and the needy,
saving the lives of the poor.

From oppression and violence they are
   redeemed;
and precious is their blood.
Long may your Chosen One live,
may gold of Sheba be given
to the one you have Anointed,
and prayers be made without ceasing,
and blessings all the day!

May there be abundance of grain in
   the land,
waving on the tops of the mountains;
may its fruit be like Lebanon;
may people flourish in the cities
like the grass in the field!

May the name of your Anointed
   endure for ever,
and continue as long as the sun!
Every tribe shall be blessed in the one
   you have chosen,
all nations bless your name.

Blessed be Yahweh, God of Israel,
who alone does wondrous things.
Blessed be your name for ever;
may your glory fill the earth.
Amen! Amen!   Glory* . . .

Ant. 3 Lamb of God, you take away the sin of the world.

Canticle: Revelation 11:17–18; 12:10b–12a

We give thanks to you, God Almighty,
who is and who was,
you have assumed your great power,
you have begun your reign.

The nations raged, but your wrath
   came,
and the time for the dead to be judged,
for rewarding your servants, the
   prophets and saints,
and those who revere your name,
the great and small alike.

Now the salvation, the power,
   and the reign have come,
of God and of the Christ,
for the accusers of our loved ones
   have been thrown down,
who accuse them day and night.

They have been conquered by the
blood of the Lamb,
and by the word of their testimony, —

for love of life did not deter them
from death.
Rejoice then, O heaven,
and you that dwell therein!
Glory* . . .

READING

RESPONSORY

You are bountiful, O God; all of your desires for us are good. —**You**. . .
Everything is a grace; —all of. . .
Glory to you, Source of all Being, Eternal Word and Holy Spirit. —**You are**. . .

CANTICLE OF MARY

Ant. You have shown your power, O God; you have scattered the proud in their
hearts' fantasy.

INTERCESSIONS

PRAYER: Jesus, our Savior and Guide, you gave yourself to us through a
meal at the end of a day, at the end of your life. Be with us at the
end of this day as we dedicate ourselves to all that you call us to
be. Help us to say to God with you, "Thy will be done." Let us
conclude this day strengthened by the remembrance of your total
gift of self. We ask this through the power of your name. Amen.

FRIDAY

MORNING PRAYER

**Ant. 1 A contrite heart, O God, is
pleasing in your sight.**

Psalm 51

Have mercy on me, O God,
according to your steadfast love;
in your abundant mercy blot out my
sins.
Wash me thoroughly from my offenses,
and cleanse me from my sin!

For I know my offenses,
and my sin is ever before me.
Against you, you alone, have I sinned,
and done what is evil in your sight,
so you are justified in your sentence
and blameless in your judgment.
Behold, I was brought forth in a
sinful world.

For you desire truth in my innermost
being;
teach me wisdom in the depths of my
heart. —

O purify me, and I shall be clean;
O wash me, I shall be whiter than snow.
Fill me with joy and gladness;
let the bones you have broken rejoice.
Hide your face from my guilt,
and blot out all my offenses.

Create in me a clean heart,
put a steadfast spirit within me.
Cast me not from your presence,
take not your spirit from me.
Give me again the joy of your
salvation,
with a willing spirit uphold me.

Then I will teach transgressors your
ways
and sinners will return to you.
Deliver me from death,
O God of my salvation,
and my tongue will sing out your
saving help.

Open my lips and my mouth will sing
  your praises.
For you take no delight in sacrifice;
were I to give a burnt offering,
you would not be pleased.
A broken spirit you accept;
a contrite heart, you will not despise.

In your goodness, show favor to Zion:
rebuild the walls of Jerusalem.
Then will you delight in just sacrifices,
in gifts offered on your altar.
  Glory* . . .

**Ant. 2 Your mercy reaches to the
  heavens; your mercy covers the earth.**

Canticle: Habakkuk 3:2–4, 13a, 15–19

O God, I have heard your renown,
and your work, O God, do I revere.
In the course of the years renew it;
in the course of the years make it
  known;
in your wrath remember mercy!

God came from Teman,
and the Holy One from Mount Paran.
Your glory covered the heavens, O God,
and the earth was full of your praise.

Your brightness was like the light,
rays flashed forth from your hand;
there you veiled your power.
You went forth to save your people,
for the salvation of your anointed.

You trampled the sea with your horses,
the surging of mighty waters.
I hear, and my body trembles,
my lips quiver at the sound;

Decay enters my bones,
my legs totter beneath me.
I wait for the day of trouble
to come on those who oppress us.

READING

RESPONSORY

Though the fig tree does not blossom,
nor fruit be on the vines,
the produce of the olive fail
and the fields yield no food.

Though the flock be cut off from the
  fold
and there be no herd in the stalls,
yet will I rejoice in the Most High
and exult in the God of my salvation.

You, O God, are my strength;
you make my feet like those of hinds,
you make me tread upon the heights.
  Glory* . . .

**Ant. 3 Hear the word of God,
  O people.**

Psalm 147:12–20

O praise the Most High, Jerusalem!
Praise your God, O Zion!

For God strengthens the bars of your
  gates,
blessing your children within you,
establishing peace in your borders,
feeding you with the finest of wheat.

You send out your word to the earth;
your command runs swiftly,
giving snow like wool,
scattering hoarfrost like ashes.

You cast forth your ice like crumbs;
who can stand before your cold?
You send forth your word, and melt
  them;
you make the wind blow, and the
  waters flow.

You make your word known to your
  people,
your statutes and decrees to Israel.
You have not dealt thus with any other
  nation;
you have not taught them your decrees.
  Glory* . . .

Who will deliver us, O God, from our weakness and sin? —**Who**. . .
Jesus Christ has saved us —**from**. . .
Glory to you, Source of all Being, Eternal Word and Holy Spirit. —**Who**. . .

CANTICLE OF ZECHARIAH

Ant.   You are compassionate, O God, and forever faithful to your promise.

INTERCESSIONS

PRAYER: O God, your son, Jesus, died giving the message of your love to us. Have mercy on us. Give us the courage to die rather than cause the death of another. Help us to allow his death to mean new life for us. Never let us stand in the way of your saving grace. Grant this through the intercession of Jesus and all who have given their lives for others. Amen.

DAYTIME PRAYER

Ant. 1 Blessed be God who comforts us in all our affliction.

Psalm 119:73–80

Your hands have made me and have fashioned me;
give me understanding that I may learn your commandments.
Those who revere you will see me and rejoice,
because I have hoped in your word.

I know that your judgments are right,
that in faithfulness you afflicted me.
Let your love be ready to comfort me according to your promise.

Let your mercy come to me, that I may live;
for your law is my delight.
Let the godless be put to shame,
who have corrupted me with guile,
while I will ponder on your precepts.

Let those who revere you turn to me,
that they may know your will.
May my heart be blameless in your commandments,
that I may not be put to shame!
Glory* . . .

Ant. 2 We have a treasure in earthen vessels, to show the power of God.

Psalm 59:1–5, 10–11, 17–18

Deliver me from evil, O my God,
protect me from those who oppress me,
deliver me from all that is wicked,
and save me from all cruelty.

Calamity lies in wait for my life;
misfortune bands together against me.
For no offense or sin of mine,
for no fault, they run and make ready.
Rouse yourself, come to my aid and see!

O my Strength, I will sing praises to you;
for you, O God, are my stronghold.
In your steadfast love you will meet me;
O God, come to my aid,
let me triumph over oppression.

As for me, I will sing of your might;
each morning sing of your love.
For you have been to me a stronghold
and a refuge in the day of distress.

O my Strength, I will sing praises to you,
for you, O God, are my stronghold,
the God who shows me love without end.   Glory* . . .

Ant. 3 Blessed are you, O God, who heal us while wounding us.

Psalm 60

O God, you have rejected us and broken our defenses;
You have turned your face; restore us.

You have made the land to quake, torn it open;
Repair its breaches for it totters.
You have made your people suffer hard things,
and gave us wine that made us reel.

You have set up a signal for those
   who fear you,
to rally to it from the bow.
That your faithful ones may be
   delivered,
help us by your hand and give answer!

You have spoken from your sanctuary:
"With exultation I will divide Schechem
and portion out the Vale of Succoth.

Gilead is mine and Manasseh;
Ephraim is my helmet,
Judah is my scepter.

Moab is my washbasin;
upon Edom I cast my shoe;
Over Philistia I will shout in triumph."

Who will bring me to the fortified city?
Who will lead me to Edom?
Have you not rejected us, O God?
You did not go forth with our armies.

Give us help against the foe,
for human help is vain.
With you we shall do valiantly;
it is you who will tread down
   oppression.   Glory* . . .

PRAYER: Lord Jesus Christ, the marvel of your love lives on and challenges everyone who comes to know you. In you we know the love of God; through you we know the will and ways of God. Be with us now that we may live for one another as you have lived and died for us. Grant this through your Spirit of Love. Amen.

EVENING PRAYER

**Ant. 1 You are gracious, O God,
and full of compassion.**

Psalm 116:1–9

I love you, O God, for you have heard
my voice and my supplications.
You have inclined your ear to me,
I will call on you as long as I live.

The snares of death encompassed me;
the pangs of the grave laid hold on me;
I suffered distress and anguish.
Then I called on your name, O God:
"O God, I pray you, save my life!"

Gracious are you and just;
merciful and full of compassion.
You preserve those with simple hearts;
when I was brought low, you saved me.

Return, my soul, to your rest;
for God has dealt kindly with you,
delivering my soul from death,
my eyes from tears,
my feet from stumbling.

I will walk before you, O God,
in the land of the living.   Glory* . . .

**Ant. 2 God is my comforter and
help in time of need.**

Psalm 121

I lift up my eyes to the hills.
From whence comes my help?
My help comes from you, O God,
who made heaven and earth.

You will not let my foot stumble,
you, who preserve me, will not sleep.
Behold, you who keep Israel
will neither slumber nor sleep.

You, O God, are our keeper;
you are our shade.
The sun shall not smite us by day,
nor the moon by night.

You will guard us from all evil;
you will preserve our lives.
You will protect our goings and comings
both now and for ever.   Glory* . . .

Ant. 3 Ruler of all the ages, just and true are your ways.

Canticle: Revelation 15:3–4

Great and wonderful are your works,
God, the Almighty One!
Just and true are your ways,
Ruler of all the ages!

Who shall refuse you honor,
or the glory due your name?
For you alone are holy,
all nations shall come and
 worship in your presence.
Your judgments are clearly seen.
 Glory* . . .

READING

RESPONSORY

Lord Jesus Christ, your yoke is easy and your burden is light. —**Lord**. . .
In you we will find rest —**for your**. . .
Glory to you, Source of all Being, Eternal Word and Holy Spirit. —**Lord Jesus**. .

CANTICLE OF MARY

Ant.   You put down the mighty from their throne and lift up the lowly.

INTERCESSIONS

PRAYER: Holy Spirit, Living Love of God, you are in the world healing the
wounds of sin and death. Warm the hearts of those embittered by
sorrow and pain, encourage those crushed by failure, enlighten the
minds of those dulled by pleasure or fatigue. Awaken in us all the
remembrance of the overwhelming love of God made known to us
in the life and death of Jesus. Help us to continue with renewed
trust. This we ask of you, Life-giving Spirit, in the name of your
Christ, God among us. Amen.

SATURDAY

MORNING PRAYER

Ant. 1 We acclaim your love in the morning and your faithfulness at night.

Psalm 92

It is good to give thanks to you,
to sing praises to your name, Most
 High,
to declare your love in the morning,
and your faithfulness by night,
to the music of the lute and the harp,
to the melody of the lyre.

For you make me glad by your deeds;
at the work of your hands I sing for joy.
How great are your works, O God!
Your thoughts are very deep!

The foolish ones cannot know;
the stupid cannot understand this:
though the wicked spring up like grass
and all evildoers flourish,
they are doomed to their own devices.
But you, O God, are on high for ever.
All wickedness shall perish;
all oppression be wiped out.

You give me the strength of the wild ox;
you pour oil over my head.
My eyes have seen the downfall of evil,
my ears have heard the doom of
 corruption.
The just shall flourish like the palm tree
and grow like a cedar in Lebanon.

They are planted in your holy house,
they flourish in your courts.
They still bring forth fruit in old age,
they are ever full of sap and green,
to show that you, O God, are just;
you are my rock; in you there is no
   injustice.   Glory* . . .

Ant. 2 **We declare your greatness,
O God.**

   Canticle: Deuteronomy 32:1–12

Give ear, O heavens, while I speak;
let the earth hear the words of my
   mouth.
May my teaching soak in like the rain,
and my speech permeate like the dew,
like a gentle rain upon the tender grass,
like a shower upon the herbs.

For I will proclaim your name, O God.
Declare your holy greatness!
"My Rock, your work is faultless;
all your ways are justice.
A faithful God, without deceit,
how just and right you are!

Yet basely have you been dealt with
   by your sinful children,
a perverse and crooked generation.
Is God to be thus requited,
you foolish and senseless people?
Is God not your source, who created
   you,
who made you and established you?

Remember the days of old,
Consider the years of many generations;
Ask your parents and they will inform
   you,
ask your elders and they will tell you.

When the Most High gave the nations
   their inheritance,
separating the children of the earth,
Yahweh fixed the boundaries of the
   peoples
according to the number of those in
   your court.
But your portion, O God, is your
   people,
Jacob, your allotted heritage.

You found them in a desert land,
in the howling waste of the wilderness;
encircling them and caring for them,
guarding them as the apple of your eye.

Like an eagle that stirs up its nest,
that flutters over its young,
so you spread your wings to catch them,
and bear them on your pinions.
You alone were their leader,
no strange god was with our God."
   Glory* . . .

Ant. 3 **How great is your name in all
the earth.**

        Psalm 8

How great is your name, O God,
   in all the earth!

You whose glory above the heavens
is chanted on the lips of babes,
have founded a defense against your
   foes,
to silence the cries of the rebels.

When I look at the heavens,
the work of your hands,
the moon and the stars which you
   established;
who are we that you should keep us in
   mind,
mortal flesh that you care for us?

Yet you have made us little less than
   God,
and crowned us with glory and honor.
You entrust us with the works of your
   hands,
to care for all your creation.

All sheep and oxen,
and even the beasts of the field,
the birds of the air, and the fish of
   the sea,
whatever passes along the paths of the
   sea.

How great is your name, Creator God,
in all the earth!   Glory* . . .

READING

RESPONSORY

Those who wait for you, O God, shall never be disappointed. —Those...
They shall see you face to face, —and shall...
Glory to you, Source of all Being, Eternal Word and Holy Spirit. —Those who...

CANTICLE OF ZECHARIAH

Ant. Guide our feet into the way of peace.

INTERCESSIONS

PRAYER: Merciful God, we often stray from your call and our own
intentions, but you meet us with forgiveness and creative love.
Give us the gift of patience and understanding that we too may
lure others to new life. May all who die this day enjoy life with
you as they see you face to face. Grant this through Mary, who
brought new life to us in Jesus. Amen.

DAYTIME PRAYER

Ant. 1 In your love spare my life, that I may keep your decrees.

Psalm 119:81–88

My soul pines for your salvation;
I hope in your word.
My eyes fail with watching for your
promise;
"When will you comfort me?"

Though parched and exhausted with
waiting
I have not forgotten your commands.
How long must your servant endure?
When will you requite me?

Evil waits to entrap me
to sin against your law.
All your commandments are sure;
then help me when oppressed by
falsehood!

Death lurks to make an end of me;
but I forsake not your precepts.
In your steadfast love spare my life,
that I may do your will.   Glory* . . .

Ant. 2 O God, you are my refuge, my stronghold against evil.

Psalm 61

Hear my cry, O God,
listen to my prayer;
from the end of the earth I call,
when my heart is faint.

Set me on the rock that is higher
than I;
for you are my refuge,
my stronghold against evil.

Let me dwell in your tent for ever!
Hide me in the shelter of your wings!
For you, O God, have heard my vows,
you have given me the heritage
of those who love your name.

May you lengthen the lives of just
rulers:
may their years cover many generations!
May they ever be enthroned before you;
bid love and truth watch over them.

So will I ever sing your praises,
as I pay my vows day after day.
Glory* . . .

Ant. 3 O God, preserve my life from corruption.

Psalm 64

Hear my voice, O God, in my
  complaint;
preserve my life from all that is evil,
hide me from the temptor's snare,
from the scheming wiles of my heart.

Evil sharpens its tongue like a sword;
aiming bitter words like arrows
shooting from ambush at the innocent,
shooting suddenly and without fear.

Holding fast to its evil purpose;
conspiring to lay secret snares
thinking: "Who can see us?
Who can search out our crimes?"

But you know well our inmost thoughts,
the depth of the heart and mind!
You will shoot your arrow at them;
they will be wounded suddenly.
Our own tongues bring us to ruin.

Then let all people fear;
they will tell what you have wrought,
and ponder what you have done.
The just will rejoice in you, Yahweh,
and fly to you for refuge.
Let the upright in heart exult.
  Glory* . . .

PRAYER: Another week has passed, O God, and we see all that we have
done and what we might have done differently. We give all of our
endeavors to you. Bless the good and heal the faulty. Inspire us to
do your will more creatively and generously in the week to come.
We ask this through Jesus who shows us the way. Amen.

WEEK III

SUNDAY, EVENING PRAYER I

**Ant. 1 Your glory is above the heavens;
we praise your name.**

Psalm 113

We your servants, praise you!
Praise your holy name!
Blessed be your name, O God,
from now and for evermore!
From the rising of the sun to its setting
your name is to be praised!

You are high above all nations,
and your glory above the heavens!
Who is like unto you, O God,
who is seated upon the heights,
who looks far down upon us,
upon the heavens and the earth?

You raise the poor from the dust,
lift the needy from the ash heap,
to set them in the company of rulers,
with the rulers of your people.
To the barren, you give a home,
and gladden their hearts with children.
Glory* . . .

**Ant. 2 I will lift up the cup of salvation
and call on your holy name.**

Psalm 116:10–19

I kept faith, even when I said:
"I am greatly afflicted;"
I said in my dismay,
"No one can be trusted."

What shall I render to you,
for all your goodness to me?
I will lift up the cup of salvation
and call on your holy name.

I will make my vows to you
in the presence of all your people.
Precious in your sight
is the death of your faithful ones.

Indeed, I am your servant;
you have loosened my bonds.
I will offer sacrifice of thanksgiving
and call on your holy name.

I will make my vows to you
in the presence of all your people,
in the courts of your holy house,
in the midst of all your saints.
Glory* . . .

**Ant. 3 Every tongue will proclaim:
Jesus Christ is Lord!**

Canticle: Philippians 2:6–11

Though he was in the form of God,
Jesus did not count equality with God
something to be grasped at.

But emptied himself,
taking the form of a slave,
being born in human likeness.

Being found in human estate,
he humbled himself and became
    obedient,
obediently accepting death,
even death on a cross!

Therefore God has highly exalted him,
and bestowed on him the name
above every other name,

So that at the name of Jesus
every knee should bow,
in heaven, on the earth,
and under the earth,
and every tongue proclaim
to the glory of God:
JESUS CHRIST IS LORD!   Glory* . . .

***Glory to you, Source of all Being,
Eternal Word, and Holy Spirit.
As it was. . .**

READING

RESPONSORY

We sing to you, O God, and bless your name. —**We**...
Tell of your salvation day after day —**and bless**...
Glory to you, Source of all Being, Eternal Word and Holy Spirit. —**We sing**...

CANTICLE OF MARY

Ant.   **You have helped your servant, Israel, remembering your mercy.**

INTERCESSIONS

PRAYER: All holy, ever-present God, at the close of this day we offer to you the world's struggle toward wholeness. We are confident that our darkness and sin have been redeemed through the death of Jesus and that your mercy has no limit. Give us the gift of mercy for ourselves and for others. We ask this in Jesus' name. Amen.

SUNDAY

MORNING PRAYER

Ant. 1 Glory to God in the highest, alleluia.

Psalm 93

O God, you are our Sovereign,
you are robed in majesty;
you are girded with strength.
The world is made firm;
it shall never be moved;
your throne is established from of old;
from all eternity, you are.

The waters have lifted up, O God,
the waters have lifted up their voice,
the waters have lifted up their thunder.
Mightier than the roaring of the
    waters,
mightier than the surgings of the sea,
You, O God, are glorious on high!

Your decrees are to be trusted.
Holiness befits your house,
O God, for evermore.   Glory* ...

Ant. 2 Praise and exalt God above all, forever, alleluia!

Canticle   Daniel 3:57–88, 56

All you works of God, praise our God.
Praise and exalt God above all forever.
All you angels, sing your praise,
you heavens and waters above.
Sun and moon, and stars of heaven,
sing praise with the heavenly hosts.

Every shower and dew, praise our God.
Give praise all you winds.
Praise our God, you fire and heat,
cold and chill, dew and rain.
Frost and chill, praise our God.
Praise God, ice and snow.
Nights and days, sing hymns of praise,
light and darkness,
lightnings and clouds.

Let all the earth bless our God.
Praise and exalt God above all forever.
Let all that grows from the earth
    give praise
together with mountains and hills.
Give praise, you springs,
you seas and rivers, −

dolphins and all water creatures.
Let birds of the air,
beasts, wild and tame,
together with all living peoples,
praise and exalt God above all forever.

O Israel, praise our God.
Praise and exalt God above all forever.
Give praise, you priests,
servants of the Most High,
spirits and souls of the just.
Holy ones of humble heart,
sing your hymns of praise.
Hananiah, Azariah, Mishael, praise our
  God.
Praise and exalt God above all forever.

Let us bless our God, Holy Mystery,
Source of All Being, Word and Spirit.
Let us praise and exalt God above all
  forever.
Blessed are you, O God, in the
  firmament of heaven.
Praiseworthy and glorious and exalted
  above all forever.

**Ant. 3 Praise God from the heavens,
  alleluia**

Psalm 148

Praise God from the heavens,
Praise God in the heights!
Praise God, all you angels,
Praise God, you heavenly hosts!

Praise God, sun and moon,
Praise God, shining stars.
Praise God, highest heavens,
and the waters above the heavens!

Let them praise the name of God,
who commanded and they were
  created.
God established them for ever;
fixed their bounds which will not pass
  away.

Praise God, all you on earth,
sea monsters and all deeps,
fire and hail, snow and frost,
stormy winds that obey God's word!

Mountains and all hills,
fruit trees and all cedars!
Beasts, wild and tame,
reptiles and birds on the wing!

All earth's rulers and peoples,
leaders and those of renown!
Young men and women,
the old together with children!

Let us praise your name, O God,
for your name alone is exalted;
your glory above heaven and earth.

You exalt the strength of your people,
you are praise for all your saints,
for all the faithful near to you.
  Glory* . . .

READING

RESPONSORY

Our hearts rejoice, O God, in your tender care. —**Our hearts**. . .
We live in peace —**in your**. . .
Glory to you, Source of all Being, Eternal Word and Holy Spirit. —**Our hearts**. . .

CANTICLE OF ZECHARIAH

Ant. You have visited and redeemed your people, O God.

INTERCESSIONS

PRAYER: God of the universe, you create the night as well as the day. You
  are with us in good fortune and bad times. You order all things for
  our well being and you lure us to truth and holiness. For these and
  all your gifts to us we sing your praise through Jesus Christ who is
  our way, our truth and our life. Amen.

DAYTIME PRAYER

**Ant. 1 You are my companion, my
helper on the way.**

Psalm 118

I

We give thanks to you, for you are good,
and your steadfast love endures for
  ever.

Let the descendants of Israel say:
"Your steadfast love endures for ever."
Let the descendants of Aaron say:
"Your steadfast love endures for ever."
Let those who fear you say:
"Your steadfast love endures for ever."

In my distress, I called to you;
you answered me and set me free.
With you at my side, I do not fear.
What can anyone do against me?
You are at my side to help me:
I shall withstand all evildoers.

It is better to take refuge in you,
than to trust in people:
it is better to take refuge in you
than to trust in our leaders.   Glory* . . .

**Ant. 2 You are my saving God; you
chastise and you bless, alleluia.**

II

All wickedness surrounded me;
in your name I crushed it.
It surrounded me, surrounded me
  on every side;
in your name I cut it off.
It surrounded me like bees;
it blazed like a fire among thorns.
In your name I crushed it.

I was pushed hard, and was falling
but you came to help me.
You are my strength and my song;
you are my salvation.

O God, your own hand has triumphed;
your hand is exalted!
Because your hand has triumphed,
I shall not die, I shall live
and recount your wondrous deeds.
You have chastened me sorely,
but have not given me over to death.
  Glory* . . .

**Ant. 3 Blessed is the one who comes
in the name of our God.**

III

Open to me the gates of justice,
that I may enter and give thanks.
This is your gate, O God;
the just shall enter through it.
I thank you for you have answered me;
you alone are my salvation.

The stone which the builders rejected
has become the cornerstone.
This is your doing, O God;
it is marvelous in our eyes.
This is the day which you have made;
let us rejoice and be glad in it.

Save us, we beseech you, O God!
O God, grant us success.
Blessed are those who enter
in your holy name.
For you, O God, are our God,
and you have given us light.

Let us go forward in procession with
  branches,
up to your holy altar.
You are my God, I thank you.
You are my God, I praise you.
We give thanks to you for you are good;
and your steadfast love endures for
  ever.   Glory* . . .

PRAYER: God of mercy, your goodness encompasses the great and the small.
Help us to know your presence in the most hidden suffering, the
most secret pain. Remind us again of your unfailing love and give
us new hope. This we ask through the intercession of all who
suffered in hope and now live with you. Amen.

EVENING PRAYER II

Ant. 1 God revealed to the Anointed One, "sit at my side, alleluia!"

Psalm 110: 1–5, 7

God's revelation to the Anointed One:
"Sit at my side:
till I put injustice beneath your feet."

God will send forth from Zion
your scepter of power;
rule in the midst of your foes.

Your people will give themselves freely
on the day you lead your host
upon the holy mountains.
From the womb of the morning
your youth will come like dew.

God has sworn an oath that will not
   be changed.
"You are a priest for ever,
after the order of Melchizedek."

The Anointed standing at your right
   hand
will shatter rulers on the day of wrath.

Drinking from your streams by the
   wayside
shall the Chosen One be refreshed.
   Glory* . . .

Ant. 2 In your gracious mercy, you cause us to remember your wonderful works, alleluia.

Psalm 111

I will give thanks to you with all my
   heart,
in the company of the great assembly.
Great are the works of the Most High;
pondered by all who delight in them.

Full of honor and majesty is your work,
your justice endures for ever.
You enable us to remember your
   wonders;
you are gracious and merciful.

You give food to those who fear you;
you are mindful of your covenant.
You have shown your people the power
   of your works,
by giving them the heritage of the
   nations.

Your works are faithful and just;
your precepts are all trustworthy,
they are established for ever and ever,
to be done in uprightness and truth.

You sent redemption to your people,
and commanded your covenant for
   ever.
Holy and awesome is your name!

To fear you is the beginning of
   wisdom;
all who do so prove themselves wise.
Your praise endures for ever!
   Glory* . . .

Ant. 3 We rejoice and exult in you, alleluia.

Canticle: Revelation 19:1, 5–7

Salvation, glory, and power
   belong to you,
your judgments are honest and true.

All of us, your servants, sing praise to
   you.
We worship you reverently, both great
   and small.

You, our almighty God, are Creator
   of heaven and earth.
Let us rejoice and exult, and give you
   glory.

The wedding feast of the Lamb has
   begun,
and the bride has made herself ready.
   Glory* . . .

READING

RESPONSORY

You create and sustain us, O God, with your love. —**You**...
From generation to generation —**with**...
Glory to you, Source of all Being, Eternal Word and Holy Spirit. —**You create**...

CANTICLE OF MARY

Ant.   **Blessed are you among women and blessed is the fruit of your womb.**

INTERCESSIONS

PRAYER: God of wisdom, your steadfast love gives meaning to our lives. Remembering your goodness from ages past, we have hope. Our very desire for you is a gift of your love. Holy Mystery, we do believe; help our unbelief. This we ask for ourselves, but most especially for those without hope and those who know no love. Hear our prayer in Jesus' name. Amen.

MONDAY

MORNING PRAYER

Ant. 1 My soul is longing for the living God.

Psalm 84

How lovely is your dwelling place,
O God of hosts!

My soul longs and yearns
for the courts of the Most High;
my heart and lips sing for joy
to you, the living God.

Even the sparrow finds a home,
and the swallow a nest for its brood,
where it may lay its young,
at your altars, O God of hosts!

Blessed are those who dwell in
    your house,
for ever singing your praise!
Blessed are those whose strength
    you are,
in whose hearts are the roads to Zion.

As they go through the Bitter Valley,
they make it a place of springs;
the early rain covers it with pools.
They go from strength to strength;
the God of gods will be seen in Zion.

O God of hosts, hear my prayer;
give ear, O God of Jacob! —

Look upon our shield, O God;
look on the face of your anointed!

For one day in your courts is better,
than a thousand anywhere else.
I would rather stand at your threshold,
than dwell in the tents of wickedness.

For you are a sun and a shield;
you bestow favor and honor.
No good do you withhold
from those who walk uprightly.

O God! God of hosts!
Blessed are those who trust in you!
    Glory* ...

Ant. 2 Let us walk in your light, O God.

Canticle   Isaiah 2:2–5

It shall come to pass in days to come,
that the mountain of the house of God
shall be established as the highest
    mountain,
and be raised above the hills.

All nations shall flow to it;
many peoples shall come and say:
"Come, let us go up to the
    mountain of God, —

to the house of the God of Jacob;
that we may be taught in God's ways,
and walk in God's paths."

For from Zion shall go forth the law,
and the word of the Most High from
  Jerusalem.
God shall judge between the nations,
and shall decide for many peoples;
they shall beat their swords into
  plowshares,
and their spears into pruning hooks;
nation shall not lift up sword against
  nation,
nor shall they teach war any more.

O house of Jacob, come,
let us walk in the light of our God!
  Glory* . . .

**Ant. 3 Let all things exult in your
presence for you come to judge
the earth.**

Psalm 96

O sing to God a new song;
sing to God, all the earth!
Sing and bless God's name.

We proclaim your salvation day by
  day,
declare your glory among the nations,
your wonders among all the peoples.

You are great and worthy to be praised;
to be feared above all gods.
The gods of the nations are idols;
but you made the heavens.
Honor and majesty are before you;
strength and beauty, in your sanctuary.

Give to God, you families of peoples,
give to God glory and power!
Give glory to God's holy name;
bring an offering, and enter God's
  courts!
Worship in the temple of Yahweh.
O earth, tremble before the Almighty.

We proclaim to all nations:
"You, O God, are sovereign.
The world you established,
it shall never be moved;
you will judge the peoples with equity."

Let the heavens be glad and the earth
  rejoice;
let the sea thunder, and all that
  fills it;
let the field exult, and everything in it!
Then shall all the trees of the wood
  sing for joy
at your presence, O God, for you come,
you come to judge the earth.

You will judge the world with justice,
and the peoples with your truth.
  Glory* . . .

READING

RESPONSORY

There is no limit, O God, to your love for us. —**There is** . . .
All that you do attests —**to your** . . .
Glory to you, Source of all Being, Eternal Word and Holy Spirit. —**There is** . . .

CANTICLE OF ZECHARIAH

Ant.   Blessed be the great God of Israel.

INTERCESSIONS

PRAYER: O God, we long to follow in the footsteps of Jesus, bringing about
your reign of love. Our weakness and sinfulness stops us over and
over again. Help us to overcome all that keeps us from loving you
and doing your will. Grant this through the intercession of all who
won eternal life by their efforts to overcome their own frailties.
Amen.

DAYTIME PRAYER

Ant. 1 I will not forget your precepts; by them you give me life.

Psalm 119:89–96

For ever, O God, your word
is firmly fixed in the heavens.
Your faithfulness endures to all
 generations;
you established the earth,
it will not be moved.

By your decree it stands to this day;
for all things are your servants.
If your law had not been my delight,
I would have died in my affliction.

I will never forget your precepts;
by them you have given me life.
Save me, for I am yours;
I have sought your precepts.

Wickedness waits to destroy me;
but I ponder your will.
I have seen a limit to all perfection,
but your commandment is exceedingly
 broad.   Glory* . . .

Ant. 2 You are my hope; my trust from the days of my youth.

Psalm 71

In you, O God, I take refuge;
let me never be put to shame!
In your justice deliver and rescue me;
incline your ear to me and save me.

Be to me a rock of refuge,
a stronghold to save me,
for you are my rock and my stronghold.
Rescue me from the throes of oppression,
from the grip of injustice and greed.

For you, O God, are my hope,
my trust, O God, from my youth.
Upon you I have leaned from my birth;
from my mother's womb you claimed
 me.
I praise you for ever and ever.

I have been a portent to many;
but you are my strong refuge.
My lips are filled with your praise,
with your glory all the day. —

Do not cast me off in old age;
forsake me not when my strength is
 spent.

O God, be not far from me;
O God, make haste to help me!
Let evil see its own destruction,
and injustice turn on itself.   Glory* . . .

Ant. 3 Even in old age, O God, do not forsake your servant.

II

But as for me, I will always hope
and praise you more and more.
My lips will tell of your justice,
of your salvation all the day,
for your goodness cannot be numbered.

I will declare your mighty deeds,
I will proclaim your justice.
You have taught me from my youth,
and I proclaim your wonders still.

Now that I am old and gray-headed,
O God, do not forsake me,
till I proclaim your power
to generations to come.
Your power and your justice, O God,
reach to the highest heavens.

You have done marvelous things,
O God, who is like you?
You who have made me see many sore
 troubles
will revive me once again;
from the depths of the earth you will
 raise me.
You will exalt and comfort me again.

So I will praise you with the harp
for your faithfulness, O God;
I will sing praises to you with the lyre,
O Holy One of Israel.

My lips will shout for joy,
when I sing praises to you;
my soul also, which you have redeemed.
My tongue will tell of your justice
 all the day long,
for evil is put to rout, and all that
 sought to harm me.   Glory* . . .

PRAYER: Help us, O God, to reach out to those in need. The poor, the elderly, the imprisoned, those who are ill call out to us as they fill out what is wanting in the suffering of Jesus. Give us the wisdom and generosity to minister to them and to manifest your love. Grant this for Jesus' sake who came to set us free. Amen.

EVENING PRAYER

Ant. 1 Our eyes look to you till you have mercy upon us.

Psalm 123

To you I lift up my eyes,
you who are enthroned in the heavens!
Behold like the eyes of servants
look to the hand of their master,

Like the eyes of a maid
look to the hand of her mistress,
so our eyes look to you, O God,
till you have mercy upon us.

Have mercy on us, O God, have mercy,
for we are filled with contempt.
Too long has our soul been sated
with the scorn of the arrogant,
the contempt of the proud.   Glory* . . .

Ant. 2 You will wipe away every tear from our eyes and death shall be no more.

Psalm 124

If you had not been on our side,
let Israel now say—
if you had not been on our side,
when oppression overwhelmed us,
then would we be swallowed alive,
when injustice raged against us.

Then the flood would have swept us
   away,
the torrent would have gone over us;
over us would have gone
   the raging waters.

Blessed be Yahweh who did not give us
a prey to its teeth!
We have escaped like a bird
from the snare of the fowler;
indeed the snare is broken,
and we have escaped.

Our help is in the name of the Most
   High,
who made heaven and earth.
   Glory* . . .

Ant. 3 O God, you chose us in Jesus to be your children.

Canticle: Ephesians 1:3–10

Praised be the God
of our Lord Jesus Christ
who has blessed us in Christ
with every spiritual blessing
   in the heavens.

God chose us in him
before the foundation of the world,
that we should be holy
and blameless in God's sight.

We have been predestined
to be God's children through Jesus
   Christ,
such was the purpose of God's will,
that all might praise the glorious favor
bestowed on us in Christ.

In Christ and through his blood,
   we have redemption,
the forgiveness of our sins,
according to the riches of God's grace
   lavished upon us.

For God has made known to us
in all wisdom and insight,
the mystery of the plan set forth in
   Christ.

A plan to be carried out in Christ,
in the fullness of time,
to unite all things in Christ,
things in heaven and things on earth.
   Glory* . . .

READING

RESPONSORY

Your mercy, O God, calls us to mercy. —**Your**...
It manifests your greatness, —**and calls**...
Glory to you, Source of all Being, Eternal Word and Holy Spirit. —**Your mercy**...

CANTICLE OF MARY

Ant.   **Your regard has blessed me, O God.**

INTERCESSIONS

PRAYER: God our creator, you have called us by name; we belong to you. Help us to believe in your truth, hope in your mercy, and love all people as you call us to love. Let our lives give joy to you and encouragement to one another. May our efforts to live in love give you praise this night and every day of our lives through all eternity. Amen.

TUESDAY

MORNING PRAYER

Ant. 1 O God, forgive the sins of your people.

Psalm 85

O God, once you favored your land,
restoring the fortunes of Rachel and
   Jacob.
You forgave the guilt of your people;
you pardoned all their sins.
You withdrew your wrath;
you calmed the heat of your anger.

Restore us again,
O God our salvation,
put away your grievance against us!
Will you be angry with us for ever,
Will you prolong it to all generations?

Will you not restore us again,
that your people may rejoice in you?
Show us your steadfast love,
and grant us your salvation.

Let me hear what you have to say,
for you will speak peace to your people,
to those who are near you,
and who turn to you in their hearts.
Your salvation is near for those who
   fear you,
that glory may dwell in our land.

Mercy and truth have embraced;
justice and peace will kiss.
Truth shall spring out of the earth,
and justice will look down from
   heaven.

You will give what is good,
our land will yield its increase.
Justice shall go before you
and make a path for your steps.
   Glory* ...

Ant. 2 O God, grant peace to all peoples.

   Canticle   Isaiah 26:1b-4, 7-9, 12

A strong city have we, O God;
you set up salvation
like walls and ramparts.
Open up the gates
that the nation which keeps faith
may enter in.

You keep those in perfect peace,
whose minds are fixed on you,
because they trust in you,
trust in you for ever.
For you are our God,
an everlasting Rock.

The way of the just is level;
you make smooth the path of the just.
In the path of your judgments,
we wait for you;
your name remembered from of old,
is the desire of our souls.

My soul yearns for you in the night,
my spirit within me keeps vigil;
when your judgments abide in the
     earth,
the inhabitants of the world learn
     justice.

O God, you ordain peace for all people,
you accomplish all our works.
   Glory* . . .

READING

RESPONSORY

It is good to give thanks to you and sing praise to your name. —It is. . .
At the works of your hands I shout for joy, —and sing. . .
Glory to you, Source of all Being, Eternal Word and Holy Spirit. —It is. . .

CANTICLE OF ZECHARIAH

Ant. I will praise you from the rising of the sun to its going down.

INTERCESSIONS

PRAYER: Giver of hope, we begin a new day confident that you come to us
in all circumstances and make all things work for the fulfillment of
your purposes. We praise you for your wonderful works through
Christ who has shown us the way. Amen.

**Ant. 3 In the light of your face there
is life, O God.**

Psalm 67

O God, be gracious to us and bless us
and make your face shine upon us.
That your ways be known upon earth,
your saving power among all nations.
Let the peoples praise you, O God;
let all the peoples praise you.

Let the nations be glad and sing for joy,
for you judge the peoples with equity
and guide the nations on earth.
Let the peoples praise you, O God;
let all the peoples praise you.

The earth has yielded its increase;
God, our God, has blessed us.
You, indeed, have blessed us;
let all the earth revere you!
   Glory* . . .

DAYTIME PRAYER

**Ant. 1 I will ponder your law within my
heart.**

Psalm 119:97–104

How I love your law, O God!
It is my meditation all the day.
Your commandment makes me wiser
     than the learned,
for it is ever with me.

I have more understanding than all
     my teachers,
for your will is my meditation. —

I have more understanding than the
     aged,
for I keep your precepts.

I turn my feet from evil ways,
to obey your word.
I turn not aside from your decrees,
for you, yourself, have taught me.

How sweet are your words to my taste,
sweeter than honey to my mouth!
Through your precepts I gain
     understanding;
therefore I hate every false way.
   Glory* . . .

Ant. 2 Restore your dwelling place
within us.

Psalm 74

Why have you cast us off for ever?
Why blaze with anger against the sheep
of your pasture?
Remember your people whom you
chose from of old,
which you redeemed as your heritage!
Remember Mount Zion where you
made your dwelling.

Direct your steps to the eternal ruins,
everything destroyed in your sanctuary!
Evil has roared in your house of prayer,
setting up its signs for symbols.

At the upper entrance they hacked
the wooden trellis with axes.
With hatchets and hammers,
broke down its carved wood.
The sanctuary they set on fire,
desecrating the place where you dwell.

They said to themselves, "We will
utterly crush them;"
and burned all the shrines in the land.
We do not see our signs any more;
there is no longer a prophet,
no one knows how long it will last.

How long, O God, is evil to conquer?
Is your name to be scoffed for ever?
Why do you hold back your hand,
Why do you keep your hand concealed?

Yet you are our ruler from of old,
working salvation in the midst of the
earth.   Glory* . . .

Ant. 3 Yours is the day, yours is
the night; all things are in
your hands.

II

It was you who divided the sea by your
might,
who shattered the heads of the monsters
in the sea.

You crushed the heads of Leviathan,
and gave them as food to the creatures
of the wilderness.
You split open springs and brooks;
dried up the ever-flowing streams.

Yours is the day and yours is the night;
you fixed the stars and the sun.
You established all the bounds of earth;
you made both summer and winter.

Remember then, how evil scoffs,
and how your name is reviled.
Do not deliver your dove to the hawk:
do not forget the lives of your poor.

Remember your covenant of old;
for violence dwells in every corner
of the land.
Let not the downtrodden be put to
shame;
let the poor and the needy bless your
name.

Arise, O God, defend your cause!
Remember how you are reviled all the
day.
Quiet those who clamor against you,
who clamor against you day after day.
Glory* . . .

PRAYER: God of love, you gave us this universe filled with your gifts. Help
us to reverence all of your creation, respecting the rights of all
species, and the integrity of the elements. Teach us to realize in
our hearts as well as in our minds that we praise you when we use
your gifts as you meant them to be used. May we unite with all
suffering creation in the struggle for liberation from all that seeks
to destroy. Grant this that all creation may live with you for all
eternity. Amen.

EVENING PRAYER

Ant. 1 You are round about your people, both now and forever.

Psalm 125

Those who put their trust in you
are like Mount Zion;
it cannot be moved, but stands forever.

As the mountains are round about
  Jerusalem,
so are you round about your people,
both now and forever.

For the scepter of wickedness shall not
  rest
over the land of the just,
lest the just put forth their hands
to turn to evil ways.

Do good, O God, to those who are good,
to those who are upright of heart!
But those who turn to evil ways,
will be chastised and punished!

On Israel, peace! Glory* . . .

Ant. 2 Blessed are those who are pure of heart.

Psalm 131

O God, my heart is not lifted up,
my eyes are not raised too high;
I have not occupied myself
with marvels beyond me.

I have calmed and quieted my soul,
like a child at its mother's breast;
like a child in its father's arms,
even so my soul.

O Israel, hope in your God
both now and for ever. Glory* . . .

Ant. 3 Let all creation serve you, for you created all things.

Canticle: Revelation 4:11, 5:9, 10, 12

Worthy are you, O God, our God,
to receive glory and honor and power.

For you have created all things;
by your will they came to be and were
  made.

Worthy are you to take the scroll
  and to open its seals,

For you were slain, and by your blood,
you purchased for God
persons of every race and tongue,
of every people and nation.

You have made of them a kingdom,
and priests to serve our God,
and they shall reign on the earth.

Worthy is the Lamb who was slain
to receive power and riches,
wisdom and strength,
honor and glory and praise. Glory* . . .

READING

RESPONSORY

Teach us to number our days that we may gain wisdom of heart. —**Teach us** . . .
Let your works be manifest to your servants, —**that we** . . .
Glory to you, Source of all Being, Eternal Word and Holy Spirit. —**Teach us** . . .

CANTICLE OF MARY

Ant. **You who are mighty have done great things for me.**

INTERCESSIONS

PRAYER: O God, you are both mother and father to us. Help us to reverence
all people with whom we share such great love and show us the
way to peace in our world. We ask this as your children through
Jesus, our brother. Amen.

WEDNESDAY
MORNING PRAYER

**Ant. 1 Gladden my soul, O God;
for to you I lift up my heart.**

Psalm 86

Incline your ear and give answer,
for I am poor and needy.
Preserve my life, for I am faithful:
save the servant who trusts in you.

You are my God, have mercy on me,
for to you I cry all the day.
Gladden the soul of your servant,
for to you I lift up my soul.

O God, you are good and forgiving,
abounding in love to all who call.
Give ear to my prayer;
hearken to my supplication.
In the day of my trouble I call on you,
for you will answer me.

There is none like you among the gods,
nor works to compare with yours.
All the nations you made
shall come and bow down,
shall glorify your name.
For you are great and do wondrous
    things,
you alone are God.

Teach me your way, O God,
that I may walk in your truth;
cause my heart to fear your name.
I give thanks to you with all my
    heart,
and glorify your name for ever.
For great toward me is your love;
you deliver my soul from the grave.

Pride has risen against me;
corruption pursues my life,
evil pays you no heed.
But you are merciful and gracious,
slow to anger, abounding in love.

Turn to me and take pity;
give strength to your servant,
and save your handmaid's child.
Show me a sign of your favor;
let injustice be put to shame,
help me and give me your comfort.
    Glory* . . .

**Ant. 2 Blessed are the just, who speak
the truth.**

Canticle   Isaiah 33:13–16

Hear, you who are far off,
what I have done;
you who are near,
acknowledge my might.

The sinners in Zion are afraid;
trembling grips the impious;
"Who of us can live with the devouring
    fire?
Who of us can live with the everlasting
    flames?"

Those who walk justly and speak
    honestly,
who spurn what is gained by oppression,
who shake their hands,
free of contact with a bribe;
who stop their ears,
lest they hear of bloodshed,
who close their eyes,
lest they look on evil.

They shall dwell on the heights;
their place of refuge
shall be the rocky fortress;
their food will be given,
their water will be sure.   Glory* . . .

**Ant. 3 Let us sing a joyful song in the
presence of our God.**

Psalm 98

We sing to you a new song,
for you have done marvelous things!
Your saving hand and your holy arm
have given the victory.

You have made known your salvation;
have revealed your justice to the nations.
You have remembered your love and
    your faithfulness
for the house of Israel.
All the ends of the earth have seen
the salvation of our God.

Make a joyful noise, all the earth;
break forth into joyous song! —

Sing praise to God with the harp,
with the lyre and the sound of music!
With trumpets and the sound of the
  horn
make a joyful noise to our God.

Let the sea roar and all that fills it;
the world and those who dwell in it!

Let the rivers clap their hands;
and the hills ring out their joy.

All creation sings before God
who comes to judge the earth.
God will judge the world with justice
and the peoples with equity.
  Glory* . . .

READING

RESPONSORY

Satisfy us in the morning with your steadfast love, that we may rejoice and be glad
  all our days. —**Satisfy us**. . .
Let the favor of God be upon us, —**that**. . .
Glory to you, Source of all Being, Eternal Word and Holy Spirit. —**Satisfy us**. . .

CANTICLE OF ZECHARIAH

Ant.   Remember the mercy you promised long ago.

INTERCESSIONS

PRAYER: God of unity and peace, may the gift of your life within us show
    itself in concrete ways so that we may make clear with our lives
    the good news of Jesus Christ. Especially today we pray for all the
    children of this world, that they may know your love and the hope
    of peace on earth. Grant this prayer that all may know the gift
    you gave in Jesus. Amen.

DAYTIME PRAYER

**Ant. 1 Your Word is the true light that
enlightens all who come into the world.**

Psalm 119:105–112

O God, your word is a lamp to my
  feet
and a light for my path.
I have sworn an oath and confirmed it
to observe your commandments.

I am sorely afflicted:
give me life according to your word!
Accept my offerings of praise,
and teach me your decrees.

Though I hold my life in my hands,
I do not forget your law.
Though the wicked try to ensnare me,
I do not stray from your precepts.

Your will is my heritage for ever,
the joy of my heart.
I incline my heart to carry out your will
for ever, to endless ages.   Glory* . . .

**Ant. 2 Hear my prayer and hasten to
help me.**

Psalm 70

Be pleased, O God, to save me!
O God, make haste to help me!
Fill me with shame and confusion
if I turn away from life!

O let me turn back in confusion,
when I delight in wrongdoing!
Let me retreat in my shame,
when I trifle with evil.

May all who seek you
rejoice and be glad!
May those who love your salvation
proclaim, "Our God is great!"

But I am poor and needy;
hasten to me, O God!
You are my help, my deliverer;
O God, do not delay.   Glory* ...

**Ant. 3 You know the hearts of all;
    your judgment is right and true.**

Psalm 75

We give thanks to you, O God;
we give you thanks;
we call on your name
and recount your wondrous deeds.

"At the time which I appoint
I will judge with equity.
When the earth totters,
and all its inhabitants,
it is I who steady its pillars.

To the boastful I say: 'Do not boast,'
to the wicked, 'Do not flaunt your
    strength,
do not flaunt your strength on high,
or speak with insolent pride.'"

For not from the east or from the west,
or from the wilderness comes judgment,
but you, O God, are the judge,
putting down one, lifting up another.

But I will rejoice for ever,
I will sing praises to you on high.
You shall break the power of wickedness,
while the strength of the just shall be
    exalted.   Glory* ...

PRAYER: O God, you both comfort us and disturb our complacency through
your Spirit. May we recognize the blind, the lame and the prisoner
in the circumstances of our lives, and understand our call to
proclaim the good news to the poor. We ask this through Jesus
who is our way, our truth and our life. Amen.

EVENING PRAYER

**Ant. 1 You will not reject me; you will
    fill my mouth with laughter.**

Psalm 126

When God restored the fortunes
    of Zion,
it seemed like a dream.
Then our mouth was filled with
    laughter,
and our tongue with shouts of joy;

then they said among the nations,
"God has done great things for them."
You have done great things for us!
Indeed we are glad.

Restore our fortunes, O God,
like the streams in the desert!
May those who sow in tears
reap with shouts of joy!

They that go forth weeping,
bearing seed for the sowing,
shall come home with shouts of joy,
bringing their sheaves with them.
    Glory* ...

**Ant. 2 Wisdom has built herself
    a house, alleluia!**

Psalm 127

If God does not build the house,
its builders labor in vain.
If God does not watch over the city,
in vain is the vigil kept.

It is vain to rise up early
and go late to rest,
eating the bread of anxious toil:
for you, O God, give sleep to your
    beloved.

Truly children are a gift from Yahweh,
the fruit of the womb, a blessing.
Like arrows in the hand of a warrior
are the children of one's youth.

Happy the couple who have
their quiver full of them!
They shall not be put to shame
when they encounter distress.
    Glory* . . .

**Ant. 3 Jesus is the firstborn of all
    creation.**

Canticle: Colossians 1:12–20

Let us give thanks to God
for having made us worthy
to share the inheritance of the
    saints in light.

God has delivered us
from the power of darkness
and transferred us
into the kingdom of God's beloved Son,
    Jesus,
in whom we have redemption,
the forgiveness of our sins.

Jesus is the image of the invisible God,
the first-born of all creation;
in him all things were created,
    in heaven and on earth,
things visible and invisible.

All things were created through him;
all were created for him.
He is before all else that is.
In him all things hold together.

He is the head of the body, the church!
He is the beginning,
the firstborn from the dead,
that in everything, he might be above
    all others.

In him all the fullness of God was
    pleased to dwell,
and, through him, to reconcile all
    things to himself,
whether on earth or in heaven,
making peace by the blood of his cross.
    Glory* . . .

READING

RESPONSORY

You will cover us with your pinions, and under your wings we will find refuge.
    —**You will**. . .
We will not fear the terror of the night; —**and under**. . .
Glory to you, Source of all Being, Eternal Word and Holy Spirit. —**You will**. . .

CANTICLE OF MARY

Ant.   Holy is the name of our God.

INTERCESSIONS

PRAYER: You, O Christ, are the light of this world. We have followed you
this day through the darkness of temptation, doubt and pain. We
thank you, O God, for all you have given us in Christ and for the
promise of an eternal dawn. May we praise you now and all the
days of our lives, forever and ever. Amen.

THURSDAY

MORNING PRAYER

Ant. 1 Blessed are those who delight in your law, O God.

Psalm 1

Blessed are those who walk not
  in the counsel of the wicked,
nor stand in the way of sinners,
nor sit with those who scoff;
but delight in your law, O God,
pondering it day and night.

They are like a tree
planted by streams of water,
that yields its fruit in due season,
and whose leaves never fade.
May they prosper in all they do.

It is not so with wickedness.
Like chaff the wind drives it away.
Evil cannot stand before you,
nor injustice before your face.

For you guide the path of the faithful,
but renounce the way of oppression.
  Glory* . . .

Ant. 2 God will come with justice for all the people.

Canticle   Isaiah 40:10–17

Behold, you come with power,
O God, the Almighty,
ruling with your strong arm;
behold, your reward is with you,
and your recompense before you.

You will feed your flock like a
  shepherd,
you will gather the lambs in your arms,
carrying them in your bosom,
gently leading the ewes with young.

Who else had measured the waters
in the hollows of their hands,
and marked off the heavens with a span,
enclosed the dust of the earth in a
  measure
weighed the mountains in scales
and the hills in a balance?

Who has directed your spirit,
or who has been your counselor?
Who did you consult for enlightenment,
who taught you the path of justice,
or showed you the way of understanding?

Behold, the nations are like a drop
  from a bucket,
accounted as dust on the scales;
you take up the isles like powder.

Lebanon would not suffice for fuel,
nor its beasts be enough for burnt
  offering.
All the nations are as nothing before
  you,
as nothing and void are they accounted.
  Glory* . . .

Ant. 3 We worship and give praise to you, Most High.

Psalm 99

O God, you reign on high;
let all the peoples tremble!
You are throned on the cherubim;
let the earth quake!
You are great in Zion.

You are exalted over all peoples.
Let them praise your name,
awesome and great!
Holy are you over all!

Mighty Sovereign, lover of justice,
you have established equity;
you have ruled with justice.
We extol you, Most High God;
worshiping at your footstool!
You alone are holy.

Moses and Aaron were among your
  priests,
among your petitioners, Judith and
  Esther.
They invoked you, and you answered.
You spoke to them in the pillar of cloud;
they kept your will,
and the precepts that you gave them.

O God, our God, you answered them;
you were a forgiving God to them,
yet you punished their offences.

We extol you, Most High God,
and worship on your holy mountain;
for you alone are holy.   Glory* . . .

READING

RESPONSORY

No one who practices deceit shall dwell in your house. —**No one**. . .
They who walk in the way that is blameless —**shall dwell**. . .
Glory to you, Source of all Being, Eternal Word and Holy Spirit. —**No one**. . .

CANTICLE OF ZECHARIAH

Ant.   Guide our feet, O God, into the way of peace.

INTERCESSIONS

PRAYER: O God, you walked with our first parents in paradise for you have
made us for communion with you and one another. As we begin
the business of this day, we recall that you alone can fill our
hearts. We ask to remain by love in your holy presence with Jesus
who incarnated your presence among us. Amen.

DAYTIME PRAYER

**Ant. 1 Sustain me, O God, according to
your promise.**

Psalm 119:113–120

I have no love for the half-hearted,
but I love your law.
You are my shelter, my shield;
I hope in your word.

Rid me of all that is evil,
that I may keep your commandments.
Uphold me according to your promise,
that I may live in your way,
let my hopes not be in vain!

Sustain me and I shall be safe
and ever observe your statutes.
Help me spurn all that is evil;
let its cunning be in vain!

You overthrow all that is wicked;
therefore I love your will.
I tremble before you in awe,
I am afraid of your judgments.
   Glory* . . .

**Ant. 2 Rescue us, O God, for the
sake of your name.**

Psalm 79:1–5, 8–11, 13

O God, the nations have invaded our
land,
they have defiled your holy temple;
Jerusalem is in ruins.
They have given the bodies of your
servants
as food to the birds of the air,
and the flesh of your faithful
to the beasts of the earth.

They have poured out blood like water
round about Jerusalem,
no one is left to bury the dead.
We have become the taunt of our
neighbors,
mocked and derided by those round
about us.

How long, O God? Will you be angry
for ever,
how long will your anger burn like fire?

Do not hold against us
   the guilt of our ancestors;
Let your compassion hasten to meet us;
for we are brought very low.

Help us, O God, our savior,
for the glory of your name;
deliver us, and forgive us our sins,
rescue us for the sake of your name.

Why should the nations say,
"Where is their God?"
Let us see oppression overthrown,
may justice come to Jerusalem!
Let the groans of the prisoners come
   before you;
let your strong arm preserve those
   condemned to die!

Then we your people, the flock of your
   pasture,
will give you thanks for ever;
from generation to generation
we will recount your praise.
   Glory* . . .

**Ant. 3 O God, you are the vinedresser;
prune the vine that it may bear fruit.**

Psalm 80

Give ear, O Shepherd of Israel,
you who lead Joseph like a flock!
You who are enthroned upon the
   cherubim,
shine forth before Ephraim, Benjamin
   and Manasseh!
Stir up your might and come to save us!

Restore us, God of hosts;
let your face shine, that we may
   be saved.

God of hosts, how long will you be
   angry with your people's prayers?
You fed them with the bread of tears,
and gave them tears to drink in full
   measure.
You made us the scorn of our neighbors,
our enemies laugh among themselves.

Restore us, God of hosts;
let your face shine, that we may
   be saved.

You brought a vine out of Egypt;
you drove out the nations to plant it.
You cleared the ground before it;
it took root and filled the land.

The mountains were covered with its
   shade,
the mighty cedars with its branches;
it sent out its branches to the sea,
and its roots to the Great River.

Then why have you broken down its
   walls?
so that all who pass by pluck its fruit?
It is ravaged by the boar of the forest,
devoured by the beasts of the field.

Turn again, O God of hosts!
Look down from heaven, and see;
have regard for this vine,
the vine that your own hand has
   planted.
It has been burned with fire and cut
   down.

Let your hand be on those you have
   chosen,
those you make strong for yourself!
Then we will never forsake you;
give us life, and we will call on your
   name.

Restore us, God of hosts!
let your face shine, that we may
   be saved.   Glory* . . .

PRAYER: Renew in our hearts, O God, the gift of your Holy Spirit, so that
we may love you fully in all that we do and love one another as
Christ loves us. May all that we do proclaim the good news that
you are God with us. Amen.

EVENING PRAYER

Ant. 1 Let us enter your courts with shouts of praise.

Psalm 132

O God, remember David,
all the many hardships he endured;
the oath he swore to you,
his vow to the Strong One of Jacob.

"I will not enter my house
or get into my bed;
I will give no sleep to my eyes,
or slumber to my eyelids,
till I find a place for Yahweh,
a dwelling for the Strong One of Jacob."

We heard of it in Ephratah,
we found the ark in the fields of
   Jaar.
"Let us go to the place of God's
   dwelling;
let us worship at God's footstool."

Go up, O God, to the place of your rest,
you and the ark of your might.
Let your priests be clothed with
   justice,
and your faithful shout for joy.
For the sake of David your servant
do not reject your anointed.
   Glory* . . .

Ant. 2 You, O God, have chosen Zion as your dwelling place.

II

You swore an oath to David;
from which you will not turn back:
"A son, the fruit of your body,
I will set upon your throne.

If your offspring keep my
   covenant in truth,
and my laws which I shall teach them,
their descendants also for ever
shall sit upon your throne."

For you have chosen Zion;
you desired it for your dwelling:
"This is my resting place for ever;
here I have desired to dwell.

I will abundantly bless its provisions;
I will satisfy its poor with bread.
I will clothe its priests with salvation
and its faithful will shout for joy.

There David's stock will flower:
I will prepare a lamp for my anointed.
Treacherous plots will be put to shame,
but on him my crown shall shine."
   Glory* . . .

Ant. 3 The glory of God is the light of the city and its lamp is the Lamb.

Canticle: Revelation 11:17–18; 12:10b–12a

We give thanks to you, God Almighty,
who is and who was,
you have assumed your great power,
you have begun your reign.

The nations raged, but your wrath
   came,
and the time for the dead to be judged,
for rewarding your servants, the
   prophets and saints,
and those who revere your name,
the great and small alike.

Now the salvation, the power,
   and the reign have come,
of God and of the Christ,
for the accusers of our loved ones
   have been thrown down,
who accuse them day and night.

They have been conquered by the
   blood of the Lamb,
and by the word of their testimony,
for love of life did not deter them
   from death.
Rejoice then, O heaven,
and you that dwell therein!
   Glory* . . .

READING

RESPONSORY

How great are your works, O God. Your thoughts are very deep. —**How**...
The dull of heart will never know. —**Your thoughts**...
Glory to you, Source of all Being, Eternal Word and Holy Spirit. —**How great**...

CANTICLE OF MARY

Ant.   **Your mercy endures through all generations.**

INTERCESSIONS

PRAYER: Most gentle God, you have fed us this day with your holy Word
and life-giving Bread. May we continue to discern your calls in
life, family, community and in the movements of our hearts. May
we always be among those who worship you in spirit and in truth.
We ask this through the intercession of all those who gave their
lives that others may have bread and a better quality of life.
Amen.

FRIDAY

MORNING PRAYER

**Ant. 1 A humble, contrite heart, O God,
you will not despise.**

Psalm 51

Have mercy on me, O God,
according to your steadfast love;
in your abundant mercy blot out my
   sins.
Wash me thoroughly from my offenses,
and cleanse me from my sin!

For I know my offenses,
and my sin is ever before me.
Against you, you alone, have I sinned;
and done what is evil in your sight,
so you are justified in your sentence
and blameless in your judgment.
Behold, I was brought forth in a
   sinful world.

For you desire truth in my innermost
   being;
teach me wisdom in the depths of my
   heart.
O purify me, and I shall be clean;
O wash me, I shall be whiter than snow.
Fill me with joy and gladness; —

let the bones you have broken rejoice.
Hide your face from my guilt,
and blot out all my offenses.

Create in me a clean heart,
put a steadfast spirit within me.
Cast me not from your presence,
take not your spirit from me.
Give me again the joy of your
   salvation,
with a willing spirit uphold me.

Then I will teach transgressors your
   ways
and sinners will return to you.
Deliver me from death,
O God of my salvation,
and my tongue will sing out your
   saving help.

Open my lips and my mouth will sing
   your praises.
For you take no delight in sacrifice;
were I to give a burnt offering,
you would not be pleased.
A broken spirit you accept;
a contrite heart, you will not despise.

In your goodness, show favor to Zion:
rebuild the walls of Jerusalem.
Then will you delight in just sacrifices,
in gifts offered on your altar.
Glory* . . .

**Ant. 2 You bring us to springs of water;
you will wipe away every tear from
our eyes.**

Canticle   Jeremiah 14:17–21

Let my eyes stream with tears
night and day, without rest,
for the virgin daughter of my people
is smitten with a great wound,
with a very grievous blow.

If I walk out into the field,
behold, those slain by the sword!
If I enter the city,
behold, the diseases of famine!
Both the prophet and the priest
ply their trade throughout the land,
ignorant of their doings.

Have you utterly rejected Judah?
Is Zion loathsome to you?
Why have you smitten us
so that there is no healing?

We looked for peace to no avail;
for a time of healing,
but terror comes instead.
We acknowledge our wickedness,
and the guilt of our ancestors,
for we have sinned against you.

Spurn us not for your name's sake;
do not dishonor your glorious throne;
remember your covenant with us,
and break it not.   Glory* . . .

**Ant. 3 We are your people, the sheep
of your pasture.**

Psalm 100

All the earth cries out to you with
   shouts of joy, O God,
Serving you with gladness;
Coming before you, singing for joy.

You, Creator of all, are God.
You made us, we belong to you,
we are your people, the sheep of your
   pasture.

We enter your gates with thanksgiving,
and your courts with songs of praise!
We give you thanks and bless your
   name.

Indeed, how good you are,
enduring, your steadfast love.
You are faithful to all generations.
Glory* . . .

READING

RESPONSORY

Return, O God! How long? Have pity on your servants. —**Return**. . .
Satisfy us in the morning with your steadfast love. —**Have**. . .
Glory to you, Source of all Being, Eternal Word and Holy Spirit. —**Return**. . .

CANTICLE OF ZECHARIAH

Ant.   **Give light to those in darkness and the shadow of death.**

INTERCESSIONS

PRAYER: Direct our activity this day, O merciful God, that we may reflect
your goodness and love to our companions. Help us to be mindful
of the many people who are oppressed this day and may we be
aware of the ways that we oppress others. We ask this in the name
of Jesus who died to set us free. Amen.

DAYTIME PRAYER

Ant. 1 The servant of God was stricken; smitten by God, and afflicted.

Psalm 22

O God, my God, why have you forsaken
   me?
Why are you so far from helping me,
from the sound of my groaning?
I cry out by day, but you do not answer;
by night, but find no rest.

Yet you alone are holy,
enthroned on the praises of Israel.
In you our ancestors trusted;
they trusted and you delivered them.
To you they cried, and were saved;
In you they trusted,
and were not disappointed.

But I am a worm and not human,
scorned and despised by the people.
All who see me mock at me,
they curl their lips, they wag their
   heads;
"You trusted in God, let God save you;
let God rescue you
for God delights in you!"

Yet it was you who took me from
   the womb;
you kept me safe upon my mother's
   breasts.
Upon you was I cast from my birth,
since my mother's womb you have been
   my God.
Be not far from me in my distress;
there is no one else to help.
   Glory* . . .

Ant. 2 By oppression and judgment, the just one was cut off from the land of the living.

II

Many bulls encompass me,
strong bulls of Bashan surround me;
they open wide their mouths,
like a ravening and roaring lion.

I am poured out like water,
disjointed are all my bones;
my heart has become like wax,
melted within my breast;
my strength is dried up like burnt clay,
my tongue cleaves to my jaws;
you lay me in the dust of death.

Many dogs are round about me;
a band of evildoers encircles me;
they pierce my hands and my feet—
I can count every one of my bones—
they stare and gloat over me;
they divide my garments among them,
for my raiment they cast lots.

But you, O God, be not far off!
O my help, hasten to my aid!
Deliver my soul from the sword,
my life from the grip of the dog!
Save me from the jaws of the lion,
my poor soul from the horns of the
   wild ox!

I will tell of your name to my kinsfolk
and praise you in the assembly.
   Glory* . . .

Ant. 3 For a moment I hid my face, but I will have compassion on you.

III

You who fear Yahweh, give praise!
You descendants of Jacob, give glory!
Stand in awe, children of Israel!

For you, O God, have not despised
nor scorned the affliction of the poor;
you have not hid your face from them,
but heard them when they cried to you.

To you comes praise from the great
   assembly;
my vows I will pay before those who
   fear you.
The poor shall eat and be satisfied;
those who seek you shall sing your
   praise!
May their hearts live for ever and ever!

All the earth shall remember
and turn to you, O God;
all families of the nations
shall worship before you.
For sovereignty belongs to you;
you rule over the nations.

All the mighty of the earth
bow down before you;
before you shall bow
all who go down to the dust.

Posterity shall serve you;
They shall tell of you
to generations yet to come,
and proclaim your deliverance
to a people yet unborn:
"These things our God has done."
Glory* . . .

PRAYER: Look upon us, most gracious God, as we gather at midday. Bless the work of our hands and hearts. May all peoples be blessed with the dignity of work, with an understanding of their gifts, and with generous spirits so that together we may further your reign among us. Help all who are unemployed and those who are disabled. May all know their worth and dignity. Grant this in Jesus' name. Amen.

EVENING PRAYER

Ant. 1 Our God is high above all other gods.

Psalm 135

We praise your name, O God,
all your servants give praise,
those who stand in your holy house,
in the courts of your house, O God!

We praise you, for you are good.
Sing to your name for you are gracious!
For you have chosen Jacob for yourself,
Israel as your own possession.

For I know that you are great,
that you are high above all gods.
You do whatever you please,
in heaven and on earth,
in the seas and all the deeps.

You summon clouds from the ends of
   the earth,
make lightning for the rain,
and bring forth wind from your
   storehouse.

You smote the firstborn of Egypt,
both of human and beast alike.
Signs and wonders you worked
in the midst of the land of Egypt,
against Pharaoh and all his servants.

You smote many nations
and slew mighty rulers,
Sihon, king of the Amorites,
Og, the king of Bashan,
and all the kingdoms of Canaan.
You gave their land as a heritage,
a heritage to your people.   Glory* . . .

Ant. 2 You are the living God come down from heaven.

II

O God, your name endures for ever,
your renown throughout all ages.
You will work justice for your people,
and have compassion on your servants.

The idols of the nations are silver
   and gold,
the work of human hands.
They have mouths, but they cannot
   speak;
they have eyes, but they cannot see;
they have ears, but they cannot hear;
nor is there any breath on their lips.
Like them be those who make them!
And everyone who trusts in them!

Descendants of Israel, bless our God!
Descendants of Aaron, bless our God! —

Descendants of Levi, bless our God!
You who fear, bless the Most High!

Blessed are you from Zion, O God,
you who dwell in Jerusalem!
    Glory* . . .

Ant. 3 Behold I make all things new, alleluia!

    Canticle: Revelation 15:3–4

Great and wonderful are your works,
God, the Almighty One! —

Just and true are your ways,
Ruler of all the ages!

Who shall refuse you honor,
or the glory due your name?

For you alone are holy,
all nations shall come and
    worship in your presence.
Your judgments are clearly seen.
    Glory* . . .

READING

RESPONSORY

When the cares of my heart are many, your consolations cheer my soul.
    —When. . .
You have become my stronghold. —Your. . .
Glory to you, Source of all Being, Eternal Word and Holy Spirit. —When. . .

CANTICLE OF MARY

Ant.   Fill the hungry with bread of earth and bread of heaven.

INTERCESSIONS

PRAYER: Most loving God, at evening's end we pray for all who near the
          evening of their lives. Grant them your peace and reconciliation
          with all who love them. May they know the hope and joy that
          awaits them when they see you face to face. This we ask through
          the intercession of Joseph and of all who died in your embrace.
          Amen.

SATURDAY

MORNING PRAYER

Ant. 1 You are near at hand, O God, and all your ways are true.

    Psalm 119:145–152

With all my heart, I cry to you;
answer me, O God.
I cry to you; save me,
that I may observe your will.

I rise before dawn and cry for help;
I hope in your words.
My eyes watch throughout the night
meditating on your promises.

Hear my voice in your steadfast love;
in your justice preserve my life.
Those who persecute me draw near:
they are far from your law.

But you, O God, are near at hand,
all your commands are true.
Long have I known that your will
endures forever.   Glory* . . .

Ant. 2 Give us your Spirit of Wisdom in all our affairs.

Canticle   Wisdom 9:1-6, 9-11

God of our ancestors, God of mercy,
you who have made all things by your
   word
and in your wisdom have established us
to care for the creatures produced by
   you,
to govern the world in holiness and
   justice,
and to render judgment in integrity of
   heart:

Give us Wisdom, the attendant at your
   throne,
and reject us not from among your
   children;
for we are your servants—weak and
   short-lived
and lacking in comprehension of
   judgment and of laws.

Indeed, though some be perfect among
   the peoples of this earth,
if Wisdom, who comes from you, be not
   with them,
they shall be held in no esteem.

Now with you is Wisdom, who knows
   your works
and was present when you made the
   world,
who understands what is pleasing in
   your eyes
and what is conformable with your
   commands.

Send her forth from your holy heavens
and from your glorious throne dispatch
   her
that she may be with us and work with
   us,
that we may know what is your
   pleasure.

For she knows and understands all
   things,
and will guide us discreetly in our affairs
and safeguard us by her glory.
   Glory* . . .

Ant. 3 O God, your faithfulness endures forever.

Psalm 117

Praise our God, all you nations!
Acclaim the Most High, all you peoples!

For great is your love for us;
And your faithfulness endures forever.
   Glory* . . .

READING

RESPONSORY

I will give heed to the way that is blameless. When will you come to me?
   —I will. . .
I will walk with integrity of heart within my house. —**When**. . .
Glory to you, Source of all Being, Eternal Word and Holy Spirit. —**I will**. . .

CANTICLE OF ZECHARIAH

Ant.   May we serve you in holiness all the days of our lives.

INTERCESSIONS

PRAYER: You are a God of Wonder, Most Holy One, as you call us into
being and set us free in your loving plan. Help us to grow in
understanding the meaning of our freedom, so that we may
discern wisely and respect the gift of freedom in all our sisters and
brothers. Grant this through the intercession of all who have died
that others may be free. Amen.

DAYTIME PRAYER

Ant. 1 Deal with us according to the greatness of your love.

Psalm 119:121–128

I have done what is right and just:
let me not be oppressed.
Guarantee the goodness of your servant
let not the proud oppress me.

My eyes grow weak watching for
    salvation,
and the fulfillment of your promise.
Treat your servant according to the
    greatness of your love,
and teach me your statutes.

I am your servant; give me knowledge,
that I may know your will!
It is time for you to act, O God,
for your law has been broken.

Therefore I love your commandments
more than finest gold.
I guide my steps by your precepts:
I hate the ways of falsehood.
    Glory* . . .

Ant. 2 Happy are those who take refuge in you.

Psalm 34

I will bless you, O God, at all times,
your praise always on my lips.
My soul makes its boast in you;
The afflicted shall hear and be glad.
Glorify our God with me.
Together let us praise God's name.

I sought you, and you answered me;
and delivered me from all my fears.
Look towards the Most High, and be
    radiant;
let your faces not be ashamed.
These poor ones cried; you heard them,
and saved them from all their troubles.

Your angel, O God, is encamped
around those who revere you, to deliver
    them.
Taste and see that God is good!
Happy are they who take refuge in you.

Revere the Most High, all you saints.
Those who revere you, have no want!
Young lions suffer want and hunger;
but those who seek you lack no blessing.
    Glory* . . .

Ant. 3 Deliver the brokenhearted from all their troubles.

II

Come children, listen to me,
I will teach you to reverence the
    Most High.
Who among you longs for life
and many days to enjoy prosperity?

Keep your tongue from evil,
your lips from speaking deceit.
Turn aside from evil and do good;
seek peace, and pursue it.

God's eyes are turned to the righteous,
God's ears toward their cry.
God's face turns away from evil,
that it not be remembered on earth.

When the just cry, the Most High hears,
and delivers them from their troubles.
God is close to the brokenhearted;
saving those whose spirits are crushed.

Many are the afflictions of the just;
they will be delivered from them all.
God will keep guard over all their bones,
not one of them shall be broken.

Evil shall be its own destruction;
oppression shall be condemned.
You redeem the lives of your servants;
those who take refuge in you shall
    not be condemned.   Glory* . . .

PRAYER: You gather us together in faith, O God, as a loving mother and a
gentle father. Help us to remember that your dwelling place is
built upon love and peace, and that to bring about your reign on
earth we must follow your way of peace. We pray for all
governments and legislatures that they may be mindful of the
rights of all peoples of this world to live in peace and dignity.
Grant this in the name of Jesus. Amen.

WEEK IV

SUNDAY EVENING PRAYER I

Ant. 1 Peace be within you!

Psalm 122

I was glad when they said to me:
"Let us go to the house of God!"
And now our feet are standing
within your gates, O Jerusalem!

Jerusalem, built as a city
bound firmly together,
to which the tribes go up,
the tribes of our God,
as was decreed for Israel,
to give thanks to your holy name.
There thrones for judgment were set,
the thrones of the house of David.

Pray for the peace of Jerusalem!
"Peace be to your homes!
Peace be within your walls,
and security within your borders!"

For love of my family and friends
I will say: "Peace be within you!"
For the sake of the house of our God,
I seek your good.   Glory* . . .

Ant. 2 From sunrise to sunset, my soul waits for you.

Psalm 130

Out of the depths I cry to you,
O God, hear my voice!
Let your ears be attentive
to the voice of my supplication.

If you should mark our iniquities,
O God, who could stand?
But with you is found forgiveness:
for this we revere you.

My soul waits for you,
in your word I hope;
my soul waits for you
more than those who watch for
    daybreak.

Let Israel hope in you!
For with you there is love,
and fullness of redemption.
And you will redeem Israel
from all its iniquities.   Glory* . . .

Ant. 3 Let every knee bow at the name of Jesus.

Canticle: Philippians 2:6–11

Though he was in the form of God,
Jesus did not count equality with God
something to be grasped at.

But emptied himself
taking the form of a slave,
being born in human likeness.

Being found in human estate,
he humbled himself and became
    obedient,
obediently accepting death,
even death on a cross!

Therefore God has highly exalted him
and bestowed on him the name
above every other name,

So that at the name of Jesus
every knee should bow,
in heaven, on the earth,
and under the earth,
and every tongue proclaim
to the glory of God:
JESUS CHRIST IS LORD!   Glory* . . .

*Glory to you, Source of all Being,
  Eternal Word, and Holy Spirit.
  As it was . . .

READING

RESPONSORY

From daybreak to sunset, we praise your name, O God. —**From**...
Your glory fills the heavens; —**we praise**...
Glory to you, Source of all Being, Eternal Word and Holy Spirit. —**From**...

CANTICLE OF MARY

Ant.   Blessed are the pure of heart, for they shall see God.

INTERCESSIONS

PRAYER: All-loving God, you restored your people to eternal life by raising
Jesus from the dead. Make our faith strong and our hope sure.
May we never doubt that you will fulfill the promises you have
made to us and to all the peoples of this world. Grant this through
the prayers of all who without seeing have believed and thereby
gained eternal life. Amen.

MORNING PRAYER

**Ant. 1 We praise you for your
    steadfast love, alleluia.**

Psalm 118

We give thanks to you, for you are good
and your steadfast love endures for ever.

Let the descendants of Israel say:
"Your steadfast love endures for ever."
Let the descendants of Aaron say:
"Your steadfast love endures for ever."
Let those who fear you say:
"Your steadfast love endures for ever."

In my distress, I called to you;
you answered me and set me free.
With you at my side, I do not fear.
What can anyone do against me?
You are at my side to help me;
I shall withstand all evildoers.

It is better to take refuge in you,
than to trust in people;
it is better to take refuge in you,
than to trust in our leaders.

All wickedness surrounded me;
in your name I crushed it.
It surrounded me, surrounded me
     on every side;
in your name I cut it off.
It surrounded me like bees;
it blazed like a fire among thorns.
In your name I crushed it.

I was pushed hard, and was falling
but you came to help me.
You are my strength and my song;
you are my salvation.

O God, your right hand has triumphed;
your right hand is exalted.
Your right hand has triumphed;
I shall not die, I shall live
and recount your wondrous deeds.
You have chastened me sorely,
but have not given me over to death.

Open to me the gates of justice,
that I may enter and give thanks.
This is your gate, O God;
the just shall enter through it.
I thank you for you have answered me
you alone are my salvation.

The stone which the builders rejected
has become the corner stone.
This is your doing, O God,
it is marvelous in our eyes.
This is the day which you have made;
let us rejoice and be glad in it.

Save us, we beseech you, O God!
O God, grant us success.
Blessed are those who enter
in your holy name.
For you, O God, are our God,
and you have given us light.

Let us go forward in procession with
branches,
up to your holy altar.
You are my God, I thank you.
You are my God, I praise you.
We give thanks to you for you are good;
and your steadfast love endures for
ever.   Glory* . . .

**Ant. 2 May all your works bless you,
alleluia.**

Canticle: Daniel 3:52–57

Blessed are you, God of our ancestors,
praiseworthy and exalted above all
forever.

Blessed be your holy and glorious
name,
praiseworthy and exalted above all for
all ages.

Blessed are you in the temple of your
glory,
praiseworthy and exalted above all
forever.

Blessed are you on the throne of your
kingdom,
praiseworthy and exalted above all
forever.

Blessed are you who look into the depths
from your throne upon the cherubim,
praiseworthy and exalted above all
forever.

Blessed are you in the firmament of
heaven,
praiseworthy and glorious forever.

We bless you, O God, and all your
works,
we praise and exalt you above all
forever.   Glory* . . .

**Ant. 3 You are wonderful in all your
works, O God.**

Psalm 150

We praise you, O God, in your holy
sanctuary;
we praise you in your mighty heavens.
We praise you for your powerful deeds;
we praise you according to your
greatness.

We praise you with trumpet sound;
we praise you with lute and harp!
We praise you with timbrel and dance,
we praise you with strings and pipe!

We praise you with sounding cymbals,
we praise you with clashing cymbals!
Let everything that breathes,
give praise to you, O God.   Glory* . . .

READING

RESPONSORY

We praise your goodness, O God, with songs of thanksgiving. —**We praise**. . .
We rejoice in your presence —**with**. . .
Glory to you, Source of all Being, Eternal Word and Holy Spirit. —**We praise**. . .

CANTICLE OF ZECHARIAH

Ant.   Give us this day our daily bread.

INTERCESSIONS

PRAYER: O God of the morning, you call us to a new day and to a life of
resurrection and union with you. Help us to live this day as a
people of hope in a world of chaos. May all who face oppression,
terror, abuse, or suffering in any way know that you call us to life
and happiness in this world as well as the world to come. We ask
this through the intercession of all who lived as people of hope in
the midst of despair and now live with you in everlasting peace.
Amen.

DAYTIME PRAYER

Ant. 1 You are the bread of life, alleluia.

Psalm 23

Yahweh, you are my shepherd;
I shall not want.
You make me to lie in green pastures.
You lead me to restful waters,
to restore my soul.

You guide me in paths of righteousness
for the sake of your name.
Even though I walk through the valley
  of the shadow of death,
I fear no evil;
for you are with me;
your crook and your staff
give me comfort.

You prepare a table before me
in the presence of my foes;
you anoint my head with oil,
my cup overflows.

Surely goodness and mercy shall follow
  me
all the days of my life.
and I shall dwell in your holy house
  for ever and ever.   Glory* . . .

**Ant. 2 More glorious are you than the
  everlasting mountains, alleluia.**

Psalm 76

O God, you are known in Judah;
your name is great in Israel.
Your abode you established in
Jerusalem, —
your dwelling place in Zion.
There you broke the flashing arrows,
the sword, and the weapons of war.

Glorious are you, more majestic
than the everlasting mountains.
Warriors were stripped of their spoil,
  sinking into death;
those engaged in war, made powerless
  at your word.
At your rebuke, O God,
the makers of war lay stunned.
  Glory* . . .

**Ant. 3 God arose in judgment to save
  the oppressed on earth, alleluia.**

II

You alone, O God, strike terror!
Who can stand before you
when your anger is aroused?
From the heavens you utter judgment;
the earth feared and was still,
when you rose to establish judgment
to save the oppressed of the earth.

Human anger will serve to praise you;
its residue gird you round.
We make vows to you, and fulfill them.
Let your faithful bring you gifts;
you, who are worthy of awe,
who cut short the lives of leaders,
who strike terror in the rulers of the
  earth.   Glory* . . .

PRAYER: Creator of all, by the paschal mystery you touch our lives with the
healing power of your love. You have given us the freedom of the
children of God. May all people know this freedom in their hearts
and in their lives, so that they may celebrate your gift and find joy
in it now and for ever. Amen.

EVENING PRAYER II

Ant. 1 We are a priestly people; let us give thanks, alleluia.

Psalm 110: 1-5, 7

God's revelation to the Anointed One:
"Sit at my right hand:
till I put injustice beneath your feet."

God will send forth from Zion
your scepter of power:
rule in the midst of your foes.

Your people will give themselves freely
on the day you lead your host
upon the holy mountains.
From the womb of the morning
your youth will come like dew.

God has sworn an oath that will not
be changed.
"You are a priest for ever,
after the order of Melchizedek."

The Anointed standing at your right
hand
will shatter rulers on the day of wrath.

Drinking from your streams by the
wayside
Shall the Chosen One be refreshed.
Glory* . . .

Ant. 2 Those who give to the poor will have treasure in heaven.

Psalm 112

Happy are they who fear the Most High,
who greatly delight in God's commands.
Their children will be mighty in the
land;
the offspring of the upright will be
blessed.

Wealth and riches are in their homes;
their justice endures for ever.
Light rises in the darkness for the
upright:
God is gracious, merciful and just.

It is well for those who are
generous and lend,
who conduct their affairs with justice.
The upright will never be moved;
they will be remembered for ever.

They have no fear of evil tidings;
their hearts are firm, trusting in God.
With steadfast hearts, they will not fear;
they will withstand all deception.

Open-handed, they give to the poor;
their justice endures for ever.
Their power is exalted in glory.

The wicked see and are angry,
gnash their teeth and melt away;
the desire of the wicked comes to
nought.   Glory* . . .

Ant. 3 May all who serve you, give you praise, alleluia.

Canticle: Revelation 19:1, 5-7

Salvation, glory, and power
belong to you,
your judgments are honest and true.

All of us, your servants, sing praise to
you
We worship you reverently, both great
and small.

You, our almighty God, are Creator
of heaven and earth.
Let us rejoice and exult, and give you
glory.

The wedding feast of the Lamb has
begun,
and the bride has made herself ready.
Glory* . . .

READING

RESPONSORY

Glorious are your works, God of the universe. —**Glorious**...
Nothing can surpass your greatness, —**God**...
Glory to you, Source of all Being, Eternal Word and Holy Spirit. —**Glorious**...

CANTICLE OF MARY

Ant.   Blessed are the meek, for they shall inherit the earth.

INTERCESSIONS

PRAYER: O holy God, as evening falls remain with us. Remember our good
deeds and forgive our failings. Help us to reflect upon and live
according to your covenant of love. Be with our lonely and elderly
sisters and brothers in the evening of their lives. May all who long
to see you face to face know the comfort of your presence. This we
ask in union with Simeon and Anna and all who have gone before
us blessing and proclaiming you by the fidelity of their lives.
Amen.

MONDAY

MORNING PRAYER

**Ant. 1 Give success to the work of our
hands, O God.**

Psalm 90

O God, you have been our shelter
from one generation to the next.
Before the mountains were formed,
or the earth or the world brought forth,
from everlasting to everlasting
you are God.

You turn us back to dust, and say:
"Go back, peoples of the earth!"
For a thousand years in your sight
are like yesterday, when it is past,
no more than a watch in the night.

You sweep us away like a dream,
like grass which is renewed in the
    morning:
in the morning it flowers and is
    renewed;
in the evening it fades and withers.

So we are consumed by your anger;
by your wrath we are overwhelmed.
You set our iniquities before you,
our secret sins in the light of your face.

All our days pass away in your anger.
Our years are over like a sigh.
The years of our life are seventy,
or eighty for those who are strong;
yet their span is but toil and trouble;
they pass swiftly and we are gone.

Who understands the power of your
    anger
and fears the strength of your wrath?
Teach us to number our days
that we may gain wisdom of heart.

Relent, O God! How long?
Have pity on your servants!
In the morning, fill us with your love,
that we may rejoice and be glad all
    our days.
Balance with joy our days of affliction,
and the years when we knew
    misfortune.

Let your word be manifest to your
    servants,
your glorious power to their children.
Let your favor, O God, be upon us:
give success to the work of our hands,
give success to the work of our hands.
    Glory* ...

**Ant. 2 You turn darkness into light
and make the rough ways smooth!**

Canticle: Isaiah 42:10-16

Sing to our God a new song,
Sing praise from the ends of the earth!

Let the sea and what fills it resound,
the coastlands and their inhabitants.
Let the desert and its cities cry out,
the villages where Kedar dwells.

Let the inhabitants of Sela exult,
let them shout from the top of the
    mountains.
Let them give glory to the Most High,
and declare God's praise in the
    coastlands.

You go forth, O God, like a hero,
like a warrior you stir up your fury;
crying out and shouting aloud,
against the oppression of your poor.

For a long time I held my peace,
I kept still and restrained myself;
now, I will cry like a woman in labor,
    gasping and panting.

I will lay waste mountains and hills,
and dry up all their herbage;
I will turn the rivers into islands,
and dry up all the streams.

I will lead the blind on their journey,
in a way that they know not,
in unknown paths I will guide them.
I will turn darkness before them into
    light,
and rough places into level ground.
    Glory* . . .

**Ant. 3 You are gracious, O God; you
call us to be your people.**

Psalm 135

We praise your name, O God,
All your servants give praise,
those who stand in your holy house,
in the courts of your house, O God!

We praise you, for you are good.
Sing to your name for you are gracious!
For you have chosen Jacob for yourself,
Israel as your own possession.

For I know that you are great,
that you are high above all gods.
You do whatever you please,
in heaven and on earth,
in the seas and all the deeps.

You make the clouds rise from the
    ends of the earth,
make lightning for the rain,
and bring forth wind from your
    storehouse.

You smote the firstborn of Egypt,
both of human and beast alike.
Signs and wonders you worked
in the midst of the land of Egypt,
against Pharaoh and all his servants.

You smote many nations
and slew mighty rulers,
Sihon, king of the Amorites,
Og, the king of Bashan,
and all the kingdoms of Canaan.
You gave their land as a heritage,
a heritage to your people.   Glory* . . .

READING

RESPONSORY

All nations rejoice and praise God our creator. —**All**. . .
Sing with joy to the Most High, —**and praise**. . .
Glory to you, Source of all Being, Eternal Word and Holy Spirit. —**All nations**. . .

CANTICLE OF ZECHARIAH

Ant.   Come to us this day and set your people free.

INTERCESSIONS

PRAYER: O God of Life, you bring us to this day and we are grateful for your gift. Enable us to be and to work for one another in order that justice may reign; that the needs of the poor be met; and, that the oppressed may be liberated. We pray this in the name of Jesus who came that we may be free. Amen.

DAYTIME PRAYER

Ant. 1 Teach me to follow in your steps, that I may be your disciple.

Psalm 119:129–136

Your will is wonderful indeed;
therefore will I obey it.
The unfolding of your words gives light;
it imparts wisdom to the simple.

I open my mouth and I sigh
as I yearn for your commandments.
Turn to me and be gracious,
treat me as one who loves your name.

Keep my steps steady in your way,
according to your promise;
let no iniquity rule over me.
Redeem me from human oppression,
that I may keep your precepts.

Let your face shine on your servant
and teach me your statutes.
My eyes shed streams of tears,
because your law is disobeyed.
    Glory* . . .

Ant. 2 Blessed are the merciful, mercy shall be theirs.

Psalm 82

God stands in the divine assembly;
holding judgment in the midst of the
    gods:

"How long will you judge unjustly
and favor the cause of the wicked?
Give justice to the weak and the orphan;
defend the afflicted and the needy.—

Rescue the weak and the destitute;
deliver them from the hand of the
    wicked."

They have neither knowledge nor
    understanding,
they walk about in darkness;
the foundations of the world are shaken.

God says, "You are gods,
children of the Most High, all of you;
yet, you shall die like human beings,
and fall like any of their leaders."

Arise, O God, judge the earth;
for to you belong all the nations.
    Glory* . . .

Ant. 3 Guide us in your way of peace.

Psalm 120

In my distress, I cry to you,
that you may answer me:
"Deliver my soul from lying lips,
and from a deceitful tongue."

What shall be given you in return,
you deceitful tongue?
The warrior's arrows sharpened
and coals, red-hot, blazing.

Alas, that I sojourn in Meshech,
dwell among the tents of Kedar!
Too long have I had my dwelling
    among those who hate peace.
I am for peace; but when I speak,
    they are for war!   Glory* . . .

PRAYER: O God, in your love you have given each of us gifts and talents to serve the common good. Help us to use them generously and lovingly, for we are your children. Free us from the desire to serve only our own interests, and help us to grow in the spirit of love that makes us your sisters and brothers. This we ask for the sake of all who are in bondage through our selfishness and that of our governments. Grant us our prayer that your love and peace may reign now and forever. Amen.

EVENING PRAYER

Ant. 1 Your love, O God, endures for ever.

Psalm 136

We give thanks to you, for you are good,
　for your love endures forever.
We thank you, O God of gods,
　for your love endures forever.
We thank you, Creator of the universe,
　for your love endures forever.

You alone have done great wonders,
　for your love endures forever.
Your wisdom made the heavens,
　for your love endures forever.
You spread out the earth upon the
　waters,
　for your love endures forever.

It was you who made the great lights,
　for your love endures forever;
the sun to rule over the day,
　for your love endures forever;
the moon and the stars to rule over the
　night, for your love endures forever.
Glory* . . .

Ant. 2 With outstretched arm you lead us out of darkenss.

II

The first born of the Egyptians you
　smote, for your love endures forever;
and brought Israel out from their midst,
　for your love endures forever;
with arm outstretched and power in
　your hand,
　for your love endures forever.

You divided the Red Sea in two,
　for your love endures forever;
you made Israel pass through the midst,
　for your love endures forever;
you flung Pharaoh and his host in the
　sea, for your love endures forever.

You led your people through the desert,
　for your love endures forever.
Nations in their greatness you struck,
　for your love endures forever.
Rulers in their splendor you slew,
　for your love endures forever.

Sihon, king of the Amorites,
　for your love endures forever;
and Og, the king of Bashan,
　for your love endures forever.

Their land you gave as a heritage,
　for your love endures forever;
a heritage to your faithful people,
　for your love endures forever.

You remembered us in our distress,
　for your love endures forever;
and you rescued us from oppression,
　for your love endures forever.
You give food to all living things,
　for your love endures forever.

We give thanks to you, God of heaven,
　for your love endures forever.
Glory* . . .

Ant. 3 In Christ, God's grace is revealed.

Canticle: Ephesians 1:3–10

Praised be the God
of our Lord Jesus Christ
who has blessed us in Christ
with every spiritual blessing
　in the heavens.

God chose us in him
before the foundation of the world,
that we should be holy
and blameless in God's sight.

We have been predestined
to be God's children through Jesus
　Christ,
such was the purpose of God's will,
that all might praise the glorious favor
bestowed on us in Christ.

In Christ and through his blood,
　we have redemption,
the forgiveness of our sins,
according to the riches of God's grace
　lavished upon us.

For God has made known to us
in all wisdom and insight,
the mystery of the plan set forth in
　Christ.

A plan to be carried out in Christ,
in the fullness of time,

to unite all things in Christ,
things in heaven and things on earth.
Glory* . . .

READING

RESPONSORY

O God, receive our prayer which is lifted up to you. —**O God,** . . .
Like the fragrance of incense, —**which is** . . .
Glory to you, Source of all Being, Eternal Word and Holy Spirit. —**O God,** . . .

CANTICLE OF MARY

Ant.   Blessed are the merciful, for they shall obtain mercy.

INTERCESSIONS

PRAYER: O God, as darkness falls, remain with us as our light. Help us to
meet you in the scriptures that we read, in the bread that we
break, and in the neighbor that we welcome into our hearts.
Grant this prayer that your reign will come; that your will be
done in us as it was in Jesus, now and for ever. Amen.

TUESDAY

MORNING PRAYER

**Ant. 1 Look with favor upon us that we
may dwell with you forever.**

Psalm 101

I will sing of fidelity and justice;
to you, O God, I will sing.
I will pay heed to the way that is
blameless.
Oh when will you come to me?

I will walk with integrity of heart
within my house;
I will not set before my eyes
anything that is base.

I renounce the ways of wrongdoers;
they shall not adhere to me.
Perverseness of heart shall be far from
me;
I will know nothing of evil.

Those who slander their neighbor
secretly
I will ignore.
Those of haughty looks and proud hearts
I will not endure.

I will look with favor on all who
are faithful,
that they may dwell with me;
they who walk in the way that is
blameless
shall minister to me.

No one who practices deceit
shall dwell in my house;
no one who utters lies
shall remain in my presence.

Morning by morning I will renounce
all the oppression in the land,
uprooting from the city of God
all that is evil.   Glory* . . .

**Ant. 2 Look upon us with compassion
O God, and heal us.**

Canticle: Daniel 3:26, 27, 29, 34–41

Blessed are you, and praiseworthy,
O God of our ancestors,
and glorious forever is your name.

For you are just in all you have done;
all your deeds are faultless, all your
ways right,
and all your judgments proper.

For we have sinned and transgressed
by departing from you,
and we have done every kind of evil.

For your name's sake, do not deliver
us up forever,
or make void your covenant.

Do not take away your mercy from us,
for the sake of those beloved by you:
Sara and Abraham, Rebecca and Isaac,
Rachel and Jacob, your holy ones,

to whom you promised to multiply their
offspring
like the stars of heaven,
or the sands on the shore of the sea.

For we are reduced beyond any other
nation,
brought low everywhere in the world
this day because of our sins.

We have in our day no ruler, prophet,
or leader,
no holocaust, sacrifice, oblation, or
incense,
no place to offer first fruits, to find favor
with you.

But with contrite heart and humble
spirit let us be received;
as though it were holocausts of rams and
bullocks, or thousands of fat lambs,
so let our sacrifice be in your presence
today as we follow you unreservedly;
for those who trust in you cannot be put
to shame.

And now we follow you with our whole
heart,
we fear you and we pray to you.
Glory* . . .

**Ant. 3 O God, you are my shield. In
you I take refuge.**

Psalm 144:1-10

Blessed are you, O God, my rock,
who trains my hands for war,
and my fingers for battle.

You are my rock and my fortress,
my stronghold and my deliverer,
my shield in whom I take refuge.
You bring peoples under your rule.

Who are we that you care for us,
mortal flesh, that you keep us in mind?
We, who are merely a breath,
whose days are like a passing shadow.

Lower your heavens and come down!
Touch the mountains that they smoke!
Flash your lightnings and scatter them,
shoot your arrows and put them to
flight.

Stretch forth your hand from on high,
rescue me from the mighty waters,
from the hands of alien foes,
whose mouths are filled with lies,
and whose hands are raised in perjury.

To you will I sing a new song.
On a ten-stringed harp I will play
to you, who give rulers their victory,
who rescue David, your servant.
Glory* . . .

READING

RESPONSORY

Answer my plea, O God; I trust in your word. —**Answer**...
Before the first rays of dawn, I come to you. —**I trust**...
Glory to you, Source of all Being, Eternal Word and Holy Spirit. —**Answer**...

CANTICLE OF ZECHARIAH

Ant. Protect us from the grasp of evil, and lead us not into temptation.

INTERCESSIONS

PRAYER: O God, you call us to begin this day in dedication to you. May all who need your help today experience your love and compassion through us and through all who have come to know you. Bless all the children of this world; protect them from abuse. May they come to know their worth and dignity as your children, rightful citizens of this earth. This we ask in union with all the innocent and pure of heart who stand in your presence now and for ever. Amen.

DAYTIME PRAYER

Ant. 1 You are true to your promise in which I delight.

Psalm 119:137–144

Just are you, O God,
    and right are your judgments.
You have decreed your will in justice
    and in all faithfulness.

I am consumed with zeal
because your words are forgotten.
Your promise is tried in the fire,
the delight of your servant.

Though I am weak and despised
I do not forget your precepts.
Your justice is righteous for ever,
and your law is true.

Trouble and anguish come upon me,
but your commands are my delight.
The justice of your will is eternal;
give me understanding that I may live.
    Glory* . . .

Ant. 2 Listen to the sound of my call, O God. I cry for your help.

Psalm 88

My God, I call for help by day;
I cry out in the night before you.
Let my prayer come into your presence,
incline your ear to my cry!
For my soul is full of troubles,
and my life draws near to the grave.

I am reckoned as one in the tomb;
I have reached the end of my strength,
like one forsaken among the dead,
like the slain that lie in the grave,
like those you no longer remember,
for they are cut off from your hand.

You have laid me in the depths of the tomb,
in the regions dark and deep.
Your anger lies heavy upon me,
you overwhelm me with all your waves.
    Glory* . . .

Ant. 3 Hide not your face from me, O God, in time of distress.

II

All my companions now shun me;
to them I am a thing of horror.
I am shut in so that I cannot escape;
my eye grows dim through sorrow.

Every day I call upon you;
to you I stretch out my hands.
Do you work wonders for the dead?
Do phantoms rise up to praise you?

Is your love declared in the grave,
or your faithfulness in the bottomless pit?
Are your wonders known in the darkness,
or your salvation in the land of forgetfulness?

But I, O God, cry out to you:
in the morning my prayer comes before you.
Why do you cast me off, O God?
Why hide your face from me?

Afflicted and close to death
    from the days of my youth,
I suffer your trials; I am helpless.
Your chastisements swept over me;
your dread assaults destroy me.

They surround me like a flood
   all day long;
they close in upon me together. —

Friend and neighbor shun me;
my companions are in darkness.
   Glory*

PRAYER: Loving God, you sent the Holy Spirit to the early Christians as their source of courage and fidelity. Send your Spirit to us that we, too, may be witnesses of your love to all peoples on this earth. We pray especially for the homeless, the displaced, the nameless, the ignored. May all come to know your love and care, for you are both mother and father to all the peoples on this earth. Help us to recognize all as our sisters and brothers. We ask this in union with Jesus, our friend and brother. Amen.

EVENING PRAYER

Ant. 1 May we remember your covenant in this land of exile.

Psalm 137:1–6

By the waters of Babylon,
we sat down and wept,
when we remembered Zion.
On the willows there
   we hung up our harps.

For there our captors
   required of us songs,
and our tormentors, mirth, saying,
"Sing us one of the songs of Zion!"

How shall we sing Yahweh's song
   in a foreign land?
If I forget you, Jerusalem,
let my hand wither!

Let my tongue cleave
   to the roof of my mouth,
if I do not remember you,
if I do not set Jerusalem
   above all my joys!   Glory* . . .

Ant. 2 Your name and your word are above all for ever.

Psalm 138

I give you thanks with all my heart;
before the gods I sing your praise;
I bow down before your holy temple
and give thanks to your name
for your steadfast love and your
   faithfulness;
for exalted above all are your name
   and your word.

On the day I called, you answered
   me;
you increased the strength of my soul.

All of earth's rulers shall praise you
for they have heard the words of your
   mouth;
they shall sing of your ways for
   great is your glory, O God.
Though you are high, you look on the
   lowly
and the haughty you know from afar.

Though I walk in the midst of trouble,
   you preserve my life;
you stretch out your hand and save me.
You will fulfill your purpose for me;
your steadfast love endures for ever.
Do not forsake the work of your hands.
   Glory* . . .

Ant. 3 Salvation and glory belong to our God, alleluia!

Canticle: Revelation 4:11, 5:9, 10, 12

Worthy are you, O God, our God,
to receive glory and honor and power.

For you have created all things;
by your will they came to be and were
   made.

Worthy are you to take the scroll
   and to open its seals,

For you were slain, and by your blood,
you purchased for God
persons of every race and tongue,
of every people and nation.

You have made of them a kingdom,
and priests to serve our God,
and they shall reign on the earth.

Worthy is the Lamb who was slain
to receive power and riches,
wisdom and strength,
honor and glory and praise.   Glory* . . .

READING

RESPONSORY

In your presence, O God, I will find all my joy. —**In your**. . .
When I see you face to face, —**I will**. . .
Glory to you, Source of all Being, Eternal Word and Holy Spirit. —**In your**. . .

CANTICLE OF MARY

Ant.   **Blessed are the poor in spirit, the reign of God is theirs.**

INTERCESSIONS

PRAYER: O gracious God, open our hearts and our eyes to the wonders of
your presence among us. May we see the signs of your beauty
within and about us and ever be in awe of the simple gifts of life.
Help us to reach beyond ourselves and to give thanks for all of
your creation that shares this universe with us: peoples of every
nation, animals of every species, all forms of vegetation, the
planets, stars, and all the elements. We pray this in union with the
incarnate Word of God in whose image all was created. May you
be blessed throughout the ages and for all eternity. Amen.

WEDNESDAY

MORNING PRAYER

**Ant. 1 I will give thanks to you among
the peoples.**

Psalm 108

My heart is steadfast, O God, my
heart is steadfast!
I will sing and make melody!
Awake, my soul!
Awake, lyre and harp!
I will awake the dawn!

I will give thanks to you among
the peoples,
I will sing praises to you among the
nations.
For your steadfast love is great above
the heavens,
your faithfulness reaches to the clouds.

Be exalted, O God, above the heavens!
Let your glory be over all the earth!
That your beloved may be delivered,
give help with your hand, and answer
me!

You have promised in your sanctuary:
"With exultation I will divide up
Shechem,
and portion out the Vale of Succoth.
Gilead is mine, and Manasseh;
Ephraim is my helmet;
Judah my scepter.
Moab is my washbasin;
upon Edom I cast my shoe;
over Philistia I shout in triumph."

Who will bring me to the fortified
city?
Who will lead me to Edom?
Have you not rejected us, O God?
You no longer go forth with our armies.
Give us help against this oppression,
for human help is vain!
With you, we shall do valiantly;
it is you who will conquer injustice.
Glory* . . .

Ant. 2 Justice and peace will spring forth before all nations.

Canticle: Isaiah 61:10–62:5

I will greatly rejoice in you, Yahweh,
in you my soul shall exult;
for you clothe me with garments of
   salvation,
you cover me with the robe of justice,
like a bridegroom bedecked with a
   garland,
like a bride adorned with her jewels.

As the earth brings forth its shoots,
and a garden makes its seeds spring up,
so will you make justice and praise
to spring forth before all the nations.

For Zion's sake I will not be silent,
for Jerusalem's sake I will not rest,
until its vindication shines forth like the
   dawn
and its salvation like a burning torch.

Nations shall behold its vindication,
   and all rulers see its glory;
it shall be called by a new name
which your own mouth will give.
It shall be a crown of beauty,
a royal diadem held in your hand,
   O God.

No more shall they call it "Forsaken,"
or its land be termed "Desolate;"
but it shall be called "My delight,"
   and its land "Espoused;"
for you, O God, delight in it,
and take it as a spouse.

For as young lovers are espoused,
so shall its children espouse Zion,
and as newlyweds rejoice in each other,
so shall you rejoice over Zion.
   Glory* . . .

Ant. 3 You set us free, O God, from the chains that bind us.

Psalm 146

My soul, give praise to my God!
I will praise the Most High as long as
   I live;
I will sing praises to my God while
   I have being.

Put no trust in sovereigns,
in mortal flesh in whom there is no
   help.
When their breath departs they return
   to the earth;
on that day their plans perish.

Happy are they whose help is the
   Most High,
whose hope is in the Creator of all,
who alone made heaven and earth,
the seas, and all that is in them;
who keeps faith forever;
who executes justice for the oppressed;
who gives food to the hungry.

For you, O God, set prisoners free;
you open the eyes of the blind.
You lift up those who are bowed down;
you love the upright of heart.
You watch over the sojourners;
uphold the bereaved and the orphaned.

O God, you will reign for ever and ever,
   through all generations.   Glory* . . .

READING

RESPONSORY

I will sing your praise, O God, every day of my life. —I will. . .
From sunrise to sunset, —every. . .
Glory to you, Source of all Being, Eternal Word and Holy Spirit. —I will. . .

CANTICLE OF ZECHARIAH

Ant.   In joy and holiness let us serve God our Savior.

INTERCESSIONS

PRAYER: See in us, O God, the face of your Christ, and forgive us our sins.
Help all who must live with the strain of broken and tense
relationships, and give us the courage to love in spite of loss, and
the mercy to forgive all who have injured us in any way. May our
work this day bring us and all the world nearer to the quality of
life to which you call us. Grant this through the intercession of the
Holy Family and of all the families like them that image your life
in the trinity of love. Amen.

DAYTIME PRAYER

**Ant. 1 Day and night I hope in your
words.**

Psalm 119:145–152

With all my heart, I cry to you;
answer me, O God.
I cry to you; save me,
that I may observe your will.

I rise before dawn and cry for help;
I hope in your words.
My eyes watch throughout the night
meditating on your promises.

Hear my voice in your steadfast love;
in your justice preserve my life.
Those who persecute me draw near:
they are far from your law.

But you, O God, are near at hand,
all your commands are true.
Long have I known that your will
  endures forever.   Glory* . . .

**Ant. 2 Do good to those who hate you,
bless those who curse you, pray for
those who abuse you.**

Psalm 94

Yahweh, avenging God,
avenging God, appear!
Judge of the earth, arise,
render injustice its deserts!
How long, O God, shall oppression,
how long shall oppression exult?

They bluster with arrogant speech,
they boast, all the evildoers.
They crush your people, O God,
they afflict the ones you have chosen.
They kill the helpless and the poor, —

and murder the parentless child.
They say: "God does not see;
their God pays no heed!"

Understand, O dullest of people!
Fools, when will you be wise?
Can God who made the ear, not hear?
The one who formed the eye, not see?
Will God who chastens nations, not
  punish?
God who imparts knowledge knows our
  thoughts,
knows they are no more than a breath.
  Glory* . . .

**Ant. 3 Judge not, and you will not be
judged; condemn not and you will
not be condemned.**

II

Happy are those whom you chasten,
whom you teach by means of your law
to give them respite from days of
  trouble,
until oppression is no more.
You will not abandon your people;
you will not forsake your heritage;
for justice will return to the righteous,
and the upright in heart will follow it.

Who will rise against oppression?
Who will stand against injustice?
If you had not been my help,
I would soon dwell in the land of
  silence.

When I think: "My foot is slipping,"
your steadfast love upholds me.
When the cares of my heart are many,
your consolations cheer my soul.

Can unjust rulers be your friends,
who do injustice under cover of law?
They attack the life of the helpless,
   and condemn the innocent to death.

But you have become my stronghold,
my God, the rock of my refuge.
Injustice will turn on itself,
and evil will destroy evil.   Glory* . . .

PRAYER: Compassionate God, we pause to rest in your presence. May the work we have begun this day find fulfillment in you, for our good and the good of all people on this earth. We ask this in the name of Jesus who is our way, our truth, and our life. Amen.

EVENING PRAYER

Ant. 1 Behold, I am with you always.

Psalm 139:1–18, 23–24

O God, you have searched me and
   you know me,
you know when I sit and when I stand;
you discern my thoughts from afar.
You mark when I walk or lie down,
with all my ways you are acquainted.

Before a word is on my tongue,
behold, O God, you know the whole
   of it.
Behind and before you besiege me,
you lay your hand upon me.
Such knowledge is too wonderful for me:
too high, beyond my reach.

O where can I go from your spirit,
or where can I flee from your presence?
If I climb to heaven, you are there!
If I lie in the grave, you are there!

If I take the wings of the morning
and dwell in the depths of the sea,
even there your hand shall lead me,
your hand shall hold me fast.

If I say: "Let darkness cover me,
and the light around me be night,"
even darkness is not dark to you
and the night is as bright as the day;
for darkness is as light to you.
   Glory* . . .

Ant. 2 O God, I praise you for the wonder of my being.

II

For it was you who formed my inmost
   parts, —

knit me together in my mother's womb.
I praise you for the wonder of my being,
for the wonder of all your works.

Already you knew me well;
my body was not hidden from you,
when I was being made in secret
and molded in the depths of the earth.

Your eyes beheld my unformed
   substance;
in your book they all were written,
the days that you had formed for me
when none of them yet were.

How precious to me are your thoughts!
How vast the sum of them!
If I count them, they are more than the
   sand.
When I awake, I am still with you.

Search me, O God, and know my heart!
O test me and know my thoughts!
See that I follow not the wrong way
and lead me in the way of life eternal.
   Glory* . . .

Ant. 3 Christ is the firstborn of all creation.

Canticle: Colossians 1:12–20

Let us give thanks to God
for having made us worthy
to share the inheritance of the
   saints in light.

God has delivered us
from the power of darkness
and transferred us
into the kingdom of God's beloved Son,
   Jesus, —

in whom we have redemption,
the forgiveness of our sins.

Jesus is the image of the invisible God,
the first-born of all creation;
in him all things were created,
    in heaven and on earth,
things visible and invisible.

All things were created through him;
all were created for him.
He is before all else that is.
In him all things hold together.

He is the head of the body, the church!
He is the beginning,
the firstborn from the dead,
that in everything, he might be above
    all others.

In him all the fullness of God was
    pleased to dwell,
and through him to reconcile all
    things to himself,
whether on earth or in heaven,
making peace by the blood of his cross.
    Glory* . . .

READING

RESPONSORY

Keep us, O God, on the path to life. —**Keep us**. . .
May your hand ever guide us —**on the**. . .
Glory to you, Source of all Being, Eternal Word and Holy Spirit. —**Keep us**. . .

CANTICLE OF MARY

Ant.   Blessed are they who mourn for they shall be comforted.

INTERCESSIONS

PRAYER: O God, look upon the poverty of our hearts with compassion and
love. Enable us to give lovingly and freely of our possessions and
gifts. May those who work with the poor and needy receive joy in
this life and fulness of life for ever. This we ask through the
intercession of all the saints, especially of those founders of
religious orders whose legacy of service we carry on today. Grant
that we may be faithful as they were faithful so that we too may
live with you forever. Amen.

THURSDAY

MORNING PRAYER

**Ant. 1 In the early morning, O God, I
remember your steadfast love.**

Psalm 143:1-11

Hear my prayer, O God;
give ear to my supplication!
In your justice and faithfulness
    answer me!
Do not call your servant to judgment
for no one is righteous before you.

For evil pursues my soul,
crushing my life to the ground,—

making me dwell in darkness
like the dead, long forgotten.
Therefore my spirit faints within me;
my heart within me is appalled.

I remember the days gone before,
I ponder on all you have done;
I muse on what you have wrought.
To you I stretch out my hands;
my soul thirsts for you like parched
    land.

O God, make haste to answer me!
My spirit fails within me! —

Hide not your face from me,
lest I be like those who go down
  to the grave.

Let me hear in the morning of your
  steadfast love,
for in you I put my trust.
Teach me the way I should go,
for to you I lift up my soul.

Deliver me, O God, from all evil!
I have fled to you for refuge!
Teach me to do your will,
for you are my God!
Let your good spirit lead me
in ways that are level and smooth!

For your name's sake, save my life!
In your justice bring me out of trouble.
  Glory* . . .

**Ant. 2 How often would I shelter you
as a hen shelters her brood!**

Canticle: Isaiah 66:10–14a

"Rejoice with Jerusalem,
  and be glad for her,
  all you who love her;
rejoice with her in joy,
all you who mourn over her;
that you may suck and be satisfied
  with her consoling breasts;
that you may drink deeply with delight
  from the abundance of her glory."

For thus says Yahweh, our God:
"Behold, I will extend prosperity
  to her like a river,
and the wealth of the nations
  like an overflowing stream.

As nurslings, you shall be carried upon
  her hip,
and fondled on her lap.

READING

RESPONSORY

As a parent comforts a child,
  so will I comfort you;
you shall be comforted in Jerusalem.

You shall see, and your hearts shall
  rejoice;
your beings flourish like the grass.
  Glory* . . .

**Ant. 3 Through you, the blind see, the
lame walk, and the poor hear your
good news.**

Psalm 147:1–11

It is good to sing praise to you;
for you are gracious and merciful;
to you our praise is due.

You, O God, build up Jerusalem;
you gather the outcasts of Israel.
You heal the broken-hearted,
and bind up their wounds.
You fix the number of the stars,
and give to each its name.

You are great and almighty,
your wisdom beyond all measure.
For you lift up the poor and
  downtrodden,
you put oppression to rout.

We sing to you with thanksgiving;
make melody upon the lyre!

You cover the heavens with clouds,
you prepare rain for the earth,
make mountains sprout with grass.
You provide beasts with their food,
and the young ravens that cry.
You delight not in the strength of the
  horse,
nor take pleasure in human indulgence;
but you delight in those who revere you,
in those who hope in your love.
  Glory* . . .

O God, you have made of us a priesthood, baptized in the blood of Christ.
  —**O God,** . . .
You send us to all nations —**baptized**. . .
Glory to you, Source of all Being, Eternal Word and Holy Spirit. —**O God,** . . .

CANTICLE OF ZECHARIAH

Ant.   Send your light and your truth to those who dwell in darkness.

INTERCESSIONS

PRAYER: O God, you call us to be your people and to minister to one another. Look with pity on all who are held captive by the bonds of addiction. Free us from our own destructive impulses that we may choose life and enable others to find what is life-giving for them. Give discernment and wisdom to all who minister to those seeking liberation from any forms of addiction that we may all know the joy of the freedom that is ours as your children. This we ask of you, who are our Mother, our Father, our Guardian, our God, Creator and Preserver of us all, both now and in eternity. Amen.

DAYTIME PRAYER

Ant. 1 Give me life according to your justice.

Psalm 119:153–160

Look on my affliction and deliver me,
for I remember your law.
Plead my cause and redeem me;
give me life according to your promise!

Salvation is far from the wicked,
for they do not seek your statutes.
Great is your mercy, O God;
give me life according to your justice.

Though my foes and oppressors are many,
I have not swerved from your will.
I look at evil with disgust,
because it seeks to snare me.

See how I love your precepts!
Preserve my life in your love.
The whole of your word is truth;
your decrees are eternal.   Glory* . . .

Ant. 2 Bless the work of our hands, O God.

Psalm 128

Blessed are they who fear you, O God,
and walk in your ways!

By the labor of their hands they shall eat.
A husband will be happy and prosper;
a wife like a fruitful vine
in the heart of her house;
their children like olive shoots
around their table.

Indeed thus shall be blessed
those who fear you, O God.

May you bless them from Zion
all the days of their lives!
May they see their children's children
in a happy Jerusalem!   Glory* . . .

Ant. 3 Deliver me for the sake of your love.

Psalm 6

O God, rebuke me not for my frailties,
nor chastise me in my weakness.
Be gracious to me for I am languishing;
heal me, for my bones are troubled.
My soul is sorely troubled.
But you, O God—how long?

Turn, O God, save my life;
deliver me for the sake of your love.
For in death there is no remembrance of you;
in the grave who can give you praise?

I am weary with my moaning;
every night I flood my bed with tears;
I drench my couch with my weeping.
My eyes waste away because of my grief,
they grow weak because of my misfortune.

Let this darkness depart from me;
hear the sound of my weeping.
You will hear my supplication;
you will accept my prayer.   Glory. . .

PRAYER: Bountiful God, you nourish us daily with the bread of life and the bread that is the work of our hands. May all the peoples and creatures of this earth have the nourishment they need to live their lives fully. Help us to solve the problems of food distribution, drought, expanding deserts, malnutrition, famine, disease; that all may share in the banquet and none will be in want. We ask this through Jesus, our Bread of Life. Amen.

EVENING PRAYER

Ant. 1 I will sing a new song to you, for you are my refuge.

Psalm 144:1–10

Blessed are you, O God, my rock,
who trains my hands for war,
and my fingers for battle.

You are my rock and my fortress,
my stronghold and my deliverer,
my shield in whom I take refuge.
You bring peoples under your rule.

Who are we that you care for us,
mortal flesh, that you keep us in mind?
We, who are merely a breath,
whose days are like a passing shadow.

Lower your heavens and come down!
Touch the mountains that they smoke!
Flash your lightnings and scatter them,
shoot your arrows and put them to
    flight.

Stretch forth your hand from on high,
rescue me from the mighty waters,
from the hands of alien foes,
whose mouths are filled with lies,
and whose hands are raised in perjury.

To you will I sing a new song.
On a ten-stringed harp I will play,
to you who give rulers their victory,
who rescues David, your servant.
    Glory* . . .

Ant. 2 Happy are the people whose God is Yahweh.

II

To you I will sing a new song;
I will play on the ten-stringed harp,
to you who give rulers their victory,
who set David your servant free.

You set him free from the evil sword,
and delivered him from alien foes,
whose mouths were filled with lies,
whose hands were raised in perjury.

Let our sons in their youth
    be like plants full grown,
our daughters like graceful columns
adorned as though for a palace.

Let our granaries be full,
    with crops of every kind;
may our sheep bring forth thousands
and ten thousands in our fields;
may our cattle be heavy with young,
suffering no mischance in bearing.

May there be no ruined wall, no exile,
no cry of distress in our streets.
Happy the people with such blessings!
Happy the people whose God is
    Yahweh.   Glory* . . .

Ant. 3 Now is the time of salvation for those who revere your name.

Canticle: Revelation 11:17–18; 12:10b–12a

We give thanks to you, God Almighty,
who is and who was.
You have assumed your great power,
you have begun your reign.

The nations raged, but your wrath
    came,
and the time for the dead to be judged,
for rewarding your servants, the
    prophets and saints,
and those who revere your name,
the great and small alike.

Now the salvation, the power,
  and the reign have come,
of God and of the Christ,
for the accusers of our loved ones
  have been thrown down,
who accuse them day and night.

They have been conquered by the
  blood of the Lamb,
and by the word of their testimony,
for love of life did not deter them
  from death.
Rejoice then, O heavens,
and you that dwell therein!
  Glory* . . .

READING
RESPONSORY

You bless the peacemakers, and call them your children. —**You**. . .
You give them your spirit, —**and call**. . .
Glory to you, Source of all Being, Eternal Word and Holy Spirit. —**You bless**. . .

CANTICLE OF MARY

Ant.   Blessed are the peacemakers, for they shall be called children of God.

INTERCESSIONS

PRAYER: God of the nations, look upon the lands devastated by war and
show us the way to peace. Turn our guns into plows and our
bombs into bread. Remove hatred from our hearts and vengeance
from our memories. Give us the wisdom and the will to end
terrorism and war whether in lands far or near, or in the confines
of our families and communities. Help us to remember that we are
one world and one family. Grant this through the intercession of
all the peacemakers of all times and all places, especially those
who suffered persecution and death for the sake of justice and
peace. Amen.

FRIDAY

MORNING PRAYER

**Ant. 1 Remember me, O God, make
yourself known in time of affliction.**

Psalm 51

Have mercy on me, O God,
according to your steadfast love;
in your abundant mercy blot out my
  sins.
Wash me thoroughly from my offenses,
and cleanse me from my sin!

For I know my offenses,
and my sin is ever before me.
Against you, you alone, have I sinned;
and done what is evil in your sight,
so you are justified in your sentence
and blameless in your judgment.
Behold, I was brought forth in a
  sinful world.

For you desire truth in my innermost
  being;
teach me wisdom in the depths of my
  heart.
O purify me, and I shall be clean;
O wash me, I shall be whiter than snow.
Fill me with joy and gladness;
let the bones you have broken rejoice.
Hide your face from my guilt,
and blot out all my offenses.

Create in me a clean heart;
put a steadfast spirit within me.
Cast me not from your presence;
take not your spirit from me.
Give me again the joy of your
  salvation,
with a willing spirit uphold me.

Then I will teach transgressors your
ways
and sinners will return to you.
Deliver me from death,
O God of my salvation,
and my tongue will sing out your
saving help.

Open my lips and my mouth will sing
your praises.
For you take no delight in sacrifice;
were I to give a burnt offering,
you would not be pleased.
A broken spirit you accept;
a contrite heart, you will not despise.

In your goodness, show favor to Zion:
rebuild the walls of Jerusalem.
Then will you delight in just sacrifices,
in gifts offered on your altar.
Glory* . . .

**Ant. 2 Your love and your kindness
extend to all the nations of the earth.**

Canticle: Tobit 13:8–11, 13–15

Let all speak of your majesty, O God,
and sing your praises in Jerusalem.

O Jerusalem, holy city,
God scourged you for the works of your
hands,
but will again pity the children of the
righteous.

Praise the goodness of God,
and bless the Sovereign of the ages,
so that Yahweh's tent may be rebuilt in
you with joy.

May God gladden within you all who
were captives;
cherishing within you all who were
ravaged
for all generations to come.

A bright light will shine to all parts of
the earth;
many nations shall come to you from
afar,
and the inhabitants of all the limits of
the earth,
drawn to you by the name of the Most
High God,
bearing in their hands their gifts for the
Almighty.

Every generation shall give joyful praise
to you,
and shall call you the chosen one,
through all ages forever.

Go, then, rejoice over the children of the
righteous,
who shall all be gathered together
and shall bless the God of the ages.

Happy are those who love you,
and happy those who rejoice in your
prosperity.
Happy are they who shall grieve over
you,
over all your chastisements,
for they shall rejoice in you
as they behold your joy forever.

My spirit blesses Yahweh, my God.
Glory* . . .

**Ant. 3 You feed us with the finest
wheat.**

Psalm 147:12–20

O praise the Most High, Jerusalem!
Praise your God, O Zion!

For God strengthens the bars of your
gates,
blessing your children within you,
establishing peace in your borders,
feeding you with the finest of wheat.

You send out your word to the earth;
your command runs swiftly,
giving snow like wool;
scattering hoarfrost like ashes.

You cast forth your ice like crumbs;
who can stand before your cold?
You send forth your word, and melt
them;
you make the wind blow, and the
waters flow.

You make your word known to your
people,
your statutes and decrees to Israel.
You have not dealt thus with any other
nation;
you have not taught them your decrees.
Glory* . . .

READING

RESPONSORY

O God, freedom is your gift to all, whether rich or poor. —**O God,** . . .
You care for all peoples of the earth, —**whether** . . .
Glory to you, Source of all Being, Eternal Word and Holy Spirit. —**O God,** . . .

CANTICLE OF ZECHARIAH

Ant.   Heal the wounds of our sins and grant us new life.

INTERCESSIONS

PRAYER: O God, look with mercy on those who are in prison. Fill their
hearts with courage and peace, and let those who minister to them
do so with justice built on compassion. Free political prisoners,
prisoners of conscience, and all those who are imprisoned unjustly.
Grant this through Jesus who was unjustly condemned but now
lives and reigns with you forever and ever. Amen.

DAYTIME PRAYER

Ant. 1 Your word is my treasure, O God.

Psalm 119:161–168

Rulers oppress me without cause
but my heart stands in awe of your
    words.
I rejoice in your word
like one who finds great treasure.

I hate and abhor falsehood,
    but I love your law.
Seven times a day I praise you
    for your just decrees.

Great peace have those who love your
    law;
nothing can make them stumble.
I hope for your salvation, O God,
I fulfill your commandments.

My soul obeys your will
    and loves it exceedingly.
I obey your precepts and your will,
for all my ways are before you.
    Glory* . . .

**Ant. 2 Let us love one another for
    love is of God.**

Psalm 133

How good and how pleasant it is,
when we live together in unity!

It is like precious oil upon the head,
running down upon the beard,
upon the beard of Aaron,
running down the collar of his robes!

It is like the dew of Hermon
which falls on the mountains of Zion!
For there God gives us the blessing,
    life for evermore.   Glory* . . .

**Ant. 3 Guard me, O God, from the
    snares of darkness.**

Psalm 140:1–9, 13–14

Rescue me from evil;
preserve me from violence.
Deliver me from an unclean heart,
from the chaos of a troubled mind.
Preserve me from a malicious tongue,
from sharp and poisonous words.

Guard me, O God, from my darkness,
and from those who lure me to evil,
who darken my light with gloom.
Pride and arrogance lay a snare;
greed and covetousness spread a net;
by my pathway they lie in wait.

I say to you: "You are my God."
Give ear to my supplication! —

O God, my strong deliverer,
you shield my head in battle.
Grant not the desires of darkness;
protect me against its snares.

I know you uphold the afflicted,
you effect justice for the needy.
Surely the just shall give thanks to
    your name;
the upright shall dwell in your
    presence.   Glory* . . .

PRAYER: O God, we remember the agonizing death of Jesus. In your
compassion deliver those who suffer from the cruelty of others and
heal the minds and hearts of those who inflict pain. Give us a
sensitivity to others that is worthy of your children. This we ask
through the intercession of all who suffered persecuton and death
for the sake of others. Amen.

EVENING PRAYER

**Ant. 1 Every day I will bless you and
praise your name for ever.**

Psalm 145

I will extol you, O God my God,
and bless your name for ever and ever.

Every day I will bless you,
and praise your name for ever.
For you are great and highly to be
    praised,
your greatness is unsearchable.

Age to age shall proclaim your works,
and declare your mighty deeds.
I will ponder your glorious splendor,
and the wonder of all your works.

Your people will proclaim the might of
    your deeds,
and I will declare your greatness.
They will pour forth the fame of your
    goodness,
and sing with joy of your justice.

You are gracious and merciful,
slow to anger, abounding in love.
Your compassion extends to all you
    have made;
how good you are to all!

All your works shall give you thanks;
all your friends shall bless you!
They shall speak of the glory of your
    creation,
and declare your marvelous might,
to make known to the children of earth
    the glory of your deeds,

and the glorious splendor of all you
    have made.

Yours is an everlasting realm,
and your dominion endures through all
    generations.   Glory* . . .

**Ant. 2 You are near to all who call to
you with sincere and upright hearts.**

II

O God, you are faithful in all your
    words,
and gracious in all your deeds.
You uphold all who are falling,
and raise up all who are bowed down.

The eyes of all creatures look to you,
to give them their food in due season.
You open wide your hand,
and satisfy the desires of every
    living thing.

You are just in all your ways,
and loving in all your deeds.
You are near to all who call on you,
who call on you from their hearts.

You fulfill the desires of those who
    revere you,
you hear their cries and save them.
You protect all who love you, O God;
but evil you will utterly destroy.

Let me speak your praises, O God,
let all humankind bless your name
for ever, for ages unending.   Glory* . . .

Ant. 3 **Your works, O God, are great
and wonderful.**

Canticle: Revelation 15:3–4

Great and wonderful are your works,
God, the Almighty One!
Just and true are your ways,
Ruler of all the ages!

Who shall refuse you honor,
or the glory due your name?

For you alone are holy,
all nations shall come and
    worship in your presence.
Your judgments are clearly seen.
    Glory* . . .

READING

RESPONSORY

Your ways are mysterious, O God, but your love is our light. —**Your ways**. . .
Your Word became flesh; —**your love**. . .
Glory to you, Source of all Being, Eternal Word and Holy Spirit. —**Your ways**. . .

CANTICLE OF MARY

Ant.   **Guide us in your truth lest we go astray.**

INTERCESSIONS

PRAYER: God, source of all life, have pity on the dying and on those who
mourn. Help them to experience this transition as a birth to new
life; this loss in time as a realization of eternity. Ease their pain
and grant them your peace which Jesus proclaimed after that first
Good Friday. We ask this in his name. Amen.

SATURDAY

MORNING PRAYER

Ant. 1 **We proclaim your love in the
morning and your faithfulness at night.**

Psalm 92

It is good to give thanks to you, O God,
to sing praise to your name, O Most
    High,
to proclaim your love in the morning,
and your faithfulness by night,
to the music of the lute and the harp,
to the melody of the lyre.

For you make me glad by your deeds;
at the work of your hands I sing for joy.
O God, how great are your works!
Your thoughts are very deep!

The foolish ones cannot know this,
and the dull cannot understand:
though wickedness sprouts like grass
and evil seems to flourish, —

they are doomed to destruction for
    ever.
But you are for ever on high.

You exalt my strength like that of the
    ox;
you pour over me fresh oil.
My eyes looked in triumph over evil,
my ears heard the doom of oppression.

The just will flourish like the palm-tree
and grow like a cedar of Lebanon.
They are planted in your holy house,
they flourish in your courts, O God.
They still bring forth fruit in old age,
they are ever full of sap and green,
to show that you are just;
you are my rock, in you is no injustice.
    Glory* . . .

Ant. 2 Give us hearts of flesh, O God, that we may serve you.

Canticle: Ezekiel 36:24–28

I will take you from the nations,
and gather you from foreign countries,
and bring you back to your own land.

I will sprinkle clean water upon you
to cleanse you from all your impurities,
and from all your idols I will cleanse
 you.

A new heart I will give you,
and a new spirit I will put within you;
and I will take out of your body the
 heart of stone
and give you a heart of flesh.

I will put my spirit within you,
and make you live by my statutes,
careful to observe my decrees.

You shall dwell in the land which I
 gave to your ancestors;
you shall be my people,
and I will be your God.   Glory* . . .

Ant. 3 Your name is great in all the earth.

Psalm 8

How great is your name, O God,
 in all the earth!

You, whose glory above the heavens
is chanted on the lips of babes,
have found a defense against your
 foes,
to silence the cries of the rebels.

When I look at the heavens,
the work of your hands,
the moon and the stars which you
 established;
who are we that you should keep us in
 mind,
mortal flesh that you care for us?

Yet you have made us little less than
 God,
and crowned us with glory and honor.
You entrust us with the works of your
 hands;
to care for all your creation.

All sheep and oxen,
and even the beasts of the field,
the birds of the air, and the fish of
 the sea,
whatever passes along the paths of the
 sea.

How great is your name, Creator God,
in all the earth!   Glory* . . .

READING

RESPONSORY

O God, you are father and mother to us; your love never ceases. —**O God,** . . .
We have sinned against you; —**your love** . . .
Glory to you, Source of all Being, Eternal Word and Holy Spirit. —**O God,** . . .

CANTICLE OF ZECHARIAH

Ant.   Fill our days with peace that we may sing your praise.

INTERCESSIONS

PRAYER: O God, your love is truth, yet we so often fear you. You regard us
 with mercy, yet we see you as judge. Open our eyes to your
 goodness and let us realize the life to which we are called. We ask
 this through the intercession of Mary, mother of Jesus, who knew
 and proclaimed your goodness to all generations. Amen.

DAYTIME PRAYER

Ant. 1 I delight in your law; teach me discernment according to your will.

Psalm 119:169–176

Let my cry come before you, O God;
give me discernment according to your
    word.
Let my supplication come before you;
deliver me as you have promised.

My lips will pour forth praise
because you teach me your commands.
My tongue will sing of your promise,
for all your commands are just.

Let your hand be ready to help me,
for I have chosen your precepts.
I long for your saving help
and your law is my delight.

Let me live, that I may praise you,
and let your precepts help me.
I have gone astray like a lost sheep;
seek your servant, for I do not forget
    your commands.   Glory* . . .

Ant. 2 Listen to my prayer, O God.

Psalm 61

Hear my cry, O God,
listen to my prayer;
from the end of the earth I call,
when my heart is faint.

Set me on the rock that is higher
    than I;
for you are my refuge,
my stronghold against evil.

Let me dwell in your tent for ever!
Hide me in the shelter of your wings!
For you, O God, have heard my vows,
you have given me the heritage of those
    who love your name.

May you lengthen the lives of just
    rulers:
may their years cover many generations!
May they ever be enthroned before you:
bid love and truth watch over them.

So will I ever sing your praises,
as I pay my vows day after day.
    Glory* . . .

Ant. 3 The needy fly to you for refuge.

Psalm 64

Hear my voice, O God, in my
    complaint;
preserve my life from all that is evil;
hide me from the temptor's snare,
from the scheming wiles of my heart.

Evil sharpens its tongue like a sword;
aiming bitter words like arrows,
shooting from ambush at the innocent,
shooting suddenly and without fear.

Holding fast to its evil purpose;
conspiring to lay secret snares.
thinking: "Who can see us?
Who can search out our crimes?"

But you know well our inmost thoughts,
the depth of the heart and mind!
You will shoot your arrow at them;
they will be wounded suddenly.
Our own tongues bring us to ruin.

Then let all people fear;
they will tell what you have wrought,
and ponder what you have done.
The just will rejoice in you, Yahweh,
and fly to you for refuge.
Let the upright in heart exult.
    Glory* . . .

PRAYER: Deliver us, O God, from those who would hurt us and from our own selfishness. Guard us from all that would prevent our growth, and let us not be stumbling blocks to others. We ask this in the name of Jesus who is our way, our truth and our life. Amen.

Let us praise our God, Holy Mystery, Source of all Being, Word and Spirit.
Let us praise and exalt God above all forever.

INDEX FOR THE NEW COMPANION
TO THE BREVIARY

Index

SUNDAY MORNING:

The earth is your masterpiece, O God, and you have made us
its stewards;
   —give us eyes to see your handiwork in every creature.
Creator is your name, and all that comes from your hand is
good;
   —cleanse our hearts and enlighten our minds that our
      choices may enhance and magnify your work in our
      world.
Your measuring rod is love;
   —give us a love that takes us out of and beyond ourselves.
Jesus, you know the strengths and weaknesses of the human
heart;
   —share with us your patience and compassion; remind us
      that another may carry a cross beyond our imagining.
Death is our last chance on earth to say yes to you, O God;
   —make us one with your will day by day.

SUNDAY EVENING:

Spirit of God, you lead each of us in a direction that is life-
giving and fruitful;
   —help us to silence all that would deafen us to your call.
As the possibilities of science continue to expand;
   —remind us of our creaturehood and give us humble hearts.
Life is your gift to us, O God, and your love for us gives
meaning to your gift;
   —show yourself to those who are tempted to despair.
Jesus, you knew the cares of family life;
   —encourage and strengthen heads of families who face the
      special challenges of our culture.
Jesus you healed on the Sabbath and were persecuted for it;
   —be with our present day prophets who make unpopular
      decisions for the cause of justice and truth.

≈

MONDAY MORNING:

O God, you bow to our weakness and need;
  —deliver us from temptation and guide us in the way of
    truth.
Your Spirit prays in us for what we know not how to ask;
  —let that same Spirit draw us to a maturity worthy of you.
Jesus, you drew your disciples to yourself and taught them
eternal truths;
  —bless the young people who must live in our streets,
    jobless and tempted to crime and despair.
Our minds and hearts are pulled in many directions;
  —let the words of your gospel unify and direct our lives.
The sick and the poor were drawn to you;
  —help us to find ways to care for all who are terminally ill.

MONDAY EVENING:

Jesus, you loved the land of your birth;
  —bless all nations torn by war and division.
You were filled with the Holy Spirit, the very Wisdom of God;
  —enlighten and guide all who labor to discover insights
    toward our spiritual and physical healing and growth.
Many believed in you because of your miracles;
  —let our love for you and for one another be the sign that
    draws others to you.
You welcomed outcasts and dined with them;
  —teach us how to reverently minister to those who are
    rejected today.
Your gospel is a call to life;
  —bring its message of peace to those who are dying.

TUESDAY MORNING:

Jesus, you enabled your disciples to hear your call and to
follow you;
  —enable all Christians to discern the promptings of your
    Spirit and to respond wholeheartedly.

Through your death and rising, we have become your Body;
your Spirit lives on in us;
> —awaken us to our responsibility as your people; let us
> meet each other with openness and good will.

Your apostle Paul prayed for an end to division within his
community;
> —teach us positive ways to heal our differences and to
> cultivate peace of mind for ourselves and our children.

Jesus, our Savior, you were taught and nourished by the
words of Scripture;
> —may our hearing of the word of God today help us to
> bring quality of life to those who are imprisoned, the
> oppressed, and the disabled.

O God, time after time you spoke to your people and drew
them to conversion of heart;
> —grant us the ability to read the signs of the times, that
> we may hear your call to a change of heart, as
> individuals and as a people.

TUESDAY EVENING:

O God, you are ever calling us to greater freedom, to walk in
the light, to grow and to deepen our lives;
> —give us the desire and the courage to respond fully to your
> goodness; make our lives pleasing to you.

Your compassion is boundless; you uphold your gift of freedom
to us;
> —deliver us from timidity and all that would keep us from
> turning to you.

Jesus, you respected those who worked with their hands;
some became your disciples;
> —preserve the dignity of those who work for others; deliver
> them from harassment of any kind.

You prayed with your people and read to them from the
Scriptures;
> —may all who lend their gifts to liturgical service enrich
> our lives and be blessed in their sharing.

You promised to be with us till the end of time;
> —may the words of your gospel keep hope alive in our
> hearts.

ઢ૭

WEDNESDAY MORNING:

O God, you know our coming and our going, and you bless our
every effort to live justly;
    —help us to remember your faithfulness and that our
      inspiration and strength is your gift.
You have power over all that you have created;
    —enable warring nations to redeem the wounds of the past
      and to discover creative ways to peace.
Jesus, you were rejected by your own people;
    —direct each of us to a milieu that is receptive of our gifts.
Love is patient and kind, but a stressful world can thin our
resources;
    —have mercy on parents who are overworked and fearful;
      guide and protect teen-agers who run away from home.
Mindful that you call us to be a light in darkness, we pray;
    —be with us in our poverty and need.

WEDNESDAY EVENING:

Faith, hope, and love are the things that last;
    —O God, make us good stewards of what we have, and grant
      us the help we need to be a sign of your kindom.
You created our bodies as temples of the Holy Spirit;
    —send your healing to victims of rape, incest, and every
      form of violence that destroys and deforms.
You call each one of us to be holy;
    —help us to reflect the divine imprint of your creativity
      in our lives.
You bless those who bear insult and persecution;
    —give wise advocates to those who are falsely accused;
      make us humble and just in our speech.
In the many voices that cry out for attention, help us to
recognize you and to pray;
    —"Speak, O God, for your servant is listening."

ઢ૭

THURSDAY MORNING:

O God, the path to holiness includes times of emptiness and darkness;
   —let us realize that you are with us as you walked with
      Jesus on his journey toward the cross.
Holy, holy, holy are you, O God; the whole earth is full of your glory;
   —help us to live compatibly with our environment.
The voice of God said, "Whom shall I send, and who will go for us";
   —with your help, may I answer: "Here I am! Send me."
Jesus, you healed many who were sick with various diseases;
   —be with all healers and health care personnel as they give
      of themselves to care for us.
Jesus, you have called us to preach the good news by the statement of our lives;
   —help us to live the truth with compassion.

THURSDAY EVENING:

Jesus, in the days of your ministry, many traveled far to listen to you;
   —keep alive our search for truth and our efforts to live by it.
You tell us not to be afraid;
   —let your Spirit guide the oppressed as they seek ways to
      freedom.
You call us "salt of the earth";
   —make us your true followers, one with the suffering of the
      world, and calling down God's blessing on your people.
You withdrew to lonely places, praying in the night;
   —remind us that you are with us in light or darkness, joy or
      sorrow—the abiding guest of our hearts.
Spirit of God, source of our deepest desires for good;
   —show us ways to be light for the world.

FRIDAY MORNING:

O God, you are Truth itself;
 —give us discerning hearts that we may live full and
   creative lives.
Jesus, you walked among the outcasts of your day, healing
them and drawing them to yourself;
 —help us to walk in your ways that those who are shunned
   by society may know your love and healing through us.
Jesus, you bless with a hundredfold our endeavors to serve
you;
 —give us the generosity to enable and support one another.
Spirit of God, you pray within us for needs we hardly know;
 —make our prayer one with yours that we may be one with
   you.
Eternal Shepherd, every person and their future is precious to
you;
 —bless those who are tempted to take negative or
   destructive paths this day.

FRIDAY EVENING:

The law of God is perfect, refreshing the soul;
 —let your love, O God, be our law of life and perfect
   guide.
Your forgiveness of humankind flows from generation to
generation;
 —bless the nations that continue to seek vengeance;
   teach us all how to forgive in the name of Jesus.
Jesus, you stayed in desert places, strengthened there by God.
 —In time of pain or trouble, help us to find God in the
   solitude of our hearts.
You are our hope in life and in death;
 —help us to live our belief in you for the strength and
   courage of all in need of your truth.
Spirit of God, your gifts abound in humankind;
 —bless the poor whose creativity is buried by a raw search
   for survival.

꩜

SATURDAY MORNING:

O God, your son Jesus prayed that we all may be one;
—help us to love one another as you love us.
All of creation cries out for healing;
—make us instruments of your peace.
You are the Center of all that is;
—teach us to listen to your life within us.
Many do not know your love and care for us;
—let our lives bear witness to your unending mercy.
You call us to live in freedom and happiness;
—give hope and peace of heart to all in prison or
bondage of any kind.

SATURDAY EVENING:

Heaven and earth will pass away, but your word will remain, O God;
—let this promise of eternal life in you give meaning to
our lives and energize us in your service.
You bless your people with a variety of talents, O God;
—give us the courage to develop our gifts for your glory
and the good of all.
Jesus, you foresaw the stark reality of the future, and you
encouraged your followers to have patience;
—help us to live the Gospel so faithfully that our lives will
be a beacon of hope to others.
We are your children and you look upon us with love.
—help us to refrain from judging others negatively and to
temper justice with mercy.
Prayer is your invitation to realize our union with you;
—awaken us to your presence in us; teach us what it
means to pray always.

≈

WEEK II

SUNDAY MORNING:

God revealing, forgiving, ever recreating us;
   —we thank you for your abiding care, and we pray for
   those who do not know your love.
You are a God of the living, and your Spirit brings us joy;
   —let our lives bear witness to the resurrection of Jesus.
Minorities, countries, the earth itself—all cry out for liberation
as never before;
   —Spirit of God, flood our lives with the wisdom to make
   all things new.
You raise up prophets today;
   —open our hearts, our church, and our world to their
   message.
Jesus, your message calls for the new wineskins of openness
to your word;
   —help us to free ourselves from what is merely familiar
   and comfortable.

SUNDAY EVENING:

Rain and clouds are your gifts of life and beauty to us, O God;
   —teach us how to use and preserve the waters of the
   earth.
You surround us with beauty on earth and in the sky;
   —bless those who have lost the gift of sight.
You are always with us, silently guiding and encouraging us;
   —help us to quiet our lives with moments for listening to
   your voice in our hearts.
You love justice, and all your ways are true;
   —give us the insight and courage to face our prejudices
   and blind spots.
Jesus is your supreme gift to us;
   —let the words of his gospel be woven into our daily lives,
   coming easily to mind for our inspiration and your
   glory.

MONDAY MORNING:

O God, you ask us to keep your words in our minds and
hearts and so we pray:
　—give us the grace to hear you in turmoil and in silence.
You came to serve and not to be served;
　—bless all who serve us daily, in inclement weather, in
　　dangerous jobs, and at work that is tedious or
　　monotonous.
Help us to recognize our sinfulness and to be grateful for your
gifts of grace;
　—give us the strength and courage to act in humility and
　　truth.
God of wisdom and source of all that is sacred;
　—help teachers to value and nourish the wisdom and
　　goodness of children.
Jesus, we are blessed by the words of your gospel;
　—make us aware of the ways we shield ourselves from its
　　challenge to us.

MONDAY EVENING:

O God, you invite us to: "Let light shine out of darkness";
　—give us the courage to embrace the darkness and walk
　　with you toward the light.
You hear the prayers of those in need;
　—give us the grace to open our hearts, our homes and
　　our spaces of worship to those who are in distress.
You marveled at the faith of the Centurion;
　—help us to recognize that truth and wisdom are often
　　found where we least expect it.
Spirit of God, guide us in our use of power;
　—let our methods be constructive and sensitive to the
　　needs of all.
May we realize that life itself is a blessing;
　—comfort those who are preparing for the blessings of
　　eternal life.

ॐ

TUESDAY MORNING:

Jesus, tax collectors and public sinners experienced your
goodness and changed their lives;
   —help us to enable others to grow and realize their worth.
You had compassion on the weak and sorrowful;
   —open our eyes and hearts to the ways we can comfort
      others.
You were a gift to all who came to you in faith;
   —fill us with love that is creative and fruitful for your
      people and the world.
No one is beyond the reach of your care;
   —bless those in refugee camps, and all who are uprooted
      from their homes and land.
Make us wise as serpents and simple as doves;
   —make us a people after your own heart.

TUESDAY EVENING:

Eternal God, you create us and call us to realize our union
with you;
   —help us to rise above all that undermines our calling.
Jesus, you were called a fool for our sake;
   —let us bear the inevitable humiliations of life with
      equanimity.
You brought joy and a new beginning to those who received
you;
   —give us a hunger for your presence and your truth.
Spirit of God, your realm of love encompasses all of creation;
   —in times of temptation and doubt, draw us ever closer to
      you.
Your love is eternal;
   —bless and heal those who are burdened with hatred or
      unforgiveness.

⁊❧

WEDNESDAY MORNING:

O God, you have made a covenant of love with us;
　—dispel from our minds and hearts the fear that belies
　　your care for us.
You have hidden yourself in every blade of grass and every
towering mountain;
　—give us eyes to see your creative love at work in our
　　world.
Jesus, you responded to women with affirmation and love;
　—show us how to encourage and support women when
　　others would prevent them from serving you.
You allowed the words of Scripture to form you and to guide
your life;
　—let the word of your life be the foundation of all we do
　　and the guide for our lives.
Spirit of God, you are the very life of the church;
　—invade us all with the wisdom, fortitude, and generosity
　　to be the people of God in deed and truth.

WEDNESDAY EVENING:

O God, you long to draw us to yourself in a realm of peace;
　—bless all who struggle with relationships in the home
　　and in the workplace.
Your gift of faith to us grows by use and for the asking;
　—make us aware of this treasure; let us taste and share
　　its fruits.
Jesus, you knew the sins of your followers, but you forgave
and encouraged them in the way of love;
　—let our awareness of our faults lead us to encourage one
　　another to turn to you.
You eased the burdens of so many by healing their sickness
and wounds;
　—give nurses and doctors the skill and compassion they
　　need to do the same.
The alien and stranger are dear to your heart;
　—give us the humility and generosity to welcome those
　　who are different from us.

❧

THURSDAY MORNING:

O God, only you know the whole truth about us and our
deeds;
   —guide us with your wisdom and compassion in our
    relationships with one another.
Every person and thing that you have created is precious to
you;
   —bless those who are handicapped and all who assist
    them.
Jesus, you crossed the sea and encountered its dangers;
   —bless sailors and all who travel the waters of our world.
We know the story of your life, O Christ, yet mystery abounds;
   —let our search for truth keep us open to the inspiration
    of the Holy Spirit.
Spirit of God, joy is among your many gifts to us;
   —bless artists of every kind—all who lift up our hearts
    and fill the world with beauty and light.

THURSDAY EVENING:

You hear our prayers and guide and protect us, O God;
   —be praised and thanked for all that we take for granted
    and for hidden gifts.
You offer us the grace to become a new person in Christ;
   —in times of boredom, awaken us to the world of the
    Spirit we so often ignore.
Jesus, you were content to hide your glory and to give in
secret;
   —strengthen our inward self that we may find our true
    peace beyond the measure of others.
You challenged the status quo; you died for being different;
   —give courage and peace to all who live on the fringes of
    society.
You promised a peace that the world cannot give;
   —banish war from our world.

ॐ

FRIDAY MORNING:

O God, you have created us for what eye has not seen and ear
has not heard;
   —give us open minds and largeness of heart that we may
     see and serve beyond ourselves.
Jesus, you served and saved others—ridicule did not shrink
your compassion;
   —make us singlehearted in our care for others.
With religious authority against you and disciples slow to
understand, you stayed your course to the end;
   —give perseverance to the new and creative in our
     culture, that your message may live on in us.
Jesus, you knew the innocence and vulnerability of childhood;
   —guide and protect the children of our disturbed and
     violent world.
Spirit of God, you promote progress—you make all things new;
   —give us the vision we need to develop for the better
     without destroying our vital heritage.

FRIDAY EVENING:

Jesus, you washed the feet of your followers;
   —teach all civic and religious leaders how to govern with
     humility and reverence.
You did not call your disciples servants but friends;
   —help us to establish your kindom by mutual collaboration
     and loving respect.
You shared a meal with one who had betrayed you;
   —give us the desire to set aside our mistrust of one
     another.
Jesus, you came into the world to testify to the truth;
   —make us credible witnesses to the truth of your
     gospel.
You suffered at the hands of those you served;
   —enable us to serve one another selflessly without regard
     to human success.

SATURDAY MORNING:

O God, you know of what we are made, and you give us all
that we need;
   —let us mirror your compassion to one another.
Jesus, many dismissed your teaching because of your common
origin;
   —help us to look beyond surface impressions to the true
     value of each person.
Our attachments and addictions lay heavy burdens upon us;
   —teach us how to listen to your freeing word written in
     our hearts.
You knew rejection and derision;
   —give us the desire to serve all and the grace to be
     at peace when we cannot please everyone.
Our culture tends to reward the strong and powerful and to
dismiss the weak;
   —make all that we do reflect your gospel—your good
     news to the poor.

SATURDAY EVENING:

O God, you grieve for all that afflicts us;
   —give those who struggle with addictions the courage and
     perseverance they need.
You are father and mother to us, and we bask in your love;
   —inspire persons of integrity and compassion to care for
     children who are separated from their parents.
You bless those who employ the talents you have given them;
   —give all in research the insight they need to develop the
     good you desire for us.
Jesus, you loved the land and fields of flowers;
   —bless farmers and all who are stewards of the soil.
You taught your followers to travel lightly through life;
   —call our consumer culture to a change of heart—to values
     that lead to life

❧

WEEK III

SUNDAY MORNING:

O God, we are one in you, and all that we do affects the whole;
   —make us aware of our power to seed the world with
     good or ill by every thought, word, and deed.
Our hearts are torn by the realization of the sufferings of
others;
   —grant that we may never be a stumbling block to others
     or a culpable cause of their pain.
Jesus, you chose laborers, and tax collectors, to be your
companions;
   —preserve us from deciding what people are by what they
     do, and let us see the worth of every person and the
     value in every kind of work.
Bless those who have lost their life companion through death
or divorce;
   —let the people of God be a saving support and comfort
     to them.
Spirit of God, enlighten the minds and renew the hearts of the
hierarchy of the churches;
   —let their ministry be a healing service for all of your
     people.

SUNDAY EVENING:

Life after death is a mystery to us, O God;
   —let the resurrection of Jesus and his Spirit among us
     witness to your eternal love and care for us.
You ask us to give, to empty ourselves, and to follow you in
faith;
   —only to fill us with solid nourishment that enables us to
     live the journey of the gospel.
We know well your law of love; your Spirit lives within us;
   —let no other rule take precedence in our lives.
You came to us bringing peace and reconciliation;
   —may your gospel be the bridge that reconciles us—
     families, communities, and nations.
Bless all who have a great fear of death;
   —grant them peace of heart and friends to support them.

ॐ

MONDAY MORNING:

You are our Creator, O God, our lives are in your hands;
—make us humble and reverent of heart as we unravel
some small part of the mystery of creation.
Jesus, people were drawn to you for you spoke with authority.
—bless our public officials with insight for our good, and
protect them from all that is not just in your sight.
You often spoke to those who were closed to your teaching;
—give us a contemplative attitude and the grace to
hear and live your message.
Spirit of God, you hovered over chaos and called forth a world
of life;
—calm us in times of anxiety; teach us how to live one
moment at a time in your loving presence.
Our hearts are drawn to glorify you, O God, and you receive
our humble praise;
—bless composers, singers and all musicians who enable
us to express our love and gratitude to you.

MONDAY EVENING:

In you, O God, resides all creative energy, and we receive our
lives from you;
—inspire us with great desires, and let our hope be larger
that our doubt.
We are a wounded people, afflicted by sin and ignorance;
—guide and protect our police and all who are missioned
to protect us; arm them with wisdom and compassion.
Jesus, for you and your people, hospitality was a sacred duty;
—help us to transform our world into a place that is safe
for mutual aid and neighborliness.
You were content to let weeds grow among wheat until harvest
time;
—give us the patience to live with our own shortcomings
and those of others.
Our days are often filled with interruptions;
—teach us how to reap the good fruit of patience from
these times.

ھو

TUESDAY MORNING:

O God, you have blessed humankind with understanding,
imagination and memory;
   —show us how to learn from the past and to plan for the
     future.
The gifts of the earth are distributed unevenly, and we long to
lift up those in need;
   —soften the hearts of those who place personal or national
     gain above the good of the whole.
Jesus, you have gifted us with the revelation of God's love;
   —let your love bear abundant fruit in our lives.
You preached to the crowds, inviting them to sit on grassy
hillsides;
   —open our eyes to the beauty of our world, and make us
     understand the need to protect our environment.
Spirit of God, life-giving presence to every person;
   —make your compassion and love known to those who
     suffer abuse, torture, and sub-human conditions.

TUESDAY EVENING:

O God, the wonders of communication have made our world
smaller but more complex;
   —bless the United Nations with wise and magnanimous
     leaders.
Jesus, you teach us of the realm of God with wonderful and
effective images;
   —inspire teachers and writers with the creativity they need
     to expand our minds and hearts.
Ask, knock, seek is your invitation to us to take our needs to
God;
   —make us quick to respond to the needs of those who ask;
     make us aware of those so needy they cannot ask.
Spirit of God, you take flesh in us and for us;
   —keep us open to all who inspire us to grow; prophets,
     athletes, philosophers, artists, and all who serve us in
     your name.

Time is your gift to us, O God; let us not take it for granted;
  —show us efficient ways to use and share it.

ಇ

WEDNESDAY MORNING:

Jesus, you preached a kindom not of this world, but you were
ever mindful to provide food for your followers;
  —grant success to those who draw food from our waters and
  fields; keep them safe and their methods environmentally
  sound.
You blessed little children and warned us against misleading
them;
  —give wisdom to those who become parents while they are
  still children themselves.
O God, you call us all to unity through Jesus;
  —show yourself to those who are estranged from one
  another, and bridge their differences with the fire of your
  love.
Jesus, you frowned upon the ambitions of your apostles;
  —let our ambition and goal be to offer you a life of love and
  dedicated service as we care for one another.
Bless the ministers of your church;
  —guide them to serve as you have served.

WEDNESDAY EVENING

Jesus, you knew a laborer's day;
  —bless those who live by the work of their hands; help all to
  find the employment they need.
The world still longs for the peace that only you can give;
  —guard and protect those whose work is to keep the peace
  in lands torn by war and revolution.
In your kindom the last shall be first and the first last;
  —encourage and liberate minorities, those whose lot is
  mostly last.
Enlighten and encourage those committed to you in religious
vocations;
  —let their lives reflect their calling.

Have mercy on all who are touched by the drug epidemic in
our world;
  —lead them to freedom through the good news enfleshed in
    those who reach out to them.

❦

THURSDAY MORNING:

O God, we praise you for the gift of faith and for all that our
baptism means to us;
  —help us to keep our commitment to you alive and active
    and to cherish and remember special moments of insight.
You answer our prayers and fulfill our needs;
  —make us aware of the needs of others and generous in
    ministering to them.
Jesus, you were called the carpenter's son, an attempt to
discredit you;
  —give us the grace we need to see one another in truth, to
    hold each other's heritage with reverence, and to realize
    that we are one in you.
Your disciples left all to follow you;
  —be praised in the missionaries who leave all that is
    familiar to them to give your message to the world.
You are resurrection and life to all who hope in you;
  —give courage and peace to those who await your coming.

THURSDAY EVENING:

Jesus, you invited Peter to follow you in ways beyond his
courage;
  —increase our faith, that we may be ready and willing
    instruments of your love.
You caution us over and over again to stay awake, to be on
guard;
  —give us the gift of discernment; help us to live consciously,
    learning from the past as we plan for the future.
O God, bless those whom you call to the single life;
  —let their commitment to the gospel be a joy to you,
    enrichment for them, and a service to others that mirrors
    your Christ.

O God, give us a desire for true and lasting values;
   —let our faith in you inform all that we are and do.
Spirit of God, you bring both peace and fire to our hearts;
   —teach us how to challenge and affirm one another in a
      spirit of harmony.

         ❧

FRIDAY MORNING:

O God, a humble heart is more pleasing to you than sacrifice;
   —lift up all who are humiliated and despised because of
      their own faults or those of others.
Faith is your free gift to us, O God;
   —enlighten us with ways of sharing it with others.
O God, your love is eternal, and we fail you "seven times a
day";
   —preserve us from measuring you by our own pettiness;
      never let fear keep us from turning to you.
Jesus, you have made yourself as available to us as bread;
   —help us to realize our need to live in your presence and to
      listen to the voice of your spirit in our hearts.
Spirit of God, love is your gift to us and the gift you desire from
us;
   —receive our desire and poor efforts to offer you our lives
      this day.

FRIDAY EVENING:

You are our Creator, O God, and you know of what we are
made;
   —have mercy on those who are forced to work beyond
      their strength or to bear their limit of suffering.
We thank and praise you for the talents you have given to
those who make our lives less burdensome by invention and
more delightful through art;
   —give them the grace to live balanced and holy lives.
The future is always a mystery to us; our lives are in your
hands;
   —grant us a childlike peace as we place our trust in you
      and do our best to serve you.

Jesus, you prayed for unity on the night before you died for
us;
    —heal us of our prejudices, and grant success to our
      efforts toward ecumenism.
You radiated the joy that is the sign of the Spirit;
    —let our joy and good humor reveal your presence in our
      lives.

ॐ

SATURDAY MORNING:

Jesus, you taught your followers the deepest lessons of life;
    —show us how to teach our children your ways of
      forgiveness, reverence for one another, and mutual
      support.
To all who would listen, you revealed God as a tender mother
and an understanding father;
    —teach us how to develop and balance the feminine and
      masculine aspects of our lives.
O God, our desires are boundless, but we are limited on every
side;
    —let the discipline of reality be a spur to our creativity.
Bless all children; let their school years be maturing and
fruitful ones for them;
    —inspire our teachers with ways to draw out the best in all.
You left your mother to follow the call of the Spirit;
    —be with those who must leave their families to find work in
      other countries.

SATURDAY EVENING:

O God, you speak to us in many ways;
    —keep us open to your guidance from sources however
      great or humble.
We cherish our call to serve you, and we endeavor to be
faithful;
    —deliver us from the plethora of idols that beckon to us
      daily.
Bless all who are united in marriage;
    —let the grace of the sacrament enable them to love and
      support one another.

Jesus, you knew the challenge of choosing your direction in life;
—send your Spirit to guide those who struggle with vocational choices.
Spirit of God, grant wisdom, understanding, and fortitude to all involved in the media;
—let the highest values and principles govern their decisions and programs.

๚

WEEK IV

SUNDAY MORNING:

O God, the whole world was changed and raised up by the coming of your son;
—let us never take his life or gospel for granted.
You give us the power to be light or darkness for one another on the way to salvation;
—show us how to transform the stumbling blocks in our lives to ladders of grace for ourselves and for others.
There are many who do not know you or your Christ;
—send laborers into your harvest.
Jesus, you ate with sinners and stayed with them;
—let the Eucharist that we share remind us of your forgiveness and constant presence in our lives.
Spirit of God, lead us to wholesome recreations that delight and nourish us;
—keep us safe as we play, and let us do so with moderation and gratitude.

SUNDAY EVENING:

O God, you are present to us, yet our minds cannot contain the mystery of your being;
—let what we know of you in the life and love of Jesus draw us to you in ever deepening faith.
It is difficult to wait with hope for what we think is good and just;
—increase our faith, and help us to hold fast to our dedication to you.

Let the harvest of our land yield enough for all;
  —banish famine from our world; teach us to share.
Eye has not seen, nor ear heard, what you have prepared for
those who love you;
  —let the hundredfold that we seek be only to love you totally
    with grateful hearts.
Jesus, you prayed that we all might be one;
  —help us to recognize those who differ from us as our
    sisters and brothers sharing this one earth that you came
    to save.

۞

MONDAY MORNING:

Jesus, you preached a gospel of love and forgiveness;
  —may those who hear your word be freed from
    unfounded guilt and a misguided conscience.
You healed those who could not hear or speak;
  —may we close our ears to falsehood and endeavor to
    speak the truth in love.
We know well how to plan for the things we want;
  —help us to plan as surely for ways to open ourselves to
    your Spirit within us.
O God, mobility is a sign of our times; the whole world is
within our reach;
  —protect us all, and guide those who are responsible for
    our trips on land, sea, and in the air.
You desire our good, and you have compassion on all who
suffer;
  —be merciful to those who are in constant pain; comfort
    and sustain them.

MONDAY EVENING:

O God, slavery is a reality in our world in many forms;
  —grant us a new consciousness of the equality of all people.
You created a new covenant of peace through your Son, Jesus,
yet we live in fear of one another;
  —show us how to re-seed the world with trust; help us to
    put love where there is no love.

You delight in those who receive your gifts with gratitude;
   —bless all who endeavor to develop their talents; encourage
      and enlighten all students, and keep them in your care.
Jesus, you revealed yourself to a woman of Samaria, an
unwelcoming land;
   —enable world leaders to overcome national rivalries and
      centuries of mutual retaliation.
You gave us the power to bind and to loose;
   —free us from our need to control, and give us the grace to
      free others from our expectations.

߿

TUESDAY MORNING:

O God, your love is greater than our guilt;
   —have mercy on those who are sentenced to death.
Too often our faith exists only in our minds and words;
   —awaken us to new and practical ways to enflesh our
      commitment to your will.
Our lives are fragile, and you surround us with men and
women in life-preserving professions;
   —guard and guide our police, fire fighters, life guards, and
      all who labor and risk their lives for our safety.
Open our minds to the ways that we are destroying the gifts of
the earth;
   —bless again the land and water and all of the life that
      sustains us.
Jesus, you knew the sweetness of friendship, and you gave
new life to those who received you;
   —keep us faithful to you and to one another.

TUESDAY EVENING:

O God, you have created us free, but our prisons are full;
   —help us to cultivate an environment that inspires life-
      giving choices.
You have created us to choose the good;
   —bless our children that they may know the good and
      pursue it.

You have created us in your image;
  —give us the joy of radiating your goodness, truth, and
    beauty.
Jesus, you experienced the worst of human weakness;
  —grant heroic courage and strength to those who are
    tortured; erase this horror from our world.
You promised to be with us to the end of the world;
  —let us never lose hope in you, and help us to trust one
    another.

꒰꒱

WEDNESDAY MORNING:

You invite us to be co-creators with you, O God; work is our
privilege;
  —bless employers with all they need to provide safe and
    satisfying work for people in their service.
You have given us stewardship over the earth;
  —make us all responsible workers in time's "vineyard."
Jesus, you teach us to serve one another and to shun
ambitious pride;
  —help us to realize that our nobility lies in our relationship
    to God, whom you have revealed to us.
You knew loneliness and misunderstanding;
  —comfort and sustain those who have been betrayed or
    abandoned.
You came to serve and not to be served;
  —let all who are elected to leadership rise to the
    responsibility of their office and serve with justice and
    integrity.

WEDNESDAY EVENING:

Your justice is governed by mercy, O God;
  —strengthen those whose work exposes them to temptations
    of greed or unjust dealings.
Inspire those who can to give aid to worthy endeavors;
  —let their hundredfold be a deepened awareness of your
    presence in their lives.

Have mercy on abused spouses and children and on those who abuse them;

—help us to enable them to begin life anew.

Spirit of God, joy and peace are your gifts to us;

—bless all who lighten our burden by their thoughtfulness, humor, and creativity.

Jesus, you remind us that we cannot serve two masters;

—give us a single heart that seeks what is good, receiving all from God with trust.

❧

THURSDAY MORNING:

O God, no one is beyond the reach of your love;

—help us to appreciate one another as we are—not expecting more than we can do or give.

Our culture is heavy with the lure of material gain;

—deliver us from the temptation to use others for our own profit.

Jesus, your Spirit dwells in our hearts;

—keep us open to the wisdom and gifts of everyone.

Wealthy men and women were among your followers, and they supported your mission;

—show us how to use whatever we have in keeping with your gospel.

We have walked on the moon, and technology reaches deeper and deeper into the galaxies;

—may scientific research deepen our thirst for the wisdom and knowledge of God.

THURSDAY EVENING:

O God, creator of all that is;

—bless the work of our hands.

Jesus, revelation of God to us;

—teach us to speak and live the truth.

Holy Spirit, dwelling in our hearts;

—deepen our love for God and for one another.

Triune God, Eternal Love;

—bless our families, communities, and the nations of the world.

Holy God, Holy Available One;
—never let us be separated from you.

꙾

FRIDAY MORNING:

O God, you have planted the seed of your word in our lives;
—let its nourishment be the deciding factor in what we
choose to see and hear.
Faith as small as a mustard seed is enough for us;
—give us an appreciation of what we have, living in your
presence day by day.
We long to be instruments of unity and peace in the world;
—teach us how to support husbands and wives in their
efforts to be faithful; show us ways to make our culture
supportive.
Jesus, again and again you assured your followers with a
calming, "Fear not!"
—Grant your peace to those who live in fear for their lives
or dignity—those for whom fear is an abiding reality.
Bless the aging who live alone, with family, or in nursing
homes;
—reveal your love for them through those who care for them.

FRIDAY EVENING:

O God, you adorn the earth with the beauty of each season;
—awaken us to your loving care as you lift up our hearts
with color and surprise.
You share your life with us through the talents you give us;
—make us worthy stewards, eager to grow, mindful of our
use of time.
Your Spirit dwells in our hearts, the very power of your love;
—let us remember that you are at work in us, never
asking what is beyond our power.
Lord Jesus, teach us to pray as you taught your apostles;
—show us how to live quietly and to know how to
distinguish want from need.
Heart of Jesus, once in agony,
—have pity on the dying.

୬

SATURDAY MORNING:

O God, we are created for eternity; time often leaves us longing
for more;
    —help us to find you within, where time and eternity are
      more clearly one.
Your commandments are guides for our way to fullness of life;
    —remind us that law follows life.
Our short lives are a history of your gifts to us;
    —may all that we do give you thanks and praise.
You are ever present to us in our need;
    —let us never be indifferent to the suffering of others.
Spirit of God, our advocate and guide;
    —teach us how to be an effective voice for the powerless.

SATURDAY EVENING:

O God, your invitation to grow is ever before us;
    —free us from the need to control; deepen our trust in your
      desire for our good.
Nothing is impossible for you;
    —let our desires be your own, then grant our requests.
Jesus, you promise to raise up those who have died with you;
    —help us to remember that the suffering of life is not
      meaningless.
Bless those who break under the stress of life;
    —give them understanding and compassionate mentors.
Help the agencies of the world that help others;
    —enable them to find homes and sustenance for all
      refugees.

SEASONAL
SUPPLEMENT

FOR FEASTS AND SOLEMNITIES

MORNING PRAYER

Psalm 63:1–9

O God, you are my God, I long for you;
my soul thirsts for you;
My body seeks for you
as in a dry and weary land without
    water.
So I have looked upon you in the
    sanctuary,
beholding your power and your glory.

For your constant love is better than
    life,
my lips will sing your praises.
So I will bless you as long as I live;
I will lift up my hands and call on your
    name.

My soul feasts on you and my mouth
    praises you,
as I think of you upon my bed,
and meditate on you in the watches
    of the night;
for you have been my help,
In the shadow of your wings I sing for
    joy.
My soul clings to you; your right hand
    upholds me.   Glory* . . .

Canticle   Daniel 3:57–88, 56

All you works of God, praise our God.
Praise and exalt God above all forever.
All you angels, sing God's praise,
you heavens and waters above.
Sun and moon, and stars of heaven,
sing praise with the heavenly hosts.

Every shower and dew, praise our God.
Give praise all you winds.
Praise our God, you fire and heat, —

cold and chill—dew and rain.
Frost and chill, praise our God.
Praise God, ice and snow.
Nights and days, sing hymns of praise,
light and darkness,
lightnings and clouds.

Let all the earth bless our God.
Praise and exalt God above all forever.
Let all that grows from the earth give
        praise
together with mountains and hills.
Give praise, you springs,
you seas and rivers,
dolphins and all water creatures.
Let birds of the air,
beasts, wild and tame,
together with all living peoples,
praise and exalt God above all forever.

O Israel, praise our God.
Praise and exalt God above all forever.
Give praise, you priests,
servants of the Most High,
spirits and souls of the just.
Holy ones of humble heart,
sing your hymns of praise.
Hananiah, Azariah, Mishael, praise
    our God.
Praise and exalt God above all forever.

Let us bless our God, Holy Mystery,
Source of All Being, Word and Spirit.
Let us praise and exalt God above all
    forever.
Blessed are you, O God, in the
    firmament of heaven.
Praiseworthy and glorious and exalted
    above all forever.

---

*Glory to you Source of all Being,
    Eternal Word and Holy Spirit.
    As it was . . .

Psalm 149

Sing a new song to our God,
Give praise in the assembly of the
   faithful.
Let Israel be glad in its maker,
let Zion's heirs exult in the Most High.
Let them praise God's name with
   dancing,
and make music with timbrel and harp.

For you take delight in your people,
   O God.
You adorn the humble with victory.
Let the faithful exult in their glory,
in their rest, let them sing for joy. —

Let the praises of God be on their lips
and two-edged swords in their hands,

to wreck vengeance on all that is
   wicked,
and chastisement on all injustice;
to bind what is evil in chains
and oppression in fetters of iron;
to carry out the sentence pre-ordained;
this is glory for all God's faithful
   ones.   Glory* . . .

INVITATORY

Psalm 95

O come, let us sing to our God;
let us make a joyful noise to the rock of
   our salvation!

We come into your presence with thanksgiving,
rejoicing with songs of praise!
For you, O God, are our God,
a great Ruler over all other gods.
In your hands are the depths of the earth;
the heights of the mountains as well.
The sea is yours, for you made it;
and your hands formed the dry land.

We bow down before you and worship,
kneeling before you, our Maker!
For you are our God, and we are your people,
the flock that you shepherd.

Today let us hearken to your voice:
"Harden not your hearts, as at Meribah,
as on the day at Massah in the desert,
when your ancestors tested me,
and put me to the test,
though they had seen my works."   Glory. . .

SUNDAYS OF ADVENT

(Psalms from the current week in the Psalter)

SUNDAY, EVENING PRAYER I

Week I

Ant 1   Behold I bring you glad tidings; our God and Savior is coming.

Ant 2   Our God is coming, bringing salvation to all. Let us rejoice! Alleluia.

Ant 3   God will come, the Holy One of Israel.

Week II

Ant 1   Bring comfort to my people, says our God.

Ant 2   Have courage, do not fear; our God is coming; the glory of God shall be revealed.

Ant 3   A savior will come to you, O Zion; the time for laughter and rejoicing is near, alleluia.

Week III

Ant 1   God indeed is my savior; with joy all will draw water at the fountain of salvation, alleluia.

Ant 2   The Savior who is to come will baptize you in the Holy Spirit and in fire.

Ant 3   O Emmanuel, Lamb of God, come and save us; free us from our sin.

Week IV

Ant 1   Say to the daughters of Zion: your salvation comes; rejoice, for the time is near, alleluia.

Ant 2   A virgin shall be with child, and will bear a son, and shall name him Emmanuel.

Ant 3   O Come, Emmanuel, promise of God; Jesus, the Word, come!

READING

RESPONSORY

O God, guide us into the way of peace and love. —**O God**...
And give light to our darkness; —**into**...
Glory to you, Source of all Being, Eternal Word, and Holy Spirit. —**O God**...

CANTICLE OF MARY

Week 1   The favors of God I will sing forever; through all generations my mouth shall proclaim your faithfulness.

Week 2   On that day it shall be said: your God is in your midst. Rejoice, O Jerusalem!

Week 3 God will shine on you; all the earth will see your splendor.

Week 4 (See the special antiphons for December 17–23.)

INTERCESSIONS: (Sundays 1 and 3)

In anticipation of your promise, O God, we pray:
> **Drop down dew, you heavens, from above;**
> **let the clouds rain down the Just One.**

Gentle God, you satisfy our thirsty hearts;
—may we respond to the needs of those thirsting for justice.
Loving God, you give us bread for our table and bread for our spirit;
—may we share our bread generously; may it never be used as a weapon in the hands of the powerful.
Peaceful God, you desire harmony for us;
—may we be free from our selfish and defensive ways.
Comforting God, you give sight to the blind;
—may we see with new eyes your life in our midst.
Liberating God, you set the captives free;
—may we support those people who are imprisoned for the sake of justice.

INTERCESSIONS: (Sundays 2 and 4)

God of a New Dawn, you are born of Mary. In confidence let us pray:
> **Come, Lord Jesus, and be one with us.**

You became human and were born in a troubled land;
—come and liberate all peoples suffering oppression.
Like us, you faced the reality of death;
—be our comfort at the hour of death, and give courage to the terminally ill.
You came to judge the poor with justice;
—save us from our blindness and place a new spirit within us.
You came as a child to call us to gentleness and simplicity;
—free us from false pretenses and from the burden of self-aggrandizement.
Your death brought us the hope of resurrection;
—grant new life to all who have died this day.

PRAYER

Week 1 We wait for you, most gracious God, for eye has not seen and ear has not heard the wonders of your deeds. In gratitude we thank you for the gift of Jesus to our world. Grant us the eyes to see beyond our limited vision and the ears to hear the joy of your message. We thank you for being one with us in your covenant of love. Amen.

Week 2 O loving God, within and about us a voice cries out to prepare a way in the wilderness. You come to restore us to new life with you and with one another. Help us to be open to every opportunity to prepare a way for you. We ask this in the name of Jesus who continues to be the voice in the wilderness. Amen.

Week 3 In joy and gladness we give praise to you, O God, for you come to share life with us. Come to us and assist us to see your loving care in the midst of our daily struggles. May you continue to grant us peace and joy that surpasses all understanding. We ask these gifts in the mystery of our God, Source of all life. Amen.

Week 4 In eagerness we await your coming, Desired One among all peoples. May we come to realize with Mary that we are your highly favored sisters and brothers and that you desire to be with us. Increase our faith and put a new spirit in our hearts so that we may give birth to you. We ask this in your name, for you are our God with us. Amen.

SUNDAY MORNING PRAYER

Week I

Ant 1 On that day, the Most High will bring forth power and glory and the fruit of the earth will be the splendor of Israel.

Ant 2 God will show mercy to a nation endangered by war and division.

Ant 3 There shall be everlasting joy for those who keep faith.

Week II

Ant 1 I will rejoice and go up to the house of my God.

Ant 2 Open wide your gates, O Jerusalem, and receive your savior.

Ant 3 In Zion I will make my salvation known, alleluia.

WEEK III

Ant 1 You who know God, rejoice, for the Just One is coming.

Ant 2 A star from Juda will arise to redeem the people.

Ant 3 The desert and the land will exult; they shall bloom with an abundance of flowers, for God, Emmanuel, is coming.

WEEK IV

Ant 1 God shall reign forever, O Zion, throughout all generations.

Ant 2 Joseph, son of David, do not fear to take Mary as your wife.

Ant 3 Behold, a virgin will conceive and bear a son and name him Emmanuel.

READING

RESPONSORY

Behold the Lamb of God, who comes to bring us salvation. —**Behold**...
Clothed in a mantle of justice, —**who**...
Glory to you, Source of all Being, Eternal Word, and Holy Spirit. —**Behold**

CANTICLE OF ZECHARIAH

Week 1   You will have joy and gladness, and many will rejoice at the savior's birth.

Week 2   Do not be afraid, Mary; you will conceive and bear a child.

Week 3   The Holy Spirit will come upon you, and the child to be born will be called holy, the child of God.

Week 4   (See the antiphons for December 17–23.)

INTERCESSIONS: (Sundays 1 and 3)

In hope we have waited for your coming, O Jesus; in confidence we pray:
Most Holy One, bring us your salvation!

Strengthen our hearts and hands;
—help us to appreciate the wonder of birth and bless the wombs of all expectant mothers.

Open our eyes to your ways;
—assist us to see beyond the borders of our vision and to cut through the prejudices that keep us in isolation.

Release us from bondage;
—may we be ready to free ourselves and others from the oppression that keeps us in slavery.

Loosen our tongues to sing your praise;
—may we proclaim your message in the way we speak to and treat one another.

Free our ears to hear your word;
—grant us a readiness to listen attentively to your voice, and assist all pastoral ministers to hear your word among the poor.

INTERCESSIONS: (Sundays 2 and 4)

We await your coming and with joyful hearts we pray:
Come, Lord Jesus!

You come to bring us hope and courage;
—may we support people who feel rejected and hopeless in their present struggles.

You come as a radiant reflection of God's love;
—assist us to be prayerful and reflective women and men before we take steps of action for the sake of justice.

You come to speak the human word of God's care and tenderness;
—help us to show our care for one another, our environment and all our endangered species.

You come to show us how to be more fully human in our giving to a needy world;
—may we share our gifts freely and willingly in a manner that gives dignity to the poor among us.

PRAYER

Week 1 We wait for you, most gracious God, for eye has not seen and ear has not heard the wonders of your deeds. In gratitude we thank you for the gift of Jesus to our world. Grant us the eyes to see beyond our limited vision and the ears to hear the joy of your message. We thank you for being one with us in your covenant of love. Amen.

Week 2 O loving God, within and about us a voice cries out to prepare a way in the wilderness. You come to restore us to new life with you and with one another. Help us to be open to every opportunity to prepare a way for you. We ask this in the name of Jesus who continues to be the voice in the wilderness. Amen.

Week 3 In joy and gladness we give praise to you, O God, for you come to share life with us. Come to us and assist us to see your loving care in the midst of our daily struggles. May you continue to grant us peace and joy that surpasses all understanding. We ask these gifts in the mystery of our God, Source of all life. Amen.

Week 4 In eagerness we await your coming, Desired One among all peoples. May we come to realize with Mary that we are your highly favored sisters and brothers and that you desire to be with us. Increase our faith and put a new spirit in our hearts so that we may give birth to you. We ask this in your name, for you are our God with us. Amen.

SUNDAY EVENING PRAYER II

Week I

Ant 1 Rejoice, nations of earth; our God comes, alleluia.

Ant 2 Jesus Christ will come to us, taking away our sins.

Ant 3 Do not lose heart, says our God; soon you will walk in my light, alleluia.

Week II

Ant 1 Look up to the heavens to see the power of God, alleluia.

Ant 2 O God, you will come and your word is true, alleluia.

Ant 3 Jesus Christ will come to heal us, alleluia.

Week III

Ant 1 Jesus Christ will come to save all people, alleluia.

Ant 2 Let the mountains rejoice and the seas rise up in joy for our Light comes to bring us peace.

Ant 3 Let us prepare for Christ's coming with lives rooted in hope.

Week IV

Ant 1 Jesus will appear in glory, and will come without delay.

Ant 2 Prepare the way for our God; make ready our hearts for the Holy One.

Ant 3 The reign of God will cover the earth; the compassion of our God will embrace all creation.

READING

RESPONSORY

Loving God, in you abides the womb of all life; show us your love and mercy.
—Loving...
Be with us in our waiting; —show us...
Glory to you, Source of all Being, Eternal Word, and Holy Spirit. —Loving...

CANTICLE OF MARY

Week 1   Hail Mary full of grace, our God is with you, alleluia.

Week 2   Blessed indeed is Mary who trusted that God's words to her would be fulfilled, alleluia.

Week 3   The Holy Spirit will come upon you and the power of the Most High will overshadow you, alleluia.

Week 4   (See the antiphons for December 17–23.)

INTERCESSIONS: (Sundays 1 and 3)

Jesus, you are the one born of Mary, and in joy we pray with eager hearts:
Maranatha! Come, Lord Jesus!

You, Jesus, are our savior;
—may we proclaim your message willingly and participate in bringing about your reign in our world.
You are the fountain of living water;
—be with all peoples who are preparing to receive baptism.
You are the Holy One of Israel;
—grant shelter to the homeless, especially children, who need food, care and companionship.
You are hope in our weariness;
—free us from our selfishness and give courage to all children and adults who are handicapped.

INTERCESSIONS: (Sundays 2 and 4)

O God of Wisdom, you come to walk with us and give us the opportunity to choose the good and the holy each day, and so we pray:
We rejoice in your coming, Jesus!

O Jesus, our brother, grant us the gift of understanding;
—may we welcome the stranger in our midst.
O Word of God, you have come to be one with us in our humanity;
—assist us to be open to our individual and communal differences.
O Light of God's radiance, you come to enlighten our darkness;
—enable us to hear the prophets of our time and to discern their message.
Proclaimer of God's love, you come to invite us to share your covenantal love;
—grant us the grace to be faithful in our commitments and covenants with one another.

PRAYER

Week 1 We wait for you, most gracious God, for eye has not seen and ear has not heard the wonders of your deeds. In gratitude we thank you for the gift of Jesus to our world. Grant us the eyes to see beyond our limited vision and the ears to hear the joy of your message. We thank you for being one with us in your covenant of love. Amen.

Week 2 O loving God, within and about us a voice cries out to prepare a way in the wilderness. You come to restore us to new life with you and with one another. Help us to be open to every opportunity to prepare a way for you. We ask this in the name of Jesus who continues to be the voice in the wilderness. Amen.

Week 3 In joy and gladness we give praise to you, O God, for you come to share life with us. Come to us and assist us to see your loving care in the midst of our daily struggles. May you continue to grant us peace and joy that surpasses all understanding. We ask these gifts in the mystery of our God, Source of all life. Amen.

Week 4 In eagerness we await your coming, Desired One among all peoples. May we come to realize with Mary that we are your highly favored sisters and brothers and that you desire to be with us. Increase our faith and put a new spirit in our hearts so that we may give birth to you. We ask this in your name, for you are our God with us. Amen.

MONDAYS OF ADVENT

(Psalms and antiphons from the current week in the Psalter.)

MORNING PRAYER

READING

RESPONSORY

Sing to God a new song, give praise from the ends of the earth. —**Sing**...
Mountains and deserts rejoice, —**give**...
Glory to you, Source of all Being, Eternal Word, and Holy Spirit. —**Sing**...

CANTICLE OF ZECHARIAH

Week 1 Look up, Jerusalem, and see the power of your God; your savior comes to free you.

Week 2 Our God proclaims: Repent, the reign of God is upon you, alleluia!

Week 3 (before December 17) From heaven you come, O Most High; to you we give honor and glory.

INTERCESSIONS: Weeks 1 and 3

O God, you share your life with us in the mystery of the Word Incarnate. In joy, let us pray:

Come, hope of all peoples!

In your light, Christ Jesus, we can walk in freedom;
—may we follow your way of truth without counting the cost.

Our hearts are open to receive you;
    —enable us to be compassionate in working with one another.
You come as a fragile child;
    —empower religious leaders to respond effectively from the experience of
    their personal vulnerability.
Teach us your law of love and mercy;
    —assist all missionaries in their efforts to give birth to your love.

INTERCESSIONS: Week 2

In joyful song we prepare for your coming as we say:
                    Come and abide with us.

As we prepare for your coming among us;
    —free our hearts from selfish desires.
Your prophets announced the joy of your coming;
    —may our lives give witness to your presence among us.
You come to us as a sign of reconciliation;
    —help all who are living in division and dissension to experience your
    forgiveness.
You bring a promise of abundance of life in our deserts;
    —give hope to prisoners and to those who are imprisoned by their fears.
You turn our sorrow into gladness;
    —may all who die this day experience the fullness of your joy.

PRAYER

Week 1   O Giver of Peace, you invite us to beat our swords into plowshares
          and our spears into pruning hooks. Enable us to translate your
          message into our daily living and to be people of peace and non-
          violence. Grant this request in the name of Jesus who comes to be
          peace with us. Amen.

Week 2   O God, open our hearts to prepare the way for the coming of Christ.
          Instruct us in your ways of compassion so that we may extend your
          love and mercy to all people. We ask this in the name of Jesus, the
          Eternal Word, who lives with you and the Holy Spirit forever. Amen.

Week 3   In you, Jesus, lies the gift of wisdom and the power of authority. You
          share these gifts with us in a caring, gentle way as given to you by
          God, our Mother and Father. Assist us in recognizing humbly the
          source of our gifts and enable us to use them in praise of you, one
          with the Source of all life. Amen.

DAYTIME PRAYER

Ant 1   Comfort, comfort my people, says our God.

Ant 2   Every valley shall be lifted up, and every mountain shall be made low,
         and the glory of God shall be revealed.

Ant 3   The grass withers, the flower fades; but the word of our God will live
         forever.

(Prayer as in Morning Prayer)

MONDAY EVENING PRAYER

READING

RESPONSORY

Come to deliver us, gentle and loving God. —Come. . .

Turn your face to us and save us; —gentle. . .

Glory to you, Source of all Being, Eternal Word, and Holy Spirit. —Come. . .

CANTICLE OF MARY

Week 1   Gabriel announced God's favor to Mary, and she conceived by the power of the Spirit of God.

Week 2   Look to see the Messiah's coming, breaking the bonds of our sinfulness.

Week 3   Every age will honor me; God, Most High, has favored me.

INTERCESSIONS: Weeks 1 and 3

In you, O God, we rejoice, for you invite us to new heights and to climb your holy mountain. In joy we proclaim:

Let us walk in your light, O God!

You are our refuge in time of need;
  —protect the homeless and give refuge to those who leave their homelands to find peace.

You are our shade in the heat of the day;
  —give hope to the elderly so that they may experience fullness in their years of apparent diminishment.

You are a light to guide us on our journey;
  —may your people find meaning in their youthful years, and a desire to create a peaceful future.

You are our shelter from storm and rain;
  —grant us the insight to see your providential care in all our struggles.

You are the source of our peace;
  —may all who die today experience peace in your light.

INTERCESSIONS: Week 2

Most provident God, you call us to be strong and not to fear for you are with us always. In trust we say:

Our God is here.

That the desert shall rejoice and bloom is the promise you give to us;
  —may all people find sufficient water of truth and spirit to satisfy their thirsty hearts.

The eyes of the blind shall be opened;
  —may you, O God of Wonders, grant us the gift to recognize our own blindness.

The highway shall be called the holy way;
  —grant us, O holy God, the understanding and courage to share in the burden of our companions on the journey.

The grass shall become reeds and rushes;
  —may you, O caring Provider, continue to give us the fruits of this earth and may we use them wisely.

Everlasting joy shall be upon their heads;
  —may you be a source of comfort to all who mourn.

PRAYER

Week 1   O Giver of Peace, you invite us to beat our swords into plowshares
and our spears into pruning hooks. Enable us to translate your
message into our daily living and to be people of peace and non-
violence. Grant this request in the name of Jesus who comes to be
peace with us. Amen.

Week 2   O God, open our hearts to prepare the way for the coming of Christ.
Instruct us in your ways of compassion so that we may extend your
love and mercy to all people. We ask this in the name of Jesus, the
Eternal Word, who lives with you and the Holy Spirit forever. Amen.

Week 3   In you, Jesus, lies the gift of wisdom and the power of authority. You
share these gifts with us in a caring, gentle way as given to you by
God, our Mother and Father. Assist us in recognizing humbly the
source of our gifts and enable us to use them in praise of you, one
with the Source of all life. Amen.

TUESDAYS OF ADVENT
(Psalms and antiphons from the current week in the Psalter.)

MORNING PRAYER

READING
RESPONSORY

Sing to God a new song, give praise from the ends of the earth. —Sing...
Mountains and deserts rejoice, —give...
Glory to you, Source of all Being, Eternal Word, and Holy Spirit. —Sing...

CANTICLE OF ZECHARIAH

Week 1   There shall come forth a shoot from the stump of Jesse, and God's
delight will fill the earth.

Week 2   A voice cries in the wilderness to make straight a highway for our God.

Week 3   Let the earth open, that salvation may come forth and justice may
spring up from the earth.

INTERCESSIONS: Weeks 1 and 3

O Giver of all gifts, you continue to reveal your goodness to us and in faith we pray:
May your spirit rest gently upon us!

O Spirit of Wisdom, you give us insight;
—grant all people the wisdom to choose effective ways to develop their
human potential through their respective governments.
O Spirit of Understanding, you show us mercy;
—help us to reach out in compassion to one another.
O Spirit of Counsel and of Strength, you give us courage;
—may we be open to your loving challenges and strengthened in our desire to
be of service.
O Spirit of Knowledge, you instruct us in your ways;
—assist us to know ourselves and to be open to your continuous revelation
in our midst.

INTERCESSIONS: Week 2

You gather us together carefully, as a mother hen gathers her chicks. In confidence, we pray:

Be merciful to us, O God!

You show us your love for all creation;
   —may we be sensitive to all living creatures.
You search after the one who wanders away;
   —assist us to confront the manner in which we wander from your way.
You call us to praise and glorify you, Creator God;
   —enable us to show our gratitude in songs of thanksgiving.
You comfort the sorrowing and give strength to the weary;
   —grant all in the health service professions the gift of compassion.
You come to bring life to the lonely;
   —be with them and touch them with transforming joy and hope.

PRAYER

Week 1   O God of Compassion, you come to be with us in our humanity. Enable us to move beyond our stagnant places to embrace your life-giving waters of new birth. We ask you to bless us in the name of the Eternal Word, who was, who is and who will always be. Amen.

Week 2   O God of Tenderness, you gather us into your arms as a shepherd gathers her lambs. Help us to demonstrate your gentleness with one another. May we gather together the diverse peoples among us and prepare to make way for your coming. We ask this through your tender care and mercy for us, God without end. Amen.

Week 3   O God of Forgiveness, you are close to the brokenhearted and to all who call upon you. As we approach the celebration of Christmas, help us to be patient with our own shortcomings and to extend forgiveness and peace to our neighbors. Grant us this grace in the name of Jesus, our brother. Amen.

DAYTIME PRAYER

Ant 1   Comfort, comfort my people, says our God.

Ant 2   Every valley shall be lifted up, and every mountain shall be made low, and the glory of God shall be revealed.

Ant 3   The grass withers, the flower fades; but the word of our God will live forever.

(Prayer as in Morning Prayer)

EVENING PRAYER

READING

RESPONSORY

Come to deliver us, gentle and loving God. —**Come**...
Turn your face to us and save us; —**gentle**...
Glory to you, Source of all Being, Eternal Word, and Holy Spirit. —**Come**...

CANTICLE OF MARY

Week 1   Jesus said to his disciples: Blessed are the eyes that see what you see!

Week 2   It is the will of your God that not one of these little ones should perish.

Week 3   Jesus said: Truly, sinners enter the fullness of God before the self-righteous.

INTERCESSIONS: Weeks 1 and 3

O God of Love, hear the cry of the poor; listen to us as we pray:
Come and save your people!
God, you invite us to work in the vineyard;
—may all peoples know the true dignity of work.
You call us to serve one another in love;
—may we be open to hear the needs of those around us.
You give us the image of peace, the wolf as a guest of the lamb;
—grant us the courage to work for peace and to support all peacemakers.
You love justice and are close to the afflicted;
—assist all women and men in their search for just institutional structures.

INTERCESSIONS: Week 2

During this season of Advent you remind us that all things are passing; in trust we pray:
Give comfort to us, O God!
You are a sign of eternal life;
—touch our hearts to recognize and work for lasting values.
In compassion you proclaim your message to us;
—assist parents to listen to their children and to act out of love.
Help us to be of service to one another;
—may the love we share be more important than the acquisition of goods.
You search tenderly after the one lost sheep;
—give us the gift of hospitality that we may open our hearts to all who seek you.

PRAYER

Week 1   O God of Compassion, you come to be with us in our humanity. Enable us to move beyond our stagnant places to embrace your life-giving waters of new birth. We ask you to bless us in the name of the Eternal Word, who was, who is and who will always be. Amen.

Week 2   O God of Tenderness, you gather us into your arms as a shepherd gathers her lambs. Help us to demonstrate your gentleness with one another. May we gather together the diverse peoples among us and prepare to make way for your coming. We ask this through your tender care and mercy for us, God without end. Amen.

Week 3   O God of Forgiveness, you are close to the brokenhearted and to all who call upon you. As we approach the celebration of Christmas, help us to be patient with our own shortcomings and to extend forgiveness and peace to our neighbors. Grant us this grace in the name of Jesus, our brother. Amen.

WEDNESDAYS OF ADVENT

(Psalms and antiphons from the current week in the Psalter.)

MORNING PRAYER

READING

RESPONSORY

Sing to God a new song, give praise from the ends of the earth. —Sing...
Mountains and deserts rejoice, —give...
Glory to you, Source of all Being, Eternal Word, and Holy Spirit. —Sing...

CANTICLE OF ZECHARIAH

Week 1 This is our God, for whom we have waited; let us rejoice in our salvation.

Week 2 You, O God, are everlasting, the creator of all the earth.

Week 3 Thus says God who formed earth and heaven: I am your God, there is no other.

INTERCESSIONS: Weeks 1 and 3

God of our salvation, you come bringing us joy and nourishment and we exclaim:
Jesus, you are the joy of our salvation!

Jesus, you are the light in our darkness;
—may we see meaning in our struggles.
You bring bread to feed us;
—assist us to move beyond our selfish desires to be a leaven for others.
In healing and forgiveness you wipe away our tears;
—help us to be a sign of healing within the brokenness around us.
You made this earth your home;
—enlighten us to discover creative ways for preserving and renewing our environment.
You taught us to have a deep respect for all life;
—be with all expectant parents and enable them to bring forth life.

INTERCESSIONS: Week 2

In your promise, Jesus, you invite us to come to you and find rest for our heavy burdens. In confidence we say:
Come, Lord Jesus!

You invite us to come to you for rest;
—may we take the time today to sit, reflect and rest in your love for us.
You show us the benefits of gentleness;
—help us to see beyond our personal and national defenses to the gentleness in all people and created things.
You remind us that your yoke is easy and your burden is light;
—enable us to ease the yoke and burdens of one another, especially those coping with addictions.
You reflect the love of a caring God;
—may our lives witness that the time of salvation is now.
You give strength to all the weary;
—be with the women and men who have the courage to challenge our unjust structures.

PRAYER

Week 1   Most compassionate God, you share your life with us in Jesus, who brings us light, healing and salvation. We are grateful for being invited to the eternal banquet. May we share generously the life we have received in your holy name. Amen.

Week 2   All loving God, you invite us in Jesus to cast aside our heavy burdens and to be gentle of heart. Help us to be open to the tender ways in which your Word of Love touches our being. We ask you to hear our prayer in the name of Jesus who lives with you and the Holy Spirit forever. Amen.

Week 3   O God, may the celebration of this holy birth fill us with the life-giving waters from your holy womb. You call us to life once again and we ask you to renew our desire to serve you in one another. Grant this in the name of the Incarnate Word who lives with you and the Holy Spirit for all ages to come. Amen.

DAYTIME PRAYER

Ant 1   Comfort, comfort my people, says our God.

Ant 2   Every valley shall be lifted up, and every mountain shall be made low, and the glory of God shall be revealed.

Ant 3   The grass withers, the flower fades; but the word of our God will live forever.

(Prayer as in Morning Prayer)

EVENING PRAYER

READING

RESPONSORY

Come to deliver us, gentle and loving God. —**Come**...
Turn your face to us and save us; —**gentle**...
Glory to you, Source of all Being, Eternal Word, and Holy Spirit. —**Come**...

CANTICLE OF MARY

Week 1   Great crowds came to Jesus and he healed them; all were filled with awe and glorified God.

Week 2   Jesus said: Come to me, all who labor and are heavy laden, and I will give you rest.

Week 3   Go tell John what you see and hear: the blind see, the lame walk, the lepers are cleansed.

INTERCESSIONS: Weeks 1 and 3

You, O God, are a loving father and mother as you share your life, your table and your inheritance with us. In gratitude we pray:
                           Show us the way, O God!
You promise us a banquet of choice food;
    —may all people find the good they need this day.

You give us guidance in your compassionate understanding;
— assist us to discern faithfully your word for us.
You invite us to choose freely the way we use our gifts and the fruits of the earth;
— help us to allow our sisters and brothers the opportunity to live in your
freedom and love.
You are a God of hospitality and you welcome us to share in your inheritance;
— enable us to be faithful to your invitation to growth, freedom and love.

INTERCESSIONS: Week 2

During this season of Advent, we celebrate your coming to be one with us, Jesus. In joy we say:

The time of salvation is now!

God of Sarah, you know us intimately and call us each by name;
— give us the strength to respond to your call.
God of Abraham, your ways are hidden and mysterious;
— may we look beyond the obvious to see with the eyes of faith.
God of Israel, you come with might and power to bring us new life;
— enable us to be a presence of your loving care for all people by walking
in your light.
God of a new dawn, you soar into our lives on eagles' wings;
— prepare us for life eternal with you, and may all who die this day find the
dawn of new life in you.

PRAYER

Week 1　Most compassionate God, you share your life with us in Jesus, who brings us light, healing and salvation. We are grateful for being invited to the eternal banquet. May we share generously the life we have received in your holy name. Amen.

Week 2　All loving God, you invite us in Jesus to cast aside our heavy burdens and to be gentle of heart. Help us to be open to the tender ways in which your Word of Love touches our being. We ask you to hear our prayer in the name of Jesus who lives with you and the Holy Spirit forever. Amen.

Week 3　O God, may the celebration of this holy birth fill us with the life-giving waters from your holy womb. You call us to life once again and we ask you to renew our desire to serve you in one another. Grant this in the name of the Incarnate Word who lives with you and the Holy Spirit for all ages to come. Amen.

THURSDAYS OF ADVENT

(Psalms and antiphons from the current week in the Psalter.)

MORNING PRAYER

READING
RESPONSORY

Sing to God a new song, give praise from the ends of the earth. —**Sing**...
Mountains and deserts rejoice, —**give**...
Glory to you, Source of all Being, Eternal Word, and Holy Spirit. —**Sing to**...

CANTICLE OF ZECHARIAH

Week 1   Trust in God forever, for God is an everlasting rock.

Week 2   It is God who holds your hand and says: Fear not, I will help you.

Week 3   My steadfast love shall not depart from you, and my covenant of peace
shall not be removed, says our God.

INTERCESSIONS: Weeks 1 and 3

O God of Goodness, you invite us to a covenant of peace and love. In faith we pray:
Show us your kindness forever!

O God, you call us to be one in you;
—give us the strength to live in your love.
You walk among us in the poor and lonely;
—help us to serve you in our sisters and brothers.
You bless the church with the gift of your Spirit;
—may we place our gifts at the service of all.
You are our messenger of light;
—assist us with the courage to share our faith life with one another.

INTERCESSIONS: Week 2

In confidence we call upon you, O God, to keep your loving promises to us and so
we pray:
Remain with us throughout this day.

Fountain of Love, you provide water for the thirsty;
—may we give thanks for your endless gifts.
Comforting God, in your mercy you drive away our fears;
—grant us the grace to reach beyond the fears that keep us in bondage.
Faithful Companion, you walk with us along our journey;
—enable us to accept the diversities among us and to bless all who walk with
integrity a different road from our own.
Liberating God, you make the desert bloom and bring hope and beauty to us;
—free us to bring beauty and hope to people in need of refreshment.

PRAYER

Week 1   O God of peace, you weave your way through our hearts to share
with us your covenantal love. May we broaden our understanding of
being peacemakers in our world today. Grant this in the name of Jesus
whose birth heralded peace on earth. Amen.

Week 2   Provident God, you take care to nurture and sustain us with the fruits
of the earth and the gifts of one another. Help us to show our
gratitude for your gifts in the way we use and respect them. We ask
this through Jesus, our brother. Amen.

Week 3   Compassionate God, you look upon our brokenness with mercy and
kindness. Help us to extend your goodness to one another. Hear our
prayer for you are our God: Creator, Redeemer and Sanctifier. Amen.

DAYTIME PRAYER

Ant 1 Comfort, comfort my people, says our God.

Ant 2 Every valley shall be lifted up, and every mountain shall be made low, and the glory of God shall be revealed.

Ant 3 The grass withers, the flower fades; but the word of our God will live forever.

(Prayer as in Morning Prayer)

EVENING PRAYER

READING
RESPONSORY

Come to deliver us, gentle and loving God. —**Come**...
Turn your face to us and save us; —**gentle**...
Glory to you, Source of all Being, Eternal Word, and Holy Spirit. —**Come**...

CANTICLE OF MARY

Week 1 Those who hear my words are like the one whose house is built on rock.

Week 2 Heed carefully what you hear!

Week 3 I send my messenger before you, who shall prepare the way for you.

INTERCESSIONS: Weeks 1 and 3

Christ, you are the Light that the darkness cannot overcome; in confidence we pray:
Come, Light of Life!

You were present at the creation of the world;
   —by your coming as one of us renew the earth.
You who dwell in the heart of God,
   —come and teach us the love of God.
John the Baptist was imprisoned for the cause of truth;
   —free those imprisoned for the sake of your name.
You are always attentive to us in our every need;
   —help us to comfort the poor by our loving efforts.

INTERCESSIONS: Week 2

O God, you joyfully embraced humanity for our sake. With gratitude we pray:
Come, Christ our Savior!

Christ our Savior, you come into our world to bring peace;
   —may peace in our world be the fruit of peace in our hearts and homes.
Christ our Savior, you walk with us in steadfast love;
   —help us to show concern for just causes and to let go of smallness of heart.
Christ our Savior, you lead us to the waters of everlasting life;
   —refresh our spirits and make us eager to share our fruitful abundance with one another.
Christ our Savior, your time of fulfillment is present among us;
   —enable us to live fully in the present, to remember our past lovingly, and to embrace our future confidently.

PRAYER

Week 1   O God of peace, you weave your way through our hearts to share with us your covenantal love. May we broaden our understanding of being peacemakers in our world today. Grant this in the name of Jesus whose birth heralded peace on earth. Amen.

Week 2   Provident God, you take care to nurture and sustain us with the fruits of the earth and the gifts of one another. Help us to show our gratitude for your gifts in the way we use and respect them. We ask this through Jesus, our brother. Amen.

Week 3   Compassionate God, you look upon our brokenness with mercy and kindness. Help us to extend your goodness to one another. Hear our prayer for you are our God: Creator, Redeemer and Sanctifier. Amen.

FRIDAYS OF ADVENT

(Psalms and antiphons from the current week in the Psalter.)

MORNING PRAYER

READING

RESPONSORY

Sing to God a new song, give praise from the ends of the earth. —**Sing**...
Mountains and deserts rejoice, —**give**...
Glory to you, Source of all Being, Eternal Word, and Holy Spirit. —**Sing to**...

CANTICLE OF ZECHARIAH

Week 1   When the reign of God appears, the deaf shall hear, the blind shall see, and the poor shall rejoice.

Week 2   Thus says your redeemer: I am your God, who leads you in the way you should go.

Week 3   My house shall be called a house of prayer for all peoples.

INTERCESSIONS: Weeks 1 and 3

Gracious Spirit, you share with us your life and light; in trust we say:
Have mercy on us!
Christ, you gave us the commandment to love one another;
   —help us to live in this convenant of love.
You send your Spirit of hope into our hearts;
   —may our lives be signs of hope for others.
Give world leaders the wisdom to work for justice;
   —that peace may become a reality for all people.
We await the celebration of Christ's birth;
   —may every family experience joy and harmony.

INTERCESSIONS: Week 2

With patience we wait for your coming and in joy we exclaim:
Come, Lord Jesus!

The world awaits your coming in joy;
   —may your grace refresh every heart and mind.
Our voices proclaim your presence among us;
   —may our lives reveal your saving work.
You come to show us your mercy;
   —forgive us for our half-heartedness.
You called us to freedom in God's will;
   —help us to listen to the gentle stirrings of the Spirit.

PRAYER

Week 1   O loving God, you remind us that living in faith is a special gift. Increase our faith in you so that we may open ourselves to the mystery of your love in our lives. We ask this in the name of Jesus, who lives and reigns with you and with the Holy Spirit forever. Amen.

Week 2   You, O God, are a loyal friend; help us to be people of wisdom. May we discern our actions in the light of our relationship with you and one another. Grant this through Jesus who lives with you, Source of all Wisdom, in the unity of the Holy Spirit. Amen.

Week 3   O holy Womb of God, guide us with your love as we await the birthing of Jesus in our hearts. Keep us faithful that we may be nurtured through life and brought to salvation. We ask this in the name of this same Jesus, God-with-us. Amen.

DAYTIME PRAYER

Ant 1   Comfort, comfort my people, says our God.

Ant 2   Every valley shall be lifted up, and every mountain shall be made low, and the glory of God shall be revealed.

Ant 3   The grass withers, the flower fades; but the word of our God will live forever.

(Prayer as in Morning Prayer)

EVENING PRAYER

READING

RESPONSORY

Come to deliver us, gentle and loving God. —**Come**...
Turn your face to us and save us; —**gentle**...
Glory to you, Source of all Being, Eternal Word, and Holy Spirit. —**Come**...

CANTICLE OF MARY

Week 1   Jesus cured the blind, saying: According to your faith, be healed.

Week 2   Jesus said to the crowds: You condemned John and rejected me, but, in time, wisdom and truth will be revealed.

Week 3   My words bear witness that God has sent me.

INTERCESSIONS: Weeks 1 and 3

We rejoice in you, the God of our salvation; you call our blindness to sight and our deafness to hearing. In joy we proclaim:

Hear our prayer, O God!

God of Love, you invite us to trust in your saving mercy;
—help us to be confident of your continuous love for us, especially in times of doubt and distress.

God of Light, increase our vision;
—help us to see the beauty around us and to celebrate it each day.

God of Wonders, you come to us in simplicity;
—enable us to be content with our basic needs.

God of Joy, increase our openness to celebrating life;
—may all children experience acceptance, love and care.

INTERCESSIONS: Week 2

God of Unconditional Love, we ask you to enlighten our minds and expand our hearts; and so we pray:

Be with your people, O God.

To hear your word and follow it will bring us to life;
—may we listen to you as you speak to us in the unusual places of our daily life.

You promise never to forsake us;
—help all lonely, isolated people to experience hope.

You teach us the path of holiness;
—assist all teachers to share the fruits of their insights.

You share with us of your bounty;
—enable those who are prosperous to see beyond their own interests that they may help those in need.

PRAYER

Week 1   O loving God, you remind us that living in faith is a special gift. Increase our faith in you so that we may open ourselves to the mystery of your love in our lives. We ask this in the name of Jesus, who lives and reigns with you and with the Holy Spirit forever. Amen.

Week 2   You, O God, are a loyal friend; help us to be people of wisdom. May we discern our actions in the light of our relationship with you and one another. Grant this through Jesus who lives with you, Source of all Wisdom, in the unity of the Holy Spirit. Amen.

Week 3   O holy Womb of God, guide us with your love as we await the birthing of Jesus in our hearts. Keep us faithful that we may be nurtured through life and brought to salvation. We ask this in the name of this same Jesus, God-with-us. Amen.

SATURDAYS OF ADVENT

(Psalms and antiphons from the current week in the Psalter.)

MORNING PRAYER

READING

RESPONSORY

Sing to God a new song, give praise from the ends of the earth. —**Sing**...
Mountains and deserts rejoice, —**give**...
Glory to you, Source of all Being, Eternal Word, and Holy Spirit. —**Sing to**...

CANTICLE OF ZECHARIAH

Week 1   God will be gracious to you at the sound of your cry and will answer you.

Week 2   The reign of God is at hand: heal the sick, raise the dead, cleanse the lepers, cast out demons.

INTERCESSIONS: Week 1

God of our Delight, invite us to walk in your way. In faith we pray:
Heal us, O God!

You are the voice that sounds in our ears;
   —help us to hear the prophetic people around us.
You are the gentle rain that brings forth the seed of life;
   —enable us to be fruitful bearers of your word.
You are the bread that nourishes our being;
   —may we share our wheat and respect the rights of agricultural workers.
You are the ointment that heals our wounds;
   —assist us to be compassionate with our sick, elderly and handicapped sisters and brothers.
You are the gift given to us for our liberation;
   —strengthen us to embrace your gift of life lovingly.

INTERCESSIONS: Week 2

In trust, O God of Hosts, we await your coming and we pray:
Come and save us, Holy One of God!

Word of God, you inflame our hearts with desire for you;
   —may we share your love with one another.
Word of God, you invite us each day to a change of heart;
   —help us to be responsive to your stirrings within us.
Word of God, you call us by name and give us new life;
   —assist all church leaders to respect the freedom and differences among their people.
Word of God, you call us to peace and wholeness;
   —may those people who have died for justice inspire us with their courage.

Advent
PRAYER

Week 1 You came among us, Jesus, to heal the brokenhearted and to show us the way to God, our Mother and Father. Help us to extend your compassion to our world. May you bless us with your generative love, for you are God-with-us, now and forever. Amen.

Week 2 Be with us, O God of Life, and help us to be faithful to our respective calls. In your love you invite us each by name to participate in the fullness of your life. We ask you to bless us in your goodness and in the name of Jesus. Amen.

DAYTIME PRAYER

Ant 1 Comfort, comfort my people, says our God.

Ant 2 Every valley shall be lifted up, and every mountain shall be made low, and the glory of God shall be revealed.

Ant 3 The grass withers, the flower fades; but the word of our God will live forever.

(Prayer as in Morning Prayer)

DECEMBER 17

(Psalms and antiphons from the current week in the Psalter.)

MORNING PRAYER

READING

RESPONSORY

Lift up your eyes, Jerusalem; the glory of God is dawning on you.
—**Lift up**...
Darkness has covered the earth and thick clouds the people; —**the glory of**...
Glory to you, Source of all Being, Eternal Word, and Holy Spirit. —**Lift up**...

CANTICLE OF ZECHARIAH

Ant Your God is coming, O Zion, to rejoice over you with gladness and renew you in tender love.

INTERCESSIONS:

Jesus Christ comes as our Savior; we rejoice in you and say:
Renew in us the light of hope.

You call all nations to universal peace;
—deliver us from all forms of violence.
You come to show us the face of Love;
—give us a readiness to forgive those who have hurt us.
May the elderly find hope and meaning
—and comfort from those who care.
You accepted with trust and love the reality of being human;
—help all who are nearing their passage through death.

PRAYER: O God of Wisdom, you who fill our hearts but transcend our thoughts, give us all things in the gift of your Incarnate Word. Make us discerning persons with formed consciences and the freedom to recognize your invitations to grow. We ask this through Jesus, Emmanuel, God with us forever. Amen.

DAYTIME PRAYER

Ant 1 Our Savior will come like rain on the grass, like showers that water the earth.

Ant 2 Christ will have dominion from sea to sea, and from the River to the ends of the earth.

Ant 3 In your day justice will flourish and peace abound until the moon be no more.

(Prayer as in morning)

EVENING PRAYER

READING

RESPONSORY

Show us, O God, your steadfast love, and grant us your salvation.
   —**Show us**...
Restore us again that we may rejoice, —**and grant**...
Glory to you, Source of all Being, Eternal Word, and Holy Spirit.
   —**Show us**...

CANTICLE OF MARY

Ant O Wisdom, Holy Word of God, you reach from one end of the earth to the other with providential and tender care. Come and teach us to live in your ways.

INTERCESSIONS:

You have revealed the Christ, O God, as the goal of human history. We pray to you:
   Enlighten our minds and hearts.

Your children, O God, are burdened with uneasiness;
   —strengthen our spirits as we try to better our world.
It is your will that all people come to the knowledge of truth;
   —give us lives of integrity to point the way.
You are the desired One of all the nations;
   —we cannot rest until we rest in you.
You have written your law in our hearts;
   —help us to love what is good and avoid what is evil.

PRAYER: O God of Wisdom, you who fill our hearts but transcend our thoughts, give us all things in the gift of your Incarnate Word. Make us discerning persons with formed consciences and the freedom to recognize your invitations to grow. We ask this through Jesus, Emmanuel, God with us forever. Amen.

DECEMBER 18

(Psalms and antiphons from the current week in the Psalter.)

MORNING PRAYER

READING

RESPONSORY

Lift up your eyes, Jerusalem; the glory of God is dawning on you. —**Lift up**...
Darkness has covered the earth and thick clouds the people; —**the glory**...
Glory to you, Source of all Being, Eternal Word, and Holy Spirit. —**Lift up**...

CANTICLE OF ZECHARIAH

Ant   Look up and raise your heads because your redemption is drawing near.

INTERCESSIONS:

Jesus, you came to witness to the truth. With trust in you we pray;
May the truth make us free.

Look with compassion on the sick and suffering;
    —may their faith in you make them whole.
At your coming all things rejoice;
    —give us respect for all living things.
You call us to deeper fidelity to the gospel;
    —free us from all forms of blindness.
You come to show us our dignity as God's children;
    —show us the way to a social order that can incarnate it.

PRAYER: O God of the Universe, your vastness is beyond our power to
imagine, but you have come among us and revealed yourself in
Christ. As we celebrate this coming, may we recognize again our
dignity and serve one another with respect for the diversity of your
gifts to us. We ask this for all creation in union with Christ who
radiates in all and through all to your honor and glory forever.
Amen.

DAYTIME PRAYER

Ant 1   You will deliver the needy when they call, the poor and those
who have no helper.

Ant 2   All peoples will be blessed in you, all nations call you blessed.

Ant 3   You will draw water in joy from the Savior's fountain.

(Prayer as in morning)

EVENING PRAYER

READING

RESPONSORY

Show us, O God, your steadfast love, and grant us your salvation.
    —**Show us**...
Restore us again that we may rejoice, —**and grant us**...
Glory to you, Source of all Being, Eternal Word, and Holy Spirit.
    —**Show us**...

CANTICLE OF MARY

Ant O Adonai and Leader of the house of Israel, who appeared to Moses in flames of a burning bush and gave him your Law on Sinai, come and free us with your outstretched arm.

INTERCESSIONS:

O God, Source of all Good, we pray to you;
> **Renew your gifts in our hearts.**

You have given us Jesus to lead us to the fullness of life;
> —we welcome in him the news of salvation.

Help us to recognize the signs of the times,
> —and to judge all things in the light of your truth.

We are aware that we are one family in you;
> —tear down the barriers that divide us.

Through Christ the riddles of sorrow and death grow meaningful;
> —comfort the grieving; console the dying.

PRAYER: O God of the Universe, your vastness is beyond our power to imagine, but you have come among us and revealed yourself in Christ. As we celebrate this coming, may we recognize again our dignity and serve one another with respect for the diversity of your gifts to us. We ask this for all creation in union with Christ who radiates in all and through all to your honor and glory forever. Amen.

DECEMBER 19

(Psalms and antiphons from the current week in the Psalter.)

MORNING PRAYER

READING
RESPONSORY

Lift up your eyes, Jerusalem; the glory of God is dawning on you. —**Lift up**...
Darkness has covered the earth and thick clouds the people; —**the glory**...
Glory to you, Source of all Being, Eternal Word, and Holy Spirit. —**Lift up**...

CANTICLE OF ZECHARIAH

Ant Let us wait for God's word as we wait for rain; may it descend upon us as dew on the grass.

INTERCESSIONS:

O Christ, you are our light, the image of God and the first born of all creation. We pray to you:
> **Come and illumine the mystery of life.**

In you we have been reconciled to God and among ourselves;
> —help us to work as one family for the liberation of all.

You are the center of all life;
> —renew us and free us from dullness of mind and heart.

Yours is the earth and its fullness;
  —help us to respect and care for our planet.
You died for all humankind;
  —may all come to live in the light of the paschal mystery.

PRAYER: O God, your holy Word became enfleshed in the Virgin Mary. With her this Advent we have reflected on the angel's promises. We know you are always coming into our lives and that we bring you forth in works of mercy and love. Help us today to live by this faith. We ask this through the intercession of all who revealed your compassionate love and now live with you in eternal joy. Amen.

DAYTIME PRAYER

Ant 1 Behold, a virgin shall conceive and bear a son and shall call his name Emmanuel.

Ant 2 Sing aloud, O daughter of Zion. Rejoice and exult with all your heart.

Ant 3 Do not fear, O Zion, your God is in your midst.

(Prayer as in morning)

EVENING PRAYER

READING

RESPONSORY

Show us, O God, your steadfast love, and grant us your salvation.
  —**Show us**...
Restore us again that we may rejoice, —**and grant us**...
Glory to you, Source of all Being, Eternal Word, and Holy Spirit.
  —**Show us**...

CANTICLE OF MARY

Ant O Root of Jesse, you stand as a sign for all people. Before you rulers keep silence; from you all nations seek help. O come to free us and do not make us wait.

INTERCESSIONS:

O God, you call us, in Christ, to holiness, grace and peace. We pray to you and say;
             Help us to live with grateful hearts.

Your word is in harmony with our deepest desires;
  —restore hope to the doubtful and despairing.
Give us a living and vibrant faith,
  —animating us to works of justice for the poor and the oppressed.
Your Spirit directs the unfolding of time;
  —renew the face of the earth.
You have created us all in love;
  —give us light to recognize that you are our true destiny.

PRAYER: O God, your holy Word became enfleshed in the Virgin Mary. With her this Advent we have reflected on the angel's promises. We know you are always coming into our lives and that we bring you forth in works of mercy and love. Help us today to live by this faith. We ask this through the intercession of all who revealed your compassionate love and now live with you in eternal joy. Amen.

DECEMBER 20

(Psalms and antiphons from the current week in the Psalter.)

MORNING PRAYER

READING
RESPONSORY

Lift up your eyes, Jerusalem; the glory of God is dawning on you. —**Lift up**...
Darkness has covered the earth and thick clouds the people; —**the glory**...
Glory to you, Source of all Being, Eternal Word, and Holy Spirit. —**Lift up**...

CANTICLE OF ZECHARIAH

Ant The angel Gabriel was sent to Mary, a virgin engaged to a man named Joseph.

INTERCESSIONS:

Jesus, you come that we might walk in newness of life. To you we pray:
Come Lord Jesus, come.
Be a deliverer to those countries ravaged by war;
   —help us to see the way to peace.
You are the center of all life;
   —teach us our responsibility for human development.
You come from God to save us from sin;
   —free us from the evil we find in our hearts.
We remember all who have died;
   —welcome them home to everlasting joy.

PRAYER: O God, Source of all peace, we have heard again your promises of old and your vision for all humankind. In the coming of Christ, we recognize the one who can free us from all that prevents their fulfillment. Help us to respond wholeheartedly to this liberating presence. This we ask through Jesus, the Eternal Word, who lives with you and the Holy Spirit, forever. Amen.

DAYTIME PRAYER

Ant 1 Our God will come from the holy place to free us from oppression.
Ant 2 Nation shall not lift up sword against nation; nor shall they learn war anymore.
Ant 3 Teach us your ways that we may walk in paths of peace.

(Prayer as in morning)

EVENING PRAYER

READING

RESPONSORY

Show us, O God, your steadfast love, and grant us your salvation.
—**Show us**...
Restore us again that we may rejoice, —**and grant us**...
Glory to you, Source of all Being, Eternal Word, and Holy Spirit.
—**Show us**...

CANTICLE OF MARY

Ant O Key of David and Scepter of the house of Israel. You open and no one
shuts. You close and no one opens. Come and deliver us from the prisons
that hold us, for we are seated in darkness, oppressed by the shadows of
death.

INTERCESSIONS:

O God, your delight is to be with the children of earth. One with you in Christ, we
pray;

Glory and praise to our God!

When we lack human resources and power,
—deepen our trust in the power of your Spirit.
We are often in darkness and aware of our weakness;
—kindle within us the light of the gospel.
You have put us at the service of your creation;
—help us use our gifts for the good of all creatures.
Sustain us in love and devotion to you;
—that we may live fully according to the truth.

PRAYER: O God, Source of all peace, we have heard again your promises of
old and your vision for all humankind. In the coming of Christ, we
recognize the one who can free us from all that prevents their
fulfillment. Help us to respond wholeheartedly to this liberating
presence. This we ask through Jesus, the Eternal Word, who lives
with you and the Holy Spirit, forever. Amen.

DECEMBER 21

(Psalms and antiphons from the current week in the Psalter.)

MORNING PRAYER

READING
RESPONSORY

Lift up your eyes, Jerusalem; the glory of God is dawning on you. —**Lift up**...
Darkness has covered the earth and thick clouds the people; —**the glory**...
Glory to you, Source of all Being, Eternal Word, and Holy Spirit. —**Lift up**...

CANTICLE OF ZECHARIAH

Ant There is no cause for fear. In five days our God will be coming to us.

INTERCESSIONS:

O God, in the gift of Jesus, we see the face of Love.
Help us to reveal this love to others.

Enlighten all church leaders and those of nations;
—may your Spirit fill the earth.
Look with compassion on the tired, disillusioned and discouraged;
—may faith enkindle new vision in the darkness.
You have blessed us with freedom for we are made in your image;
—keep our consciences true and our choices wise.
You call us to commune with you and to share your happiness;
—may this gift of friendship be realized in our lives.

PRAYER: O God, Source of all good, you constantly broke through our
history calling us to love, peace and justice. Your Word made flesh
in Jesus is a new call and a new beginning. This Advent we ask to
renew this vision and our fidelity to Jesus who is the way. We ask
this in Jesus' name. Amen.

DAYTIME PRAYER

Ant 1 Come let us walk in the light of our God.

Ant 2 The night is far gone; the day is at hand.

Ant 3 Let us cast off the works of darkness and put on the armor of light.

(Prayer as in morning)

EVENING PRAYER

READING
RESPONSORY

Show us, O God, your steadfast love, and grant us your salvation.
—**Show us...**
Restore us again that we may rejoice, —**and grant us...**
Glory to you, Source of all Being, Eternal Word, and Holy Spirit.
—**Show us...**

CANTICLE OF MARY

Ant O Rising Sun, splendor of Eternal Light and brilliant Sun of Justice, come
and light up the darkness concealing from us the path to life.

INTERCESSIONS:

You have revealed the Christ, O God, as the goal of human history. We pray to you:
Enlighten our minds and hearts.

You draw to yourself the marginal and alienated;
—heal all families, communities and nations that have lost your Spirit as the
bond of union.
You alone search the heart;
—deliver us from all harmful judgments of ourselves and others.
May new possibilities in science and technology,
—lead to wise and moral choices.
We recognize our freedom but also new kinds of social slavery;
—come and save us from all forms of death.

PRAYER: O God, Source of all good, you constantly broke through our history calling us to love, peace and justice. Your Word made flesh in Jesus is a new call and a new beginning. This Advent we ask to renew this vision and our fidelity to Jesus who is the way. We ask this in Jesus' name. Amen.

DECEMBER 22

(Psalms and antiphons from the current week in the Psalter.)

MORNING PRAYER

READING

RESPONSORY

Lift up your eyes, Jerusalem; the glory of God is dawning on you. —**Lift up**...
Darkness has covered the earth and thick clouds the people; —**the glory**...
Glory to you, Source of all Being, Eternal Word, and Holy Spirit. —**Lift up**...

CANTICLE OF ZECHARIAH

Ant When the voice of your greeting came to my ears, the babe in my womb leaped for joy.

INTERCESSIONS:

O Christ, we long for your coming as we say:

Come Lord Jesus, Come!

As Sarah longed for Isaac,
 —our barren and sorrow-laden world longs for your fullness.
As Hannah longed for Samuel,
 —our deafened ears long to hear your voice.
As Elizabeth rejoiced in the babe in her womb,
 —let all expectant mothers rejoice in their fruitfulness.
As Zachary sang a song of blessing for his son,
 —let all expectant fathers rejoice in the gift of new life.
As Mary waited in mystery and longing,
 —may all who await your second coming be born into eternal life.

PRAYER: O God of tender mercy, your love for us has drawn you to be one with us in Christ. You are breaking down the barriers between nations by the force of that love in our hearts. Help us always to be persons of peace in union with those who actively build it in society. Grant this through your Christ whose gift is the blessing of peace in the midst of chaos. Amen.

DAYTIME PRAYER

Ant 1 No one has seen a God like you who rewards those who await you.

Ant 2 You bless the ones who joyfully work for justice, who remember you in your ways.

Ant 3 The days are coming when I will fulfill the promise I made to the house of Judah and the house of Israel.

(Prayer as in morning)

EVENING PRAYER

READING

RESPONSORY

Show us, O God, your steadfast love, and grant us your salvation.
—**Show us**...
Restore us again that we may rejoice, —**and grant us**...
Glory to you, Source of all Being, Eternal Word, and Holy Spirit.
—**Show us**...

CANTICLE OF MARY

Ant O Ruler of all nations and true desire of our hearts! You are the
cornerstone binding us all into a home for God. Come and free us whom
you formed from earth.

INTERCESSIONS:

O God, you made the world in the image of your Word; with grateful hearts, we
pray:

Come, Lord Jesus, come!

In the image of the Word all things were made;
—teach us to reverence all of creation.
Your hands fashioned the moon and the stars;
—may our adventures into space further the cause of peace.
You created the waters and all that dwell in them;
—may we keep them free of all pollution.
The birds and animals reflect the joy of your bounty;
—may we respect their rights to survive for their own sake rather than ours.
You created us as your own children;
—may your image shine forth in us.

PRAYER: O God of tender mercy, your love for us has drawn you to be one
with us in Christ. You are breaking down the barriers between
nations by the force of that love in our hearts. Help us always to be
persons of peace in union with those who actively build it in
society. Grant this through your Christ whose gift is the blessing of
peace in the midst of chaos. Amen.

DECEMBER 23

(Psalms and antiphons from the current week in the Psalter.)

MORNING PRAYER

READING

RESPONSORY

Lift up your eyes, Jerusalem; the glory of God is dawning on you. —**Lift up**...
Darkness has covered the earth and thick clouds the people; —**the glory**...
Glory to you, Source of all Being, Eternal Word, and Holy Spirit. —**Lift up**...

CANTICLE OF ZECHARIAH

Ant   Behold, all things spoken to Mary by an angel have now been completed.

INTERCESSIONS:

To the One who is and who is to come, we pray:

O Come, O Come, Emmanuel!

Because we are poor and needy,
—we long for your fullness.
Because your people are oppressed and in chains,
—teach us how to break the bonds that enslave them.
Because your word falls on barren ground,
—send us the saving waters that we may make barren land fruitful.
Because our hearts are stone and our eyes are blind,
—create in us hearts of flesh to see your suffering world.
Because we await your coming at the dawning of each day,
—may those who await your final coming see the dawn of eternal life.

PRAYER: O God of Life, Mary became the mother of Jesus by embracing your will with a full heart. Help us to enter into the mystery of salvation by an active and responsible obedience. Free us from the attitudes that limit our responses to your inspirations. We ask this in union with all who journey with Jesus to fullness of life. Amen.

DAYTIME PRAYER

Ant 1   In those days I will cause a branch to spring forth for David. Justice will be seen in the land.

Ant 2   Proclaim to all peoples the glad tidings. God, our Savior, is coming to us.

Ant 3   Behold, a virgin shall conceive and bear a son and shall call his name Emmanuel.

(Prayer as in morning)

EVENING PRAYER

READING

RESPONSORY

Show us, O God, your steadfast love, and grant us your salvation.
—**Show us**...
Restore us again that we may rejoice, —**and grant us**...
Glory to you, Source of all Being, Eternal Word, and Holy Spirit.
—**Show us**...

CANTICLE OF MARY

Ant   O Emmanuel, Giver of a new law to all nations, come and save us, for you are our God.

INTERCESSIONS:

To Christ who longed to live among us, we pray:

Glory to you, Lord Jesus Christ!

Leaping from the eternal womb of God, you come into our world,
—may we reverence this world that you love.
Encircled in the loving womb of Mary,
—may we reverence all children born into this world.
Experiencing our weakness and littleness,
—teach us to reverence the sick, the elderly and the lonely.
Enjoying the blessings of family life,
—give comfort to the homeless, the abandoned and the forgotten.
Returning to the One you loved and served,
—may all who die know your welcoming and loving embrace.

PRAYER: O God of Life, Mary became the mother of Jesus by embracing your will with a full heart. Help us to enter into the mystery of salvation by an active and responsible obedience. Free us from the attitudes that limit our responses to your inspirations. We ask this in union with all who journey with Jesus to fullness of life. Amen.

DECEMBER 24

(Psalms from the current week in the Psalter.)

MORNING PRAYER

Ant 1   Do not be afraid, Mary, for you have found favor with God.

Ant 2   The Holy Spirit will come upon you, and the power of the Most High will overshadow you.

Ant 3   You will call his name Jesus, for he will save his people from their sins.

READING
RESPONSORY

Tomorrow our sinfulness will be taken away and salvation shall be ours.
—**Tomorrow**...
The one who frees us will be our ruler; —**and salvation**...
Glory to you, Source of all Being, Eternal Word, and Holy Spirit.
—**Tomorrow**...

CANTICLE OF ZECHARIAH

Ant   The Savior of the world shall appear like the sun and descend into the Virgin's womb as rain on the grass.

INTERCESSIONS:

The time has come; the day is at hand. With joyful hearts we pray:
Today is the day of salvation!
We eagerly await your coming;
—come to all your people, especially those who are most destitute.
We eagerly await your coming,
—to the homeless, the addicted, and all held in bondage.
We eagerly await your coming,
—to free the waters, the animals and the planets from human destruction and negligence.

We eagerly await your coming,
   —to those longing to be taken to their eternal home.
We eagerly await your coming,
   —to praise the One who sent you, the Source of all Life and fruitfulness.

PRAYER: Most loving God, in the silence of this Advent season we have
contemplated the mystery of your coming in Christ. We thank you
for your great mercy and for the hope that gives meaning to all our
striving. Renew that hope in our hearts at the dawning of each day
that we may not tire in the work we must do. Grant this through
Jesus, the Incarnate Word who lives with you and the Spirit for all
eternity. Amen.

DAYTIME PRAYER

Ant 1   The child to be born will be called holy, the holy one of God.

Ant 2   Blessed is she who has believed in the word spoken to her from God.

Ant 3   O that you would rend the heavens and come down, that the mountains
would quake at your presence.

(Prayer as in Morning Prayer)

CHRISTMAS

EVENING PRAYER I

Ant 1   Christ, our peace, comes in glory; the universe welcomes its redeemer.
(Psalm 113)

Ant 2   This day God sends forth the Eternal Word to the earth. (Psalm 147).

Ant 3   O Eternal Word, for our salvation you emptied yourself and became
one of us. (Phil. 2:6–11)

READING

RESPONSORY

Today you will see the coming of the Promised One. —**Today**...
At dawn you will see God's glory, —**the coming**...
Glory to you, Source of all Being, Eternal Word, and Holy Spirit. —**Today**...

CANTICLE OF MARY

Ant   At sunrise you will see the coming of the Most High. Like the morning
star, God will shine in our darkness.

INTERCESSIONS:

A child is born in Bethlehem, alleluia.
                    Come, let us rejoice, alleluia, alleluia.

This is the day we have long awaited, the reality foretold by all the prophets.
   —We thank you, we praise you, we rejoice in you.
You are our God who shares divinity with us.
   —We thank you, we praise you, we rejoice in you.
You are our God, Emmanuel, ever in our hearts and lives each day.
   —We thank you, we praise you, we rejoice in you.

PRAYER: O God, the long-awaited day has come when your Eternal Word becomes one of us in Jesus. May every child born into this world also incarnate your Word, that the good news of your life with us and in us is relived in every time and every age, today and forever. Amen.

MORNING PRAYER

(Psalms and canticle from Feasts and Solemnities)

Ant 1   Shepherds, tell us what you have seen and heard. We saw the newborn savior, and hosts of angels singing God's praises, alleluia.

Ant 2   The angel said to them: I bring you good news of great joy; to you is born this day Christ the savior, alleluia.

Ant 3   To us a child is born; today the Mighty God shares our humanity, alleluia.

READING

RESPONSORY

Christ has made known our salvation, alleluia, alleluia. —**Christ**. . .
Salvation by our God, —**alleluia, alleluia**. . .
Glory to you, Source of all Being, Eternal Word, and Holy Spirit. —**Christ**. . .

CANTICLE OF ZECHARIAH

Ant   Glory to God in the highest; peace to all people on earth, alleluia.

INTERCESSIONS:

In the beginning was the Word, and the Word was God, who became flesh and dwells among us this day.

Christ shall be called Wonderful! Christ shall be called Peace!

On this day new joy entered our world;
   —may we try by our lives to share joy with others each day.
On this day fresh hope entered our world;
   —may we bring hope to those who are heavily burdened.
On this day love was visible in a child;
   —may we show our love for others in concrete ways of friendship and service.
On this day the promise of peace on earth was proclaimed;
   —may we be lovers of peace and demonstrate this love by reflective responses to life's challenges and trials.

PRAYER: Morning has broken with new glory this Christmas day; we rejoice in our brother, Jesus. May we deepen our relationships with God and with one another in ever-growing love and reverence. This we ask through Jesus born this day and through all ages. Amen.

DAYTIME PRAYER

Ant 1   The parents of Jesus were filled with awe at all that was said of him, alleluia. (Psalm 19:7–14)

Ant 2   Mary kept all these things, pondering them in her heart, alleluia. (Psalm 47)

Ant 3   My eyes have seen your salvation, which you have prepared in the presence of all peoples, alleluia. (Psalm 48)

PRAYER: At this noontime hour we thank you for the time you offer us to praise you anew and to grow in knowing, loving, and serving you in one another. May all know your gift of peace in the midst of chaos. Grant this through Jesus who promised us peace the world cannot give. Amen.

EVENING PRAYER II

Ant 1   You are honored by the Most High; before the dawning of time, before the creation of the sun, you were begotten, alleluia. (Psalm 110:1–5, 7)

Ant 2   The love of God is eternal; the power of the Most High will not fail. (Psalm 130)

Ant 3   In the beginning was the Word, who is God; today the Word comes to save the world. (Col. 1:12–20)

READING

RESPONSORY

The Word was made flesh, alleluia, alleluia. —**The Word**. . .
And dwelt among us, —**alleluia**. . .
Glory to you, Source of all Being, Eternal Word, and Holy Spirit.
    —**The Word**. . .

CANTICLE OF MARY

Ant   Your Christ is born today and has appeared among us. All creation joins in song with angel choirs to sing your praise. Today your people delight in your glory, alleluia.

INTERCESSIONS:

With bright hope we confide our weary, war-torn, suffering world to you, son of Mary, Word of God,
                May your birth bring new peace to all.
We confide all young people to you,
    —increase their faith in your love so that they find more joy in life and more courage in the challenge of following your ways.
We confide all the suffering of our world to you;
    —may they know your presence and healing grace at this difficult time.
We confide the unemployed, the homeless, the suicidal to your tender concern;
    —be light in the darkness of their pain and grant them hope.

We confide all the elderly to you;
—may they be strengthened and comforted by faith in the eternal life that
   lies ahead of them.
We confide all the children of the world to you;
—may they experience love and compassion, food and shelter, and the joy
   of carefree play.

PRAYER: O holy Womb of God, birth each of us into your image and
likeness that Christ may again reveal your love and concern to our
world. We pray especially for all who are most vulnerable that they
may experience your care. Grant this in the name of Jesus and
through the intercession of all the children who play with you in
your eternal home. Amen.

HOLY FAMILY

(Sunday in the Octave of Christmas.)

EVENING PRAYER I

Ant 1   Jacob was the father of Joseph, the husband of Mary, of whom Jesus
was born, who is called the Christ. (Psalm 113)

Ant 2   Joseph, son of David, do not fear to take Mary as your wife, for the
one who is conceived in her is of the Holy Spirit. (Psalm 147:12–20)

Ant 3   The shepherds went with haste and found Mary and Joseph, and the
babe lying in a manger. (Eph. 1:3–10)

READING

RESPONSORY

The Word was made flesh, alleluia, alleluia. —**The Word**...
And dwelt among us, —**alleluia, alleluia**...
Glory to you, Source of all Being, Eternal Word, and Holy Spirit.
   —**The Word**...

CANTICLE OF MARY

Ant   The boy Jesus stayed behind in Jerusalem. His parents did not know it,
but supposing him to be among their friends and relatives, they went a
day's journey.

INTERCESSIONS:

O God, you image life in relationship through the gift of our families, and so we
pray:

Blessed are you, Most Holy Trinity.

O God, beloved Father, giver of all gifts,
—we thank you for your provident care.
O God, beloved Mother, birthing us into new life,
—we thank you for life-giving waters.
O God, Word made flesh in Jesus,
—we thank you for drawing us into the mystery of incarnating Christ in
   our lives.

O Holy Trinity,
    —grant that we may be generative and fruitful bearers of your
      life-giving Spirit.

PRAYER: O God, you call us to life in relationship. Help us to know ourselves
that we may be compassionate to others. Forgive the many times
we have failed to be forgiving to those nearest us, and grant us the
humility to ask pardon. This we ask through the intercession of
Jesus, Mary, and Joseph. Amen.

MORNING PRAYER

(Psalms from Feasts and Solemnities)

Ant 1   The parents of Jesus went to Jerusalem every year at the feast
of the Passover.

Ant 2   The child grew and became strong and filled with wisdom; the favor
of God was upon him.

Ant 3   His father and mother marveled at what was said about their child.

READING

RESPONSORY

Christ, come forth from the living God, have mercy on us. —**Christ**...
Obedient to Mary and Joseph, —**have mercy**...
Glory to you, Source of all Being, Eternal Word, and Holy Spirit. —**Christ**...

CANTICLE OF ZECHARIAH

Ant   Son, why have you treated us so? Your father and I have been anxiously
looking for you.

INTERCESSIONS:

Christ, you came to us from the depths of Mystery. Your vision always drew you
forward and so we pray:

        May we seek our God in sincerity of heart.

Christ, our brother and companion, teach us how to communicate with gentle
understanding and love;
    —be with us each day in our families and communities as we try to grow in
      loving relationships.
You were obedient to Mary and Joseph;
    —may we learn to follow you by listening to each other with
      discerning hearts.
You showed your love for your parents;
    —let us be creative and generous in responding to those who fostered and
      nurtured us.
Be with those families wounded by alienation and pain;
    —enable them to understand differences and support one another
      in suffering.
Comfort loved ones who grieve for missing, kidnapped, or run-away children;
    —give them strength to keep the light of hope burning in their homes and
      in their hearts.

PRAYER: O Holy Trinity, look with compassion on all families where love
          and understanding have long been absent. In your merciful
          kindness, bring peace, comfort, and joy to all members today.
          Grant this through the intercession of Jesus, Mary and Joseph.
          Amen.

DAYTIME PRAYER

(See Psalter for Psalms: Sunday, Week I)

Ant 1   Mary and Joseph marveled at what was spoken of Jesus.

Ant 2   The mother of Jesus kept these words in her heart.

Ant 3   My eyes have seen your salvation which you have prepared in the
        presence of all peoples.

PRAYER: Creator, Redeemer, and Sanctifier, bless all family units
          this day and give them strength in forgiving one another and in
          patient love, so that they will daily find comfort and
          encouragement in their homes. This we ask through the intercession
          of all our family members who live with you in the communion of
          saints. Amen.

EVENING PRAYER II

Ant 1   After three days, Mary and Joseph found Jesus in the temple, sitting
        among the teachers, listening to them and asking them questions.

Ant 2   Jesus went with his parents to Nazareth, and was obedient to them.

Ant 3   Jesus increased in wisdom and stature, in the favor of God and of
        the people.

READING

RESPONSORY

Let us adore the Christ who was pleased to be born of a virgin. —Let us...
Flesh of our flesh, —who was...
Glory to you, Source of all Being, Eternal Word, and Holy Spirit. —Let us...

CANTICLE OF MARY

Ant   All who heard him were amazed at his understanding and his answers.

INTERCESSIONS:

O God, you image life in relationship through the gift of our families, and so we
pray:
Blessed are you, Most Holy Trinity.
O God, beloved Father, giver of all gifts,
  —we thank you for your provident care.
O God, beloved Mother, birthing us into new life,
  —we thank you for life-giving waters.

O God, Word made flesh in Jesus,
  —we thank you for drawing us into the mystery of incarnating Christ
  in our lives.
O Holy Trinity,
  —grant that we may be generative and fruitful bearers of your life-giving
  Spirit.

PRAYER: O God, you call us to life in relationship. Help us to know ourselves
that we may be compassionate to others. Forgive the many times
we have failed to be forgiving to those nearest us, and grant us the
strength to forgive one another with patient love. Give us the grace
to find comfort and encouragement daily in our lives together.
Amen.

DECEMBER 26

FEAST OF ST. STEPHEN

MORNING PRAYER

(Psalms from Feasts and Solemnities)

Ant 1   I have been faithful to you, my God, even in the face of death.

Ant 2   Filled with the Holy Spirit, Stephen gazed into heaven and saw the
glory of God.

Ant 3   Stephen saw Jesus standing at the side of the Most High.

READING

RESPONSORY

The heavens opened, and Stephen beheld your glory. —**The heavens**...
Forgiving those who stoned him, —**Stephen**...
Glory to you, Source of all Being, Eternal Word, and Holy Spirit.
  —**The heavens**...

CANTICLE OF ZECHARIAH

Ant   Stephen prayed, "Lord, receive my spirit." He entered heaven and was
crowned the first of martyrs.

INTERCESSIONS:

In Christ, O God, we have received every spiritual blessing; we lift our hearts and
pray:

May your perfect love cast out all fear.

We praise you and ask for the courage to accept life's sufferings;
  —hide us in the shelter of your wings.
We give you thanks for Stephen and all the early martyrs;
  —may we learn to be nonviolent when we are challenged and confronted.
We give you thanks for the martyrs of today;
  —give them strength and courage in their time of trial.
You taught us in Jesus to forgive those who hurt us;
  —turn our hearts of stone to hearts of flesh.

PRAYER: O God, as we celebrate your coming into our world, we also celebrate the feast of your martyr, Stephen, born into eternal life. Give us the grace to understand both the joy and the cost of discipleship. We pray especially for all of our sisters and brothers who are serving you in life-threatening situations. Be their strength and comfort. This we ask through the intercession of Stephen and all who gave their lives for you. Amen.

DAYTIME PRAYER

(Psalms from the current weekday in the Psalter)

Ant 1   Mary and Joseph marveled at what was spoken of Jesus.

Ant 2   The mother of Jesus kept these words in her heart.

Ant 3   My eyes have seen your salvation which you have prepared in the presence of all peoples.

PRAYER: Christ Jesus, give us the courage to forgive and love those who do harm to us, and to our sisters and brothers all over the world. Then, like your martyr, Stephen, may we one day rejoice in your presence, beholding the glory of God Most Holy. Amen.

EVENING PRAYER

(Antiphons and psalms as in Evening Prayer II of Christmas)

READING

RESPONSORY

The Word was made flesh, alleluia, alleluia, —**The Word**...
And dwelt among us, —**alleluia**...
Glory to you, Source of all Being, Eternal Word, and Holy Spirit. —**The Word**...

CANTICLE OF MARY

Ant   In the silent darkness of night, the Word of God came down from heaven.

INTERCESSIONS:

O God, you have come to earth that we might live with you for all eternity. Let us sing out in joy:

Glory to God in the highest!

God of compassion, you did not condemn Paul at the time of Stephen's death;
   —teach us to withhold judgment and give us patient hearts.
You chose Stephen to serve the needs of your people;
   —may all called to ministry be enabled to serve your people according to their gifts.
You graced Stephen with the gifts of wisdom and goodness;
   —help us to appreciate and affirm the gifts of our friends and companions.
You enabled Stephen to forgive those who persecuted him;
   —give us the gift of compassion toward those who misunderstand us, and toward those who oppress others.

PRAYER: O God, as we celebrate your coming into our world, we also celebrate the feast of your martyr, Stephen, born into eternal life. Give us the grace to understand both the joy and the cost of discipleship. We pray especially for all of our sisters and brothers who are serving you in life-threatening situations. Be their strength and comfort. This we ask through the intercession of Stephen and all who gave their lives for you. Amen.

DECEMBER 27

St. John, Apostle and Evangelist

(Psalms from Feasts and Solemnities)

MORNING PRAYER

Ant 1   John, evangelist and apostle, was beloved of Christ.

Ant 2   Christ on the cross put the care of his mother, Mary, into the hands of John.

Ant 3   The disciple whom Jesus loved said: It is the Lord!

READING

RESPONSORY

The Word was made flesh, alleluia, alleluia. —**The Word**...
And dwelt among us, —**alleluia**...
Glory to you, Source of all Being, Eternal Word, and Holy Spirit.
  —**The Word**...

CANTICLE OF ZECHARIAH

Ant   The Word became flesh and dwelt among us, and we have witnessed the glory of God bestowed on Jesus.

INTERCESSIONS:

Christ Jesus, you chose women and men to preach the good news, and so we pray:
              Give us the grace of discipleship.

You called John to preach the gospel of love;
  —break down the barriers that separate us from others.
Your disciples, Mary and John, stood beneath the cross;
  —give us the courage to be faithful in times of trial.
You entrusted to John the care of your mother;
  —help us grow in trust toward one another.
John was called a "Son of Thunder";
  —teach us to accept ourselves as we are and to appreciate the gifts we
    have been given.

PRAYER: O God, may the celebration of the birth of Jesus enkindle our desires to be his disciples. Teach us to be loving and responsive to those in need, and help us to grow in intimacy with you. This we ask in the name of Jesus, God-with-us, now and forever. Amen.

DAYTIME PRAYER

Ant 1 Mary and Joseph marveled at what was spoken of Jesus.

Ant 2 The mother of Jesus kept these words in her heart.

Ant 3 My eyes have seen your salvation which you have prepared in the presence of all peoples.

(Prayer as in Morning Prayer)

EVENING PRAYER

(Antiphons and psalms as in Evening Prayer II of Christmas)

READING
RESPONSORY

The Word was made flesh, alleluia, alleluia. —**The Word**...
And dwelt among us, —**alleluia**...
Glory to you, Source of all Being, Eternal Word, and Holy Spirit.
   —**The Word**...

CANTICLE OF MARY

Ant The prophet's words, O Mary, have been fulfilled through you; Christ was born of a virgin.

INTERCESSIONS:

Your Word, O God, came down from heaven to set us free, and so we pray:
   Glory to God in the highest!

Through the mouths of children, you perfected praise;
   —teach us to be meek and humble of heart.
John preached the message: Love one another;
   —help us to persevere in our efforts to grow in relationship.
John accepted the cup you asked him to drink;
   —give us the courage to accept the circumstances of our daily lives.
You chose women and men to witness to your coming,
   —may we give witness to our world that you still live among us.

PRAYER: O God, as evening comes, we thank you for the gift of Christ, the Light of the World. We thank you for the early followers of Jesus who passed the light on to us. May we be light for our world that all may know you live and dwell among us. Grant this through Jesus and all who preached in his name. Amen.

DECEMBER 28

Holy Innocents, Martyrs

MORNING PRAYER

(Psalms from Feasts and Solemnities)

Ant 1 These holy ones, who shed their blood for Christ, will dwell in heaven forever.

Ant 2 By their death and not by words, do these infants proclaim their witness to the gospel.

Ant 3 Out of the mouths of children you have found perfect praise, O God.

READING
RESPONSORY

In the heavens, O God, your friends praise you forever. —**In the**...
You have prepared a place for them. —**your friends**...
Glory to you, Source of all Being, Eternal Word, and Holy Spirit. —**In the**...

CANTICLE OF ZECHARIAH

Ant We praise you, O God; the glorious company of martyrs acclaim you.

INTERCESSIONS:

O God, at the birth of Jesus the angels sang songs of glory and peace,
>   **Grant us peace the world cannot give.**

As Rachel mourned her children,
>   —comfort all parents who mourn the death of their children.

As Jacob wept for Joseph,
>   —bring solace and hope to those whose children are missing or have run away.

The Israelites in Egypt grieved over the slaughter of their children;
>   —protect children from all forms of violence.

Mary and Joseph fled with the child into Egypt;
>   —may all exiled and refugee children find loving care and support.

Through the intercession of Joachim and Anne,
>   —give patience and wisdom to young mothers and fathers.

PRAYER: Most loving God, the Holy Innocents were martyrs for Christ. May we, in our lives, bear witness to our love for you, showing by our deeds what we profess. Grant courage to women and men who strive by non-violent action to influence others for the good of those suffering and deprived. This we ask through the intercession of those who were victims of violence and now share eternal life with you. Amen.

DAYTIME PRAYER

(Psalms are from the current weekday in Psalter)

Ant 1 Mary and Joseph marveled at what was spoken of Jesus.

Ant 2 The mother of Jesus kept these words in her heart.

Ant 3 My eyes have seen your salvation which you have prepared in the presence of all peoples.

PRAYER: Merciful God, we ask your blessing on young people who are tempted to end their lives because of the experience of abuse or a sense of meaninglessness. Send them a friend who can encourage or enlighten them and share their burdens with them. We ask this through Jesus who is our way, our truth, and our life. Amen.

EVENING PRAYER

(Antiphons and psalms as in Evening Prayer II of Christmas)

READING

RESPONSORY

The Word was made flesh, alleluia, alleluia. —The Word. . .
And dwelt among us, —alleluia. . .
Glory to you, Source of all Being, Eternal Word, and Holy Spirit.
   —The Word. . .

CANTICLE OF MARY

Ant   God took flesh of the holy Virgin and became her only child. Let us
   worship God who is our salvation.

INTERCESSIONS:

Today innocent people suffer because of jealousy and fear and so we pray:
                 Create in us a new heart, O God.
Christ Jesus, you answered insult with silence;
   —teach us how to be nonviolent in our responses.
Christ Jesus, you forbade Peter to use the sword;
   —enable us to resolve conflicts between nations and persons through
     dialogue rather than violence.
Christ Jesus, you invited the children to come to you;
   —may all children come to know their worth and their dignity.
Christ Jesus, you came to forgive our sins;
   —forgive all who have perpetrated violence in any way and give them the
     help they need to live peacefully.
Christ Jesus, you call us to justice;
   —give us discerning hearts that we may follow your example.

PRAYER: Splendor of God, brighten our lives with your humanity so that
            we are guided in our actions by your words and deeds. May we
            follow your example so that all will know you, Emmanuel, God-
            with-us, now and forever. Amen.

DECEMBER 29

MORNING PRAYER

(Antiphons and psalms as in Morning Prayer at Christmas)

READING

RESPONSORY

Christ has made known our salvation, alleluia, alleluia. —Christ. . .
Salvation by our God, —alleluia. . .
Glory to you, Source of all Being, Eternal Word, and Holy Spirit. —Christ. . .

CANTICLE OF ZECHARIAH

Ant The shepherds said to one another, "Let us go over to Bethlehem and see this thing that has happened which God has made known to us."

INTERCESSIONS:

The Word of God lives among us. Let us cry out in joy,
Praise be to you, Christ Jesus.

In you we find true peace,
—give patient endurance to all who work for justice and peace between peoples and nations.
You spoke words of truth in the midst of hostility;
—may all those who disseminate information speak with integrity and honesty.
You treated all people with respect and reverence;
—teach us to appreciate diversity in persons and cultures.
You fully entered into family and social gatherings;
—lift our burdens of stress and help us to enjoy family and friends.
You commended yourself into the hands of God;
—may all who die this day find themselves in God's embrace.

PRAYER: Most Loving God, in Jesus you gave us the best of gifts. He is our companion on the way, leading us toward fullness of life in you. May we respond each day to the way you lure us in the many choices that we make, and so incarnate your life in us. We ask this through Jesus, our bread of life. Amen.

DAYTIME PRAYER

(Psalms from the current weekday in the Psalter)

Ant 1 Mary and Joseph marveled at what was spoken of Jesus.

Ant 2 The mother of Jesus kept these words in her heart.

Ant 3 My eyes have seen your salvation which you have prepared in the presence of all peoples.

(Prayer as in Morning Prayer)

EVENING PRAYER

(Antiphons and psalms as in Evening Prayer II of Christmas)

READING

RESPONSORY

The Word was made flesh, alleluia, alleluia. —**The Word**...
And dwelt among us, —**alleluia**...
Glory to you, Source of all Being, Eternal Word, and Holy Spirit.
—**The Word**...

CANTICLE OF MARY

Ant O Christ, you humbled yourself by taking on our humanity that you might restore humanity to the inheritance of heaven.

INTERCESSIONS:

As evening comes, we sing a new song to our God, for a light has shone in our darkness. In confidence we pray:

In your light we find life.

Christ, our Light, we rejoice in your redeeming love;
   —may we share our resources, our time, and our gifts with one another and
     especially with those in need of love.
Christ, our Light, we give thanks for your compassion;
   —enlighten our hearts that we may understand and lovingly support the
     many people who are burdened with emotional trauma during this season.
Christ, our Light, we are touched by your humility;
   —assist us in our efforts to act with integrity and justice and to
     speak truthfully.
Christ, our Light, we are honored with your humanity;
   —teach us to respect and care for our own bodies, and by reverencing
     ourselves to embrace all life.
Christ, our Light, we are humbled by your simplicity;
   —show us creative ways to live simply and to conserve our natural resources
     for future generations.

PRAYER: Most Loving God, you shared your Word with us as a light in our
           darkness. May we be open to the awe and mystery of life that
           surrounds us in so many ways. Help us to recognize the light of
           Christ in our own inner poverty and to reach out courageously to
           share our light with others. We pray this in the wonder of your
           love. Amen.

DECEMBER 30

MORNING PRAYER

(Antiphons and psalms as in Morning Prayer at Christmas)

READING

RESPONSORY

Christ has made known our salvation, alleluia, alleluia. —**Christ**...
Salvation by our God, —**alleluia**...
Glory to you, Source of all Being, Eternal Word, and Holy Spirit. —**Christ**...

CANTICLE OF ZECHARIAH

Ant   Angels sang to greet the birth of Christ: Glory to God and to the
      Anointed One, alleluia.

INTERCESSIONS:

In the birth of Christ we are reminded of our own fragile humanity and God's enduring love, and so we pray:

Word of God, stay with us.

Word of God, the prophetess Anna spoke of our redemption;
—open our hearts to listen to the prophets of today.
Word of God, the parents of young children need your comfort;
—grant all parents the patience and wisdom to nurture their children.
Word of God, you call us to live in this world and yet not be part of it;
—help us to carry out our business affairs with integrity.
Word of God, you remind us that we belong to you;
—touch our hearts that we may have confidence in your love and live in
your freedom.
Word of God, you call us to eternal life;
—give comfort to the dying and be with all those people who mourn the
death of their loved ones this day.

PRAYER: O Holy Word of God, you call us to walk with you each day in the
mystery of your love. We are often anxious and worried about our
own well-being. Help us to put aside false anxiety and to trust in
your care for us. Grant us the grace to discern wisely, to act
confidently, and to let go courageously. We ask this in your name,
Word incarnate among us. Amen.

DAYTIME PRAYER

(Psalms from the current weekday in the Psalter)

Ant 1   Mary and Joseph marveled at what was spoken of Jesus.

Ant 2   The mother of Jesus kept these words in her heart.

Ant 3   My eyes have seen your salvation which you have prepared in the
presence of all peoples.

(Prayer as in Morning Prayer)

EVENING PRAYER

(Antiphons and psalms as in Evening Prayer II of Christmas)

READING

RESPONSORY

The Word was made flesh, alleluia, alleluia. —**The Word**...
And dwelt among us, —**alleluia**...
Glory to you, Source of all Being, Eternal Word, and Holy Spirit.
—**The Word**...

CANTICLE OF MARY

Ant   Holy Mary, mother of our Redeemer, we praise you; watch over all
those saved by your son.

INTERCESSIONS:

In joy and thanksgiving we call to you, Christ Jesus;
                    May we find hope in your birth.

Christ, be our strength in our struggle for justice;
—may oppressed and abused children find hope in your birth.

Christ, be our wisdom in our efforts to further world progress;
  —may we use our gifts wisely and treat one another justly.
Christ, be our vision of wholeness in our search for integration;
  —may we bind up our own wounds and in our healing find hope in
    your birth.
Christ, be our sign of grace in times of despair;
  —in times of rejection may young people find hope in us and choose life.
Christ, you are the Light of the World. Be a light to us;
  —may we experience joy in one another's gifts and may we all find hope
    in your birth.

PRAYER: O Giver of Hope, you delight us with the birth of Christ in whom
we find strength, wisdom, and grace. Renew our vision during this
season that we may reach out to the needs of others in our families,
our neighborhood, and places of work. In confidence we pray that
we may always find hope in your birth. Amen.

DECEMBER 31

MORNING PRAYER

(Antiphons and psalms as in Morning Prayer at Christmas)

READING

RESPONSORY

Christ has made known our salvation, alleluia, alleluia. —**Christ**. . .
Salvation by our God, —**alleluia**. . .
Glory to you, Source of all Being, Eternal Word, and Holy Spirit. —**Christ**. . .

CANTICLE OF ZECHARIAH

Ant   And suddenly there was with the angel a multitude of the heavenly host
praising God and saying: Glory to God in the highest; peace, good
will to all.

INTERCESSIONS:

In the fullness of time you came to share life with us. With the evangelist
we proclaim in awe:
         The Word became flesh and dwells among us.
In the beginning was the Word; you, O God, are timeless and your patience
is without end;
  —help the many people who are in prison for their beliefs to experience
    inner peace.
The Word was in God's presence; you, O God, are with us always;
  —may we live and work mindful of your presence, and may our own actions
    reflect your love.
The Word was God; you, O God, are wonder in the flesh;
  —assist us to respect all forms of life and to support efforts to improve the
    quality of life among the poor.

Through you, O God, all things come into being;
  —may we make time today to reflect upon your generosity to us, and to
    show compassion to those people with heavy burdens.
You are the true light, O God, that enlightens each of us;
  —shed light this day upon those places within us that cry out for healing,
    that we may find wholeness in you.

PRAYER: O Christ, you are the Word become flesh, you are our God. You
                know both the love and the struggle experienced in human families.
                Teach us to extend ourselves beyond our immediate families to
                embrace a broader vision of your gospel challenge. May this day be
                a time of reflection on our past gifts and a time of conversion to
                hear your continuous call. Amen.

DAYTIME PRAYER

(Psalms from the current weekday in the Psalter)

Ant 1   Mary and Joseph marveled at what was spoken of Jesus.

Ant 2   The mother of Jesus kept these words in her heart.

Ant 3   My eyes have seen your salvation which you have prepared in the
       presence of all peoples.

(Prayer as in Morning Prayer)

JANUARY 1

MARY, MOTHER OF GOD

EVENING PRAYER I

Ant 1   Great is your love, O God. You were born of the Virgin Mary to
       share in our humanity, so that we may become one with you in your
       divinity. (Psalm 113)

Ant 2   The Scriptures have been fulfilled, O Christ, in your birth to a
       virgin. You have come like dew upon the earth to refresh your people.
       (Psalm 147:12–20)

Ant 3   The burning bush on Sinai symbolized your faithful virginity, O Mary.
       Pray for us who look to you for help. (Eph. 1:3–10)

READING

RESPONSORY

The Word was made flesh, alleluia, alleluia. —**The Word**...
And dwelt among us, —**alleluia**...
Glory to you, Source of all Being, Eternal Word, and Holy Spirit.
  —**The Word**...

CANTICLE OF MARY

Ant   In the depth of your love for us, O God, you sent your Word, born of
      Mary, to take on mortal flesh and live under the law of Moses.

INTERCESSIONS:

Most Loving God, you sent forth Jesus to share your life with us, and so we pray:

Christ Jesus, born of Mary, hear our prayer.

Breath of Life, you continue to sustain your people;
—may we reverence the gift of life within ourselves, our companions, and all of creation.

God, our Father, you show your compassion for us in the gift of Jesus;
—may we be grateful for your mercy and extend your tenderness to those living in our midst who are oppressed.

God, our Mother, you share with us the strength and beauty of giving birth;
—may we draw upon your strength in times of birthing new energy, insight, and integrity into our institutional structures.

God of Wonder, you surprise us with the mystery of your love and joy;
—may we delight in the good humor that surrounds us and calls us to shed light where there is darkness.

Womb of God, you surround us with sustenance and life-giving water;
—may we use fruitfully the gifts of nourishment; may addicted people find hope and help this day.

PRAYER: You, O God, are the Holy One who gathers us together in the womb of our earth. May we reverence the life you give us in Jesus through Mary, our mother. We give thanks for you bring us life and salvation through Jesus, our way, our truth, and our life. We ask you to bless us as we celebrate your life with us in the name of Jesus. Amen.

MORNING PRAYER

(Psalms from Feasts and Solemnities)

Ant 1   God became the child of Mary, we have been made the children of God.

Ant 2   John saw Jesus and said: Behold the Lamb of God, who takes away the sin of the world.

Ant 3   Mary, virgin and mother, treasured in her heart what was spoken of her son, Jesus.

READING

RESPONSORY

Christ has made known our salvation, alleluia, alleluia. —**Christ**...
Salvation by our God, —**alleluia**...
Glory to you, Source of all Being, Eternal Word, and Holy Spirit. —**Christ**...

CANTICLE OF ZECHARIAH

Ant   God has renewed us by becoming one of us in Jesus. We rejoice at this wondrous work of love.

INTERCESSIONS:

A new dawn gives us joy as we celebrate Mary, Mother of God, who brings peace in Christ to all people, and so we pray:

Christ, be a sign of peace to all.

Christ, way of peace, enlighten our hearts to embrace the ways of non-violence;
   —may we resist violence within our hearts and within our homes.
Christ, giver of peace, share your gifts this day with all leaders;
   —may they find ways to pursue peaceful solutions to issues of injustice.
Christ, proclaimer of peace, enable us to speak honestly and truthfully for the
   sake of peace and justice;
      —may all peoples working in justice systems be open to the ways
      of non-violence.
Christ, sign of peace, be with us in our efforts to be women and men with
   peaceful hearts;
      —may the prayers of contemplative people bring peace to those in need
      of healing.
Christ, teacher of peace, spur us on today to take renewed steps as people
   of peace;
      —may all parents and teachers strive to show and share attitudes of peace
      with our youth.

PRAYER: You, O God, are the Holy One who gathers us together in the
             womb of our earth. May we reverence the life you give us in Jesus
             through Mary, our mother. We give thanks for you bring us life and
             salvation through Jesus, our way, our truth, and our life. We ask
             you to bless us as we celebrate your life with us in the name of
             Jesus. Amen.

DAYTIME PRAYER

Ant 1   Mary and Joseph marveled at what was spoken of Jesus. (Psalm 122)

Ant 2   Mary kept all these things, pondering them in her heart. (Psalm 127)

Ant 3   My eyes have seen your salvation, which you have prepared in the
          presence of all peoples. (Psalm 131)

(Prayer as in Morning Prayer)

EVENING PRAYER II

Ant 1   Great is your love, O God. You were born of the virgin Mary to share
          in our humanity, so that we may become one with you in your divinity.
          (Psalm 122)

Ant 2   The Scriptures have been fulfilled, O Christ, in your birth to a virgin;
          you have come like dew upon the earth to refresh your people. (Psalm
          127)

Ant 3   The burning bush on Sinai symbolizes your faithful virginity, O Mary.
          Pray for us who look to you for help. (Eph. 1:3–10)

READING

RESPONSORY

The Word was made flesh, alleluia, alleluia. —**The Word**...
And dwelt among us, —**alleluia**...
Glory to you, Source of all Being, Eternal Word, and Holy Spirit.
   —**The Word**...

CANTICLE OF MARY

Ant Blessed is your mother, O Christ, for she heard the word of God and kept it, alleluia.

INTERCESSIONS:

You are blessed among all people for you are the mother of God, and so we pray:
Christ, born of Mary, hear us.

Sun of Justice, show us new ways to be people of justice;
—may we protect the rights of peoples, animals and all creation.
You are called Wonderful, Counselor, O God; you share the wonder of life with women and men in the parenting of children;
—may we support parents of the young in word and deed.
Christ, you gladden our hearts with the announcement of salvation;
—may all who proclaim your gospel of peace receive the unction of your joy.
In Mary you found warmth, love, and nourishment for your journey among us;
—may all mothers be blessed with creative insight and wisdom and find delight in their children.
You are our comforter in time of affliction;
—be with those who are dying today and bring them to your dwelling place.

PRAYER: You, O God, are the Holy One who gathers us together in the womb of our earth. May we reverence the life you give us in Jesus through Mary, our mother. We give thanks, for you bring us life and salvation through Jesus, our way, our truth, and our life. We ask you to bless us as we celebrate your life with us in the name of Jesus. Amen.

From January 2 to Epiphany

MONDAY

(Psalms and antiphons from the current weekday in the Psalter)

MORNING PRAYER

READING

RESPONSORY

Jesus revealed in glory, alleluia, alleluia. —Jesus...
The salvation by our God, —alleluia, alleluia...
Glory to you, Source of all Being, Eternal Word, and Holy Spirit. —Jesus...

CANTICLE OF ZECHARIAH

Ant A child is given to us, the Eternal Word of God.

INTERCESSIONS:

At the name of Jesus, every knee must bend in heaven and on earth, and so we pray:
Come, let us adore.

Jesus, in your name our sins are forgiven and we are healed;
  —let your name in our minds and hearts protect us from harm.
Jesus, in your name the deaf hear, the blind see, and the dumb speak;
  —give us the grace to use our faculties with reverence, as instruments of
    praise to you.
Jesus, in your name the hungry are fed and anxious hearts are comforted;
  —teach us to share our bread, your word, and ourselves, that all may have
    what they need.
Jesus, for the sake of your name, the disciples faced suffering and death;
  —help us to endure whatever is necessary for the sake of truth and justice.

PRAYER: O God, you have called us to follow Jesus as a model of dedication
          to you. Have mercy on our weakness and give us the insight and
          strength we need to grow in grace and wisdom before you. This we
          ask in the name of Jesus. Amen.

DAYTIME PRAYER

Ant 1   Joseph and Mary, the parents of Jesus, wondered at what was said
            of him.

Ant 2   Mary, the mother of Jesus, kept all these things, pondering them in
            her heart.

Ant 3   My eyes have seen your salvation, which you have prepared in the
            presence of all people.

(Prayer as in Morning Prayer)

EVENING PRAYER

READING
RESPONSORY

The Word became flesh, alleluia, alleluia. —**The Word**...
And dwelt among us. —**alleluia**...
Glory to you, Source of all Being, Eternal Word, and Holy Spirit.
  —**The Word**...

CANTICLE OF MARY

Ant   O glorious child, you brought light and healing to us at your birth,
          coming to us like the sun rising in the east.

INTERCESSIONS:

Child of God, child of the poor, named by God: they named him Jesus.
In faith we proclaim:
          Child of Bethlehem, you are the Christ of God.

Mary and Joseph were faithful to the law; Jesus was circumcised on the eighth
  day;
  —O God, guide us to formulate laws that serve the needs of the people.
Jesus, you submitted to the rites asked of every child;
  —deliver us from the corruption of pride and vainglory.

Mary, your mother, was full of grace; Joseph was called "just";
—bless all children with good parents and guides.
Jesus, in your name your mother will suffer much; you will one day be her widow's mite;
—draw us to give all that we have to be one with you.

PRAYER: O God, you have called us to follow Jesus as a model of dedication to you. Have mercy on our weakness and give us the insight and strength we need to grow in grace and wisdom before you. This we ask in the name of Jesus. Amen.

TUESDAY

(Psalms and antiphons from the current weekday in the Psalter)

MORNING PRAYER

READING

RESPONSORY

Jesus revealed in glory, alleluia, alleluia. —Jesus. . .
The salvation by our God, —alleluia. . .
Glory to you, Source of all Being, Eternal Word, and Holy Spirit. —Jesus. . .

CANTICLE OF ZECHARIAH

Ant   The Word became flesh and dwelt among us, from whose fullness we have all received.

INTERCESSIONS:

Prophets and rulers, exiles and slaves, all people had awaited the coming of the savior. You come as a child, O Christ, and your name is Jesus, and so we pray:
Blessed be the name of Jesus.

To those who seek you with a sincere heart,
—grant the light of faith and the courage to embrace it.
To those who wait for deliverance in our prisons,
—bring peace of heart, and caring personnel that will enable their rehabilitation.
To all who serve you in the single life,
—grant the support of human companionship and the awareness of your presence.
To our hidden poor,
—give the opportunity to find adequate employment and all that is needed for their livelihood and development.

PRAYER: O God, you delight to be with the children of the earth. We know your love and we praise you for your goodness to us. Keep us open to your Spirit. Let our joy be in doing your will that we may praise you now and forever. Amen.

DAYTIME PRAYER

Ant 1 Joseph and Mary, the parents of Jesus, wondered at what was said of him.

Ant 2 Mary, the mother of Jesus, kept all these things, pondering them in her heart.

Ant 3 My eyes have seen your salvation, which you have prepared in the presence of all people.

(Prayer as in Morning Prayer)

EVENING PRAYER

READING

RESPONSORY

The Word became flesh, alleluia, alleluia. —**The Word**...
And dwelt among us —**alleluia**...
Glory to you, Source of all Being, Eternal Word, and Holy Spirit.
   —**The Word**...

CANTICLE OF MARY

Ant The presence of Jesus among us fills us with song. Our salvation has come, allelulia.

INTERCESSIONS:

Jesus, the new high priest, calls us all to share in his priesthood. We pray:
                  O God, we come to do your will.

For your church:
   —may those who are guided by your Spirit be enabled to serve as leaders.
For the people of all nations, large or small:
   —teach us to live as sisters and brothers born of your love.
For all minorities:
   —may their voices be heard and their persons be respected as children of God.
To those who plan and wait for a better future:
   —send your Spirit that they may renew the face of the earth.

PRAYER: O God, you delight to be with the children of the earth. We know your love and we praise you for your goodness to us. Keep us open to your Spirit, Let our joy be in doing your will that we may praise you now and forever. Amen.

WEDNESDAY

(Psalms and antiphons from the current weekday in the Psalter)

MORNING PRAYER

READING

RESPONSORY

Jesus revealed in glory, alleluia, alleluia. —**Jesus**...
The salvation by our God, —**alleluia**...
Glory to you, Source of all Being, Eternal Word, and Holy Spirit. —**Jesus**...

CANTICLE OF ZECHARIAH

Ant For love of us, O Christ our God, you emptied yourself and took
on our nature, restoring our humanity, alleluia.

INTERCESSIONS:

O God, you have created us and all your ways are holy. With gratitude we pray:
Make us a holy people.

You call us to unity but we are a church divided;
—break the barriers among us and bring us to truth.
The earth is yours and all it contains;
—teach us to use its resources with reverence and discipline.
You delight in all your creatures: animals and plants, fish and fowl;
—help us to share the earth with them in responsible ways.
Your rain sings the song of the heavens;
—forgive our pollution of the seas and rivers, and make us generous and
persevering in restoring and preserving them.

PRAYER: O God, you called us all to be your people, inviting us to fullness of
life and joy in your presence. Let us never forget your mercy to us
throughout the ages. Make us ever attentive to your Spirit. This we
ask in the name of Jesus who lives with you and the Spirit, now and
forever. Amen.

DAYTIME PRAYER

Ant 1 Joseph and Mary, the parents of Jesus, wondered at what was said
of him.

Ant 2 Mary, the mother of Jesus, kept all these things, pondering them
in her heart.

Ant 3 My eyes have seen your salvation, which you have prepared in
the presence of all people.

(Prayer as in Morning Prayer)

EVENING PRAYER

READING

RESPONSORY

The Word became flesh, alleluia, alleluia. —**The Word**...
And dwelt among us, —**alleluia**...
Glory to you, Source of all Being, Eternal Word, and Holy Spirit.
—**The Word**...

CANTICLE OF MARY

Ant   I have come into the world to do not my will but the will of the One who sent me.

INTERCESSIONS:

Jesus, son of God, son of David, son of Mary, you are flesh of our flesh. We pray:
O Christ, you are the glory of our race.

O Christ, you fulfilled the desires of your people;
  —deepen in us the desire for union with you.
Enslaved, your people dreamed of your coming in power;
  —let the power of your love transform the hearts of all oppressors.
Your people renewed their hope through prayer and song;
  —help us to keep alive the hope of your gospel.
The hope of your birth, O Christ, brought joy and courage;
  —let our lives incarnate your message to the world.

PRAYER: O God, you called us all to be your people, inviting us to fullness of life and joy in your presence. Let us never forget your mercy to us throughout the ages. Make us ever attentive to your Spirit. This we ask in the name of Jesus who lives with you and the Spirit, now and forever. Amen.

THURSDAY

(Psalms and antiphons from the current weekday in the Psalter)

MORNING PRAYER

READING

RESPONSORY

Jesus revealed in glory, alleluia, alleluia. —**Jesus**. . .
The salvation by our God, —**alleluia**. . .
Glory to you, Source of all Being, Eternal Word, and Holy Spirit. —**Jesus**. . .

CANTICLE OF ZECHARIAH

Ant   You have come to your people, O God, to release them from sorrow and sin.

INTERCESSIONS:

God, you hide yourself from the worldly wise and show yourself to the lowly, and so we pray to you:
Make us meek and humble of heart.

Your Spirit abides in all who believe in you;
  —teach us to listen to one another with openness and respect.
To all who labor to open to us the lessons of history,
  —send your Spirit with gifts of understanding and wisdom.
To all who share wealth, time, and talents to serve underdeveloped countries,
  —give insight and creativity in all their endeavors.
To all who are mentally ill or handicapped,
  —grant your peace and help us to facilitate a wholesome life for them.

PRAYER: God, our Creator, you have given us the freedom to choose between good and evil. Have mercy on our blindness and let the coming of Jesus enlighten us. Fill our minds with his truth and our memories with his goodness. Let our hearts be totally dedicated to you. This we ask in the name of Jesus who is our way. Amen.

DAYTIME PRAYER

Ant 1 Joseph and Mary, the parents of Jesus, wondered at what was said of him.

Ant 2 Mary, the mother of Jesus, kept all these things, pondering them in her heart.

Ant 3 My eyes have seen your salvation, which you have prepared in the presence of all people.

(Prayer as in Morning Prayer)

EVENING PRAYER

READING

RESPONSORY

The Word became flesh, alleluia, alleluia. —**The Word**...
And dwelt among us, —**alleluia**...
Glory to you, Source of all Being, Eternal Word, and Holy Spirit.
   —**The Word**...

CANTICLE OF MARY

Ant   Mary and Joseph named the child, Jesus, for he would save his people from their sins.

INTERCESSIONS:

Jesus, at your birth, angels sang of peace, and shepherds rejoiced at your coming; and now, we, your people, pray to you:
   O Christ, grant us the peace that the world cannot give.

To those who proclaim war as a way to peace,
   —grant the heart, mind and attitude of Jesus.
To those who oppose the destruction of human life in any way,
   —grant the courage of their convictions and let their efforts bear fruit.
To all who bear the wounds of war,
   —grant your peace and consolation.
For all who have died in war,
   —bless their generosity and courage with eternal life.

PRAYER: God, our Creator, you have given us the freedom to choose between good and evil. Have mercy on our blindness and let the coming of Jesus enlighten us. Fill our minds with his truth and our memories with his goodness. Let our hearts be totally dedicated to you. This we ask in the name of Jesus who is our way. Amen.

FRIDAY

(Psalms and antiphons from the current weekday in the Psalter)

MORNING PRAYER

READING

RESPONSORY

Jesus revealed in glory, alleluia, alleluia. —Jesus...
The salvation by our God, —alleluia...
Glory to you, Source of all Being, Eternal Word, and Holy Spirit. —Jesus...

CANTICLE OF ZECHARIAH

Ant   Jesus Christ came by water, blood, and Spirit.

INTERCESSIONS:

In Christ, you have called us each by name, and so we pray:
> **Open our minds to your way, your truth and your life.**

By your birth, human life is raised to a new dignity;
> —make us diligent in preserving and enabling quality of life for all.

You were sent by God, not to judge, but to bring us to new life;
> —give us the grace to hear and to live your gospel.

By your birth you filled the lives of Mary and Joseph with joy;
> —bless all who desire to have children with the gift of new life.

You were called the son of Joseph;
> —give joy and fulfillment to adopted and foster children, and bless their families.

By your birth, you revealed the fidelity of God;
> —make us worthy of your promises.

By your birth, human life is changed forever,
> —open our minds and hearts to transformation. Make us witnesses of your love.

PRAYER: O God, giver of all gifts, you clothe us with love and lead us to truth. Let us realize the wonder of your call to life. Let us respond by giving all to you and by sharing life creatively with one another. Grant this through Jesus, who lives and reigns with you, Source of all Being, and with your Holy Spirit, forever and ever. Amen.

DAYTIME PRAYER

Ant 1   Joseph and Mary, the parents of Jesus, wondered at what was said of him.

Ant 2   Mary, the mother of Jesus, kept all these things, pondering them in her heart.

Ant 3   My eyes have seen your salvation, which you have prepared in the presence of all people.

(Prayer as in Morning Prayer)

EVENING PRAYER

READING

RESPONSORY

The Word became flesh, alleluia, alleluia. —The Word...
And dwelt among us, —alleluia...
Glory to you, Source of all Being, Eternal Word, and Holy Spirit.
   —The Word...

CANTICLE OF MARY

Ant   The Spirit descended upon Jesus, and a voice from heaven proclaimed:
You are my beloved; with you I am well pleased.

INTERCESSIONS:

Jesus, named by an angel, you will be obedient unto death. We pray:
   Your law, O God, is a light to our path.
Jesus, born a helpless child, cared for by Mary and Joseph,
   —have compassion on children who are abused. Heal them and those who
   abuse them.
Jesus, mighty in God's love for you,
   —enlighten all who look upon themselves with disdain. Let them know your
   love and care.
Jesus, marked by circumcision a child of Israel,
   —claim us as your own. Make us true disciples.
Jesus, open to life and death, given totally to God's will,
   —make us fearless in following you.

PRAYER: O God, giver of all gifts, you clothe us with love and lead us to
truth. Let us realize the wonder of your call to life. Let us respond
by giving all to you and by sharing life creatively with one another.
Grant this through Jesus, who lives and reigns with you, Source of
all Being, and with the Holy Spirit, forever and ever. Amen.

SATURDAY

(Psalms and antiphons from the current weekday in the Psalter)

MORNING PRAYER

READING

RESPONSORY

Jesus revealed in glory, alleluia, alleluia. —Jesus...
The salvation by our God, —alleluia...
Glory to you, Source of all Being, Eternal Word, and Holy Spirit. —Jesus...

CANTICLE OF ZECHARIAH

Ant   You are the One of whom the prophets wrote: In Israel the Anointed One
is born; eternal will be your reign.

INTERCESSIONS:

You, O Christ, are just and all your ways are holy; we pray to you:
You have the words of eternal life.

By your coming, you break through the clouds of our darkness;
—help us to know and to live the truth that is our peace.
By your coming you brought a marvelous love into the world;
—heal the wounds of the past, and let us run toward the lure of God's call.
By your coming you conquer sin and death;
—give us the courage to stop the flow of anger and revenge by returning
good for evil.
By your coming you revealed the equality of all women and men;
—guide us to the unity that you share with God.

PRAYER: O God, you sent Jesus to save us and to teach us to love one
another. Heal our prejudices; expand our hearts. Give us a hunger
to see the beauty and goodness that you see in us. Let the birth of
Jesus be a new birth for us, that we may be children in whom you
are well pleased. This we ask in Jesus' name. Amen.

DAYTIME PRAYER

Ant 1   Joseph and Mary, the parents of Jesus, wondered at what was said
of him.

Ant 2   Mary, the mother of Jesus, kept all these things, pondering them
in her heart.

Ant 3   My eyes have seen your salvation, which you have prepared in
the presence of all people.

(Prayer as in Morning Prayer)

EPIPHANY

EVENING PRAYER I

Ant 1   Begotten before the daystar and before the ages, Jesus our savior
has appeared this day to our world. (Psalm 135, I)

Ant 2   Your light has come, Jerusalem; the glory of our God has risen
upon you; the nations shall walk by your light, alleluia.
(Psalm 76)

Ant 3   That star, like a flame of fire, pointed the way to God, Ruler of
rulers; the Magi saw the star and brought their gifts in homage.

Canticle   1 Timothy 3:16

Praise our Savior, all you nations.
Christ manifested in the flesh,
Christ justified by the Spirit.

Praise our Savior, all you nations.
Christ seen by the angels,
Christ proclaimed to unbelievers.

Praise our Savior, all you nations.
Christ believed in by the world,
Christ taken up in glory.

Praise our Savior, all you nations.
Glory. . .

READING

RESPONSORY

All humankind will be blessed in Jesus, people of every race. —**All
humankind**...
Every nation will glorify Christ, —**people of**...
Glory to you, Source of all Being, Eternal Word, and Holy Spirit.
   —**All humankind**...

CANTICLE OF MARY

Ant   The Magi, seeing the star, said to one another, "This is the sign of the
      great king! Let us go and seek him, bringing him our gifts of gold,
      frankincense and myrrh, alleluia."

INTERCESSIONS:

Led by the light of a star, magi came to worship the child. In our longing for truth
let us pray:

Guide all who seek you, O God.

Creator of the world, complete the work which you have begun;
   —help us to hear and live the message of Jesus.
God of the nations, you see us all as your children;
   —draw us to unity that mirrors your own.
Source of all truth, you dwell within us, the light of our minds;
   —let us never silence your voice.
Word of God made flesh, the magi adored you in a Child;
   —help us to recognize you in one another.
Eternal God, you know our needs and you care for us;
   —help us to see the things that you see.

PRAYER: Lord Jesus, you are the star inviting all nations to fullness of life.
          Give us the wisdom to follow you and to lead others to walk in your
          light. This we ask in your name. Amen.

MORNING PRAYER

(Psalms from Feasts and Solemnities)

Ant 1   The magi worshiped the child and offered him their treasures of gold,
        frankincense, and myrrh, alleluia.

Ant 2   Bless God, seas and rivers; springs and fountains exalt God forever,
        alleluia.

Ant 3   Arise, shine, O Jerusalem, for your light has come, the glory of God;
        nations shall come to your light, alleluia.

READING

RESPONSORY

All the rulers of the earth will come to adore. —**All the rulers**...
Men and women of every nation, —**will come**...
Glory to you, Source of all Being, Eternal Word, and Holy Spirit.
   —**All the rulers**...

CANTICLE OF ZECHARIAH

Ant This day earth unites with heaven, for Christ has become one with us and has revealed God's glory to the people.

INTERCESSIONS:

Jesus, son of God, son of Mary, you are the glory of our race. To you we pray:
Come and set us free.

You are the revelation of God to us;
—help us to be your revelation to one another.
Splendor of God's glory, you came as a child;
—teach us to see you in the great and the small.
Your light drew the magi to a foreign land;
—open our minds to new insights, new vision.
Your parents received the magi with the courtesy of the poor;
—be with us as we encourage those who seek you.

PRAYER: Lord Jesus, you are the star inviting all nations to fullness of life. Give us the wisdom to follow you and to lead others to walk in your light. This we ask in your name. Amen.

DAYTIME PRAYER

Ant 1 Rise in splendor, Jerusalem! Your light is come, the glory of our God has dawned upon you.

Ant 2 Raise your eyes, see, they all gather and come to you; your sons come from afar, and your daughters rise up at your side.

Ant 3 All shall come bearing gold, frankincense and myrrh, and proclaiming the praises of God.

(Prayer as in Morning Prayer)

EVENING PRAYER II

Ant 1 Jesus, our peace, you come in glory; you are ruler of all the earth, alleluia. (Psalm 110:1–5, 7)

Ant 2 Daylight has dawned upon God's people; you, O Christ, bring us grace, mercy, and justice, alleluia. (Psalm 112)

Ant 3 All nations shall come and worship you, for your justice has been revealed, allelulia. (Rev. 15:3–4)

READING

RESPONSORY

All humankind will be blessed in Jesus, people of every race. —**All humankind...**
Every nation will glorify Christ, —**people of...**
Glory to you, Source of all Being, Eternal Word, and Holy Spirit.
—**All humankind...**

CANTICLE OF MARY

Ant   Seeing the star the magi were filled with joy; and entering the house, they offered the child gold, frankincense, and myrrh, alleluia.

INTERCESSIONS:

Led by the light of a star, magi came to worship the child. In our longing for truth let us pray:

Guide all who seek you, O God.

Creator of the world, complete the work which you have begun;
  —help us to hear and live the message of Jesus.
God of the nations, you see us all as your children;
  —draw us to unity that mirrors your own.
Source of all truth, you dwell within us, the light of our minds;
  —let us never silence your voice.
Word of God made flesh, the magi adored you in a child;
  —help us to recognize you in one another.
Eternal God, you know our needs and you care for us;
  —help us to see the things that you see.

PRAYER: Lord Jesus, you are the star inviting all nations to fullness of life. Give us the wisdom to follow you and to lead others to walk in your light. This we ask in your name. Amen.

MONDAY

(Psalms and antiphons from the current weekday in the Psalter)

MORNING PRAYER

READING

RESPONSORY

All the rulers of the earth will come to adore. —**All**. . .
Women and men of every nation, —**will**. . .
Glory to you, Source of all Being, Eternal Word, and Holy Spirit —**All**. . .

CANTICLE OF ZECHARIAH

Ant   From the East the magi came to worship the Savior, offering gold to Christ our Ruler, frankincense to Christ our God, and myrrh to Christ our Redeemer, alleluia.

INTERCESSIONS:

The Word became flesh bringing light out of darkness. Come let us adore:

Glory to you, O God.

Your light, O Christ, means life to us;
  —make us bearers of life to others.
Your light, O Christ, reveals the mysteries of God to us;
  —help us to recognize the "gifts of God."

Your light, O Christ, brings healing to our hearts;
  —teach us to be compassionate with one another.
Your light, O Christ, brings peace to the world;
  —have mercy on us lest we cloud it with conflict.

PRAYER: Jesus, you light our way through the centuries; you guide us day by
           day. Give us the courage to remain steadfast in our commitment to
           you when our weakness darkens the way. We ask this in your holy
           name. Amen.

DAYTIME PRAYER

Ant 1   Rise in splendor, Jerusalem! Your light is come, the glory of our God
        has dawned upon you.

Ant 2   Raise your eyes, see, they all gather and come to you; your sons come
        from afar, and your daughters rise up at your side.

Ant 3   All shall come bearing gold, frankincense and myrrh, and proclaiming
        the praises of God.

(Prayer as in Morning Prayer)

EVENING PRAYER

READING

RESPONSORY

All humankind will be blessed in Jesus, people of every race.
—**All**. . .
Every nation will glorify Christ, —**people of**. . .
Glory to you, Source of all Being, Eternal Word, and Holy Spirit. —**All**. . .

CANTICLE OF MARY

Ant   When the magi saw the star, they rejoiced; going into the house, they
      offered the child gifts: gold, frankincense, and myrrh, alleluia.

INTERCESSIONS:

Jesus, the Sun of Justice, is born for our salvation. We pray to him::
                    Draw us, O Christ, we will follow you.
In your light our sins are forgiven and we are healed;
  —help us to forgive one another.
In your light all who seek will find you;
  —deliver us from all that blinds us to you.
In your light our hope is renewed and nourished;
  —teach us how to encourage one another.
In your light the poor discover the way to fullness of life;
  —teach us to discern and cherish true human values.
Your light is eternal;
  —keep us faithful to your teaching.

PRAYER: Jesus, you light our way through the centuries, you guide us day by day. Give us the courage to remain steadfast in our commitment to you when our weakness darkens the way. We ask this in your holy name. Amen.

TUESDAY

(Psalms and antiphons from the current weekday in the Psalter)

MORNING PRAYER

READING
RESPONSORY

All the rulers of the earth will come to adore. —**All**. . .
Women and men of every nation, —**will**. . .
Glory to you, Source of all Being, Eternal Word, and Holy Spirit —**All**. . .

CANTICLE OF ZECHARIAH

Ant   The magi offered the child their treasures, alleluia.

INTERCESSIONS:

Jesus, Word made flesh, you came bringing peace, yet rulers would seek to destroy you. Hear us as we pray:

Have mercy on us.

Your peace, O Christ, is a challenge to our lethargy;
   —call us again to be your disciples.
In your peace, O Christ, we can hear the voice of your Spirit;
   —make us faithful to your call.
In your peace, O Christ, we die and rise daily;
   —give us the courage to live this mystery.
Your peace, O Christ, is peace the world cannot give;
   —let our lives be open to your gifts.

PRAYER: Jesus, our Savior, you knew the homage of the wise and the wrath of rulers. Bless all who must flee from their homeland. Guide and protect those who are displaced by war or poverty. Show us the way to justice for all. This we ask in your name and through the intercession of those who have given their lives for the sake of others. Amen.

DAYTIME PRAYER

Ant 1   Rise in splendor, Jerusalem! Your light is come, the glory of our God has dawned upon you.

Ant 2   Raise your eyes, see, they all gather and come to you; your sons come from afar, and your daughters rise up at your side.

Ant 3   All shall come bearing gold, frankincense and myrrh, and proclaiming the praises of God.

(Prayer as in Morning Prayer)

EVENING PRAYER

READING

RESPONSORY

All humankind will be blessed in Jesus, people of every race. —**All**...
Every nation will glorify Christ, —**people**...
Glory to you, Source of all Being, Eternal Word, and Holy Spirit. —**All**...

CANTICLE OF MARY

Ant   Christ, our Light, when you dawned upon the nations, the magi offered
you their gifts, alleluia.

INTERCESSIONS:

Jesus, Word made flesh, is revealed to the shepherds and the sages; let us praise
God as we say:

           O God, we long to see your face.

Christ Jesus, you reveal yourself to the singlehearted;
   —help us to seek and to do your will all the days of our lives.
You promise your fullness to the poor in spirit;
   —help us to hear the cry of the poor.
You chose to live among the poor and the lowly;
   —make us humble of heart.
You answer all who call upon you;
   —let us walk in the way of your mercy.

PRAYER: Jesus, our Savior, you knew the homage of the wise and the wrath
of rulers. Bless all who must flee from their homeland. Guide and
protect those who are displaced by war or poverty. Show us the
way to justice for all. This we ask in your name and through the
intercession of those who have given their lives for the sake of
others. Amen.

WEDNESDAY

(Psalms and antiphons from the current weekday in the Psalter)

MORNING PRAYER

READING

RESPONSORY

All the rulers of the earth will come to adore. —**All**...
Women and men of every nation, —**will**...
Glory to you, Source of all Being, Eternal Word, and Holy Spirit —**All**...

CANTICLE OF ZECHARIAH

Ant   We have seen the star in the East, and have come to worship the Savior.

INTERCESSIONS:

A Child is born for us; God has visited the people of the earth. Let us pray:

Come, let us adore.

Word of God, you came to save us, born in a stable;

—teach us to see you in the poor and lowly.

You came to make all things new;

—liberate us from the prison of the familiar.

You revealed yourself to magi from a foreign land;

—save us from our hidden prejudices.

Visitors from the East brought you royal gifts;

—help us to give you the best of our lives.

PRAYER: Jesus, our Savior, you came as a child to bring new life to the world. Open our minds and hearts to the message of your life. Transform our lives and make us instruments of your peace. Grant this through the power of your name. Amen.

DAYTIME PRAYER

Ant 1   Rise in splendor, Jerusalem! Your light is come, the glory of our God has dawned upon you.

Ant 2   Raise your eyes, see, they all gather and come to you; your sons come from afar, and your daughters rise up at your side.

Ant 3   All shall come bearing gold, frankincense and myrrh, and proclaiming the praises of God.

(Prayer as in Morning Prayer)

EVENING PRAYER

READING

RESPONSORY

All humankind will be blessed in Jesus, people of every race.

—**All**...

Every nation will glorify Christ, —**people of**...

Glory to you, Source of all Being, Eternal Word, and Holy Spirit. —**All**...

CANTICLE OF MARY

Ant   The magi said to Herod: We saw the star of the Savior rise in the East; its brightness fills the heavens and the earth.

INTERCESSIONS:

The Word of God has come to satisfy the longing of all people from ages past. With one voice let us pray:

Be praised forever, O Christ.

Through your coming, Christ Jesus, we know the way to fullness of life;

—teach us to be poor in spirit.

Through your coming, Christ Jesus, we see the face of God;

—teach us to see you in one another.

Through your coming, Christ Jesus, we share the Bread of Life;

—give us the courage to share your cross.

Through your coming, Christ Jesus, our sins are forgiven, our lives renewed;
—we thank and praise you for your mercy and love.

PRAYER: Jesus, our Savior, you came as a child to bring new life to the
world. Open our minds and hearts to the message of your life.
Transform our lives and make us instruments of your peace. Grant
this through the power of your name. Amen.

THURSDAY

(Psalms and antiphons from the current weekday in the Psalter)

MORNING PRAYER

READING

RESPONSORY

All the rulers of the earth will come to adore. —**All**...
Women and men of every nation, —**will**...
Glory to you, Source of all Being, Eternal Word, and Holy Spirit —**All**...

CANTICLE OF ZECHARIAH

Ant   All nations will come from afar bearing their gifts, alleluia.

INTERCESSIONS:

Jesus is born in Bethlehem. Angels sing and shepherds adore; let us join them as we
say:

Glory to God in the highest!

We praise you, O God, in the gift of Jesus, our way;
—keep us ever true to his teaching.
We praise you in the angels and saints;
—following their example, may we also lead others to you.
We praise you for the daily bread of life that you give us;
—give us the wisdom to nourish and support one another.
We praise you for your constant mercy;
—fill our minds with understanding and our hearts with compassion.

PRAYER: O God, we marvel at your goodness to us. We are the work of your
hands and you invite us to labor with you in building the city of
God. Keep us faithful to you, and may our service be worthy of our
calling. Grant this in the name of Jesus who lives with you and the
Holy Spirit. Amen.

DAYTIME PRAYER

Ant 1   Rise in splendor, Jerusalem! Your light is come, the glory of our God
has dawned upon you.

Ant 2   Raise your eyes, see, they all gather and come to you; your sons come
from afar, and your daughters rise up at your side.

Ant 3   All shall come bearing gold, frankincense and myrrh, and proclaiming the praises of God.

(Prayer as in Morning Prayer)

EVENING PRAYER

READING

RESPONSORY

All humankind will be blessed in Jesus, people of every race.
—**All**...
Every nation will glorify Christ, —**people of**...
Glory to you, Source of all Being, Eternal Word, and Holy Spirit. —**All**...

CANTICLE OF MARY

Ant   All are coming from every land! They bear gold and frankincense, alleluia.

INTERCESSIONS:

God guides the humble to truth; God protects the stranger. In gratitude we pray:
Loving Guardian of us all, may you be praised forever.

Jesus, our brother, you loved the poor and lived among them;
—help us to serve those who cannot support themselves.
Jesus, faithful friend, grazing animals first befriended you and your parents;
—teach us to respect the animals of our world and give them the care and space they need.
A rocky cave housed you and straw gave you rest;
—help us to give our planet, its plants, rocks, and all of its substance the reverence that we owe to all that you have created.
You were the son of a carpenter and you labored with your hands;
—bless all people with labor and wages sufficient for a wholesome life.

PRAYER: O God, we marvel at your goodness to us. We are the work of your hands and you invite us to labor with you in building the city of God. Keep us faithful to you, and may our service be worthy of our calling. Grant this in the name of Jesus who lives with you and the Holy Spirit. Amen.

FRIDAY

(Psalms and antiphons from the current weekday in the Psalter)

MORNING PRAYER

READING

RESPONSORY

All the rulers of the earth will come to adore. —**All**...
Women and men of every nation, —**will**...
Glory to you, Source of all Being, Eternal Word, and Holy Spirit —**All**...

CANTICLE OF ZECHARIAH

Ant   Those who were once in darkness will come to adore you.

INTERCESSIONS:

Jesus, your law is love and your gospel is peace. Savior of the world we sing to you:
Come and set us free.

By the power of your life you raised the human race to new dignity;
  —help us to free all women and men who are denied their human rights.
By the power of your love you taught us that love is stronger than death;
  —give us the courage to risk our lives, if necessary, to be faithful to you.
Your power is just and merciful;
  —give us leaders who are capable, honest, and compassionate.
By the power of your death and resurrection, you have overcome the world;
  —help us to hope and to give hope to others.

PRAYER: O God of peace and love, you raise up the lowly and call sinners to
repentance. Heal our weakness and show us how to use our gifts for
the good of others. Transform our lives that we, too, may live by
the power of love. Grant this that your reign may be manifest even
in this our day and for all eternity. Amen.

DAYTIME PRAYER

Ant 1   Rise in splendor, Jerusalem! Your light is come, the glory of our God
has dawned upon you.

Ant 2   Raise your eyes, see, they all gather and come to you; your sons come
from afar, and your daughters rise up at your side.

Ant 3   All shall come bearing gold, frankincense and myrrh, and proclaiming
the praises of God.

(Prayer as in Morning Prayer)

EVENING PRAYER

READING

RESPONSORY

All humankind will be blessed in Jesus, people of every race.
—**All**...
Every nation will glorify Christ, —**people of**...
Glory to you, Source of all Being, Eternal Word, and Holy Spirit. —**All**...

CANTICLE OF MARY

Ant   Warned in a dream, the magi departed to their own country by another
way.

INTERCESSIONS:

Bountiful God, all that you do is done with love. In joy we sing of your care:
God has done marvelous deeds for us.

You are our God, and you call us to union with you;
   —lead us out of our selfishness—we cannot do it alone.
You are our Creator, and you share this world with us;
   —help us to heal the inequities that scar our society.
You sent your Word, not to judge, but to call us to fullness of life;
   —teach us how to take your message to the ends of the earth.
You are love, O God, and those who seek you live in you;
   —fill our hearts with longing, that, living in you, we may reveal your love
    in our lives.

PRAYER: O God of peace and love, you raise up the lowly and call sinners to repentance. Heal our weakness and show us how to use our gifts for the good of others. Transform our lives that we, too, may live by the power of love. Grant this that your reign may be manifest even in this our day and for all eternity. Amen.

SATURDAY

(Psalms and antiphons from the current weekday in the Psalter)

MORNING PRAYER

READING

RESPONSORY

All the rulers of the earth will come to adore. —**All**...
Women and men of every nation, —**will**...
Glory to you, Source of all Being, Eternal Word, and Holy Spirit —**All**...

CANTICLE OF ZECHARIAH

Ant   Jesus worked the first of his signs at Cana in Galilee, and manifested his glory; his disciples believed in him.

INTERCESSIONS:

Jesus Christ, born of a woman, has revealed the love of God to us. Let us pray:
      Savior of the world, come and set us free.

O God, you called a humble virgin to be the mother of the savior;
   —help us to respond to your call as Mary did.
Magi, persecution, and exile wove a cloak of mystery around the child;
   —give us the faith to live the questions in our lives.
You sent a savior for all the nations, yet many do not know you;
   —inspire teachers and preachers to take the gospel to the whole world.
O God, you sent a savior to give us life;
   —have mercy on the dying and those who are in pain.

PRAYER: Mother and God, God and Father, you revealed yourself to us in Jesus, our brother. You call us to recognize all humanity as your children, our sisters and brothers. Help us to reverence each other. May the diversity that exists among us not be a cause of division but of enrichment. Grant this in Jesus' name. Amen

DAYTIME PRAYER

Ant 1   Rise in splendor, Jerusalem! Your light is come, the glory of our God has dawned upon you.

Ant 2   Raise your eyes, see, they all gather and come to you; your sons come from afar, and your daughters rise up at your side.

Ant 3   All shall come bearing gold, frankincense and myrrh, and proclaiming the praises of God.

(Prayer as in Morning Prayer)

BAPTISM OF THE LORD JESUS

EVENING PRAYER I

Ant 1   Today is the mystery, hidden from all ages, revealed to us. (Psalm 135, I)

Ant 2   Arise, Jerusalem, your light is come and the glory of our God is risen upon you, alleluia. (Psalm 100)

Ant 3   Today, when Jesus was baptized in the Jordan, a voice from the clouds thundered: This is my Beloved, in whom I am well pleased.

Canticle   1 Timothy 3:16

Praise our Savior, all you nations.
Christ manifested in the flesh,
Christ justified by the Spirit.

Praise our Savior, all you nations.
Christ seen by the angels,
Christ proclaimed to unbelievers.

Praise our Savior, all you nations.
Christ believed in by the world,
Christ taken up in glory.

Praise our Savior, all you nations.
Glory. . .

READING

RESPONSORY

O Christ, anointed of God, hear the plea of your people. —**O Christ**. . .
Let living water flow for them, —**hear**. . .
Glory to you, Source of all Being, Eternal Word, and Holy Spirit.
    —**O Christ**. . .

CANTICLE OF MARY

Ant   Our Savior came to John to be baptized in the Jordan. Through these cleansing waters we are restored to new life, our sinful nature is healed, and we are clothed in holiness.

INTERCESSIONS:

Jesus was baptized in the river Jordan by John, and the heavens opened. We cry out in expectation:

Come, Holy Spirit.

Jesus, beloved of God, you were led by the Spirit throughout your mission;
    —teach us to follow that same Spirit on our way through life.

Jesus, Word of God, you embraced our humanity totally;
—help us to live your gospel and so transform our lives.
Jesus, son of Mary, you left your family and home to proclaim God's love;
—draw us to follow you in the service of others.
Jesus, sent by God to teach us, you went to John as a disciple to a master;
—teach us to respect all people, whatever their age or state in life.
Jesus, our Savior, you allowed John to cover you with the waters of baptism;
—give us a spirit of reverence that we may heal and encourage one another.

PRAYER: Jesus, sent by God to save us, you so loved the world that your every deed was inspired by the Holy Spirit. Your mission was God's mission, and you gave your life to fulfill it. Teach us to listen to the Spirit in our hearts. Help us to love as you have loved us that we may continue your mission. We ask this in your name. Amen.

MORNING PRAYER

(Psalms from Feasts and Solemnities)

Ant 1   In those days, Jesus came from Nazareth of Galilee and was baptized in the Jordan, alleluia.

Ant 2   When Jesus came out of the water, the heavens opened and the Spirit descended upon him, alleluia.

Ant 3   Rivers of water were made holy as Christ Jesus revealed the glory of our God to the world, alleluia.

READING

RESPONSORY

Lord Jesus Christ, have mercy on us. —**Lord**...
Make known your ways to us, —**have**...
Glory to you, Source of all Being, Eternal Word, and Holy Spirit. —**Lord**...

CANTICLE OF ZECHARIAH

Ant   You springs and fountains, rivers and seas, clap your hands, for your Creator has manifested a sign of salvation in you.

INTERCESSIONS:

The Holy Spirit hovered over Jesus and a voice declared him the beloved One of God. We pray to him:
Blessed be God who comes to save us.

Jesus, servant of God, you listened to the Spirit and were led to the Jordan to be baptized;
—open our minds and hearts to your call to conversion.
Jesus, Word made flesh, you listened to the Spirit and were led to the desert to prepare for your mission;
—teach us to pray that our ministry may proclaim the good news of the fullness of life.

Jesus, savior of us all, you listened to the Spirit and encouraged John in his time of doubt;

 —help us to live the truth of our own baptism so deeply that we may be guides to one another.

Jesus, our peace, you listened to the spirit and were covered with the waters of the Jordan;

 —bless all who are dying and enfold them in your mercy.

PRAYER: Jesus, sent by God to save us, you so loved the world that your every deed was inspired by the Holy Spirit. Your mission was God's mission, and you gave your life to fulfill it. Teach us to listen to the Spirit in our hearts. Help us to love as you have loved us that we may continue your mission. We ask this in your name. Amen.

DAYTIME PRAYER

Ant 1 When Jesus had been baptized and was praying, the heavens were opened.

Ant 2 You purged our guilt by fire and the Holy Spirit. We praise you, our God and Savior.

Ant 3 John bore witness: I saw the Spirit descend as a dove from heaven and it remained on him.

(Prayer as in Morning Prayer)

EVENING PRAYER II

Ant 1 A wondrous mystery has been made manifest this day. We praise you, our God! Alleluia. (Psalm 110: 1–5, 7)

Ant 2 We have seen and have borne witness, this is the anointed of God, alleluia. (Psalm 112)

Ant 3 Seas and rivers, mountains and hills, all you living creatures sing with us the praises of our God, alleluia. (Rev. 15:3–4)

READING

RESPONSORY

Jesus comes in water, blood and Spirit. —Jesus...
The Christ who saves us, —in water...
Glory to you, Source of all Being, Eternal Word, and Holy Spirit. —Jesus...

CANTICLE OF MARY

Ant The one on whom the Spirit descends and remains, this is the one who baptizes with the Holy Spirit.

INTERCESSIONS:

Jesus was baptized in the river Jordan by John, and the heavens opened, and so we pray:

Come, Holy Spirit.

Jesus, beloved of God, you were led by the Spirit throughout your mission;
—teach us to follow that same Spirit on our way through life.
Jesus, Word of God, you embraced our humanity totally;
—help us to live your gospel and so transform our lives.
Jesus, son of Mary, you left your family and home;
—draw us to follow you in the service of others.
Jesus, sent by God to teach us, you went to John as a disciple to a master;
—teach us to respect all people, whatever their age or state in life.
Jesus, our savior, you allowed John to cover you with the waters of baptism;
—give us a spirit of reverence that we may heal and encourage one another.

PRAYER: Jesus, sent by God to save us, you so loved the world that your every deed was inspired by the Holy Spirit. Your mission was God's mission, and you gave your life to fulfill it. Teach us to listen to the Spirit in our hearts. Help us to love as you have loved us that we may continue your mission. We ask this in your name. Amen.

February 2

PRESENTATION OF THE LORD JESUS

EVENING PRAYER I

Ant 1 The parents of Jesus brought him to Jerusalem to present him to God according to the Law of Moses. (Psalm 113)

Ant 2 Open your hearts, people of God, to receive your redeemer. (Psalm 147:12–20)

Ant 3 Simeon and Anna, prophets of God, gave witness to Christ, the fulfillment of God's promises. (Phil. 2:6–11)

READING

RESPONSORY

You reveal, O God, your salvation for us. —**You**...
In the sight of all you have prepared —**your**...
Glory to you, Source of all Being, Eternal Word, and Holy Spirit. —**You**...

CANTICLE OF MARY

Ant You, Most High, have prepared your salvation in the presence of all the people.

INTERCESSIONS:

Mary and Joseph brought Jesus to the temple to be presented to God. Let us pray:
Christ, be our light.

Jesus, light of the world, you revealed the love of God to us;
—let our lives lead others to the truth of God's mercy.
Jesus, longed for savior, you are presented with the gifts of the poor;
—help us to dedicate our lives to those in need.

Jesus, child of mystery, your mother's heart was pierced by prophecy;
   —strengthen all women whose dedication to you brings pain and sorrow.
Jesus, child of promise, Simeon had waited and prayed for your coming;
   —give us patience and hope as we pray for the fulfillment of your gospel.
Jesus, joy of all who seek God, Anna had given you lifelong service;
   —bless the aging and teach us how to give them joy and encouragement.

PRAYER: Bountiful God, you are father and mother to us. You receive the
dedication of the infant Son, Jesus, with two turtle doves. You
inspire aged Simeon and Anna to bless and announce his mission. O
gentle, strong God, we rejoice in your care for us. Help us to draw
those who turn away from you in fear. Let the saving light of Jesus
bring truth and peace to our world. This we ask in his name.
Amen.

MORNING PRAYER

(Psalms from Feasts and Solemnities)

Ant 1   Simeon, just and devout, looked for the consolation of Israel.

Ant 2   Inspired by the Holy Spirit, they received the child in their arms
and gave thanks to God.

Ant 3   Anna gave thanks to God for the child and spoke of him to all who
were looking for the redemption of Jerusalem.

READING

RESPONSORY

We adore you, O God, and bow down before you. **—We**...
We sing your praise, **—and**...
Glory to you, Source of all Being, Eternal Word, and Holy Spirit. **—We**...

CANTICLE OF ZECHARIAH

Ant   You grant peace to your servant, O God, according to your word.

INTERCESSIONS:

Jesus was presented in the temple; Anna and Simeon gave praise to God. Let us
proclaim:

God has come to save us.

Jesus, you were dedicated to God in the temple, and Simeon blessed you;
   —have mercy on children who have no one to guide them in the path of
   holiness.
Jesus, hope of the ages, women and men of good will prayed for and longed for
you for generations;
   —show your compassion to all who are exiled or cut off from their roots.
Jesus, light of the world, your people longed for freedom;
   —enlighten and change the hearts of governments that enslave others.
Jesus, infant son, you embraced our human helplessness;
   —bless all who are in need, and fill us all with compassion for them.

PRAYER: Bountiful God, you are father and mother to us. You receive the
dedication of the infant Son, Jesus, with two turtle doves. You
inspire aged Simeon and Anna to bless and announce his mission. O
gentle, strong God, we rejoice in your care for us. Help us to draw
those who turn away from you in fear. Let the saving light of Jesus
bring truth and peace to our world. This we ask in his name.
Amen.

DAYTIME PRAYER

Ant 1   You have prepared in the presence of all, a light of revelation to the
nations.

Ant 2   Blessed are you, O God, who have fulfilled your word to your people.

Ant 3   The child Jesus grew and became strong, and the favor of God was
upon him.

(Prayer as in Morning Prayer)

EVENING PRAYER II

Ant 1   It had been revealed to Simeon by the Holy Spirit that he should not see
death before he saw the Christ of God.

Ant 2   Simeon prayed: Your salvation is a light of revelation to the nations and
the glory of your people.

Ant 3   Joseph and Mary marveled at what was said about the child.

READING

RESPONSORY

You reveal, O God, your salvation for us. —**You**. . .
In the sight of all, you have prepared —**your**. . .
Glory to you, Source of all Being, Eternal Word, and Holy Spirit. —**You**. . .

CANTICLE OF MARY

Ant   This day, Mary brought the child Jesus into the temple.

INTERCESSIONS:

Mary and Joseph brought Jesus to the temple to be presented to God. Let us pray to
him:

Christ, be our light.

Jesus, light of the world, you revealed the love of God to us;
—let our lives lead others to the truth of God's mercy.
Jesus, longed for savior, you are presented with the gifts of the poor;
—help us to dedicate our lives to those in need.
Jesus, child of mystery, your mother's heart was pierced by prophecy;
—strengthen all women whose dedication to you brings pain and sorrow.
Jesus, child of promise, Simeon had waited and prayed for your coming;
—give us patience and hope as we pray for the fulfillment of your gospel.

Jesus, joy of all who seek God, Anna had given you lifelong service;
—bless the aging and teach us how to give them joy and encouragement.

PRAYER: Bountiful God, you are father and mother to us. You receive the
dedication of the infant Son, Jesus, with two turtle doves. You
inspire aged Simeon and Anna to bless and announce his mission. O
gentle, strong God, we rejoice in your care for us. Help us to draw
those who turn away from you in fear. Let the saving light of Jesus
bring truth and peace to our world. This we ask in his name.
Amen.

ASH WEDNESDAY

(Psalms as in Friday, Week III in psalter)

MORNING PRAYER

Ant 1   Rend your hearts and not your garments.

Ant 2   You, O God, are slow to anger and rich in compassion.

Ant 3   A contrite, humble heart, O God, you will not spurn.

READING

RESPONSORY

Spare us, O God, and have pity on your people. —**Spare**...
We have sinned against you, —**have pity**...
Glory to you, Source of all Being, Eternal Word, and Holy Spirit.
—**Spare**...

CANTICLE OF ZECHARIAH

Ant   When you fast, do not look gloomy like the hypocrites.

INTERCESSIONS:

We pray that we will be filled with the Holy Spirit, that our hearts will be renewed,
and our vision clarified in love, and so we ask:

O loving Creator, fill us with your Spirit.

O God, grant that we may be sensitive to your presence in our lives,
—by taking time to pause for reflection and remembrance.
May we use the freedom you have given us,
—to liberate those with burdens too heavy to bear.
Give us world leaders who govern with integrity and honesty,
—so that all people may live their lives in peaceful environments.
Strengthen our inner resources with your power,
—that we may grow in gentleness when our lives are confronted
with difficulties.
Be with those who are terminally ill,
—and grant them peace of mind as they await your coming.

PRAYER: As we begin Lent, O holy God, strengthen us in our endeavors against evil. Bless our efforts to live in union with you and all the people of the world. Help us to discover whatever interferes with loving each other. We ask this in union with all people who begin this season in your name. Amen.

DAYTIME PRAYER

Ant 1 The season of deliverance has come; the time of salvation is at hand.

Ant 2 Turn to me with all your heart, says our God.

Ant 3 Believing in God's strength and mercy, let us be fortified with patience.

(Prayer as in Morning Prayer)

EVENING PRAYER

Ant 1 Wash me from my guilt and cleanse me of my sin.

Ant 2 I acknowledge my offense; my sins are before me always.

Ant 3 I turn to you, O God, and seek your salvation.

READING

RESPONSORY

Have mercy on me, O God, in your goodness. —Have...
In the greatness of your compassion, wipe out my offense; —**O God**...
Glory to you, Source of all Being, Eternal Word, and Holy Spirit. —**Have**...

CANTICLE OF MARY

Ant A clean heart create for me, O God, and a steadfast spirit renew within me.

INTERCESSIONS:

O God, giver of life, we ask during this lenten time to be united with the suffering, death and resurrection of Jesus. We raise our hearts to you in prayer:
Draw us ever closer to you.

O God, you desire peace and harmony for all;
—comfort those who are experiencing the devastation of war.
Your Christ healed the sick and forgave sins;
—bless all in this world who relieve physical and psychological pain.
Through the ministry of Jesus, the poor were fed and the blind given sight;
—refresh all those who continue to work with the helpless and the needy.
Strengthen all those dedicated to your service;
—that their lives may give witness to your love and compassion.
You look with gracious mercy on all who seek you;
—ease the burdens of the elderly and all who are in need of your help.

PRAYER: Make us reconciled to you, O God, that we may put on the holiness of Christ and give you glory. Help us to live this season as true disciples on our way to transformation and fullness of life. Grant this as we journey to you with Jesus, our brother. Amen.

THURSDAY AFTER ASH WEDNESDAY

(Antiphons and psalms as in Psalter for Thursday, Week IV)

MORNING PRAYER

READING

RESPONSORY

Spare us, O God, and have pity on your people. —**Spare**...
We have sinned against you, —**have pity**...
Glory to you, Source of all Being, Eternal Word, and Holy Spirit.—**Spare**...

CANTICLE OF ZECHARIAH

Ant   Happy are they who walk in your ways.

INTERCESSIONS:

O God, we pray that we may grow in your Spirit during these days of Lent
and so we say:

Renew our hearts and fill us with your love.

May leaders of nations choose life for their people,
  —that all may have employment, food and shelter for their families.
May church leaders choose life for the faithful,
  —that consciences be not burdened but formed to make reflective decisions.
May parents choose life for their children,
  —that they may grow in wisdom and reverence for others.
May all peoples of this earth choose life for our planet,
  —that our natural resources may be preserved and all species continue
    to exist.
May all of us choose life now and for all time,
  —that we may live in your presence for all eternity.

PRAYER: O God, grant us the strength to bear our sufferings and our
              weaknesses. Help us to carry our burdens with a renewed faith and
              continued belief in your love for us. Give us lightness of heart and
              compassion for those we live and work with. This we ask in Jesus'
              name. Amen.

DAYTIME PRAYER

Ant 1   The season of deliverance has come; the time of salvation is at hand.

Ant 2   Turn to me with all your heart, says our God.

Ant 3   Believing in God's strength and mercy, let us be fortified with patience.

(Prayer as in Morning Prayer)

EVENING PRAYER

READING

RESPONSORY

Have mercy on me, O God, in your goodness. —**Have**...
In the greatness of your compassion, wipe out my offense; —**O God**...
Glory to you, Source of all Being, Eternal Word, and Holy Spirit. —**Have**...

CANTICLE OF MARY

Ant   Happy are they who delight in God's law and meditate on it night
and day.

INTERCESSIONS:

In your mercy look on us with kindness. Hear our prayer as we say:
Increase our faith and fill us with your Spirit.

God of compassion, look with tender mercy on all who grieve the loss of a
loved one;
—comfort them in their affliction.
God of wisdom, inspire scientists and those engaged in research,
—to find cures for fatal illnesses and to promote quality of human life
in ethical ways.
God of the universe, give us a lively curiosity,
—that we may explore the planets and the atoms in ways that benefit all of
creation.
God of providence, order our minds and hearts,
—that our daily choices will further the coming of your reign on earth.
God of the living, receive those who die this day,
—that they may see you face to face.

PRAYER: O God, grant us the strength to bear our sufferings and our
weaknesses. Help us to carry our burdens with a renewed faith and
continued belief in your love for us. Give us lightness of heart and
compassion for those we live and work with. This we ask in Jesus'
name. Amen.

FRIDAY AFTER ASH WEDNESDAY

(Antiphons and psalms as in Psalter for Friday, Week IV)

MORNING PRAYER

READING

RESPONSORY

Spare us, O God, and have pity on your people. —**Spare**...
We have sinned against you, —**have pity**...
Glory to you, Source of all Being, Eternal Word, and Holy Spirit.—**Spare**...

CANTICLE OF ZECHARIAH

Ant   A broken, humble heart, O God, you will not scorn.

INTERCESSIONS:

During this lenten season, O God, you enlighten us to walk in truth and love. Lead us to share the blessings we receive with others. We pray:
			Guide us into the paths of goodness.

Uplift those who suffer the anguish of mental illness,
	—and fill those who care for them with strength and compassion.
Inspire lawyers and judges to be just in all circumstances,
	—so that the welfare of all may become their main concern.
Liberate all men and women who are suffering persecution,
	—help them to be faithful and fill them with the love that conquers hatred.
Dissipate our inertia of mind and body;
	—strengthen our efforts toward wholeness.

PRAYER:	O God, in your gentle way, free us from the sin that keeps us bound to the familiar and the comfortable. May the light of Easter joy encourage us in the way of discipleship. We ask this in the name of Jesus who died for us and was raised to new life. Amen.

DAYTIME PRAYER

Ant 1	The season of deliverance has come; the time of salvation is at hand.

Ant 2	Turn to me with all your heart, says our God.

Ant 3	Believing in God's strength and mercy, let us be fortified with patience.

(Prayer as in Morning Prayer)

EVENING PRAYER

READING

RESPONSORY

Have mercy on me, O God, in your goodness. —**Have**...
In the greatness of your compassion, wipe out my offense; —**O God**...
Glory to you, Source of all Being, Eternal Word, and Holy Spirit. —**Have**...

CANTICLE OF MARY

Ant	Save your servant who trusts in you.

INTERCESSIONS:

O God, accept our lenten efforts. May they bear fruit in the ways we relate to others and to our planet. Fill us with your compassion and tenderness as we say:
			Cleanse us and heal our brokenness.

Grant to artists, musicians, and writers,
	—the ability to lift our hearts to the Source of all harmony and beauty.
Give parents patience, tolerance and happiness,
	—as they meet the daily challenge of their problems and possibilities.
Instill in each of us the desire to be responsible,
	—for the preservation of all living things within our environment.
Enkindle within our hearts,
	—a cheerfulness of spirit as we approach each day.

PRAYER: O God, in your gentle way, free us from the sin that keeps us bound to the familiar and the comfortable. May the light of Easter joy encourage us in the way of discipleship. We ask this in the name of Jesus who died for us and was raised to new life. Amen.

SATURDAY AFTER ASH WEDNESDAY

(Antiphons and psalms as in Psalter for Saturday, Week IV)

MORNING PRAYER

READING

RESPONSORY

Spare us, O God, and have pity on your people. —**Spare**. . .
We have sinned against you, —**have pity**. . .
Glory to you, Source of all Being, Eternal Word, and Holy Spirit.—**Spare**. . .

CANTICLE OF ZECHARIAH

Ant God will renew your strength.

INTERCESSIONS:

God of abundant life, you call us to become a loving people. We pray with confidence:

Give us your Holy Spirit.

You are life for our searching minds;
—give wisdom and insight to educators.
You are love for our hungry hearts;
—help us to be patient with our brokenness.
You are the truth that sets us free;
—help those seeking truth to bring integrity and accuracy to the media.
You are the dawn when the night is over;
—welcome into your joy all those who have died.

PRAYER: God, our Creator, as we fast and pray and share our resources with those in need, may we find in ourselves a renewed dedication to walk in the way of truth as Jesus has taught us. We ask this in his name. Amen.

DAYTIME PRAYER

Ant 1 The season of deliverance has come; the time of salvation is at hand.
Ant 2 Turn to me with all your heart, says our God.
Ant 3 Believing in God's strength and mercy, let us be fortified with patience.

(Prayer as in Morning Prayer)

SUNDAY—Weeks 1 to 4

(Antiphons and psalms from the current week in the Psalter)

EVENING PRAYER I

READING
RESPONSORY

My soul waits for God; in your word I hope. —**My**...
For with you there is steadfast love, —**in your word**...
Glory to you, Source of all Being, Eternal Word, and Holy Spirit. —**My**...

CANTICLE OF MARY

Sun. 1 Jesus was in the wilderness forty days, and was tempted by Satan.

Sun. 2 I will indeed bless you, and I will multiply your descendants as the stars of heaven and as the sands on the shore.

Sun. 3 God said to Moses: Strike the rock, and water shall come out of it, that the people may drink!

Sun. 4 The Most High is my shepherd; I shall dwell in the house of God all the days of my life.

INTERCESSIONS: Sundays 1 and 3

Let us praise Jesus Christ, bread of life and living water. In homage we pray:
You alone are holy.

By your prayer and fasting,
  —teach us to rid our lives of all that blinds us to your Holy Spirit.
By your faithfulness to the word of God,
  —help us to keep your gospel alive and meaningful in our culture.
You revealed yourself to the woman at the well and she became your disciple
  announcing your truth to the others;
  —let the voices of women be heard in your church, that your message to
    them may be given to the world.
You are the temple destroyed by human hands;
  —help us to remember that we are temples of the Holy Spirit.

INTERCESSIONS: Sundays 2 and 4

Let us praise God who at various times and places is revealed to us. Let us rejoice
in the revelation of Jesus. In God's presence let us acclaim:
It is good for us to be here.

You called Abraham to serve you with obedience and love and did not allow the
  death of his son;
  —teach us to discern what is pleasing to you, always keeping the welfare
    and rights of others in mind.
You chose David, a youthful shepherd, to lead your people;
  —help us to look beyond outward appearances as we choose our leaders.
You made Jesus a vessel of your healing love;
  —show us how to reach out to the sick in healing ways, with respect and
    reverence.
You sent manna for your people to eat in the desert,
  —let your word nourish our minds and enkindle our hearts toward the
    transformation of our lives.

PRAYER

Sun. 1 Jesus, our Savior, you bore hunger, thirst, and temptation as you prepared to preach the good news to your people. You offer the bread of heaven and living water to those who hear you with faith. During this holy season of Lent, let us hunger and thirst anew for your word. Grant us all that we need to be totally dedicated to you, that we may live with you forever. Amen.

Sun. 2 O God, we praise you for your call to renew our lives during this season of Lent. Make us ready and eager to accept your invitation to grow. We confess our weakness and ask for new strength to serve you more faithfully. Let our efforts be pleasing to you. This we ask through Jesus, who is our way, our truth, and our life. Amen.

Sun. 3 O God, you shepherd us with tender care and you draw us to yourself in a covenant of love. Help us to heed the words of Jesus to follow the call of your Spirit. Let this season of Lent be a turning point in our lives toward greater fidelity to you. We ask this in Jesus' name. Amen.

Sun. 4 O God, you are our light and without you, all our ways are darkness. Heal our blindness and lead us to the light of your truth. Help us to overcome all that keeps us from following your commandments. During this season of Lent, may we grow in love for you and for one another. This we ask through Christ Jesus, the light of the world. Amen.

MORNING PRAYER

READING

RESPONSORY

Christ, Chosen One of the living God, have mercy on us. —**Christ**...
Delivered up to death on a cross, —**have mercy**...
Glory to you, Source of all Being, Eternal Word, and Holy Spirit. —**Christ**...

CANTICLE OF ZECHARIAH

Sun. 1 You shall worship God alone; you shall serve only your God.

Sun. 2 If God is for us, who can be against us?

Sun. 3 To those who are called, Christ is the power of God.

Sun. 4 Once you were in darkness, but now you are light in Christ Jesus.

INTERCESSIONS: Sundays 1 and 3

Let us praise Jesus Christ, model of faithfulness, hope of our salvation.
With sincere hearts we pray:

O Christ, guide us to truth.

You knew the burden of temptation;
  —make us strong in resisting evil.
You drove away those who desecrated the temple of God;
  —help us to make our worship pleasing to you and a blessing for all.
Moses was called to lead his people to water in the desert;
  —lead those who thirst for truth to the words of the gospel.

You taught your disciples patience and long-suffering;
  —teach us to set aside our own convenience and comfort to enable the
    growth of others.

INTERCESSIONS: Sundays 2 and 4

As Moses lifted up the serpent in the desert, so Jesus was lifted up on the cross for
our salvation. In homage we pray:
                    We adore you, O Christ.
Whoever believes in you will not be condemned;
  —we do believe, help our unbelief.
You have come to reconcile us to God and to one another;
  —make us effective ambassadors of your mission of peace.
You seek out those who are lost, forgiving us again and again;
  —let our lives so mirror your compassion that those who are wounded by
    sin will be drawn to you.
Your mercy reached out to all in need;
  —bless the sick and the dying; let them know your presence.

PRAYER

Sun. 1 Jesus, our Savior, you bore hunger, thirst, and temptation as you prepared
to preach the good news to your people. You offer the bread of heaven
and living water to those who hear you with faith. During this holy
season of Lent, let us hunger and thirst anew for your word. Grant us
all that we need to be totally dedicated to you, that we may live with
you forever. Amen.

Sun. 2 O God, we praise you for your call to renew our lives during this season of
Lent. Make us ready and eager to accept your invitation to grow. We
confess our weakness and ask for new strength to serve you more
faithfully. Let our efforts be pleasing to you. This we ask through Jesus,
who is our way, our truth, and our life. Amen.

Sun. 3 O God, you shepherd us with tender care and you draw us to yourself in
a covenant of love. Help us to heed the words of Jesus to follow the call
of your Spirit. Let this season of Lent be a turning point in our lives
toward greater fidelity to you. We ask this in Jesus' name. Amen.

Sun. 4 O God, you are our light and without you, all our ways are darkness.
Heal our blindness and lead us to the light of your truth. Help us to
overcome all that keeps us from following your commandments. During
this season of Lent, may we grow in love for you and for one another.
This we ask through Christ Jesus, the light of the world. Amen.

DAYTIME PRAYER

Ant 1 The season of deliverance has come; the time of salvation is at hand.

Ant 2 Turn to me with all your heart, says our God.

Ant 3 Believing in God's strength and mercy, let us be fortified with patience.

(Prayer as in Morning Prayer)

EVENING PRAYER II

READING

RESPONSORY

My soul waits for God; in your word I hope. —**My**...
For with you there is steadfast love, —**in your word**...
Glory to you, Source of all Being, Eternal Word, and Holy Spirit. —**My**...

CANTICLE OF MARY

Sun. 1 The time is fulfilled, the reign of God is at hand; repent and believe the good news.

Sun. 2 Jesus took Peter, James and John, and led them up a high mountain where he was transfigured before them.

Sun. 3 Jesus knew human nature and needed no one to explain it to him; he, himself, knew what was in the human heart.

Sun. 4 Jesus said: I have come into the world that those who do not see may be given light.

INTERCESSIONS: Sundays 1 and 3

Let us praise Jesus Christ who calls us to worship in spirit and in truth.
With confidence we ask:
                          Teach us to pray.

You turned away from the honor of this world;
   —help us to seek only the glory that is your presence in our lives.
You seek to satisfy the deepest longings of the human heart;
   —help us to discern what is of real value in our lives.
You called tax collectors and sinners to conversion by your care for them;
   —help us to remember your unfailing love and follow you with a new heart.
After your Transfiguration, you set your face toward Jerusalem;
   —may times of consolation and insight renew us and give us courage.

INTERCESSIONS: Sundays 2 and 4

O God, you are rich in mercy, sending leaders and prophets, and your Eternal
Word to lead us to life. With hope and trust we pray:
                   We will serve you all the days of our lives.

You have called us out of darkness to be light in Jesus Christ;
   —soften our hardened hearts, and call us again during this season of Lent.
O God, you rejoice at the conversion of one sinner,
   —give us the grace to give every person the reverence due your people.
O God, you gave us a law of live to enable us to live as sisters and brothers;
   —help us to grow in grace and truth that choosing life may be the law of our lives.
Abraham and Sarah believed and you made them the founders of your people;
   —give us faith in you that will bear fruit a hundredfold in your service.

PRAYER

Sun. 1 Jesus, our Savior, you bore hunger, thirst, and temptation as you prepared to preach the good news to your people. You offer the bread of heaven and living water to those who hear you with faith. During this holy season of Lent, let us hunger and thirst anew for your word. Grant us all that we need to be totally dedicated to you, that we may live with you forever. Amen.

Sun. 2 O God, we praise you for your call to renew our lives during this season of Lent. Make us ready and eager to accept your invitation to grow. We confess our weakness and ask for new strength to serve you more faithfully. Let our efforts be pleasing to you. This we ask through Jesus, who is our way, our truth, and our life. Amen.

Sun. 3 O God, you shepherd us with tender care and you draw us to yourself in a covenant of love. Help us to heed the words of Jesus to follow the call of your Spirit. Let this season of Lent be a turning point in our lives toward greater fidelity to you. We ask this in Jesus' name. Amen.

Sun. 4 O God, you are our light and without you, all our ways are darkness. Heal our blindness and lead us to the light of your truth. Help us to overcome all that keeps us from following your commandments. During this season of Lent, may we grow in love for you and for one another. This we ask through Christ Jesus, the light of the world. Amen.

MONDAY—Weeks 1 to 4

(Antiphons and psalms from the current week in the Psalter)

MORNING PRAYER

READING

RESPONSORY

Spare us, O God, and have pity on your people. —**Spare**...
We have sinned against you, —**have pity**...
Glory to you, Source of all Being, Eternal Word, and Holy Spirit. —**Spare**...

CANTICLE OF ZECHARIAH

Week 1 You shall be holy, as I, your God, am holy.

Week 2 To you, O God, belong mercy and forgiveness.

Week 3 Now I know that there is no God but you in all the earth.

Week 4 For behold, I create a new heaven and a new earth.

INTERCESSIONS: Week 1 and 3

We praise you, O Christ, for your fidelity unto death. We cry out in hope:
  Fill us with the fullness of life.

You count as done to you all that we do for others;
  —help us to love others as you love them.

You did not spare yourself in the service of those in need;
>—show us the way to spend ourselves for others, for their welfare and your glory.

You bore insult and abuse from the people of your own town,
>—teach us to respect people and things that are familiar to us, ever open to hidden truths.

You came to set us free from our small ideas and from our limited notions of God;
>—let your forgiving love and healing word enlighten our minds and change our hearts.

INTERCESSIONS: Weeks 2 and 4

Jesus Christ, you have shown us the narrow gate and promised that it is the entrance to life. With trust we pray:
>**Lead us and we will follow.**

You showed us the way of mercy and compassion;
>—give us understanding and patience with the weaknesses of others.

You had pity on public sinners and shared their ignominy;
>—enlighten governments that claim an eye for an eye and a life for a life.

You call us to conversion to life, not to death,
>—enlighten our lenten efforts that they may enrich our lives and give praise to you.

For a father's faith, you healed a child: increase our faith;
>—let our belief be a sharing in your life and healing ministry.

PRAYER

Week 1 O God, we thank you for your mercy and love. Your law of love guides our way, and your mercy heals and restores our courage. Help us to persevere in our lenten efforts to serve you more faithfully. This we ask through Jesus who showed us the way. Amen.

Week 2 O God, you keep your merciful covenant of love with us even when we sin and fail you generation after generation. During this lenten season, as we renew our efforts to serve you and to love one another, give us the grace we need to persevere in our resolutions. Free us from all that separates us from you; help us to follow the way of Jesus, your incarnate Word, who lives with you in the unity of the Holy Spirit. Amen.

Week 3 O God, each morning we awaken anew to your gift of life. In this season of Lent grant us also the gift of renewed fervor in following your way of truth and love. Give us the mind and heart of Jesus and never let us be separated from you. We ask this in his name. Amen.

Week 4 O God, be with us during this season of Lent as we seek to serve you more faithfully. Bless our country and our world. Enlighten our leaders; make them instruments of your peace. Bless all in research; reward their efforts with healing for our people and regeneration for our environment. Let this be a time of salvation for us and of glory and praise to you. We ask this in Jesus' name. Amen.

DAYTIME PRAYER

Ant 1   The season of deliverance has come; the time of salvation is at hand.

Ant 2   Turn to me with all your heart, says our God.

Ant 3   Believing in God's strength and mercy, let us be fortified with patience.

(Prayer as in Morning Prayer)

EVENING PRAYER

READING

RESPONSORY

Have mercy on me, O God, in your goodness. —**Have**...
In the greatness of your compassion wipe out my offense, —**O God**...
Glory to you, Source of all Being, Eternal Word, and Holy Spirit. —**Have**...

CANTICLE OF MARY

Week 1   Come and receive your inheritance, for I was hungry and you gave me food; I was thirsty and you gave me drink.

Week 2   Give and it shall be given to you; for the measure you give will be the measure you receive.

Week 3   Jesus came to Nazareth and spoke to the people in the synagogue.

Week 4   The royal official believed the word that Jesus spoke to him and went his way.

INTERCESSIONS: Weeks 1 and 3

When the Word made flesh comes again in glory, we will stand before your holiness. We cry out to you:

Have mercy on us on that day.

Jesus, you come each day in glory, your Spirit abides in our hearts;
   —help us to minister to those in need.
Jesus, you bless those who clothe the naked and shelter the homeless;
   —bless, too, our fashion-conscious culture, and enlighten our use of our resources.
Jesus, our spirits, hungry and thirsty for your inspiration, are weakened by our own selfishness;
   —break through the resistance of our fears and apathy; renew our will and strength to serve you.
Jesus, you care for the least of us as well as the greatest;
   —heal our pride; dissolve our prejudices; let us love as we are loved.

INTERCESSIONS: Weeks 2 and 4

Jesus has come, creating a new heaven and a new earth; let us praise him saying:
O Christ, all your works are wonderful.

By your life among us you have taught us how to live;
   —during this season of Lent, let us put aside all that keeps us from being your disciples.

You sought out what was lost; you blessed the poor in spirit;
—hear us as we plead for zeal and direction for without you we can do
nothing.
Only you are just and all your ways are holy;
—forgive us for our self-righteous ways; let us see ourselves in truth.
You guard the weak and care for the lowly;
—have pity on all children who have no one to care for them; help us to
come to their aid.

PRAYER

Week 1 O God, we thank you for your mercy and love. Your law of love guides
our way, and your mercy heals and restores our courage. Help us to
persevere in our lenten efforts to serve you more faithfully. This we
ask through Jesus who showed us the way. Amen.

Week 2 O God, you keep your merciful covenant of love with us even when we
sin and fail you generation after generation. During this lenten season,
as we renew our efforts to serve you and to love one another, give us
the grace we need to persevere in our resolutions. Free us from all that
separates us from you; help us to follow the way of Jesus, your
incarnate Word, who lives with you in the unity of the Holy Spirit.
Amen.

Week 3 O God, each morning we awaken anew to your gift of life. In this season
of Lent grant us also the gift of renewed fervor in following your way
of truth and love. Give us the mind and heart of Jesus and never let us
be separated from you. We ask this in his name. Amen.

Week 4 O God, be with us during this season of Lent as we seek to serve you more
faithfully. Bless our country and our world. Enlighten our leaders;
make them instruments of your peace. Bless all in research; reward
their efforts with healing for our people and regeneration for our
environment. Let this be a time of salvation for us and of glory and
praise to you. We ask this in Jesus' name. Amen.

TUESDAY—Weeks 1 to 4

(Antiphons and psalms from the current week in the Psalter)

MORNING PRAYER

READING

RESPONSORY

Spare us, O God, and have pity on your people. —**Spare**...
We have sinned against you, —**have pity**...
Glory to you, Source of all Being, Eternal Word, and Holy Spirit. —**Spare**...

CANTICLE OF ZECHARIAH

Week 1 The word that goes forth from my mouth shall not return to
me empty.

Week 2   Cease to do evil, learn to do good; seek justice, correct oppression; defend the orphan, plead for the helpless.

Week 3   Deliver us by your marvelous works, O God, and give glory to your name.

Week 4   I saw the water issuing from the temple, flowing from the temple to renew the world.

INTERCESSIONS: Weeks 1 and 3

Let us praise God who forgives us our sins and gives us the power to forgive one another. In gratitude we pray:

May you be blessed forever, O God.

Jesus, you reveal God to us as father and mother;
  —help us to respond with confidence and love.
Jesus, you teach us to ask for our daily bread;
  —give us the generosity to share what we have with those in need.
Jesus, you were put to the test; you were delivered into the hands of evil;
  —give us the wisdom to shun evil and to choose what is good for ourselves and others.
Jesus, you prayed for the fidelity of your disciples;
  —pray for us that we will stand firm in time of trial.

INTERCESSIONS: Weeks 2 and 4

God promises forgiveness: though your sins are like scarlet, they shall be as white as snow. Let us pray with confidence:

Save us, O God.

Jesus, your yoke is easy and your burden is light;
  —show us the way to live your gospel in sincerity and truth.
Jesus, you did not seek a name or place of honor;
  —help us to simplify our lives and the trends of our culture.
Jesus, you were persecuted for healing on the sabbath;
  —console and enlighten those who are called to choose between law and mercy.
O God, you hear our secret prayer, you are present to us always;
  —help us to remember your love and to live in hope in times of doubt and pain.

PRAYER

Week 1   God, our Creator, you care for us with the love of a father and a mother. You know our weakness, and you raise us up. You know our strength, and you challenge us to grow. Teach us to love and forgive one another with patience and good will. Make us worthy to be called your children. We ask this in the name of Jesus, our brother. Amen.

Week 2   O God, no sin is so great that it cannot be forgiven when we come to you in faith. In times of doubt, help us to see that the whole world is a message of your sustaining love. You do not leave us orphans. You are present to our every thought and desire. Help us to let you fill our lives with grace and to draw us to the fullness of joy, that we may live with you forever and ever. Amen.

Week 3   O God, you have created us all, and all that we have belongs to you. Help us to share what we now have, to heal old wounds, and to free one another from the bondage of debt. Raise up leaders for the nations and for the church who will bring us to unity and peace. This we ask in the name of Jesus who promised peace the world cannot give. Amen.

Week 4   O God, in this season of Lent, we recall the suffering of Jeusus. Our pain and struggle is very present to us. Help us to remember the power of Jesus' resurrection, that eye has not seen nor ear heard what you have prepared for those who love you. Help us to persevere in our service to you and to one another. We ask this in Jesus' name, who is our companion on the way. Amen.

DAYTIME PRAYER

Ant 1   The season of deliverance has come; the time of salvation is at hand.

Ant 2   Turn to me with all your heart, says our God.

Ant 3   Believing in God's strength and mercy, let us be fortified with patience.

(Prayer as in Morning Prayer)

EVENING PRAYER

READING

RESPONSORY

Have mercy on me, O God, in your goodness. —**Have**...
In the greatness of your compassion wipe out my offense, —**O God**...
Glory to you, Source of all Being, Eternal Word, and Holy Spirit. —**Have**...

CANTICLE OF MARY

Week 1   If you forgive the sins of others, God will forgive you.

Week 2   Those who exalt themselves will be humbled; those who humble themselves will be exalted.

Week 3   You must forgive from your heart those who wrong you as God forgives you.

Week 4   Jesus said: "Do you want to be healed? Rise, take up your mat and walk."

INTERCESSIONS: Weeks 1 and 3

O God, a contrite and humble heart is pleasing to you, more than holocausts of rams on your altars. We pray to you, saying:
> **We praise you for your mercy.**

Jesus, those who trust in you are never disappointed;
  —teach us to realize our limitations and to live in peace with the limitations of others.

Jesus, you teach us to forgive our sisters and brothers seventy-times seven times;
  —help us to bring peace to the world by being nonjudgmental toward one another.

Jesus, you call us to abide in you as branches on the vine;
  —guide us in our efforts to live the truths of your gospel.
Jesus, we did not choose you; you have chosen us to follow you;
  —make us generous and creative in sharing the gift of your word.

INTERCESSIONS: Weeks 2 and 4

Eternal life is knowing God, and Jesus Christ whom God has sent, and so we pray:
  Christ Jesus, you have the words of eternal life.

You taught your disciples to pray in your name;
  —in your name, we ask for the grace to persevere in your love.
You spoke the truth in love; your words were words of life;
  —help us to guard our tongue by using the gift of speech with responsibility
  and reverence.
You were held in derision and contempt;
  —teach us how to serve the outcasts of society, and how to respect and
  accept their gifts.
You hid from those who would destroy you and falsify your message;
  —come to the aid of those who are abused by the misuse of law and who
  have no one to defend them.

PRAYER

Week 1   God, our Creator, you care for us with the love of a father and a
          mother. You know our weakness, and you raise us up. You know our
          strength, and you challenge us to grow. Teach us to love and forgive
          one another with patience and good will. Make us worthy to be called
          your children. We ask this in the name of Jesus, our brother. Amen.

Week 2   O God, no sin is so great that it cannot be forgiven when we come to
          you in faith. In times of doubt, help us to see that the whole world is a
          message of your sustaining love. You do not leave us orphans. You are
          present to our every thought and desire. Help us to let you fill our lives
          with grace and to draw us to the fullness of joy, that we may live with
          you forever and ever. Amen.

Week 3   O God, you have created us all, and all that we have belongs to you.
          Help us to share what we now have, to heal old wounds, and to free
          one another from the bondage of debt. Raise up leaders for the nations
          and for the church who will bring us to unity and peace. This we ask
          in the name of Jesus who promised peace the world cannot give.
          Amen.

Week 4   O God, in this season of Lent, we recall the suffering of Jeusus. Our
          pain and struggle is very present to us. Help us to remember the power
          of Jesus' resurrection, that eye has not seen nor ear heard what you
          have prepared for those who love you. Help us to persevere in our
          service to you and to one another. We ask this in Jesus' name, who is
          our companion on the way. Amen.

WEDNESDAY—Weeks 1 to 4

MORNING PRAYER

READING

RESPONSORY

Spare us, O God, and have pity on your people. —**Spare**...
We have sinned against you, —**have pity**...
Glory to you, Source of all Being, Eternal Word, and Holy Spirit. —**Spare**...

CANTICLE OF ZECHARIAH

Week 1 Create in me a clean heart, O God, and put a new spirit within me.

Week 2 One who wishes to be great must serve the needs of all.

Week 3 Moses said to the people: Give heed to the statutes and ordinances
I teach you and do them, that you may live.

Week 4 Sing for joy, O heavens, and exult, O earth; break forth, O mountains,
into song.

INTERCESSIONS: Weeks 1 and 3

Jesus, you are the sign of Jonah; death will not destroy you, and so we proclaim:
Glory and praise to you.

You came with truth and healing, but the crowds asked for a sign;
—open our eyes to the life-giving message of the gospel.
You ministered to all who came to you;
—help us to see through our prejudices and free ourselves to serve all people.
You suffered from the dullness of your apostles and the unbelief of the crowds;
—strengthen us when our labor seems fruitless and we doubt your call.
Remember all who have brought your word to us: our parents, teachers, clergy,
religious, and friends;
—let them know the gift of God they have been to us.

INTERCESSIONS: Weeks 2 and 4

Jesus came not to be served but to serve and to give his life as a ransom for many.
We cry out to you:
O Christ, you are the savior of the world.

Your call is a call to service;
—inspire people of all ages to work in your vineyard.
Bless those who are difficult to serve, those who harm themselves, and the
people who minister to them;
—may they have the courage to trust and the willingness to endure.
Bless our families; give them the material sustenance they need;
—enable them to hear your word and keep it with a joyful spirit.
Bless the aging and the dying;
—help us to make their last years a time of contentment and peace.

PRAYER

Week 1 O God, our hearts are longing for your peace, and the whole world cries out for justice and mercy. During this season of Lent, give us the grace to deepen our efforts to make peace among ourselves. Let us fan the flames of justice so that the starving will be fed, the naked clothed, and all in need will know your saving power. We ask this in the name of Jesus who lived and walked among us. Amen.

Week 2 Jesus, you came among us as a servant, lording it over no one, wielding only the power of love. Help us to care as much for the concerns of others as we do for our own. Let us hear your voice in every cry for help; to think your thoughts, and love what pleases you. This we ask through the power of your holy name. Amen.

Week 3 O God, you created all things, the great and the small. Your care extends to all. During this season of Lent, help us to see your sustaining presence everywhere. Teach us to live responsibly, sharing the gifts of creation with discipline and reverence as well as with satisfaction and joy. Grant this through Jesus, your Word of life, who teaches us the way. Amen.

Week 4 Christ Jesus, to follow you is to follow the way of the cross to new life. In this season of Lent, give us the grace to take up the challenge of each day and to live as your faithful disciples. Strengthen us when we waver and help us to persevere in our efforts to grow. Through our lives let the world hear your words and see your good works. May all one day live with you forever in the unity of the Holy Trinity. Amen.

DAYTIME PRAYER

Ant 1 The season of deliverance has come; the time of salvation is at hand.

Ant 2 Turn to me with all your heart, says our God.

Ant 3 Believing in God's strength and mercy, let us be fortified with patience.

(Prayer as in Morning Prayer)

EVENING PRAYER

READING

RESPONSORY

Have mercy on me, O God, in your goodness. —**Have**...
In the greatness of your compassion wipe out my offense, —**O God**...
Glory to you, Source of all Being, Eternal Word, and Holy Spirit. —**Have**...

CANTICLE OF MARY

Week 1 As Jonah became a sign for the people of Nineveh, so will the Christ be a sign to this generation.

Week 2 Jesus said: "You do not know what you ask. Are you able to drink the cup I am to drink?"

Week 3 Till heaven and earth pass away, nothing will pass from the law until all is accomplished.

Week 4 Even if a mother forgets her child and be without tenderness, I will never forget you, says our God.

INTERCESSIONS: Weeks 1 and 3

Jesus is the fulfillment of the law; his love is everlasting. Let us pray with confidence:

Christ Jesus, lead us on the path of salvation.

Jesus, you are never alone; God is always with you;
—help us to realize the presence of God in our lives.
You came to cast fire on the earth;
—enkindle in our hearts a love that bears fruit in service and praise.
You came that we might have life, now and forever;
—awaken us to our responsibility to build a world based on justice and compassion.
Jesus, you are the way, the truth, and the life;
—come to the aid of those who search for meaning in life.

INTERCESSIONS: Weeks 2 and 4

The goodness and kindness of God follows us all the days of our lives. With trust in your word we pray:

O God, all our hope is in your promise.

Jesus, your days were long with work and prayer;
—free those who must labor beyond their strength.
You are the living bread come down from heaven;
—help us to discern those things that nourish us and those that destroy our bodies and minds.
You reign from the cross but your realm is not of this world;
—give men and women the courage and creativity to lead our nations in ways of peace and justice.
Jesus, your word is a light for our way; you know our weakness;
—send your Spirit to those who interpret your gospel, lest they burden the consciences of those seeking truth.

PRAYER

Week 1 O God, our hearts are longing for your peace, and the whole world cries out for justice and mercy. During this season of Lent, give us the grace to deepen our efforts to make peace among ourselves. Let us fan the flames of justice so that the starving will be fed, the naked clothed, and all in need will know your saving power. We ask this in the name of Jesus who lived and walked among us. Amen.

Week 2 Jesus, you came among us as a servant, lording it over no one, wielding only the power of love. Help us to care as much for the concerns of others as we do for our own. Let us hear your voice in every cry for help; to think your thoughts, and love what pleases you. This we ask through the power of your holy name. Amen.

Week 3   O God, you created all things, the great and the small. Your care extends to all. During this season of Lent, help us to see your sustaining presence everywhere. Teach us to live responsibly, sharing the gifts of creation with discipline and reverence as well as with satisfaction and joy. Grant this through Jesus, your Word of life, who teaches us the way. Amen.

Week 4   Christ Jesus, to follow you is to follow the way of the cross to new life. In this season of Lent, give us the grace to take up the challenge of each day and to live as your faithful disciples. Strengthen us when we waver and help us to persevere in our efforts to grow. Through our lives let the world hear your words and see your good works. May all one day live with you forever in the unity of the Holy Trinity. Amen.

THURSDAY—Weeks 1 to 4

(Antiphons and psalms from the current week in the Psalter)

MORNING PRAYER

READING

RESPONSORY

Spare us, O God, and have pity on your people. —**Spare**...
We have sinned against you, —**have pity**...
Glory to you, Source of all Being, Eternal Word, and Holy Spirit. —**Spare**...

CANTICLE OF ZECHARIAH

Week 1   Ask and it will be given you; seek and you will find; knock and it will be opened to you.

Week 2   Amend your ways and your doings and do not trust in deceptive words, says our God.

Week 3   Obey my voice; I will be your God and you shall be my people.

Week 4   My judgment is just because I seek not my own will but the will of the One who sent me.

INTERCESSIONS: Weeks 1 and 3

You, O Christ, have come to call sinners and not the just. With contrite hearts we pray:

Be merciful for we have sinned.

You call us to turn from sin through persons, events and inner urgings;
   —strengthen us in the way of your truth.
You were led by the Spirit into the wilderness;
   —give us courage to face the emptiness of our lives.
You call us to works of justice and mercy;
   —let us see your face in the poor and homeless.
By your passion and death you have opened the gates of heaven;
   —draw to yourself all those who have died.

INTERCESSIONS: Weeks 2 and 4

Christ is at work in our hearts through the energy of the Spirit, renewing the face of the earth, and so we pray:

Let us walk each day in love.

We remember those whose search for justice has led to the cross;
—strengthen them in the light of the resurrection.
You taught us wisdom by using examples from daily life;
—bless all teachers dedicated to youth.
Free us from the love of self,
—to bring our gifts into the service of humanity.
May leaders of nations work in harmony for the good of the earth;
—be for all the way, the truth, and the life.

PRAYER

Week 1 God of mercy, as we begin this season of Lent, opening ourselves to your grace, we ask that you will guide us into a true change of heart and reorientation of our lives. We ask this in the name of Jesus. Amen.

Week 2 We are aware, O God, of our sin which inhibits a free response to your grace and word. We confess our failures but look to the promise given to us in the death and resurrection of Jesus. As we share his cross, may we share his glory. We ask this in his name. Amen.

Week 3 O Christ, you have taught us to let go and to love to the end, persevering to the other side of death which is resurrection. During this lenten season, call us to prayer that will make our hearts ready for this depth of love. We ask this grace in your name. Amen.

Week 4 O God, you have given us this life to know you, to love you and to be at home with you. Help us to experience you in our hearts as we find you anew in the works and deeds of Jesus. This we ask through Jesus who is our way to you. Amen.

DAYTIME PRAYER

Ant 1 The season of deliverance has come; the time of salvation is at hand.

Ant 2 Turn to me with all your heart, says our God.

Ant 3 Believing in God's strength and mercy, let us be fortified with patience.

(Prayer as in Morning Prayer)

EVENING PRAYER

READING

RESPONSORY

Have mercy on me, O God, in your goodness. —Have...
In the greatness of your compassion wipe out my offense, —O God...
Glory to you, Source of all Being, Eternal Word, and Holy Spirit. —Have...

CANTICLE OF MARY

Week 1   How much more will God who loves you give good things to those who ask.

Week 2   If you do not hear Moses and the prophets you will not be convinced if some one should rise from the dead.

Week 3   They who are not with me are against me, and they who do not gather with me scatter.

Week 4   How can you believe: you, who receive glory from one another, and do not seek the glory that comes from the one true God?

INTERCESSIONS: Weeks 1 and 3

The God of peace is preparing a new dwelling place and a new earth where justice will abide. Let us pray with confidence:

In you, O God, we place all our hope.

Jesus has given us a pledge of hope and strength in the Eucharist;
   —may we always walk in the strength of this food.
You have sent your Christ to preach the good news to the poor;
   —free us from our prisons and our blindness.
We remember those who are lost, frightened and despairing;
   —send forth your Spirit to comfort their hearts.
We will one day overcome death and be raised in Christ;
   —what was sown in weakness will be raised in power.

INTERCESSIONS: Weeks 2 and 4

Christ, you have entrusted to your church the mystery of God and the meaning of our existence, and so we pray to you:

Teach us to worship in spirit and truth.

You are the fully human one;
   —in following you may we become more human.
May the great movements in the world be penetrated by the spirit of the gospel;
   —open our eyes to see what is false.
You healed the sick by the touch of your hands;
   —bless all those who serve us in hospitals and nursing homes.
Help us to overcome all forms of violence between nations and races;
   —strengthen those human associations which are just and impartial.

PRAYER

Week 1   God of mercy, as we begin this season of Lent, opening ourselves to your grace, we ask that you will guide us into a true change of heart and reorientation of our lives. We ask this in the name of Jesus. Amen.

Week 2   We are aware, O God, of our sin which inhibits a free response to your grace and word. We confess our failures but look to the promise given to us in the death and resurrection of Jesus. As we share his cross, may we share his glory. We ask this in his name. Amen.

Week 3   O Christ, you have taught us to let go and to love to the end, persevering to the other side of death which is resurrection. During this lenten season, call us to prayer that will make our hearts ready for this depth of love. We ask this grace in your name. Amen.

Week 4   O God, you have given us this life to know you, to love you and to be at home with you. Help us to experience you in our hearts as we find you anew in the works and deeds of Jesus. This we ask through Jesus who is our way to you. Amen.

FRIDAY—Weeks 1 to 4

(Antiphons and psalms from the current week in the Psalter)

MORNING PRAYER

READING

RESPONSORY

Spare us, O God, and have pity on your people. —**Spare**...
We have sinned against you, —**have pity**...
Glory to you, Source of all Being, Eternal Word, and Holy Spirit. —**Spare**...

CANTICLE OF ZECHARIAH

Week 1   Unless your holiness exceeds that of the scribes and pharisees, you will never enjoy the fullness of life.

Week 2   When Joseph came to his brothers, they stripped him of his robe, and they took him and cast him into a pit.

Week 3   I will heal their faithlessness; I will love them freely, for my anger has turned from them.

Week 4   "Let us condemn him to a shameful death." Their sin blinded them; they did not know the secret purposes of God.

INTERCESSIONS: Weeks 1 and 3

Led by the Spirit into the desert of Lent, we are called to purify and renew ourselves. Let us earnestly pray:
   May the light of Christ shine brightly on our world, O God.

May we hear and interpret the many voices of our age,
   —and judge them in the light of your word.
You raised Jesus from the dead;
   —Christ is the center of our race, the joy of every heart and the answer to our yearnings.
We remember the elderly who feel useless or forgotten;
   —have mercy on your people, and let them know your love.
Teach us to be simple and disciplined in our needs,
   —and to share our abundance with those in want.

INTERCESSIONS: Weeks 2 and 4

In God we live and move and have our being. Immersed in the mystery of this presence we humbly pray:
   Let us cling to you in love.

May we see your will in every event, see Christ in every person,
   —and judge all things in the light of faith.

Your love is poured forth in our hearts by the Holy Spirit;
  —help us to live the spirit of the beatitudes in our lives.
We remember those imprisoned because of their convictions;
  —let them know your saving help.
Into your hands we commend the dead and dying;
  —may they see your face in glory.

PRAYER

Week 1 Jesus, you are God's own compassion. You are one with the victimized,
the wounded, the weak and the forgotten. May we abandon our
struggles for power and learn to minister in a spirit of service and
self-emptying. We ask this in your holy name, for you are one with
our Source and with the Spirit, for all ages. Amen.

Week 2 God of peace, purify our hearts through fasting, prayer, words and
works of kindness, that we may be new people who celebrate the
paschal mystery. We ask this in the name of Jesus, the Eternal Word,
who lives with you and the Holy Spirit, now and forever. Amen.

Week 3 Christ Jesus, may we join you in your passion by letting go of our
selfish ways and plans. Help us learn true sacrifice and thus prepare
for our union with you in the victory of resurrection. We ask this in
your name. Amen.

Week 4 Merciful God, may we imitate Jesus in the deep love revealed in his
passion and accept the kind of suffering that leads to true freedom and
resurrection. We ask this in the name of Jesus, the Eternal Word who
lives with you and with the Holy Spirit, forever. Amen.

DAYTIME PRAYER

Ant 1 The season of deliverance has come; the time of salvation is at hand.

Ant 2 Turn to me with all your heart, says our God.

Ant 3 Believing in God's strength and mercy, let us be fortified with patience.

(Prayer as in Morning Prayer)

EVENING PRAYER

READING

RESPONSORY

Have mercy on me, O God, in your goodness. —**Have**...
In the greatness of your compassion wipe out my offense, —**O God**...
Glory to you, Source of all Being, Eternal Word, and Holy Spirit. —**Have**...

CANTICLE OF MARY

Week 1 First be reconciled to your sister or brother and then come and offer
your gift.

Week 2 Jesus said to them: "Have you never read in the scriptures: 'The very
stone which the builders rejected has become the cornerstone' ?"

Week 3 You shall love your God with all your heart, with all your soul, with
all your mind, and with all your strength.

Week 4 I have not come of my own accord. The One who sent me is true and unknown by you.

INTERCESSIONS: Weeks 1 and 3

Christ Jesus, you call us to share in your mission and to deepen our belief in the mystery of creation and redemption. We wish to be sensitive to your Spirit and so we pray:

Renew your gifts in our hearts.

We believe the life of each person in our world is sacred;
   —may we incarnate your love in a global way.
We confess to you our sins and addictions;
   —forgive us and lead us on the path to life.
You have given us the gift of life;
   —help us live with grateful hearts.
Look upon all countries divided by fear and hatred;
   —may their people know the gift of peace.

INTERCESSIONS: Weeks 2 and 4

We are called to a new hope and to a new vision that we must live without fear and without oversimplification. Aware of our weakness, we pray:

Jesus, make us free.

We are aware of the challenge of this moment in history;
   —form your church as a model of justice.
Renew in us the grace of baptism;
   —draw us to deeper friendship with you.
May we renounce our selfishness and bear our daily cross;
   —open our hearts to live with your compassion.
We remember those who have died and those who grieve;
   —may the light of Christ shine in their hearts.

PRAYER

Week 1 Jesus, you are God's own compassion. You are one with the victimized, the wounded, the weak and the forgotten. May we abandon our struggles for power and learn to minister in a spirit of service and self-emptying. We ask this in your holy name, for you are one with our Source and with the Spirit, for all ages. Amen.

Week 2 God of peace, purify our hearts through fasting, prayer, words and works of kindness, that we may be new people who celebrate the paschal mystery. We ask this in the name of Jesus, the Eternal Word, who lives with you and the Holy Spirit, now and forever. Amen.

Week 3 Christ Jesus, may we join you in your passion by letting go of our selfish ways and plans. Help us learn true sacrifice and thus prepare for our union with you in the victory of resurrection. We ask this in your name. Amen.

Week 4 Merciful God, may we imitate Jesus in the deep love revealed in his passion and accept the kind of suffering that leads to true freedom and resurrection. We ask this in the name of Jesus, the Eternal Word who lives with you and with the Holy Spirit, forever. Amen.

SATURDAY—Weeks 1 to 4

(Antiphons and psalms from the current week in the Psalter)

MORNING PRAYER

READING

RESPONSORY

Spare us, O God, and have pity on your people. —**Spare**...
We have sinned against you, —**have pity**...
Glory to you, Source of all Being, Eternal Word, and Holy Spirit. —**Spare**...

CANTICLE OF ZECHARIAH

Week 1   Love your enemies and pray for those who persecute you so that you may be children of the One who makes the sun rise on the evil and on the good.

Week 2   While he was yet at a distance, his father saw him and had compassion. He ran and embraced him and kissed him.

Week 3   Those who exalt themselves will be humbled and those who humble themselves will be exalted.

Week 4   When they heard these words, some of the people said, "This is really the prophet." Others said, "This is the Christ."

INTERCESSIONS: Week 1 and 3

Our vocation as disciples calls us to a change of heart, a conversion expressed in praise of God and in deeds of justice and service. We turn to God and pray:
Help us and heal us, O God.

Enable us to grow in a spirit of self-giving,
   —showing care and concern for all people.
Break through the evil in our hearts and our social structures;
   —we are burdened with a sense of guilt.
Teach us to pray and to know the beauty of silence;
   —fill us with your faithful love.
Enlighten the leaders of nations,
   —to make the choices that lead to peace.

INTERCESSIONS: Weeks 2 and 4

We believe in the redemptive love of God. As those who have experienced God's forgiving mercy in Christ we pray:
You have redeemed us and set us free.

May your mother, Mary, draw us to reflect on your gifts to us,
   —and join with her in a song of praise.
You learned obedience by the things you suffered;
   —give us patience and a spirit of wisdom.
Comfort the elderly and those who feel useless;
   —renew in them an undying hope.
May the remembrance of what God has done in you through the Spirit,
   —be a wellspring of creativity for the future.

PRAYER

Week 1   Merciful God, in this season of Lent we wish to discipline ourselves so that we can learn to say a fuller yes to all you call us to become. We ask for this grace in the name of Jesus, your Incarnate Word, who lives with you in the Holy Spirit, now and forever. Amen.

Week 2   Jesus, in a fullness of knowledge and trust you embraced the reality and truth of being human. Help us by our lenten renewal to be free of our illusions and evasions. We ask this of our God in your name. Amen.

Week 3   God of mercy and love, may the discipline of Lent strengthen us to say yes to the hard choices that lead to life. We ask this in union with Jesus who has shown us the way. Amen.

Week 4   God, our Creator, may our lenten journey teach us not to fill the void of our incompleteness with material things, but to find hope in the brightness of your promises. We ask this through Jesus Christ who lives and reigns with you, Source of all Being, and with your Holy Spirit, forever and ever. Amen.

DAYTIME PRAYER

Ant 1   The season of deliverance has come; the time of salvation is at hand.

Ant 2   Turn to me with all your heart, says our God.

Ant 3   Believing in God's strength and mercy, let us be fortified with patience.

(Prayer as in Morning Prayer)

FIFTH SUNDAY OF LENT

(Psalms and antiphons from the current weekday in the Psalter)

EVENING PRAYER I

READING

RESPONSORY

My soul waits for God; in your word I hope. —My soul...
For with you there is steadfast love, —in your...
Glory to you, Source of all Being, Eternal Word, and Holy Spirit. —My soul...

CANTICLE OF MARY

Ant   Unless a grain of wheat falls into the earth and dies, it remains alone; but if it dies, it bears much fruit.

INTERCESSIONS:

Christ Crucified is the power of God and the wisdom of God. With trust we pray to him:

Save us by your Holy Cross.

You are one with God in glory;
   —help us to serve and follow you.

You wanted to gather your people as a hen gathers her young;
  —free us from the forces that divide us.
Through you a new law is written in our hearts;
  —may our thoughts and actions spring from love.
You cured **Lazarus** and brought him to life;
  —heal the sick and comfort the dying.

PRAYER: Compassionate One, free us from the sins and attachments that
keep us from the fullness of life you have given us in Christ. May
our fidelity be strengthened in him who was obedient unto death on
a cross. Amen.

MORNING PRAYER

READING

RESPONSORY

Christ, Chosen One of the living God, have mercy on us. —**Christ**...
Delivered up to death on a cross, —**have**...
Glory to you, Source of all Being, Eternal Word, and Holy Spirit. —**Christ**...

CANTICLE OF ZECHARIAH

Ant   Our friend, Lazarus, has fallen asleep. Let us go to awaken him from
sleep.

INTERCESSIONS:

We are not our own; we were bought with a price, and so we proclaim:
          We are yours, O Christ, and you are God's!

O God, we are burdened with our own concerns and forget the needs of others;
  —make us caring people.
We are confused by a multitude of voices;
  —give us discerning hearts.
We are drawn in opposite ways from our deepest yearnings;
  —strengthen us in truth.
We feel the loss of many whom we love;
  —bring them to eternal life in you.

PRAYER: Compassionate One, free us from the sins and attachments that
keep us from the fullness of life you have given us in Christ. May
our fidelity be strengthened in him who was obedient unto death on
a cross. Amen.

DAYTIME PRAYER

Ant 1   The season of deliverance has come; the time of salvation is at hand.

Ant 2   Turn to me with all your heart, says our God.

Ant 3   Believing in God's strength and mercy, let us be fortified with patience.

(Prayer as in Morning Prayer)

EVENING PRAYER II

READING

RESPONSORY

My soul waits for God; in your word I hope. —My soul...
For with you there is steadfast love, —in your...
Glory to you, Source of all Being, Eternal Word, and Holy Spirit. —My soul...

CANTICLE OF MARY

Ant   When I am lifted up from the earth, I will draw all people to myself.

INTERCESSIONS:

O God of Salvation, you have raised Christ Jesus. We, too, shall be raised by your power, and so we pray:

Help us to live in union with you.

Lent is the season to renew our lives;
  —may your Spirit help and guide us.
You have given us a world rich in resources;
  —encourage those who see solutions to the problem of equitable distribution.
Through fear and distrust we collect weapons of war;
  —lead us into the path of peace.
You led the Israelites through the desert to the promised land;
  —may the discipline of prayer and fasting bring us joy of heart.

PRAYER: Compassionate One, free us from the sins and attachments that keep us from the fullness of life you have given us in Christ. May our fidelity be strengthened in him who was obedient unto death on a cross. Amen.

MONDAY

(Psalms and antiphons from the current weekday in the Psalter)

MORNING PRAYER

READING

RESPONSORY

Christ, Chosen One of the living God, have mercy on us. —Christ...
Delivered up to death on a cross, —have...
Glory to you, Source of all Being, Eternal Word, and Holy Spirit. —Christ...

CANTICLE OF ZECHARIAH

Ant   The one who follows me will not walk in darkness but will have the light of life.

INTERCESSIONS:

We pray to you, O Christ, whose death has brought life to the world:

Remove our sins from us.

You know the recesses of the human heart;
  —help us to seek God's will in all things.

We are aware of dark forces in our world;
   —remind us that in you victory is already ours.
You stood for truth against the pain of opposition;
   —we pray for integrity in those who lead us.
Because you trusted God, you accepted the cross;
   —may the promise of resurrection help us through the narrow gate.

PRAYER: Christ Jesus, you emptied yourself and appeared in human likeness.
          Lead us always in the way of truth and a loving acceptance of the
          burdens of life. We ask this in the power of your name. Amen.

DAYTIME PRAYER

Ant 1   The season of deliverance has come; the time of salvation is at hand.

Ant 2   Turn to me with all your heart, says our God.

Ant 3   Believing in God's strength and mercy, let us be fortified with patience.

(Prayer as in Morning Prayer)

EVENING PRAYER

READING

RESPONSORY

My soul waits for God; in your word I hope. —My soul...
For with you there is steadfast love, —in your...
Glory to you, Source of all Being, Eternal Word, and Holy Spirit. —My soul...

CANTICLE OF MARY

Ant   I bear witness to myself, and the One who sent me bears witness to me.

INTERCESSIONS:

Most loving God, you have given us, in Jesus, the bread of life and the cup of
salvation. We turn to him and say:
                 We proclaim your death until you come!
Jesus was led like a sheep to the slaughter;
   —comfort those who face a cruel death.
May our fasting from food and self-indulgence,
   —free us to love you and one another.
Jesus died that we all may be one;
   —end the prejudices that divide women and men, races and nations.
You call us to intimate union with you;
   —encourage those who seek you in silence and solitude.

PRAYER: Christ Jesus, you emptied yourself and appeared in human likeness.
          Lead us always in the way of truth and a loving acceptance of the
          burdens of life. We ask this in the power of your name. Amen.

TUESDAY

(Psalms and antiphons from the current weekday in the Psalter)

MORNING PRAYER

READING

RESPONSORY

Christ, Chosen One of the living God, have mercy on us. —**Christ**...
Delivered up to death on a cross, —**have**...
Glory to you, Source of all Being, Eternal Word, and Holy Spirit. —**Christ**...

CANTICLE OF ZECHARIAH

Ant You are from below, I am from above; you are of this world, I am not of
this world.

INTERCESSIONS:

Lord Jesus, you were baptized by the Spirit and missioned to call us to union with
God. We pray as one people:

May your Spirit help and guide us.

For those in difficult periods of transition,
   —we pray for trust.
For victims of mass starvation,
   —we pray for relief and a change in the inequitable possession of our world's
   resources.
For those addicted to drugs and alcohol,
   —we pray for healing and freedom.
For our beloved dead,
   —we pray for life eternal.

PRAYER: Jesus, our Brother, you are the cornerstone rejected by builders but
exalted by God. Help us to believe that the power of Love at work
in our world is in all things and above all things to the glory of
God's name. Amen.

DAYTIME PRAYER

Ant 1   The season of deliverance has come; the time of salvation is at hand.

Ant 2   Turn to me with all your heart, says our God.

Ant 3   Believing in God's strength and mercy, let us be fortified with patience.

(Prayer as in Morning Prayer)

EVENING PRAYER

READING

RESPONSORY

My soul waits for God; in your word I hope. —**My soul**...
For with you there is steadfast love, —**in your**...
Glory to you, Source of all Being, Eternal Word, and Holy Spirit. —**My soul**...

CANTICLE OF MARY

Ant The One who sent me is with me, never leaving me alone, because I always do God's will.

INTERCESSIONS:

You are the truthful One, who sends us the gift of our salvation in the living word of Jesus; therefore we proclaim:

Blessed are you, Lord Jesus Christ!

Strengthen leaders of church and state;
   —help them to see new and creative possibilities in problem areas.
There are many who are sick in mind as well as in body;
   —be light in their darkness and help us to lessen the stress and enervating tensions in which we live.
Help us to transform our sinful ways,
   —so that we may be of service to one another.
Give hope to all people who are oppressed;
   —enable them to find freedom and support within their communities and families.

PRAYER: Jesus, our Brother, you are the cornerstone rejected by builders but exalted by God. Help us to believe that the power of Love at work in our world is in all things and above all things to the glory of God's name. Amen.

WEDNESDAY

(Psalms and antiphons from the current weekday in the Psalter)

MORNING PRAYER

READING

RESPONSORY

Christ, Chosen One of the living God, have mercy on us. —**Christ**...
Delivered up to death on a cross, —**have**...
Glory to you, Source of all Being, Eternal Word, and Holy Spirit. —**Christ**...

CANTICLE OF ZECHARIAH

Ant If you live by my word, you are truly my disciples; and you will know the truth, and the truth will make you free.

INTERCESSIONS:

You, O liberating God, call us from slavery to freedom and from death to life. In joy we cry out:

We come to do your will.

You invite us to be slaves no longer;
   —free us from the selfishness that keeps us in bondage.
You call us to a life of freedom;
   —help us to bear the stress necessary to develop and grow in wholesome ways.

You draw us from death to life;
—enable us to confront our addictions and to support one another in our process to recovery.
God of our freedom, we are open to your will;
—help us to discern your ways for us.

PRAYER: God of Love, you have called us to the life of resurrection by raising us, in Christ, from the dead. Strengthen us and those preparing for baptism to be wholly given to the Easter mystery. We ask this in Jesus' name. Amen.

DAYTIME PRAYER

Ant 1   The season of deliverance has come; the time of salvation is at hand.

Ant 2   Turn to me with all your heart, says our God.

Ant 3   Believing in God's strength and mercy, let us be fortified with patience.

(Prayer as in Morning Prayer)

EVENING PRAYER

READING
RESPONSORY

My soul waits for God; in your word I hope. —**My soul**. . .
For with you there is steadfast love, —**in your**. . .
Glory to you, Source of all Being, Eternal Word, and Holy Spirit. —**My soul**. . .

CANTICLE OF MARY

Ant   Now you seek to kill me, a man who has told the truth which I heard from God.

INTERCESSIONS:

O God of our ancestors, in Christ we are sisters and brothers to one another, and so we pray:

May we be one in you!

O God, you are a father to us;
—help us to break down the barriers that keep us from respecting our differences.
O God, you are a mother to us;
—aid us in our efforts to care for our earth and to protect our environment for future generations.
You, most faithful companion, journey with us;
—enable us to serve one another in humility.
You, Spirit of life, breathe your life within us;
—may all preparing for baptism find support in their faith communities.

PRAYER: God of Love, you have called us to the life of resurrection by raising us, in Christ, from the dead. Strengthen us and those preparing for baptism to be wholly given to the Easter mystery. We ask this in Jesus' name. Amen.

THURSDAY

(Psalms and antiphons from the current weekday in the Psalter)

MORNING PRAYER

READING

RESPONSORY

Christ, Chosen One of the living God, have mercy on us. —**Christ**...
Delivered up to death on a cross, —**have**...
Glory to you, Source of all Being, Eternal Word, and Holy Spirit. —**Christ**...

CANTICLE OF ZECHARIAH

Ant   Jesus said to them: They who are of God hear the words of God; the
reason why you do not hear them is that you are not of God.

INTERCESSIONS:

Most Loving God, you invite us to a covenantal relationship with you and with one
another. In confidence we proclaim:

Your faithfulness will last forever!

You promise to keep your covenant with us throughout the ages;
   —give hope to our children who do not experience love and care.
You give us the land as part of our inheritance;
   —may we design a future where peace will reign.
You gift us through our ancestors, our cultural heritage and our relationships
      with one another;
   —bring us to a growing awareness of interdependence in our global family.
You mystify us in being the I AM, our God;
   —increase our faith in you, Holy Mystery, triune God.

PRAYER: God of Mercy, you light up what is hidden in darkness and reveal
the purposes of the heart. Give us the mind and heart of Christ that
our thoughts and inclinations may lead to work worthy of you.
Grant this in the power of Jesus' name. Amen.

DAYTIME PRAYER

Ant 1   The season of deliverance has come; the time of salvation is at hand.

Ant 2   Turn to me with all your heart, says our God.

Ant 3   Believing in God's strength and mercy, let us be fortified with patience.

(Prayer as in Morning Prayer)

EVENING PRAYER

READING

RESPONSORY

My soul waits for you; in your word I hope. —**My soul**...
For with you there is steadfast love, —**in your**...
Glory to you, Source of all Being, Eternal Word, and Holy Spirit. —**My soul**...

CANTICLE OF MARY

Ant   You are not yet fifty years old, and have you seen Abraham? Truly, I say to you, before Abraham was, I am.

INTERCESSIONS:

Jesus, you are the way, the truth and the life. In confidence we say:
May we walk in the light of your life.

Jesus, seeker of truth, you spoke your truth and were stoned;
—may we have the courage to speak honestly in the face of violence and oppression.
Jesus, sign of peace, your suffering gives us your gift of peace;
—help us to transform our suffering and to recognize its redemptive qualities.
Jesus, seeker of justice, your life challenges all oppressors to face their destructive ways;
—may we be open to look at the subtle ways that we oppress one another.
Jesus, source of light, you are a beacon in our darkness;
—enable all leaders within church communities to offer credible, just, and collegial leadership.

PRAYER: God of Mercy, you light up what is hidden in darkness and reveal the purposes of the heart. Give us the mind and heart of Christ that our thoughts and inclinations may lead to work worthy of you. Grant this in the power of Jesus' name. Amen.

FRIDAY

(Psalms and antiphons from the current weekday in the Psalter)

MORNING PRAYER

READING

RESPONSORY

Christ, Chosen One of the living God, have mercy on us. —**Christ**. . .
Delivered up to death on a cross, —**have**. . .
Glory to you, Source of all Being, Eternal Word, and Holy Spirit. —**Christ**. . .

CANTICLE OF ZECHARIAH

Ant   I have shown you many good works from the One who sent me. For which of these do you seek to kill me?

INTERCESSIONS:

Your works, Christ Jesus, reflect the goodness of the Holy One who sent you. In faith let us pray:
Show us your mercy!

God of Holiness, you give us the healing gifts of Jesus;
—may all who experience the incurable illnesses of our day find comfort in your healing touch.
Most provident God, in Jesus we know the effects of fruitful ministry;
—help us to work diligently and prayerfully to be signs of your living presence.

God of Wonders, we marvel at the miracles of life;
   —enable us to enter joyously and fully into our personal and communal
      commitments.
Spirit of God, you broke the bonds of death;
   —may all who die this day experience the fullness of your life.

PRAYER: Everlasting God, you have brought us into union with Christ Jesus,
          who is our way to you. By him we have become your people and
          are set free. May we always rejoice in your love until we behold you
          in glory. Amen.

DAYTIME PRAYER

Ant 1   The season of deliverance has come; the time of salvation is at hand.

Ant 2   Turn to me with all your heart, says our God.

Ant 3   Believing in God's strength and mercy, let us be fortified with patience.

(Prayer as in Morning Prayer)

EVENING PRAYER

READING

RESPONSORY

My soul waits for God; in your word I hope. —**My soul**. . .
For with you there is steadfast love, —**in your**. . .
Glory to you, Source of all Being, Eternal Word, and Holy Spirit. —**My soul**. . .

CANTICLE OF MARY

Ant   If I do the works of God, even though you do not believe me, believe
         my works.

INTERCESSIONS:

In the mystery of faith we are invited to be one with you, gracious God. In awe
we pray:
                You, O God, are our strength!
Jesus, you show us how much God, your father, loves us;
   —in times of doubt increase our faith.
You tell us of the love of God as mother;
   —enable health care ministers to show gentleness and love to all terminally ill
      people and their families.
Jesus, you present God as a persistent friend;
   —may we respond to the fullness of life to which our God calls us.
You reflect the image of the compassionate God;
   —help all teachers and leaders of youth to exhibit your courage and mercy.

PRAYER: Everlasting God, you have brought us into union with Christ Jesus,
          who is our way to you. By him we have become your people and
          are set free. May we always rejoice in your love until we behold you
          in glory. Amen.

SATURDAY

(Psalms and antiphons from the current weekday in the Psalter)

MORNING PRAYER

READING

RESPONSORY

Christ, Chosen One of the living God, have mercy on us. —Christ...
Delivered up to death on a cross, —have...
Glory to you, Source of all Being, Eternal Word, and Holy Spirit. —Christ...

CANTICLE OF ZECHARIAH

Ant   Jesus dies to bring together into one body all the scattered children
of God.

INTERCESSIONS:

O God, you make your dwelling place with us and give us the promise of your
fidelity; in trust we proclaim:

You are the God of everlasting love!

You promise to make a covenant of peace with us;
—enable all women and men to put aside their defenses and weapons to make
peace a reality.
Your dwelling place is with us in the midst of our struggles;
—give us the insight to recognize that you dwell with all your people and
that each person has the right to human dignity.
You, indeed, are our God; there is no other God but you;
—help us to place our trust in you and to put aside the idols of consumerism,
and all that keeps us from allowing you to be our God.
You call us to a covenantal relationship as your people;
—may all who experience brokenness in relationships find healing and
forgiveness in their faith communities.

PRAYER: O God, Source of all blessings, we have not received the spirit of
the world but the Spirit which is from you. May our lenten path of
penance open us to a renewal of life in the Spirit. We ask this in
Jesus' name. Amen.

DAYTIME PRAYER

Ant 1   The season of deliverance has come; the time of salvation is at hand.

Ant 2   Turn to me with all your heart, says our God.

Ant 3   Believing in God's strength and mercy, let us be fortified with patience.

(Prayer as in Morning Prayer)

PASSION SUNDAY (PALM SUNDAY)

(Psalms and antiphons from the current weekday in the Psalter)

EVENING PRAYER I

READING

RESPONSORY

We adore you, O Christ, and we bless you. —**We**...
By your death you redeemed the world. —**we bless**...
Glory to you, Source of all Being, Eternal Word, and Holy Spirit. —**We**...

CANTICLE OF MARY

Ant   O Just One, the world has not known you, but I have known you
because you have sent me.

INTERCESSIONS:

Jesus wept for his people in their blindness; he mourned their future destruction.
When his time had come he entered the city of Jerusalem. Let us greet him saying:
Praise to you, O Christ, our Savior.

Jesus, many whom you had healed and consoled would betray you;
—make us grateful for the gift of your life and death and keep us
faithful to you.
Your disciples would leave you when the glory changed to scorn;
—help us to sustain the cost of discipleship.
You received the praise of children and would not let them be silenced;
—make us pure of heart, ever open to your truth.
You freely exchanged a political throne for the reign of love on the cross;
—give us the wisdom to know and the courage to live by the values
of the gospel.

PRAYER: Jesus, our Savior, you came with a message of love and forgiveness;
you offered us joy and fullness of life. Generation after generation
we have scorned your love and destroyed your life among us. Have
mercy on us. Let your Holy Spirit overcome our weakness that we
may rise courageously to the challenge of following you. This we
ask in your name, Eternal Word, one with the Source of all Being
and with the Holy Spirit for all ages. Amen.

MORNING PRAYER

READING

RESPONSORY

Hosanna on high, Christ our Savior. —**Hosanna**...
You gave your life for us, —**Christ**...
Glory to you, Source of all Being, Eternal Word, and Holy Spirit. —**Hosanna**...

CANTICLE OF ZECHARIAH

Ant   The multitude, gathered for the feast, cried out: Blessed be the one who
comes in the name of our God! Hosanna in the highest!

INTERCESSIONS:

Jesus enters Jerusalem riding on a donkey; the people would make him king. Let us join the children and sing:

Hosanna to the Son of David.

Jesus, your realm is not of this world;
—help us to build here a world of justice and love.
You knew the hearts of those who hailed you as king;
—show us our true selves and keep us faithful to you.
You came as giver of mercy and love and disdained a political crown;
—bless our leaders with integrity and wisdom.
You declared your beliefs openly even in the face of death;
—give us the courage to seek and live the truth no matter what the cost.

PRAYER: Jesus, our Savior, you came with a message of love and forgiveness; you offered us joy and fullness of life. Generation after generation we have scorned your love and destroyed your life among us. Have mercy on us. Let your Holy Spirit overcome our weakness that we may rise courageously to the challenge of following you. This we ask in your name, Eternal Word, one with the Source of all Being and with the Holy Spirit for all ages. Amen.

DAYTIME PRAYER

Ant 1 The Hebrew children bearing olive branches went out to meet Jesus, crying: Hosanna in the highest!

Ant 2 The people spread their garments on the road shouting: Hosanna to the son of David! Blessed be the one who comes in the name of our God!

Ant 3 To you, God, defender of my life, I have entrusted my cause.

(Prayer as in Morning Prayer)

EVENING PRAYER II

READING

RESPONSORY

We adore you, O Christ, and we bless you. —**We**...
By your death you redeemed the world. —**we bless**...
Glory to you, Source of all Being, Eternal Word, and Holy Spirit. —**We**...

CANTICLE OF MARY

Ant It is written: I will strike the shepherd, and the sheep of the flock will be dispersed. But after I have risen, I will go before you into Galilee. There you will see me.

INTERCESSIONS:

Jesus wept for his people in their blindness; he mourned their future destruction. When his time had come he entered the city of Jerusalem. Let us greet him saying:

Praise to you, O Christ, our Savior.

Jesus, many whom you had healed and consoled would betray you;
—make us grateful for the gift of your life and death and keep us faithful
   to you.
Your disciples would leave you when the glory changed to scorn;
—help us to sustain the cost of discipleship.
You received the praise of children and would not let them be silenced;
—make us pure of heart, ever open to your truth.
You freely exchanged a political throne for the reign of love on the cross;
—give us the wisdom to know and the courage to live by the values of
   the gospel.

PRAYER: Jesus, our Savior, you came with a message of love and forgiveness;
you offered us joy and fullness of life. Generation after generation
we have scorned your love and destroyed your life among us. Have
mercy on us. Let your Holy Spirit overcome our weakness that we
may rise courageously to the challenge of following you. This we
ask in your name, Eternal Word, one with the Source of all Being
and with the Holy Spirit for all ages. Amen.

MONDAY OF HOLY WEEK

(Psalms and antiphons from the current weekday in the Psalter)

MORNING PRAYER

READING

RESPONSORY

Hosanna on high, Christ our Savior. —**Hosanna**...
You gave your life for us, —**Christ**...
Glory to you, Source of all Being, Eternal Word, and Holy Spirit. —**Hosanna**...

CANTICLE OF ZECHARIAH

Ant   O God, glorify me in your presence with the glory I had with you before
   the world was made.

INTERCESSIONS:

Jesus, you came a gentle savior, not breaking the bruised reed, not quenching the
smoldering wick. We pray to you:
Show us your mercy, O Christ.

Jesus, before your passion you welcomed the company of your friends;
—help us to recognize those in need of consolation and to know how to
   support them.
You let Mary anoint your feet with perfume in preparation for your burial;
—give us the grace to serve the sick selflessly.
You knew your time had come;
—have mercy on those on death row, who count the remaining days of their
   lives.
You hid from your enemies and could not walk freely in your own land;
—give strength, patience and courage to all who are in prison.

PRAYER:　Jesus, on the eve of your passion and death, you found comfort in the company of your friends. In the truest sign of friendship, you gave your life for them and for us. Help us to live the call of the gospel more deeply. Let our relationship with one another be a sign of your presence. Help us to live and die in your love, that we may live with you forever. Amen.

DAYTIME PRAYER

Ant 1　With you at my side, of whom shall I be afraid?

Ant 2　O God, you have pleaded the cause of my soul; you the defender of my life.

Ant 3　My people, what have I done to you, or in what have I grieved you? Answer me.

(Prayer as in Morning Prayer)

EVENING PRAYER

READING

RESPONSORY

We adore you, O Christ, and we bless you. —**We**...
By your death you redeemed the world. —**we bless**...
Glory to you, Source of all Being, Eternal Word, and Holy Spirit. —**We**...

CANTICLE OF MARY

Ant　You would have no power over me unless it were given you from above.

INTERCESSIONS:

Six days before the Passover, Jesus came to Bethany, where Lazarus was, whom Jesus had raised from the dead. Let us pray:

　　　　We remember your mercies, O Christ.

Jesus, faithful to the end, you blessed the house of Lazarus;
　—give us the grace to live lovingly in union with one another.
Jesus, you defended Mary and received her costly gift;
　—give us the wisdom to judge values in the light of your truth.
Jesus, you would remain the faithful servant of God to the end;
　—give us all the gift of perseverance in following you.
Jesus, you knew that your death would mean suffering for your friends;
　—give us the courage to follow God's will through all of the mystery of suffering for ourselves and others.

PRAYER:　Jesus, on the eve of your passion and death, you found comfort in the company of your friends. In the truest sign of friendship, you gave your life for them and for us. Help us to live the call of the gospel more deeply. Let our relationship with one another be a sign of your presence. Help us to live and die in your love, that we may live with you forever. Amen.

TUESDAY OF HOLY WEEK

(Psalms and antiphons from the current weekday in the Psalter)

MORNING PRAYER

READING

RESPONSORY

Hosanna on high, Christ our Savior. —**Hosanna**...
You gave your life for us, —**Christ**...
Glory to you, Source of all Being, Eternal Word, and Holy Spirit. —**Hosanna**...

CANTICLE OF ZECHARIAH

Ant   Before the festival day of the Passover, Jesus knew that his hour had come
to depart from this world. Having loved his own who were in the world,
he loved them to the end.

INTERCESSIONS:

Jesus said to his disciples: Where I am going, you cannot follow me now. Later on
you shall come after me. Let us pray to him:
Draw us, we shall come after you.

Jesus, you knew that Peter would deny you three times, yet your forgave him;
—help us to be forgiving of one another.
Jesus, all would betray you; your only refuge was in God;
—be with us when we have no one to help us.
Your disciples were without understanding even to the end;
—we praise you for your patience with us as we strive to follow you.
You remained steadfast in your mission when all seemed doomed to failure;
—let us always choose faithfulness to you above worldly success.

PRAYER: O God, we praise you in the gift of Jesus, given to us for our
salvation. We ask you to forgive us for our sins and failings that
prevent the coming of your reign and continue to nail his followers
to a cross. Give us the grace to change our lives and to let the life of
Jesus bear fruit in us. We ask this in his name. Amen.

DAYTIME PRAYER

Ant 1   With you at my side, of whom shall I be afraid?

Ant 2   O God, you have pleaded the cause of my soul; you the defender of my
life.

Ant 3   My people, what have I done to you, or in what have I grieved you?
Answer me.

(Prayer as in Morning Prayer)

EVENING PRAYER

READING

RESPONSORY

We adore you, O Christ, and we bless you. —**We**...
By your death you redeemed the world. —**we bless**...
Glory to you, Source of all Being, Eternal Word, and Holy Spirit. —**We**...

CANTICLE OF MARY

Ant I have the power to lay my life down and I have power to take it up again.

INTERCESSIONS:

Jesus, Truth itself, confronts the Prince of Lies. Let us pray:
O Christ, be our light.

O Christ, generation upon generation awaited your coming, and now you
die unknown;
—keep us in your truth that we may never deny you.
You spent yourself in healing and preaching to the people;
—give us the generosity to serve you and others without seeking a reward.
You spent many nights in prayer during the time of your ministry;
—teach us to make prayer the foundation of our service to you.
You knew that your passion and death would pierce your mother's heart;
—bless all parents who suffer with their children.

PRAYER: O God, we praise you in the gift of Jesus, given to us for our
salvation. We ask you to forgive us for our sins and failings that
prevent the coming of your reign and continue to nail his followers
to a cross. Give us the grace to change our lives and to let the life of
Jesus bear fruit in us. We ask this in his name. Amen.

WEDNESDAY OF HOLY WEEK

(Psalms and antiphons from the current weekday in the Psalter)

MORNING PRAYER

READING
RESPONSORY

Hosanna on high, Christ our Savior. —**Hosanna**...
You gave your life for us, —**Christ**...
Glory to you, Source of all Being, Eternal Word, and Holy Spirit. —**Hosanna**...

CANTICLE OF ZECHARIAH

Ant Simon, are you asleep? Could you not watch one hour with me?

INTERCESSIONS:

At the name of Jesus, every knee should bow, in heaven, on earth and under the
earth. In adoration we proclaim:
Jesus Christ is Lord.

Jesus, you shared your bread with one who would betray you;
  —teach us the ways of non-violence.
Jesus, the betrayer broke your heart, but you did not condemn him;
  —help us to give one another time to rise from weaknesses.
Jesus, you were sold for thirty pieces of silver;
  —give us the courage always to prefer you above all things.
You celebrated the paschal meal with your people on the eve of your death;
  —imprint on our hearts the depths of your dedication.

PRAYER: Jesus, you spent the years of your ministry sharing the word of God and your healing power with all who would receive them. You approached your passion with a heart broken by sorrow but overflowing with love for God and for us. Have mercy on us. Keep us faithful to your gospel that we may end our days faithful to you. We ask this for the glory of your name. Amen.

DAYTIME PRAYER

Ant 1 With you at my side, of whom shall I be afraid?

Ant 2 O God, you have pleaded the cause of my soul; you the defender of my life.

Ant 3 My people, what have I done to you, or in what have I grieved you? Answer me.

(Prayer as in Morning Prayer)

EVENING PRAYER

READING

RESPONSORY

We adore you, O Christ, and we bless you. —**We**...
By your death you redeemed the world. —**we bless**...
Glory to you, Source of all Being, Eternal Word, and Holy Spirit. —**We**...

CANTICLE OF MARY

Ant The maid said to Peter: Surely you are one of them for even your speech betrays you.

INTERCESSIONS:

Your heart was broken with insults, O Christ. You looked for comfort and there was none. With contrite hearts, we pray:

Come, let us adore.

Jesus, your love is stronger than death;
  —help us to overcome our selfishness; give us hearts of flesh.
Light of the world, you were forced to hide from your enemies;
  —bless all who are exiled for their works of justice.
You suffered the ignominy of a captured criminal;
  —give us the creativity and generosity to improve the lives of all prisoners.
You became obedient for us, even to death;
  —give us the grace to seek and do the will of God all the days of our lives.

PRAYER: Jesus, you spent the years of your ministry sharing the word of God and your healing power with all who would receive them. You approached your passion with a heart broken by sorrow but overflowing with love for God and for us. Have mercy on us. Keep us faithful to your gospel that we may end our days faithful to you. We ask this for the glory of your name. Amen.

HOLY THURSDAY

(Psalms and antiphons from the current weekday in the Psalter)

MORNING PRAYER

READING

RESPONSORY

Hosanna on high, Christ our Savior. —**Hosanna**...
You gave your life for us, —**Christ**...
Glory to you, Source of all Being, Eternal Word, and Holy Spirit. —**Hosanna**...

CANTICLE OF ZECHARIAH

Ant   Now his betrayer had given them a sign, saying; "Whomsoever I kiss, that is he. Hold him!"

INTERCESSIONS:

Jesus rose from supper and began to wash the feet of his disciples, and so we pray:
O Christ, free us from our sins.

You came to serve and not to be served;
   —help us to realize the nobility of serving you and one another.
In your last hour you were lonely, even among friends;
   —be present to all who face death alone.
You are the Good Shepherd, who dies for the sheep;
   —raise up leaders who will enable their people to live wholesome lives.
The disciple whom you loved rested his head on your breast; he would stand beneath the cross;
   —give us the grace to live and die faithful to your calling.

PRAYER: Christ Jesus, our Savior, you have given us a memorial of your life and death. As we are nourished by your body and blood, open our minds and hearts to your Spirit that we too may give ourselves totally to the salvation of your people. Let the bread of life make us one with you and with one another. Amen.

DAYTIME PRAYER

Ant 1   With you at my side, of whom shall I be afraid?
Ant 2   O God, you have pleaded the cause of my soul; you the defender of my life.
Ant 3   My people, what have I done to you, or in what have I grieved you? Answer me.
(Prayer as in Morning Prayer)

EVENING PRAYER

(Evening prayer is said only by those who do not participate in the evening Eucharist)

READING

In place of the responsory the following is said:

Ant   Christ Jesus humbled himself and became obedient unto death, even death on a cross.

CANTICLE OF MARY

Ant   Jesus said to them: "How I have longed to eat this passover with you before I suffer, for I tell you I shall not eat it again until all is fulfilled."

INTERCESSIONS:

Jesus sat at table with his disciples and said: I have earnestly desired to eat this passover with you before I suffer. Let us pray:

How can we repay you, O Christ, for your goodness to us?

You gave us your body and blood in the sacrament of thanksgiving;
—let this sign of your love transform us into true followers of your gospel.
You would shield your people as a mother hen hides her nestlings, but there was no one to comfort you in your suffering;
—forgive us and awaken us to the many who suffer from our mindless neglect.
You sweat blood in fear and sorrow for our sins;
—strengthen all who live in fear of any kind.
You asked that the cup of suffering might be removed from you, yet you acquiesced to God's will for you and your ministry;
—let us always begin and complete all that we do in accord with God's will no matter what the cost.
You prayed that we all may be one as you are one with the Creator;
—make us instruments of your peace, signs of your love on earth.

PRAYER: Christ Jesus, our Savior, you have given us a memorial of your life and death. As we are nourished by your body and blood, open our minds and hearts to your Spirit that we too may give ourselves to the salvation of your people. Let the bread of life make us one with you and with one another. Amen.

GOOD FRIDAY

MORNING PRAYER

Ant 1   They divided my garments among them and for my vesture they cast lots. (Psalm 51)

Ant 2   Daughters of Jerusalem, weep not for me but for your children.

Canticle   Habakkuk 3:2–4, 13a, 15–19

O God, I have heard reports of you and your work, O God, I fear.
In the course of the years renew it; —

In the course of the years make it known.
In your wrath remember mercy!

God came from Teman;
the Holy One from Mount Paran.
Your glory covered the heavens,
and the earth was full of your praise.

Your brightness was like the light,
rays flashed from your hand;
there you veiled your power.
You went forth for the salvation of
    your people,
to save your anointed.

You trampled the sea with your horses,
amid the surging of mighty waters.
I hear, and my body trembles,
my lips quiver at the sound.

Decay enters into my bones,
my steps totter beneath me.
I will wait for the day of reckoning
to come upon the earth.

Though the fig tree does not blossom
nor fruit be on the vines,
the produce of the olive fail
and the fields yield no food,

the flock be cut off from the fold
and there be no herd in the stalls,
yet will I rejoice in you, Most High,
and rejoice in the God of my salvation.

For you, O God, are my strength;
you make my feet like hinds' feet,
you make me tread upon high places.
    Glory...

Ant 3 Truly, I say to you, today you will be with me in paradise.
(Psalm 147: 12–20)

READING

In place of the responsory the following is said:

Ant Christ Jesus humbled himself and became obedient unto death, even
death on a cross.

CANTICLE OF ZECHARIAH

Ant Let every spirit praise you, Most Holy Trinity, who has given us
victory through the cross.

INTERCESSIONS:

We adore you, O Christ, for by the wood of the cross, you brought joy to the world.
    Glory and praise to you, Lord Jesus Christ.

Jesus, you were taken prisoner in the darkness of night; all your friends
    abandoned you;
    —be with all who are abducted and strengthen all who mourn those who
    are missing.
You were crowned with thorns and beaten by soldiers;
    —help us to end torture throughout the world; have pity on those so afflicted.
Your face was covered with spittle and you wore a robe of shame;
    —heal the wounds that make us act less than human; remind us that we are
    made in the image of God.
You accepted the help of Simon and Veronica;
    —awaken us to the ways that we can help those who are suffering.
Carrying your cross, you continued to show concern for others, for those who
    would come after you.
    —let our burdens make us compassionate toward the burdens of others.

PRAYER: Merciful God, you so loved the world that you sent Jesus to save us. He showed his love for us by his life and his death on the cross. Give us the grace to respond with all our minds and hearts with a love that transforms us into a people worthy of you. Teach us to live in you and for one another as Jesus taught us. Amen.

DAYTIME PRAYER

Ant 1   And when they crucified him, they divided his garments among them by casting lots; then they sat down and kept watch over him.

Ant 2   Now at the sixth hour there was darkness over all the land.

Ant 3   Standing by the cross were the mother of Jesus and his mother's sister, Mary, the wife of Clopas, and Mary Magdalen.

(Prayer as in Morning Prayer)

EVENING PRAYER

Ant 1   Into your hands, O God, I commend my spirit. (Psalm 116:10–19)

Ant 2   Behold the Lamb of God! (Psalm 143:1–11)

Ant 3   They took the body of Jesus, bound it in linen cloth and spices and laid it in a tomb. (Phil. 2:6–11)

(In place of the responsory the following is said)

Ant   Christ, for our sake, became obedient to death, even death on a cross.

CANTICLE OF MARY

Ant   When Jesus had taken the wine he said: It is consummated! And bowing his head, he gave up his spirit.

INTERCESSIONS:

Mary, the mother of Jesus, stood before the cross of her dying son, and so we pray:
Blessed is she who has believed.

Jesus, you entrusted the care of your mother to the disciple whom you loved;
   —instill in us a deep respect and love for the aging and abandoned.

You forgave Peter with a look of love and you promised the believing thief the fullness of life;
   —give us undying faith in your mercy; let us never turn from you in our sins.

At your death, the veil of the temple was rent in two;
   —protect your church from all blindness; keep us ever open to your truth.

You hung naked on the cross, at the mercy of those who reviled you;
   —heal victims of rape and those who molest them. Give our society a respect for life.

In derision you were hailed as king, king of fools;
   —Ruler of the nations, bless all nations with just and wise leaders, that the people of the earth may become your glory.

PRAYER: Merciful God, you so loved the world that you sent Jesus to save us. He showed his love for us by his life and his death on the cross. Give us the grace to respond with all our minds and hearts with a love that transforms us into a people worthy of you. Teach us to live in you and for one another, as Jesus taught us. Amen.

HOLY SATURDAY

MORNING PRAYER

Ant 1   Truly he has borne our iniquities and carried our sorrows. (Psalm 64)

Ant 2   Our Shepherd who led us to living waters is gone; at his passing the sun was darkened. (Isaiah 38:10–14, 17–20)

Ant 3   In peace I shall sleep and take my rest, for my body rests in hope. (Psalm 150)

READING

In place of the responsory the following is said:

Ant   Christ Jesus humbled himself and became obedient unto death, even death on a cross. Therefore God also exalted him and gave him a name above all other names.

CANTICLE OF ZECHARIAH

Ant   The women sitting at the sepulchre were weeping and lamenting.

INTERCESSIONS:

The body of Jesus was taken from the cross and wrapped in a linen shroud and laid in a rock-hewn tomb, where no one had ever yet been laid. We cry to you:
Spare us, O God.

Jesus, your betrayer despaired of your love;
—let us never lose hope of forgiveness, however grave our guilt.
Your mother held your broken body; her heart was pierced with sorrow;
—have pity on all mothers who must bury their children or lose them by abduction.
Jesus, covered with wounds, you died for a wounded world;
—heal us, bring light out of our darkness, let us know the things that are to our peace.
One with the Creator of the earth, by your burial you became one with the earth;
—teach us to reverence our earth and all its resources.
The women who had followed you prepared spices for your anointing;
—bless all women who minister to your people at the risk of their reputations and their lives.

PRAYER: O God, by his life and his death on the cross, Jesus has revealed the depth of your love for us. One in our flesh, he became one in our dying and burial. Have mercy on us, forgive us our sins, and once again call us to life that we may be one with him in his resurrection. This we ask through Jesus, who lives and reigns with you and the Holy Spirit, one God, forever. Amen.

DAYTIME PRAYER

Ant 1   They shall mourn for him as for an only child; for the savior who is innocent has been slain! (Psalm 27)

Ant 2   O death, I will be your death! Hell, I will be your destruction! (Psalm 30)

Ant 3   I know that my Redeemer lives and in my flesh I shall see God. (Psalm 76)

(Prayer as in Morning Prayer)

EVENING PRAYER

Ant 1   Now in the place where Jesus was crucified there was a garden, and in the garden a new tomb where no one had ever lain. It was there that they laid him. (Psalm 116:10–19)

Ant 2   The women who had come from Galilee followed, and saw the tomb and how the body was laid. Then they returned and prepared spices and ointments. (Psalm 143:1–11)

Ant 3   Joseph of Arimathea laid the body in his own new tomb, rolled a great stone to the door of the tomb and departed. (Phil. 2:6–11)

READING

In place of the responsory the following is said:

Ant   Christ Jesus humbled himself and became obedient unto death, even death on a cross. Therefore God also exalted him and gave him a name above all other names.

CANTICLE OF MARY

Ant   After three days I will rise again.

INTERCESSIONS:

Jesus, son of God, come to set us free, lies bound in the earth. All who hoped in him await a new day, and so we pray:

O Christ, deliver us.

Jesus, you died to set us free;
    —give true freedom to those bound because of race, color or creed.
Jesus, you died that we might have life to the full;
    —inspire and encourage women in their quest for equality.
Jesus, you died revealing God's love for us;
    —enlighten those who have no love for themselves; befriend and heal them.
Jesus, you died leaving your mother in the care of another;
    —bless those who leave all to serve you; encourage and comfort their families.
Death released you from the agony of the cross;
    —be present to all who are ill; have pity on the elderly and the dying.

PRAYER: O God, by his life and his death on the cross, Jesus has revealed the depth of your love for us. One in our flesh, he became one in our dying and burial. Have mercy on us, forgive us our sins, and once again call us to resurrection. This we ask through Jesus, who lives and reigns with you and the Holy Spirit, one God, forever. Amen.

EASTER SUNDAY

MORNING PRAYER

(Psalms from Feasts and Solemnities)

Ant 1 I am risen and still with you, alleluia!

Ant 2 And behold, there was a great earthquake; for an angel came down from heaven, rolled back the stone and sat upon it, alleluia!

Ant 3 The angel spoke and said to the women, "Do not be afraid; for I know that you seek Jesus," alleluia!

READING

(In place of the responsory the following is said:)

Ant This is the day our God has made; let us give praise in song, alleluia!

CANTICLE OF ZECHARIAH

Ant Early on the first day of the week, at sunrise, the women went to the tomb, alleluia.

INTERCESSIONS:

God has raised up for us a mighty savior who chose to lay down his life for us. With renewed confidence, let us pray:

Raise us up with you, Christ Jesus!

Lamb of God, you returned from death to bring peace;
—may we learn to return blessing for injury.
Servant of God, you showed us the way to reveal your God and ours;
—live in us your spirit of service to all without discrimination.
Passionate Lover of humanity, you emptied yourself to become like us;
—may the fire of your Spirit transform us to your likeness.
Rising Dawn of our universe, First-born of all creation,
—draw us with you into eternal light.
Giver of life, bring to new birth in water and Spirit all our catechumens;
—may they find unending joy as your people.

PRAYER: Most merciful, loving God, you have been revealed in Christ Jesus as he rises to bring us the message of forgiveness and all-embracing love. May we who have passed with him from death to life in the mysteries we have celebrated, be signs of your living among us. We ask this through Jesus, our risen Savior. Amen.

DAYTIME PRAYER

Ant 1   Christ, having risen from the dead, will die no more; death shall no longer have dominion over him, alleluia. (Psalm 8)

Ant 2   Put to death indeed in the flesh, Jesus was brought to life in the spirit, alleluia. (Psalm 19a)

Ant 3   The cross has become our victory; let us live in the holiness of Christ, alleluia. (Psalm 19:7–14)

(Prayer as in Morning Prayer)

EVENING PRAYER

Ant 1   After the Sabbath, toward the dawn of the first day of the week, Mary Magdalen and the other Mary went to see the tomb, alleluia. (Psalm 110:1–5, 7)

Ant 2   Go quickly, tell his disciples that he has risen from the dead, alleluia. (Psalm 114)

Ant 3   Jesus said to them: Do not be afraid; see, I was dead, but now I live and am among you, alleluia. (Rev. 19:1, 5–7)

READING

(In place of the responsory the following is said:)

Ant   This is the day our God has made; let us give praise in song, alleluia!

CANTICLE OF MARY

Ant   On the evening of that day, the first day of the week, the doors being shut where the disciples were, Jesus came and stood among them and said to them: "Peace be with you," alleluia!

INTERCESSIONS:

You broke the reign of death, O Christ, and we are free! With joyful voice we proclaim:

Glory and praise to you!

Redeemer of all, enlighten us who still walk in the shadow of death,
    —that with your new life we may conquer our addictions and prejudices.

Risen Savior, you appeared first to women, and sent them with the glad tidings;
    —free all women bound by traditions and cultures that inhibit their human development.

Hallowed Stranger, you appeared this evening to the disillusioned disciples on the road to Emmaus;
    —enkindle our hearts to recognize you in the unlikely circumstances of our lives.

Savior of the world, your message is peace in a world racked with violence;
    —teach us the way of non-violence toward all creation.

PRAYER: Most merciful, loving God, you have been revealed in Christ Jesus as he rises to bring us the message of forgiveness and all-embracing love. May we who have passed with him from death to life in the mysteries we have celebrated, be signs of your living among us. We ask this through Jesus, our risen Savior. Amen.

EASTER MONDAY

(Antiphons and psalms as on Easter Sunday)

MORNING PRAYER

READING

(In place of the responsory the following is said:)

Ant   This is the day our God has made; let us give praise in song, alleluia!

CANTICLE OF ZECHARIAH

Ant   Go and tell his disciples that Christ is alive again, alleluia.

INTERCESSIONS:

Christ Jesus appears among us today as the Morning Star rising in our hearts.
In gratitude we cry out:
> **Light of Christ, we praise you!**

You are among us as light for our world; awaken us to new consciousness,
  —that your Spirit may have full sway in our lives.
You are among us as truth; open the ears of our hearts,
  —that we may listen untiringly for the good, the true and the beautiful
    which emanates from you.
You are among us as the Way; lure us into your ways,
  —that all our paths may be peaceful and all our ways, love.
You are among us as Life; may we surrender to that life,
  —that all peoples may be irresistibly drawn toward unending life in you.

PRAYER: O God, through this paschal mystery you have saved the world.
Uphold your people with your grace that they may walk in perfect
freedom on their way to life eternal. This we ask through Jesus, our
risen Savior. Amen.

DAYTIME PRAYER

Ant 1   Christ, having risen from the dead, will die no more; death shall no
longer have dominion over him, alleluia. (Psalm 8)

Ant 2   Put to death indeed in the flesh, Jesus was brought to life in the
spirit, alleluia. (Psalm 19a)

Ant 3   The cross has become our victory; let us live in the holiness of Christ,
alleluia. (Psalm 19:7–14)

(Prayer as in Morning Prayer)

EVENING PRAYER

READING

(In place of the responsory the following is said:)

Ant   This is the day our God has made; let us give praise in song, alleluia!

CANTICLE OF MARY

Ant   The angel said: Why do you seek the living among the dead? He is not here but has risen, alleluia!

INTERCESSIONS:

Jesus is the Evening Star which lights our path to heaven; in joy let us cry out:
Stay with us, for the day is now far spent.

O Christ, your resurrection sounds the death knell of sin;
  —may we live out courageously our struggle for true freedom and wholeness.

The tomb could not contain you, O Jesus, who had freely submitted to death;
  —lead us out of our sterile selfishness to genuine surrender.

You won paradise for the thief; grant eternal joy to all who have died,
  —that they may praise your mercy forever.

In taking flesh among us you raised all creation to a new dignity;
  —teach us to have an ever-growing reverence for the work of your hands and a sense of responsibility for its preservation.

PRAYER: O God, through this paschal mystery you have saved the world. Uphold your people with your grace that they may walk in perfect freedom on their way to life eternal This we ask through Jesus, our risen Savior. Amen.

EASTER TUESDAY

(Antiphons and psalms as on Easter Sunday)

MORNING PRAYER

READING

(In place of the responsory the following is said:)

Ant   This is the day our God has made; let us give praise in song, alleluia!

CANTICLE OF ZECHARIAH

Ant   Woman, why are you weeping, whom do you seek? Sir, if you have carried him away, tell me where you have laid him and I will take him away!

INTERCESSIONS:

God raised up the temple of your body, as you prophesied, O Christ. By that power won for us we joyfully cry out:
May the whole world come to fullness of life.

Christ Jesus, your victory has changed our sorrow into joy;
  —help us share that joy with all we meet today.

You have overcome death by your total acceptance of death;
  —let your courage live in us as we strive for a non-violent way of life.

It was love that overcame your fear and dread;
  —strengthen in that love all who face mortal anguish.

You breathed peace into your disciples, and sent them to share the good news;
  —fill us with that peace that brands us as your own.
Your death has swallowed up death;
  —may all who have died awake to life with you.

PRAYER: O God, we praise you in the victory of life over death in Jesus, our Savior. Help us to comprehend the awesome mystery of its effects in our life and make us tireless witnesses of this good news. We ask this in his name. Amen.

DAYTIME PRAYER

Ant 1   Christ, having risen from the dead, will die no more; death shall no longer have dominion over him, alleluia. (Psalm 8)

Ant 2   Put to death indeed in the flesh, Jesus was brought to life in the spirit, alleluia. (Psalm 19a)

Ant 3   The cross has become our victory; let us live in the holiness of Christ, alleluia. (Psalm 19:7–14)

(Prayer as in Morning Prayer)

EVENING PRAYER

READING

(In place of the responsory the following is said:)

Ant   This is the day our God has made; let us give praise in song, alleluia!

CANTICLE OF MARY

Ant   Jesus said to Mary: Do not cling to me, for I have not yet ascended, but go to my sisters and brothers and say to them, I am ascending to my God and your God.

INTERCESSIONS:

As we recall your return to those you loved, our hearts cry out in joy as we say:
  Remain with us, Jesus, for the day is now far spent!

You sent your holy women, Christ Jesus, to be apostles to the apostles;
  —show your special regard for all women who are still shackled by the slavery of our culture and free them to be good news for the world.
You rewarded the undaunted search of Mary Magdalen with your glorified presence;
  —grant that we may be persevering in the cause of peace.
You have opened a new way of hope for our world;
  —may our lives incarnate that hope to the despairing, the indifferent, and the lonely.
Your resurrection, O Christ, has transformed our universe;
  —sensitize us to a new, all-embracing concern for our environment and a humble regard for all creatures who share a common source, a loving creator.

PRAYER: O God, we praise you in the victory of life over death in Jesus, our Savior. Help us to comprehend the awesome mystery of its effects in our life and make us tireless witnesses of this good news. We ask this in his name. Amen.

EASTER WEDNESDAY

(Antiphons and psalms as on Easter Sunday)

MORNING PRAYER

READING

(In place of the responsory the following is said:)

Ant   This is the day our God has made; let us give praise in song, alleluia!

CANTICLE OF ZECHARIAH

Ant   O foolish and slow of heart to believe all that the prophets have spoken! Was it not necessary that the Christ should suffer these things and so enter into glory? Alleluia.

INTERCESSIONS:

Behold the lion of the tribe of Juda, the root of David, has overcome death to open the scroll and its seven seals. In grateful praise we cry out, saying:

Thanksgiving, power, honor, and glory to you, Christ Jesus!

You have shown your power, O Jesus, in taking on our weakness;
—help us share in your victory by standing with the oppressed whenever the opportunity presents itself.
You have freed us by your blood;
—help us to accept that freedom and to use it responsibly for the building up of our world and for lifting up the down-trodden.
You have called us to be liberators of our inner powers;
—give us the humility to cultivate those lesser talents, which we prefer to overlook, for the sake of wholeness.
You taught us to visit prisoners;
—may our prayers this day touch all those imprisoned for any reason, that healing may come to the suffering, perseverance, steadfast faith and hope to all prisoners of conscience.

PRAYER: O God, through the self-emptying of the Word made flesh you have raised up our fallen world and showed us the way of true glory. Help us to abide in this love that we, too, may radiate Christ's humble, self-giving love to all. We ask this in Jesus' name. Amen.

DAYTIME PRAYER

Ant 1   Christ, having risen from the dead, will die no more; death shall no longer have dominion over him, alleluia. (Psalm 8)

Ant 2   Put to death indeed in the flesh, Jesus was brought to life in the spirit, alleluia. (Psalm 19a)

Ant 3   The cross has become our victory; let us live in the holiness of Christ, alleluia. (Psalm 19:7–14)

(Prayer as in Morning Prayer)

EVENING PRAYER

READING

(In place of the responsory the following is said:)

Ant This is the day our God has made; let us give praise in song, alleluia!

CANTICLE OF MARY

Ant They drew near to the village to which they were going. He appeared to be going further, but they constrained him, saying, "Stay with us, for it is towards evening and the day is now far spent." Alleluia.

INTERCESSIONS:

Christ Jesus is risen as he promised, yet disguised in many ways. In faith, let us pray:

Let us see your glory, O Christ!

You come to us in our deprived sisters and brothers; show us how to lighten their burdens,
—that they may retain their dignity and hope.
You come to us in the helplessness of little children seeking affirmation; touch our hearts,
—that we may recognize and alleviate those needs.
You come to us in the weariness and powerlessness of the elderly. Give us your wisdom,
—that we may recognize you in them with tender, reverent love, and heartfelt gratitude, and service.
You come to us in the breaking of the bread,
—that we may celebrate our oneness with all humankind and give our lives in service.

PRAYER: O God, through the self-emptying of the Word made flesh you have raised up our fallen world and showed us the way of true glory. Help us to abide in this love that we, too, may radiate Christ's humble self-giving love to all. We ask this in Jesus' name. Amen.

EASTER THURSDAY

(Antiphons and psalms as on Easter Sunday)

MORNING PRAYER

READING

(In place of the responsory the following is said:)

Ant This is the day our God has made; let us give praise in song, alleluia!

CANTICLE OF ZECHARIAH

Ant Jesus stood in the midst of his disciples and said to them: Peace to you! It is I, do not be afraid, alleluia.

INTERCESSIONS:

Jesus has gone down into the valley of death for our sake and has come back in triumph. Let us cry out with confidence:

Good Shepherd, bring us to wholeness.

You have known the depths of suffering; grant solace to all the sick and dying,
— that they may experience the joy of your saving help.

You have known the anguish of betrayal, loss, and desolation; draw near to all who suffer,
— that they may know the power of your resurrection in their lives.

You have always taken the part of the lonely and the orphan; now you have left their care to us. Guide us,
— that we may have the wisdom to aid them according to their needs.

You are yearning for the hearts of the young; help us to live lives that inspire, encourage and befriend them, especially in difficult times,
— that discouragement may be transformed into enthusiasm by our understanding and care.

PRAYER: O God, in the paschal mystery you have saved the world. Support the weakness of your people by your grace, that they may attain to true freedom and walk in the way of eternal life, following the steps of Jesus, our shepherd. We ask this in his name. Amen.

DAYTIME PRAYER

Ant 1 Christ, having risen from the dead, will die no more; death shall no longer have dominion over him, alleluia. (Psalm 8)

Ant 2 Put to death indeed in the flesh, Jesus was brought to life in the spirit, alleluia. (Psalm 19a)

Ant 3 The cross has become our victory; let us live in the holiness of Christ, alleluia. (Psalm 19:7–14)

(Prayer as in Morning Prayer)

EVENING PRAYER

READING

(In place of the responsory the following is said:)

Ant This is the day our God has made; let us give praise in song, alleluia!

CANTICLE OF MARY

Ant While they still disbelieved in joy and wonder, he said to them: Have you anything to eat? They gave him a piece of broiled fish, and he took it and ate before them, alleluia.

INTERCESSIONS:

Christ, our Pasch, is sacrificed. In joy let us cry out:

Worthy are you, O Christ, to receive honor, glory and praise!

You laid down your life that we might live;
— give us courage to die to all selfishness that we may live for others.
You were the joy of the disciples;
— be our joy and perennial hope.
You call us out of disbelief by your care for our daily needs;
— may we revel in such love and pass it on.
You are the first-born from the dead;
— may all who have died experience the joy of your salvation.

PRAYER: O God, in the paschal mystery you have saved the world. Support the weakness of your people by your grace, that they may attain to true freedom and walk in the way of eternal life, following the steps of Jesus, our shepherd. We ask this in his name. Amen.

EASTER FRIDAY

(Antiphons and psalms as on Easter Sunday)

MORNING PRAYER

READING

(In place of the responsory the following is said:)

Ant This is the day our God has made; let us give praise in song, alleluia!

CANTICLE OF ZECHARIAH

Ant Just as the day was breaking, Jesus stood on the shore; yet the disciples did not know that it was Jesus, alleluia.

INTERCESSIONS:

Christ, risen from the dead, is the crown of all creation. Let us give praise, saying:
Glory, honor, praise and thanksgiving be to you, Christ Jesus!

In your rising, Jesus, you gave us your Spirit,
— that we may live out the vocation to which we are called.
You broke the reign of death, O Christ,
— that divisions may be healed and new life spring up again.
You rescued us from the power of darkness,
— that you might bring us to the fullness of light.
You, Christ Jesus, are the fullness of God among us;
— through you may we be reconciled and be people of peace.

PRAYER: All powerful, ever-living God, you have reconciled humanity through the paschal mystery. Grant that what we celebrate today in faith we may activate in our lives. We ask this through Jesus, our savior. Amen.

DAYTIME PRAYER

Ant 1 Christ, having risen from the dead, will die no more; death shall no longer have dominion over him, alleluia. (Psalm 8)

Ant 2 Put to death indeed in the flesh, Jesus was brought to life in the spirit, alleluia. (Psalm 19a)

Ant 3 The cross has become our victory; let us live in the holiness of Christ, alleluia. (Psalm 19:7–14)

(Prayer as in Morning Prayer)

EVENING PRAYER

READING

(In place of the responsory the following is said:)

Ant This is the day our God has made; let us give praise in song, alleluia!

CANTICLE OF MARY

Ant None of the disciples dared to ask him, "Who are you?" They knew it was the Christ, alleluia.

INTERCESSIONS:

Let us praise the wonderful works of our God as we say:
                    Your mighty works are clearly seen!
When Christ arose, you filled the earth with glory, O God;
   —may we radiate that glory to all we meet today.
Through the mystery of Christ's rising may we begin anew,
   —to direct all our desires to the coming of the fullness of life.
Light of the world, help us recognize your presence,
   —that we may cultivate discernment as a way of life.
May the redemption which Jesus won for us make us joyful,
   —that we may in thought and deed be alleluia people.

PRAYER: All powerful, ever-living God, you have reconciled humanity through the paschal mystery. Grant that what we celebrate today in faith we may activate in our lives. We ask this through Jesus, our savior. Amen.

EASTER SATURDAY

(Antiphons and psalms as on Easter Sunday)

MORNING PRAYER

READING

(In place of the responsory the following is said:)

Ant This is the day our God has made; let us give praise in song, alleluia!

CANTICLE OF ZECHARIAH

Ant Now when Jesus was risen early on the first day of the week, he appeared first to Mary Magdalen, alleluia.

INTERCESSIONS:

O splendor of eternal light and sun of justice, to you, risen from death, we pray:

Illumine our pathway to heaven!

You appeared first to Mary Magdalen and the other women and sent them as your first witnesses;

—break down the barriers that inhibit women from following your call.

You died reviled, and returned to us breathing peace,

—that we may be schooled to non-violence.

You died with passionate love for all;

—teach us an all-embracing love of every race, and creed, and nation.

You were risen from death as promise of our future life;

—grant to all who have died a share in your glory.

PRAYER: O most loving God, grant that we who have celebrated these paschal mysteries with great joy, may come to share in the joy that is eternal. We ask this through Jesus, our risen savior. Amen.

DAYTIME PRAYER

Ant 1 Christ, having risen from the dead, will die no more; death shall no longer have dominion over him, alleluia. (Psalm 8)

Ant 2 Put to death indeed in the flesh, Jesus was brought to life in the spirit, alleluia. (Psalm 19a)

Ant 3 The cross has become our victory; let us live in the holiness of Christ, alleluia. (Psalm 19:7–14)

(Prayer as in Morning Prayer)

SECOND SUNDAY OF EASTER

EVENING PRAYER I

(Antiphons and psalms as in Easter Evening Prayer)

READING

(In place of the responsory the following is said:)

Ant This is the day our God has made; let us give praise in song, alleluia.

CANTICLE OF MARY

Ant After that Jesus appeared to his followers as they sat at table, alleluia.

INTERCESSIONS:

Handed over to death, Christ Jesus was raised to life for our justification. In living hope we pray:

Free us, Christ Jesus, from what still binds us!

You, who have shared our human condition, look on the oppressed and the deprived,

—that they may be aided in their struggle for self-determination.

You, who have revealed in your being the compassion of God,
  —grant relief to the sick and the dying through our own compassion.
You, who call us to use our God-given talents,
  —give courage to further our own human development.
You, who call us each to wholeness, unsettle our complacencies,
    —that we recognize our blindness and surrender to the guidance of your
    Spirit.

PRAYER: Most loving God, we have just celebrated the gift of the paschal
          mysteries. Grant that we may preserve their spirit in our way of life
          by the support of your abiding grace. We ask this through Jesus,
          our risen savior. Amen.

MORNING PRAYER
(Antiphons from Easter; psalms from Feasts and Solemnities)

READING

(In place of the responsory the following is said:)

Ant   This is the day our God has made; let us give praise in song, alleluia!

CANTICLE OF ZECHARIAH

Ant   Peace be with you! As I have been sent, so do I send you, alleluia.

INTERCESSIONS:

The tomb of Christ has become death's burial place. In joy we cry out:
  You have risen, O Christ, let heaven and earth rejoice!
You taught the ways of peace and forgiveness in your return to us, Christ Jesus;
  —transform our own longing into deeds of mercy.
You appeared to many in their varied needs;
  —help us to respect the differences we see in one another and learn to
  appreciate them.
You died for us and have risen to help us come to wholeness and holiness;
  —may we, with renewed courage, uphold the human rights of all peoples.
Lamb of God, in your brokenness you sought to mend;
  —through your passion and death may we become healers of relationships
  and true lovers of humanity.

PRAYER: Most loving God, we have just celebrated the gift of the paschal
          mysteries. Grant that we may preserve their spirit in our way of life
          by the support of your abiding grace. We ask this through Jesus,
          our risen savior. Amen.

DAYTIME PRAYER

Ant 1   Christ, having risen from the dead, will die no more; death shall no
        longer have dominion over him, alleluia. (Psalm 8)

Ant 2   Put to death indeed in the flesh, Jesus was brought to life in the
        spirit, alleluia. (Psalm 19a)

Ant 3   The cross has become our victory; let us live in the holiness of Christ, alleluia. (Psalm 19:7–14)

(Prayer as in Morning Prayer)

EVENING PRAYER II

(Antiphons and Psalms as on Easter)

READING

(In place of the responsory the following is said:)

Ant   This is the day our God has made; let us give praise in song, alleluia!

CANTICLE OF MARY

Ant   On the evening of that day, the first day of the week, Jesus came and stood among them and said: "Peace!" Alleluia.

INTERCESSIONS:

Now triumphant, Christ displays the spoils of victory, peace. In grateful praise we cry out:

Glory to you, Christ Jesus!

Your death has freed all creation from endless death;
 —make us liberators of our earth's ecology.
Your free acceptance of death has overcome death;
 —free all prisoners of conscience from every bondage.
You showed us the way of true leadership;
 —inspire all church leaders in the ways of loving service.
In your death you relinquished loving relationships,
 —so that broken relationships might be mended and faithful ones
  strengthened.

PRAYER: Most loving God, we have just celebrated the gift of the paschal mysteries. Grant that we may preserve their spirit in our way of life by the support of your abiding grace. We ask this through Jesus, our risen savior. Amen.

SUNDAYS OF EASTER
Weeks 3 to 6

(Antiphons and psalms from the current week in the Psalter)

EVENING PRAYER I

READING

RESPONSORY

Christ our hope has risen, alleluia, alleluia. —**Christ**...
Let us rejoice and give thanks, —**alleluia**...
Glory to you, Source of all Being, Eternal Word, and Holy Spirit. —**Christ**...

CANTICLE OF MARY

Sun 3   Beginning with Moses and the prophets, Jesus interpreted in all the
         scriptures the things concerning him, alleluia.

Sun 4   I came that you may have life and have it abundantly, alleluia.

Sun 5   Let not your hearts be troubled. Believe in God; believe also in me,
         alleluia.

Sun 6   If you love me, you will keep my commandment; my commandment is
         that you love one another, alleluia.

INTERCESSIONS: Sundays 3 and 5

Christ Jesus has loved us and redeemed us by his death and rising. In joy let us
proclaim:
        Worthy is the Lamb to receive honor and glory, wisdom and praise!

Savior God, you have made us partakers of your priesthood;
    —may we offer you continual thanks and praise.
You have conquered death; raise us to new life,
    —that we may be your resurrection people.
You walked the way of Calvary's anguish;
    —in your powerful compasssion succor all prisoners of conscience and those
      unjustly detained.
In your resurrection, you promised life after death;
    —may all who have died enjoy fullness of life with you.

INTERCESSIONS: Sundays 4 and 6

You, Christ Jesus, are the sign of our hope and joy. In gratitude we pray:
        Christ yesterday, today and forever, alleluia!

You are the Good Shepherd; you know us and call us by name;
    —may we recognize the good shepherds in our midst and heed their prophetic
      calls.
You give us your gift of peace;
    —enable us to use our energies to create a world of peace and harmony.
You are the Lamb of God;
    —help us to see the signs of resurrection and new life around us.
You promise to make your home with us;
    —grant us the faith to believe that you truly desire to dwell within each of us.

PRAYER

Sun 3   O God, you call us to the banquet table of your eucharist that we may
         realize our union with you. You overcome our lack of faith with
         everlasting fidelity. God of our life and our salvation, grant that we
         may always recognize you in the breaking of the bread and learn again
         and again the message of your Christ, that you are a God of love. We
         ask this in the name of Jesus, our risen savior. Amen.

Sun 4   O God, you sent Christ Jesus to be our shepherd and the lamb of
         sacrifice. Help us to embrace the mystery of salvation, the promise of
         life rising out of death. Help us to hear the call of Christ and give us the
         courage to follow it readily that we, too, may lead others to you. This
         we ask through Jesus, our shepherd and guide. Amen.

Sun 5   O God, you are One and all your works are holy. Who can fathom your wondrous love? Through Jesus, you call us all to life and count our love for each other as love for you. As we celebrate this Easter season, we ask you to increase our faith, to renew our hope, and to let our love abound to the praise of your glory, that we may live with you forever and ever. Amen.

Sun 6   O God, we praise you in the resurrection of Jesus, sign of victory over death, the proclamation of your union with creation. As we endeavor to live the message and mystery of his life, grant us the grace to remain faithful to you. Let us rise from our daily deaths, and let our lives bear witness to our union with you. Grant this through Jesus who lives with you in the unity of the Holy Spirit for all eternity. Amen.

MORNING PRAYER

READING

RESPONSORY

You are our savior, O Christ, alleluia, alleluia. —**You**...
Your death brings us life, —**alleluia**...
Glory to you, Source of all Being, Eternal Word, and Holy Spirit. —**You**...

CANTICLE OF ZECHARIAH

Sun 3   Thus it is written, that the Christ should suffer and on the third day rise from the dead, and that repentance and forgiveness should be preached to all nations, alleluia.

Sun 4   I am the Good Shepherd; I lay down my life for my sheep, alleluia.

Sun 5   I am the vine; you are the branches, alleluia.

Sun 6   As God has loved me, so have I loved you; abide in my love, alleluia.

INTERCESSIONS: Sundays 3 to 5

Handed over to death, Christ Jesus was raised to life for our justification. In living hope we pray:

Free us, Christ Jesus, from what still binds us!

You, who have shared our human condition, look on the oppressed and the deprived,
—that they may be aided in their struggle for self-determination.
You, who have revealed in your being the compassion of God,
—grant relief to the sick and the dying through our own compassion.
You, who call us to use our God-given talents,
—give courage to further our own human development.
You, who call us each to wholeness, unsettle our complacencies,
—that we recognize our blindness and surrender to the guidance of your Spirit.

INTERCESSIONS: Sundays 4 and 6

Let us praise God who calls us all to new life through faith in Jesus. In confidence we pray:

Blessed be God whose mercy endures forever.

O God, we crucified your Son and you offer us resurrection and life;
—teach us your ways of mercy and forgiveness.
O Christ, loving shepherd, you walk before us in life and in death;
—help us to support and encourage leaders who seek to serve you and your people with integrity.
You call us to die daily to all that would separate us from you;
—through the celebration of your resurrection may we grow in courage and joy in following you.
Once rejected, you are raised up, the cornerstone of our faith;
—in times of failure and pain let your resurrection be a wellspring of hope in our hearts.

PRAYER

Sun 3   O God, you call us to the banquet table of your eucharist that we may realize our union with you. You overcome our lack of faith with everlasting fidelity. God of our life and our salvation, grant that we may always recognize you in the breaking of the bread and learn again and again the message of your Christ, that you are a God of love. We ask this in the name of Jesus, our risen savior. Amen.

Sun 4   O God, you sent Christ Jesus to be our shepherd and the lamb of sacrifice. Help us to embrace the mystery of salvation, the promise of life rising out of death. Help us to hear the call of Christ and give us the courage to follow it readily that we, too, may lead others to you. This we ask through Jesus, our shepherd and guide. Amen.

Sun 5   O God, you are One and all your works are holy. Who can fathom your wondrous love? Through Jesus, you call us all to life and count our love for each other as love for you. As we celebrate this Easter season, we ask you to increase our faith, to renew our hope, and to let our love abound to the praise of your glory, that we may live with you forever and ever. Amen.

Sun 6   O God, we praise you in the resurrection of Jesus, sign of victory over death, the proclamation of your union with creation. As we endeavor to live the message and mystery of his life, grant us the grace to remain faithful to you. Let us rise from our daily deaths, and let our lives bear witness to our union with you. Grant this through Jesus who lives with you in the unity of the Holy Spirit for all eternity. Amen.

DAYTIME PRAYER

Ant 1   Alleluia, Christ is risen, alleluia, alleluia.
Ant 2   The women and men who believed in Jesus rejoiced, alleluia, alleluia.
Ant 3   Stay with us, for it is toward evening and the day is far spent, alleluia, alleluia.

(Prayer as in Morning Prayer)

EVENING PRAYER II

READING

RESPONSORY

Christ is the sun that never sets, alleluia, alleluia. —**Christ**...
Giving light to our hearts, —**alleluia**...
Glory to you, Source of all Being, Eternal Word, and Holy Spirit. —**Christ**...

CANTICLE OF MARY

Sun 3   The disciple whom Jesus loved said to Peter, "It is the Lord." Alleluia.

Sun 4   My sheep hear my voice; I know them and they follow me, alleluia.

Sun 5   By this will all know that you are my followers, if you have love for one another, alleluia.

Sun 6   Peace I leave with you, my peace I give you, alleluia.

INTERCESSIONS: Sundays 3 and 5

Let us rejoice with Christ Jesus who manifests himself in the breaking of the bread. In joy we pray:

You are risen indeed!

O Christ, you showed yourself to your disciples and assured them with your touch;
  —give us the grace we need to embrace the mysteries of your life with our minds and hearts.
Your disciples recognized you in the miraculous catch of fish;
  —help us to see you in your care for us each day of our lives.
You challenged Peter's love and commissioned him to lead your church;
  —fill our hearts with the love and zeal we need to fulfill our mission on earth.
Throughout your life and to the last, your message was a call to love;
  —teach us how to hear and live your message in the complexity of our lives.

INTERCESSIONS: Sundays 4 and 6

Those who have died with Christ will rise with him; God will wipe away every tear from their eyes, and so we rejoice:

Worthy is the Lamb that was slain.

Jesus, you are the way, the truth, and the life; we go to God only through you;
  —let us always hear and follow your spirit of truth.
Your resurrection heralds a new heaven and a new earth;
  —help us to live daily with minds and hearts open to your Holy Spirit.
You tell us that people of faith will do works even greater than your own;
  —increase our faith that we, too, may bring healing and new life to the world.
We praise you for the bread of thanksgiving and the words of your gospel;
  —give us the grace to let these gifts of God bear fruit a hundredfold to God's glory.

PRAYER

Sun 3 O God, you call us to the banquet table of your eucharist that we may realize our union with you. You overcome our lack of faith with everlasting fidelity. God of our life and our salvation, grant that we may always recognize you in the breaking of the bread and learn again and again the message of your Christ, that you are a God of love. We ask this in the name of Jesus, our risen savior. Amen.

Sun 4 O God, you sent Christ Jesus to be our shepherd and the lamb of sacrifice. Help us to embrace the mystery of salvation, the promise of life rising out of death. Help us to hear the call of Christ and give us the courage to follow it readily that we, too, may lead others to you. This we ask through Jesus, our shepherd and guide. Amen.

Sun 5 O God, you are One and all your works are holy. Who can fathom your wondrous love? Through Jesus, you call us all to life and count our love for each other as love for you. As we celebrate this Easter season, we ask you to increase our faith, to renew our hope, and to let our love abound to the praise of your glory, that we may live with you forever and ever. Amen.

Sun 6 O God, we praise you in the resurrection of Jesus, sign of victory over death, the proclamation of your union with creation. As we endeavor to live the message and mystery of his life, grant us the grace to remain faithful to you. Let us rise from our daily deaths, and let our lives bear witness to our union with you. Grant this through Jesus who lives with you in the unity of the Holy Spirit for all eternity. Amen.

MONDAY — Weeks 2 to 6

MORNING PRAYER

READING

RESPONSORY

Christ rose from the grave, alleluia, alleluia. —**Christ**...
Conquering sin and death, —**alleluia**...
Glory to you, Source of all Being, Eternal Word, and Holy Spirit. —**Christ**...

CANTICLE OF ZECHARIAH

Week 2 I say to you, unless you are truly born anew, you cannot see the reign of God, alleluia.

Week 3 Do not labor for the food which perishes, but for the food which endures to eternal life, alleluia.

Week 4 I am the Good Shepherd. I lay down my life for my sheep, alleluia.

Week 5 Whatever you ask in my name I will do it, that God may be glorified, alleluia.

Week 6 When the Counselor comes, the Spirit of truth whom I shall send you, you will bear witness to me, alleluia.

INTERCESSIONS: Weeks 2, 4 and 6

Christ Jesus, you rose from the dead and showed yourself to the women.
With joyful hearts we proclaim:
Wonderful are your works, O Christ.

Jesus, through your resurrection you call us to be born again;
—help us to recognize and to be open to your Spirit in our lives.
You are the Good Shepherd and you guide us with tender care;
—enlighten our civil and religious leaders; give them your mind and heart.
You promise to send the Comforter to witness on your behalf;
—empowered with your Spirit, may we bear witness to you in word and deed.
O God, you have created all things, and all that you have created is good;
—help us to see others and all things as you see them.

INTERCESSIONS: Weeks 3 and 5

Jesus, by your resurrection, you conquered sin and death and revealed the power
of God's love. We praise you and say:
We will sing of your mercy forever.

Christ Jesus, your disciples hasten to give their lives for you;
—let the sacrifice of all who serve you throughout the ages give life to your
Church.
Christ Jesus, you fed your people bread in the wilderness;
—nourish our hungry minds and hearts, and teach us to seek the things that
are to our peace.
Christ Jesus, you promised to send the Paraclete to teach us all things;
—teach us to live your word of love that the fruits of your resurrection may
encompass the whole world.
Jesus, our risen Lord, you showed yourself to your disciples and their eyes
were opened;
—let us know your presence in our lives that we may love and serve you
faithfully.

PRAYER

Week 2   O God, you granted to Nicodemus the consolation of the words of your
beloved Christ, and the challenge to transform his life. Bless all who
seek you and encourage those who are too fearful to listen to your
word. Let your creative love call us once again that we, too, may be
living witnesses of your goodness. We ask this through Christ Jesus,
risen from the dead. Amen.

Week 3   Jesus, our risen Savior, you offer us the bread of heaven, yet we cling
to what will perish. We praise your long-suffering love and ask you,
through the grace of your resurrection, to conquer our blindness and
free us from our attachment to all that keeps us from following you.
We ask this in your holy name, for you are one with our Source and
with the Spirit for all ages. Amen.

Week 4   O God, you gave Peter the wisdom and largeness of heart to open the
sheepfold of your church to the Gentiles and to all who would believe
in your Word. Give us the vision and the generosity to remove the

barriers that we place before those who seek to know and love you. Teach us how to share the fruits of the life, death, and resurrection of Jesus. Amen.

Week 5   Christ Jesus, you promise to dwell in those who love you and are true to your word. We ask you to give us loving hearts. Make us faithful to you, that with you in us, we may labor for the reign of God. We ask this in your holy name. Amen.

Week 6   Jesus, our risen Savior, you teach us to live in love and to be prepared for persecution and death. You teach us to live as you have lived. Help us to realize the presence of your Spirit in us. In your goodness, teach, heal, forgive sins, and give new life to others through us, to the glory of your name. Amen.

DAYTIME PRAYER

Ant 1   Alleluia, Christ is risen, alleluia, alleluia.

Ant 2   The women and men who believed in Jesus rejoiced, alleluia, alleluia.

Ant 3   Stay with us, for it is toward evening and the day is far spent, alleluia, alleluia.

(Prayer as in Morning Prayer)

EVENING PRAYER

READING

RESPONSORY

The followers of Jesus were filled with joy, alleluia, alleluia. —**The**. . .
When they saw him risen from the dead, —**alleluia**. . .
Glory to you, Source of all Being, Eternal Word, and Holy Spirit. —**The**. . .

CANTICLE OF MARY

Week 2   That which is born of the flesh is flesh; and that which is born of the Spirit is spirit, alleluia.

Week 3   This is the work of God, that you believe in the Anointed One sent by God, allelulia.

Week 4   I have other sheep, not of this fold; they will heed my voice, so there shall be one flock and one shepherd, alleluia.

Week 5   The Counselor will be with you and dwell in you forever, alleluia.

Week 6   I have said all this that you may be faithful, alleluia.

INTERCESSIONS: Weeks 2, 4 and 6

Jesus, you rose from the dead and your disciples recognized you in the breaking of the bread. We proclaim in faith:
Jesus is risen indeed.

Christ Jesus, through your Spirit you transformed your frightened apostles into fearless proclaimers of your word;
—bless all missionaries with fortitude and perseverance.

By your life, death, and resurrection you invite all the nations of the world to
   be the people of God;
   —help us to live as true sons and daughters of our loving Creator.
Through your resurrection you give hope to all who believe in you;
   —through our daily deaths, transform our lives evermore into your likeness.
Following your example, Peter prayed for guidance in time of decision;
   —help us to realize the necessity of prayer in our lives.
By your death and resurrection you conquered death;
   —have pity on the dying; be their light and their peace.

INTERCESSIONS: Weeks 3 and 5

Jesus, risen from the dead, you promise to live in those who love you. In homage
we pray:
     Christ Jesus, keep us faithful to you all the days of our lives.

Jesus, our salvation was your pearl of great price;
   —teach us to live and die for others and so rise with you.
You blessed little children and had time for them;
   —give us the wisdom, creativity and generosity to provide for them and those
     who care for them.
Your apostles left all to follow you; at your death you seemed to leave them;
   —help us to keep alive the hope of your resurrection both for ourselves and
     for those burdened with trials.
You taught, healed and comforted many, yet how many gave you thanks?
   —give us grateful hearts that lead us to use the gifts you give us for the
     praise and glory of God.
Jesus, you knew the sorrow that death brings;
   —comfort those who mourn.

PRAYER

Week 2   O God, you granted to Nicodemus the consolation of the words of your
beloved Christ, and the challenge to transform his life. Bless all who
seek you and encourage those who are too fearful to listen to your
word. Let your creative love call us once again that we, too, may be
living witnesses of your goodness. We ask this through Christ Jesus,
risen from the dead. Amen.

Week 3   Jesus, our risen Savior, you offer us the bread of heaven, yet we cling
to what will perish. We praise your long-suffering love and ask you,
through the grace of your resurrection, to conquer our blindness and
free us from our attachment to all that keeps us from following you.
We ask this in your holy name, for you are one with our Source and
with the Spirit, for all ages. Amen.

Week 4   O God, you gave Peter the wisdom and largeness of heart to open the
sheepfold of your church to the Gentiles and to all who would believe
in your Word. Give us the vision and the generosity to remove the
barriers that we place before those who seek to know and love you.
Teach us how to share the fruits of the life, death, and resurrection of
Jesus. Amen.

Week 5   Christ Jesus, you promise to dwell in those who love you and are true to your word. We ask you to give us loving hearts. Make us faithful to you, that with you in us, we may labor for the reign of God. Grant this in your name. Amen.

Week 6   Jesus, our risen Savior, you teach us to live in love and to be prepared for persecution and death. You teach us to live as you have lived. Help us to realize the presence of your Spirit in us. In your goodness, teach, heal, forgive sins, and give new life to others through us, to the glory of your name. Amen.

DAYTIME PRAYER

Ant 1   Alleluia, Christ is risen, alleluia, alleluia.

Ant 2   The women and men who believed in Jesus rejoiced, alleluia, alleluia.

Ant 3   Stay with us, for it is toward evening and the day is far spent, alleluia, alleluia.

(Prayer as in Morning Prayer)

TUESDAY — Weeks 2 to 6

MORNING PRAYER

READING

RESPONSORY

Christ rose from the grave, alleluia, alleluia. —**Christ**. . .
Conquering sin and death, —**alleluia**. . .
Glory to you, Source of all Being, Eternal Word, and Holy Spirit. —**Christ**. . .

CANTICLE OF ZECHARIAH

Week 2   I am the Alpha and the Omega, the first and the last, the beginning and the end, alleluia.

Week 3   Truly I tell you: it was not Moses who gave you bread from heaven; God gives you the true bread from heaven, alleluia.

Week 4   The works that I do in God's name bear witness to me, alleluia.

Week 5   Peace I leave with you, my peace I give to you, alleluia.

Week 6   I will see you again and your hearts will rejoice, and no one will take your joy from you, alleluia.

INTERCESSIONS: Weeks 2, 4 and 6

Jesus, risen from the dead, you dined with the women and men who followed you, served them, and strengthened their faith in you; and so we pray:
> **How can we repay you, O God, for your goodness to us.**

Jesus, you came to do the will of God, and in death you were raised up in glory;
> —have mercy on those who despair of meaning in life.

Your resurrection gave new hope to your small community of followers;
  —let the celebration of that same resurrection bring new life to your church
    today.
You asked those who followed you to sell all and give to the poor;
  —teach us effective ways to feed the hungry and house the homeless of our
    world.
You never cease to call us to greater intimacy with you;
  —transform the mustard seed of our faith into total dedication.

INTERCESSIONS: Weeks 3 and 5

Jesus, risen from the dead, you forgave your disciples and gave them the power to
forgive sins. We humbly pray:
                    In your mercy, remember us.
O Christ, your wounds have become your sign of victory;
  —help us to transform our suffering and labor into means of growth.
You bless those who, without seeing you, believe in your word;
  —bless those who have not heard your word; send laborers into your harvest.
You promised to be with your church until the end of time;
  —make us willing instruments in building the unity of your church throughout
    the world.
You showed your wounds to your disciples and they believed in you;
  —enfold those who inflict torture on others; transform their lives and let
    them see your loving presence in themselves and in all people.
You lived and died a person of peace;
  —grant peace to all who have died in war and to all who live with its scars.

PRAYER

Week 2 Jesus, by your death, you taught us how to stop the flow of revenge
and evil that wounds our world. By your resurrection, you show us
the fruit of self-giving love. We remember your love day by day. Help
us to be your true disciples, never counting the cost, faithful to the
end as you were faithful. Grant this in your name. Amen.

Week 3 Jesus, risen from the dead, your gift of faithful love is the bread that
nourishes us unto eternal life, and the living water that quenches our
thirst. Give us the wisdom to persevere in our love for you, that, lured
away from empty attachments, we may always choose life, to the
praise and glory of your name. Amen.

Week 4 O God, you have sent Jesus to call us into the unity of one flock.
Through his life, death and resurrection, he has revealed your love for
us and has freed us from the bondage of sin. Have mercy on us again
and again. Help us to hear his voice and to proclaim the message of
the gospel with our lives. This we ask in the name of our Risen Savior.
Amen.

Week 5 O God, our Risen Savior is the source of the peace the world cannot
give. From that eternal well, let us inundate the world with the
justice and mercy that flows from your very heart. This we ask
through this same Christ who lives with you forever. Amen.

Week 6 O God, we praise you in the life, death and resurrection of Jesus. You sent him into the world; you send us into the world. Fill our minds with his words of life and our hearts with his unsurpassing love. Let us live for one another as he did for us, to the praise and glory of your name. Amen.

DAYTIME PRAYER

Ant 1 Alleluia, Christ is risen, alleluia, alleluia.

Ant 2 The women and men who believed in Jesus rejoiced, alleluia, alleluia.

Ant 3 Stay with us, for it is toward evening and the day is far spent, alleluia, alleluia.

(Prayer as in Morning Prayer)

EVENING PRAYER

READING

RESPONSORY

The followers of Jesus were filled with joy, alleluia, alleluia. —**The**...
When they saw him risen from the dead, —**alleluia**...
Glory to you, Source of all Being, Eternal Word, and Holy Spirit. —**The**...

CANTICLE OF MARY

Week 2 Did not our hearts burn within us while Jesus opened to us the scriptures? Alleluia.

Week 3 The bread of God is that which comes down from heaven and gives life to the world, alleluia.

Week 4 My sheep hear my voice and they follow me, and I give them eternal life, alleluia.

Week 5 If you love me, you would have rejoiced, because I go to the One who sent me, alleluia.

Week 6 It is to your advantage that I go away, for if I do not go, the Counselor will not come to you, alleluia.

INTERCESSIONS: Weeks 2, 4 and 6

Jesus, risen from the dead, you have filled the world with light and hope. With joy we sing:
This is the day that our God has made.

Jesus, your resurrection frees us from the bondage of death;
—free those who are enslaved or oppressed in any way.
Your resurrection is a promise of new life;
—give hope and new opportunity for wholesome labor to migrant workers and to all who receive an inadequate wage.
By your resurrection you were freed from suffering and death;
—have mercy on all those who suffer from illness or abuse.
You rose from the dead and appeared to your mother and to your friends;
—bless our families and friends and all who show us your love and mercy.

INTERCESSIONS: Weeks 3 and 5

Jesus, you rose from the dead, the hope of all who believe in you. In faith we pray:
Christ is our light and our salvation.

Jesus, by your resurrection you herald a new heaven and a new earth;
—give us the grace to grow in love for you and in dedication to your gospel.

You are the vine and we are the branches;
—help us to remember that whatever we say or do affects everyone and everything else.

You call us not servants, but friends, for you have revealed to us the will of God;
—make us worthy of your gifts and your promises; help us to live the challenge of your gospel.

Jesus, to rise with you, we must take up our cross and follow you;
—teach us to meet the challenge of each day as a gift and a call to serve you, accepting our limitations and sharing our strengths.

Jesus, our risen Savior, your forgiving heart reveals the mercy of God to us;
—grant your peace to those who approach death with fear or sadness.

PRAYER

Week 2 Jesus, by your death, you taught us how to stop the flow of revenge and evil that wounds our world. By your resurrection, you show us the fruit of self-giving love. We remember your love day by day. Help us to be your true disciples, never counting the cost, faithful to the end as you were faithful. Grant this in your name. Amen.

Week 3 Jesus, risen from the dead, your gift of faithful love is the bread that nourishes us unto eternal life, and the living water that quenches our thirst. Give us the wisdom to persevere in our love for you, that, lured away from empty attachments, we may always choose life, to the praise and glory of your name. Amen.

Week 4 O God, you have sent Jesus to call us into the unity of one flock. Through his life, death and resurrection, he has revealed your love for us and has freed us from the bondage of sin. Have mercy on us again and again. Help us to hear his voice and to proclaim the message of the gospel with our lives. This we ask in the name of our Risen Savior. Amen.

Week 5 O God, our Risen Savior is the source of the peace the world cannot give. From that eternal well, let us inundate the world with the justice and mercy that flows from your very heart. This we ask through this same Christ who lives with you forever. Amen.

Week 6 O God, we praise you in the life, death and resurrection of Jesus. You sent him into the world; you send us into the world. Fill our minds with his words of life and our hearts with his unsurpassing love. Let us live for one another as he did for us, to the praise and glory of your name. Amen.

WEDNESDAY— Weeks 2 to 6

MORNING PRAYER

READING

RESPONSORY

Christ rose from the grave, alleluia, alleluia. —**Christ**...
Conquering sin and death, —**alleluia**...
Glory to you, Source of all Being, Eternal Word, and Holy Spirit. —**Christ**...

CANTICLE OF ZECHARIAH

Week 2 O God, you so loved the world that you gave your eternal Word, that all who have faith should not perish but have eternal life, alleluia.

Week 3 This is the will of the Most High, that all who see and believe in the Anointed One should have eternal life, alleluia.

Week 4 I have come as light into the world, that whoever believes in me may not remain in darkness, alleluia.

Week 5 I am the vine, you are the branches, alleluia.

Week 6 I have yet many things to say to you, but you cannot bear them now. The Spirit of truth will come and guide you into all truth, alleluia.

INTERCESSIONS: Weeks 2, 4 and 6

Jesus is risen from the dead, a mystery revealed to little ones. With sincere hearts we pray:

Christ Jesus, make us humble of heart.

Jesus, by your resurrection, you bring light to our darkness, hope to despair;
    —give us a hunger for your words of life.
You will not leave us orphans;
    —help us to be aware of your presence throughout the day.
You have chosen us to follow your disciples in bringing our world to fullness of life;
    —make us responsible Christians; let our lives proclaim our faith in you.
You promised the Spirit who would pray within us;
    —quiet our minds and hearts; teach us to pray.

INTERCESSIONS: Weeks 3 and 5

On the third day, the Sun of Justice arose, and darkness was conquered forever. We joyfully sing your praises:

Glory to you, O God!

O Christ, you receive all who come to you;
    —enlighten all who turn away from religion because of negative experiences.
Jesus, powerless in death, you rose in the power of God's love;
    —teach us the wisdom and necessity of non-violence for the salvation of our planet.
Jesus, you rose from the dead, making known to all the power of God's love for us;
    —help us to banish servile fear from our lives and to love as we are loved.
You appeared to your friends, each according to their need;
    —open our minds and hearts to your loving guidance in our lives.

PRAYER

Week 2 O God, you sent Christ Jesus to be our light and our salvation. Give us the grace to live with integrity and let our faith be manifested in all that we do. Heal the wound of falsehood in the world, and help us to love the light of truth. This we ask through Jesus, who is our way, our truth and our life. Amen.

Week 3 Jesus, Bread of Life, Word of God, you nourish our minds and hearts and surround us with all that is good. As we celebrate your resurrection, help us to rise from our weaknesses and let the life of your Spirit renew us day by day. We ask this in the power of your name. Amen.

Week 4 O God, you sent Christ Jesus into the world not to judge but to save it, to enable all people to live wholesome lives in the image of their Creator. Let this Easter Season renew our hope as we endeavor to do your will and to grow in love. We ask this in the name of Jesus. Amen.

Week 5 Christ Jesus, by your resurrection you have made all things new. Give us the courage to pass beyond the familiar and to heed the voice of your Spirit in our lives. Let your healing and life-giving ways be a part of all that we do, and let us welcome all that magnifies your name. Amen.

Week 6 O God, you have created us and you sustain us daily with loving care. As we celebrate the resurrection of Jesus, confirm our faith in our own life after death. Help us to live in your presence, to hear your voice and follow it, that we may live with you now and in eternity, forever and ever. Amen.

DAYTIME PRAYER

Ant 1 Alleluia, Christ is risen, alleluia, alleluia.

Ant 2 The women and men who believed in Jesus rejoiced, alleluia, alleluia.

Ant 3 Stay with us, for it is toward evening and the day is far spent, alleluia, alleluia.

(Prayer as in Morning Prayer)

EVENING PRAYER

READING

RESPONSORY

The followers of Jesus were filled with joy, alleluia, alleluia. —**The**...
When they saw him risen from the dead, —**alleluia**...
Glory to you, Source of all Being, Eternal Word, and Holy Spirit. —**The**...

CANTICLE OF MARY

Week 2 Christ came to save the world, not to condemn it, alleluia.

Week 3   I have come down from heaven to do the will of the One who sent me, alleluia.

Week 4   Put your faith in me and in the One who sent me, alleluia.

Week 5   If you live in me, and my words dwell in you, ask whatever you will, and it shall be done for you, alleluia.

INTERCESSIONS: Weeks 2, 4 and 6

Jesus is risen from the dead and we, too, shall rise. We lift our voices as we say:
Wonderful are your ways, O God.

Jesus, by your resurrection, you have overcome tyranny and injustice;
—strengthen and encourage those who are victims of greed and misplaced power.
You appeared to your followers to free them from fear;
—let us never allow our sins to keep us from turning to you.
Jesus, risen from the dead, you are the Good Shepherd, seeking those who are lost;
—teach us how to proclaim the good news to those who do not know you.
You revealed the secrets of God's designs to your followers;
—help us to live the graces of our baptism.
You spoke to Peter about how he would die;
—prepare us for death by a life of dedication to you.

INTERCESSIONS: Weeks 3 and 5

Jesus rose from the dead and worked many signs and wonders in the presence of his disciples, and so we pray:
O God, we long to see your face.

Jesus, you commission those who follow you to bear much fruit;
—give us the zeal to live disciplined lives, opening ourselves to your Spirit.
You promise that what we ask in your name will be granted;
—never let us be separated from you.
You kept the law of Moses and fulfilled it;
—give us the wisdom to discern those things that are for the glory of God.
You rose from the dead in the secret of night;
—keep us watchful and ready for the coming of your grace in our lives.
Your resurrection healed the hearts of your mother and your disciples;
—be with those who mourn the death of their loved ones.

PRAYER

Week 2   O God, you sent Christ Jesus to be our light and our salvation. Give us the grace to live with integrity and let our faith be manifested in all that we do. Heal the wound of falsehood in the world, and help us to love the light of truth. This we ask through Jesus, who is our way, our truth and our life. Amen.

Week 3   Jesus, Bread of Life, Word of God, you nourish our minds and hearts and surround us with all that is good. As we celebrate your resurrection, help us to rise from our weaknesses and let the life of your Spirit renew us day by day. We ask this in the power of your name. Amen.

Week 4   O God, you sent Christ Jesus into the world not to judge but to save
it, to enable all people to live wholesome lives in the image of their
Creator. Let this Easter Season renew our hope as we endeavor to do
your will and to grow in love. We ask this in the name of Jesus.
Amen.

Week 5   Christ Jesus, by your resurrection you have made all things new. Give
us the courage to pass beyond the familiar and to heed the voice of
your Spirit in our lives. Let your healing and life-giving ways be a
part of all that we do, and let us welcome all that magnifies your
name. Amen.

Week 6   O God, you have created us and you sustain us daily with loving
care. As we celebrate the resurrection of Jesus, confirm our faith in
our own life after death. Help us to live in your presence, to hear your
voice and follow it, that we may live with you now and in eternity,
forever and ever. Amen.

THURSDAY— Weeks 2 to 5

MORNING PRAYER

READING

RESPONSORY

Christ rose from the grave, alleluia, alleluia. —**Christ**...
Conquering sin and death, —**alleluia**...
Glory to you, Source of all Being, Eternal Word, and Holy Spirit. —**Christ**...

CANTICLE OF ZECHARIAH

Week 2   The Christ whom God has sent speaks the words of God, alleluia.

Week 3   Everyone who has heard and learned from the Most High comes
to me, alleluia.

Week 4   I tell you all these things that you may know that I am the one sent
from God, alleluia.

Week 5   If you keep my commandments, you will abide in my love, alleluia.

INTERCESSIONS: Weeks 2 and 4

O Christ, by your resurrection from the dead, the sorrow of the world is turned
into joy. We cry out:

Alleluia, alleluia, alleluia!

O Christ, whoever believes in you has life eternal;
— bless all those who do not know your name or your gospel.
Through the love you bear for us,
— help us to love and care for one another.
By your resurrection you transcend the needs of the flesh;
— have mercy on those who live in deprivation of any kind.
In our daily dyings and risings,
— be with us as we strive to enrich our quality of life and deepen our love
for you.

INTERCESSIONS: Weeks 3 and 5

Jesus, the lamb that was slain, is risen as he said, alleluia. Therefore, we proclaim:
By your wounds, O Christ we are healed.

O Christ, you met violence with peace, lies with truth, and death with
immortality;
—be with those who defend the innocent in our courts, and bless all who
labor to put an end to violence in our society.

You commissioned women to proclaim the good news of your resurrection;
—let those you send today to proclaim a new word be heard.

Your resurrection consoled the pierced heart of your mother;
—give comfort and courage to families of missing children; protect the
children and return them to their homes.

You came to heal the sick;
—give us insight into our brokenness, and draw us to your healing love.

PRAYER

Week 2   O God, your Word Incarnate, Jesus Christ, was obedient even to
death on a cross. As we celebrate his resurrection from the dead, grant
us the grace so to love you that we, too, will spend our lives in your
service. We ask this with Jesus who lives with you in the unity of the
Holy Spirit, now and forever. Amen.

Week 3   Christ Jesus, you are the bread come down from heaven. Nourished
on this manna, we shall never die. As we celebrate your glorious
resurrection, revive in us a longing to be one with you, and give us
grace to proclaim your gospel in word and deed. We ask this in your
name. Amen.

Week 4   O God, you know our hearts. Through the resurrection of Christ
Jesus, call us to new growth; strengthen our weakness and direct our
strength, that transformed in Christ, we may bring his healing and
forgiving word to the world. Grant this through Jesus who lives with
you and the Holy Spirit forever. Amen.

Week 5   Jesus Christ, come to cast fire on the earth, you have forgiven us,
healed us, raised our dead to life, and died for us. We give glory to
God in this celebration of your resurrection and ask you to live on in
our lives, forgiving, healing, raising up, and dying for others; that we,
too, may rise and live with you forever. Amen.

DAYTIME PRAYER

Ant 1   Alleluia, Christ is risen, alleluia, alleluia.

Ant 2   The women and men who believed in Jesus rejoiced, alleluia, alleluia.

Ant 3   Stay with us, for it is toward evening and the day is far spent,
alleluia, alleluia.

(Prayer as in Morning Prayer)

EVENING PRAYER

READING

RESPONSORY

The followers of Jesus were filled with joy, alleluia, alleluia. —**The**...
When they saw him risen from the dead, —**alleluia**...
Glory to you, Source of all Being, Eternal Word, and Holy Spirit. —**The**...

CANTICLE OF MARY

Week 2 The one who believes in the Christ has eternal life, alleluia.

Week 3 I am the living bread which came down from heaven; those who eat of this bread will live forever, alleluia.

Week 4 If you know the things of God, blessed are you if you do them, alleluia.

Week 5 These things I have spoken to you, that my joy may be in you, and that your joy may be full, alleluia.

INTERCESSIONS: Weeks 2 and 4

The risen Christ appeared to Mary Magdalen and called her by name, and so we pray:

O Christ, call us again and again.

Jesus Christ, risen in glory, death could not contain you;
— call to new life all that is dead or barren within us.
O Christ, on the cross you prayed for deliverance;
— you were heard for your reverence and raised up in glory.
Jesus, through love for the earth and all of its fruits,
— help us to redeem the harm we have done to this planet.
Rising from the dead, you returned to those with whom you had shared life;
— be with all who are lonely or handicapped in society.

INTERCESSIONS: Weeks 3 and 5

Jesus has risen from the dead. The shroud of death is laid aside and in its place—
the robe of immortality! We sing and proclaim:

Your reign shall last forever!

O God, we are your creatures and our lives are in your hands;
— make us worthy of the life, death, and resurrection of Christ.
Not a sparrow falls that you do not know it ;
— through the resurrection of Jesus, let all see the face of your love turned
    to every person of whatever race, color, or creed.
Jesus, you loved sinners and cared for them;
— reassure those who suffer from the guilt or brokenness of their past lives;
    grant them your peace.
You ask us to forgive seventy times seven times;
— strengthen and encourage those who strive to overcome addictions of
    any kind.
You wept for Lazarus, your friend, and raised him to life;
— befriend those who are ill; let them know your loving presence.

PRAYER

Week 2 O God, your Word Incarnate, Jesus Christ, was obedient even to
death on a cross. As we celebrate his resurrection from the dead, grant
us the grace so to love you that we, too, will spend our lives in your
service. We ask this with Jesus who lives with you in the unity of the
Holy Spirit, now and forever. Amen.

Week 3 Christ Jesus, you are the bread come down from heaven. Nourished
on this manna, we shall never die. As we celebrate your glorious
resurrection, revive in us a longing to be one with you, and give us
grace to proclaim your gospel in word and deed. We ask this in your
name. Amen.

Week 4 O God, you know our hearts. Through the resurrection of Christ
Jesus, call us to new growth; strengthen our weakness and direct our
strength, that transformed in Christ, we may bring his healing and
forgiving word to the world. Grant this through Jesus who lives with
you and the Holy Spirit forever. Amen.

Week 5 Jesus Christ, come to cast fire on the earth, you have forgiven us,
healed us, raised our dead to life, and died for us. We give glory to
God in this celebration of your resurrection and ask you to live on in
our lives, forgiving, healing, raising up, and dying for others; that we,
too, may rise and live with you forever. Amen.

FRIDAY — Weeks 2 to 5

MORNING PRAYER

READING

RESPONSORY

Christ rose from the grave, alleluia, alleluia. —**Christ**...
Conquering sin and death, —**alleluia**...
Glory to you, Source of all Being, Eternal Word, and Holy Spirit. —**Christ**...

CANTICLE OF ZECHARIAH

Week 2 Jesus took the bread and when he had given thanks, distributed it
to those who were with him, alleluia.

Week 3 The one who eats my flesh and drinks my blood has eternal life,
alleluia.

Week 4 Let not your hearts be troubled; believe in God, believe also in me,
alleluia.

Week 5 This is my commandment, that you love one another as I have
loved you, alleluia.

INTERCESSIONS: Weeks 2 and 4

Jesus risen from the dead, has turned all our grief into joy, and so we pray:
Let all the earth sing praise!

Christ Jesus, you had compassion on the multitude in the desert and fed them;
—help us to do all in our power to feed the hungry and care for all in need.

You fled from those who would make you king;
> —give all in public office the courage to maintain their integrity and to labor for the public good.

You are our way to God, the Source of all that is;
> —give us the grace to heed your words and to embrace your gospel with our lives.

You taught and encouraged your disciples to the very end;
> —make us tireless in sharing your gospel, patient and compasssionate with those who are slow to hear.

INTERCESSIONS: Weeks 3 and 5

Christ Jesus, who fed the multitude in the desert, rises now as the bread of eternal life. We humbly ask:
> **Give us this bread, today and always.**

Jesus, you gave your life as food for eternal life;
> —help us to see the needs of others and to give our time and energies in their service.

You have called us to bear fruit for the healing of the world;
> —during this Easter season remind us of the gift of our baptism and renew our zeal in following you.

In you we are many parts, but one body living your gospel throughout the ages;
> —let us fulfill our mission through your Holy Spirit to the glory and praise of your name.

You wept for a people who had not known you;
> —through your resurrection, help us to recognize you in one another, in all creation, and in all of the ways that you come to us.

PRAYER

Week 2 Christ Jesus, you fed your people in the desert and you feed us with the bread of life. Let our celebration of your life, death and resurrection fill our minds and hearts with zeal for the good of our earth. Help us to bring it your peace. This we ask in your name. Amen.

Week 3 O God, you promise eternal life to all who believe in you. As we celebrate the resurrection of Jesus Christ, open our minds and hearts to his message of love. Make of us the good earth that bears fruit a hundredfold. Grant this through Jesus , who lives with you in the unity of the Holy Spirit, now and always. Amen.

Week 4 O God, you have sent Christ Jesus to be our way, our truth, and our life. Through his resurrection remove from our lives all that prevents us from following the gospel, all that would lead us into error, and all that would keep us from embracing your call wholeheartedly. We ask this in the name of Jesus. Amen.

Week 5 Christ Jesus, you call us friends and ask that we love one another. Help us to see the ways that selfishness rules our lives and to learn to live for others. Help us to give all and to be cheerful in giving. This we ask in your name. Amen

DAYTIME PRAYER

Ant 1   Alleluia, Christ is risen, alleluia, alleluia.

Ant 2   The women and men who believed in Jesus rejoiced, alleluia, alleluia.

Ant 3   Stay with us, for it is toward evening and the day is far spent, alleluia, alleluia.

(Prayer as in Morning Prayer)

EVENING PRAYER

READING

RESPONSORY

The followers of Jesus were filled with joy, alleluia, alleluia. —**The**...
When they saw him risen from the dead, —**alleluia**...
Glory to you, Source of all Being, Eternal Word, and Holy Spirit. —**The**...

CANTICLE OF MARY

Week 2   When the people saw the signs Jesus worked they said: "This is indeed the prophet who has come into the world," alleluia.

Week 3   By his death and resurrection, our living Christ has redeemed all people, alleluia.

Week 4   I go to prepare a place for you, that where I am you also may be, alleluia.

Week 5   I have called you friends, for I have told you all I have heard from the One who has sent me, alleluia.

INTERCESSIONS: Weeks 2 and 4

Christ Jesus, rising from the dead, gives glory to God and new vision to all who believe. With hearts full of joy, we cry out:

Glory and praise to you, O Christ!

Jesus, you rose from the dead and proved that all your words are true;
  —in time of doubt let the light of your glory shine in our minds and hearts.
You rose from the dead and all your works are magnified;
  —give us the courage to face necessary deaths when new life beckons.
You rose from the dead, having forgiven those who had crucified you;
  —help us always to return good for evil and to pray for those who harm us.
Christ Jesus, you rose from the dead and you call us to unity;
  —teach us to realize that all we think and do affects everyone and everything in the world.

PRAYER

Week 2   Christ Jesus, you fed your people in the desert and you feed us with the bread of life. Let our celebration of your life, death and resurrection fill our minds and hearts with zeal for the good of our earth. Help us to bring it your peace. This we ask in your name. Amen.

Week 3　O God, you promise eternal life to all who believe in you. As we celebrate the resurrection of Jesus Christ, open our minds and hearts to his message of love. Make of us the good earth that bears fruit a hundredfold. Grant this through Jesus , who lives with you in the unity of the Holy Spirit, now and always. Amen.

Week 4　O God, you have sent Christ Jesus to be our way, our truth, and our life. Through his resurrection remove from our lives all that prevents us from following the gospel, all that would lead us into error, and all that would keep us from embracing your call wholeheartedly. We ask this in the name of Jesus. Amen.

Week 5　Christ Jesus, you call us friends and ask that we love one another. Help us to see the ways that selfishness rules our lives and to learn to live for others. Help us to give all and to be cheerful in giving. This we ask in your name. Amen

SATURDAY — Weeks 2 to 5

MORNING PRAYER

READING

RESPONSORY

Christ rose from the grave, alleluia, alleluia. —Christ...
Conquering sin and death, —alleluia...
Glory to you, Source of all Being, Eternal Word, and Holy Spirit. —Christ...

CANTICLE OF ZECHARIAH

Week 2　Peace to you, it is I; do not be afraid, alleluia.

Week 3　Simon Peter said: "Lord, to whom shall we go? You have the words of eternal life; we have believed and have come to know that you are the Holy One of God," alleluia.

Week 4　The one who believes in me will also do the works I do, and greater works than these, alleluia.

Week 5　Christ Jesus died and rose from the grave. In death and in life, Christ is our hope, alleluia.

INTERCESSIONS: Weeks 2 and 4

Jesus, risen from the dead, lives on, fulfilling the works of God, and so we pray:
O Christ, live on in us.

Jesus, you call us to complete the work you have begun on earth;
　—teach us to put no limits on the power of your Spirit in our lives.
Jesus, Lord of heaven and earth, the winds and the seas obey you;
　—be merciful to us and guide our human freedom that we may serve you with upright hearts.
Christ Jesus, your mother beheld your death and your resurrection;
　—bless all mothers with the strength and grace they need to bear and to guide their children.

Christ Jesus, those who have seen you have seen God;
  —let not the familiarity of your gospel blind us to seeing you as you are, son
  of Mary, son of God.

INTERCESSIONS: Weeks 3 and 5

Christ Jesus, dying you destroyed death; rising you restored life. In confidence
let us pray:
May we walk in the land of the living forever.
Jesus, you were hated by many in your lifetime, but God raised you in glory;
  —help us to rise above the opinions and rejection of others as we strive
  to be faithful to you.
You chose your disciples because they did not adhere to this world;
  —bless our world and our culture with values, directions, and leaders that
  derive their power from the gospel.
You told your disciples that they would suffer for your sake;
  —let the joy of your resurrection fill us with courage to live and die for you
Jesus, you spent your life doing good;
  —may our celebration of this Easter season enable us to bring your word
  and work to life again.

PRAYER

Week 2 O God, your love abounds in our lives and you are our help in time
of need. As we celebrate the resurrection of Jesus, bring new life to
our church and to each of us. Give us a hunger to know you better
and zeal to do your will. We ask this through Jesus, our way. Amen.

Week 3 Christ Jesus, your words are spirit and life; we long to follow you
unreservedly. Through your resurrection, give us the grace to love and
respect the gift of life each day and to be open to the depths and
heights of the new life to which you call us. Grant that someday we
may live with you for all eternity. Amen.

Week 4 O God, giver of all that is good, we praise you in the life, death and
resurrection of Jesus Christ. During this Easter season, let his saving
light live in us in abundance, bringing guidance, healing, and the
peace that only you can give. We ask this in Jesus' name. Amen.

Week 5 O God, you have sent your eternal Word, born of a woman, to reveal
your love and to call us to new life. Through his resurrection give us
the grace to recognize your love and to respond with open and loving
hearts. This we ask of you in the name of Jesus. Amen.

DAYTIME PRAYER

Ant 1 Alleluia, Christ is risen, alleluia, alleluia.

Ant 2 The women and men who believed in Jesus rejoiced, alleluia, alleluia.

Ant 3 Stay with us, for it is toward evening and the day is far spent,
alleluia, alleluia.

(Prayer as in Morning Prayer)

ASCENSION

EVENING PRAYER I

Ant 1   I go to prepare a place for you, so that you can be with me forever, alleluia. (Psalm 113)

Ant 2   As Jesus blessed his followers, he parted from them and was carried up into heaven, alleluia. (Psalm 117)

Ant 3   I will be with you until the end of time, alleluia. (Rev. 11:17–18; 12:10b–12a)

READING

RESPONSORY

Christ ascends into splendor, alleluia, alleluia —**Christ**...
The glory of God fills all creation, —**allelulia**...
Glory to you, Source of all Being, Eternal Word, and Holy Spirit. —**Christ**...

CANTICLE OF MARY

Ant   You are my witnesses. Proclaim the good news to all the earth, alleluia, alleluia.

INTERCESSIONS:

We give you thanks, Christ Jesus, for your appearances to your early followers and the many ways you appear to us. We cry out in joy:
Alleluia, alleluia, alleluia!

Christ Jesus, before your Ascension you instructed the women and men who believed in you;
—continue to instruct all your faithful people, especially those responsible for the formation of the young and those troubled in conscience.
You promised to send the Holy Spirit to empower us;
—help us to recognize and claim the gifts we have been given.
Christ Jesus, you cautioned your disciples to wait for the coming of the Spirit;
—protect us from impulsiveness and give us discerning hearts that we may act with prudence and wisdom.
Christ Jesus, after you ascended, your disciples hoped for your return;
—give us faith to believe that you have returned and are still with us as we carry on our daily activities.

PRAYER: O God, we believe that Jesus, your Incarnate Word, lives in you and in us. Strengthen our faith, hope and love that your reign will be proclaimed in our lives and the presence of your Spirit be manifested in our thoughts, words and actions. This we ask of you through Jesus and in the Holy Spirit. Amen.

MORNING PRAYER

(Psalms from Feasts and Solemnities)

Ant 1   After his resurrection, Jesus appeared to his disciples, speaking often of the reign of God, alleuia.

Ant 2   When the Spirit comes, you shall remember all that I taught you, alleluia.

Ant 3   Jesus was taken from their sight and ascended into heaven, alleluia.

READING

RESPONSORY

Jesus is glorified in heaven and we have seen his glory.   —**Jesus**...
Shining through all creation   —**we have**...
Glory to you, Source of all Being, Eternal Word, and Holy Spirit.   —**Jesus**...

CANTICLE OF ZECHARIAH

Ant   It is better for you that I go, that the Spirit of God may come to you, alleluia.

INTERCESSIONS:

You mount your throne amid shouts of joy and so we sing your praise:
                        Praise to you, Christ Jesus!

O God, you invest some members of your church with authority;
   —grant them the wisdom and vision to govern with love and forbearance.
You distribute your gifts to all your people;
   —give them the vision to recognize their talents and the opportunity to use them in your service.
You empower us with your Spirit;
   —enable us to claim our power that the good news may continue to be proclaimed in us.
Your fullness is manifested in Christ, filling the universe in all its parts;
   —give us reverence and respect for our universe, the temple of your glory.

PRAYER: O God, we believe that Jesus, your Incarnate Word, lives in you and in us. Strengthen our faith, hope and love that your reign will be proclaimed in our lives and the presence of your Spirit be manifested in our thoughts, words and actions. This we ask of you through Jesus and in the Holy Spirit. Amen.

DAYTIME PRAYER

Ant 1   Glory to God in heaven and on earth, alleluia.

Ant 2   I am the Alpha and the Omega, the beginning and the end, alleluia.

Ant 3   I am the bright Morning Star rising in the heavens, alleluia.

(Prayer as in Morning Prayer)

EVENING PRAYER II

Ant 1 Shout to God with shouts of joy, alleluia.

Ant 2 The Christ of God reigns over all the earth, alleluia.

Ant 3 Christ enlightens our innermost vision and calls us to hope, alleluia.

READING

RESPONSORY

Christ ascends in splendor, alleluia, alleluia. —Christ...
The glory of God fills all creation, —alleluia...
Glory to you, Source of all Being, Eternal Word, and Holy Spirit. —Christ...

CANTICLE OF MARY

Ant We praise you, O Christ. You have ascended to your place with the Most High, yet you remain in our midst forever, alleluia.

INTERCESSIONS:

Jesus promised to be with us till the end of time. With confidence we pray:
You are the Way, the Truth and the Life.

Christ Jesus, you sent your followers to preach the good news to all creation;
— may all people and all creatures experience your justice and love through those who profess faith in you.

You told us that signs and wonders would accompany our profession of faith;
— safeguard us from literalism and give us the wisdom and insight to hear your words in the reality of our lives.

After leaving your disciples, you continued to work with them;
— strengthen our faith in your presence in times of darkness and disillusionment.

Your disciples were to be found in the temple speaking the praises of God;
— make us women and men of prayer that we may be your glory and your rest.

PRAYER: O God, we believe that Jesus, your Incarnate Word, lives in you and in us. Strengthen our faith, hope and love that your reign will be proclaimed in our lives and the presence of your Spirit be manifested in our thoughts, words and actions. This we ask of you through Jesus and in the Holy Spririt. Amen.

FRIDAY AFTER ASCENSION
(Antiphons and psalms from the Psalter, Week II)

MORNING PRAYER

READING

RESPONSORY

Christ rose from the grave, alleluia, alleluia. —Christ...
Conquering sin and death, —alleluia...
Glory to you, Source of all Being, Eternal Word, and Holy Spirit. —Christ...

CANTICLE OF ZECHARIAH

Ant   I was dead but now I live; I hold the keys of life eternal, alleluia.

INTERCESSIONS:

Christ Jesus, you ascended into heaven to prepare a place for us. In joyful hope we pray:

Be with us now and forever.

Christ Jesus, when we experience you as absent,
   —enhance our longing and desire for your presence.
When we experience you as present,
   —fill us with gratitude.
In the death of our loved ones,
   —may our grief be turned into joy.
Christ Jesus, you took leave of those you loved on earth;
   —ascend again in glory in those who will die this day.

PRAYER: O God, in times of darkness and in times of grief, give us the faith
                 to believe that you will return again with your gift of peace. Grant
                 this through Jesus in whom we place our trust. Amen.

DAYTIME PRAYER

(Concluding prayer as in Morning Prayer)

EVENING PRAYER

READING

RESPONSORY

The Spirit of truth will come, alleluia, alleluia. —**The**...
And guide you into all truth, —**alleluia**...
Glory to you, Source of all Being, Eternal Word, and Holy Spirit. —**The**...

CANTICLE OF MARY

Ant   If you have faith, God will grant whatever you ask in my name, alleluia.

INTERCESSIONS:

You promised to send the Spirit, Christ Jesus, and so we pray:

Come, Holy Spirit, renew our hearts.

Send forth your Spirit over our earth;
   —bless our land and protect it from toxic waste.
Breathe forth your Spirit into our air;
   —encourage with success those who strive to keep it free from smog and acid
      rain.
Rain down your Spirit upon our waters,
   —and upon those responsible for decisions concerning our seas and rivers.
Enkindle your Spirit in tongues of fire,
   —that fire may be used to replenish our store of energy rather than to destroy
      our plains and forests.

PRAYER: O God, in times of darkness and in times of grief, give us the faith to believe that you will return again with your gift of peace. Grant this through Jesus in whom we place our trust. Amen.

SATURDAY AFTER ASCENSION

(Antiphons and psalms from the Psalter, Week II)

MORNING PRAYER

READING

RESPONSORY

Christ rose from the grave, alleluia, alleluia. —**Christ**...
Conquering sin and death, —**alleluia**...
Glory to you, Source of all Being, Eternal Word, and Holy Spirit. —**Christ**

CANTICLE OF ZECHARIAH

Ant The Spirit, the Counselor, will teach you all things, alleluia.

INTERCESSIONS:

Christ Jesus, you assured us that whatever we ask in your name will be given to us and so we pray:

Holy be your name.

Christ Jesus, by the power of your name,
— may all people come to realize their individual dignity and respect the rights and dignity of others.
You assured us of God's love for us;
— help us to respect our bodies and spiritual welfare by the moderate use of the goods of this world.
You came from God and returned to God;
— make us ever aware that we, too, are God's children and in God is our true home.
Christ Jesus, you are the firstborn, the risen Savior;
— may all who have died, live with you for all eternity.

PRAYER: Most loving God, you call us to make our home in you as you make yours in us. Graft us onto you that your life may flow through us in Jesus, who is our way, our truth and our life. Fill us with your Spirit and help us renew all creation. We ask this in Jesus' name. Amen.

DAYTIME PRAYER

(Concluding prayer as in Morning Prayer)

SEVENTH SUNDAY OF EASTER

(Psalms from Sunday, Week III in the Psalter)

EVENING PRAYER I

Ant 1 If you suffer in the name of Christ, you will share in the glory of Christ, alleluia.

Ant 2 Eternal life is this, to know the Most High God and Jesus Christ, the One sent by God, alleluia.

Ant 3 God gave glory to Christ, so that Christ in turn might give glory to God, alleluia.

READING

RESPONSORY

The Holy Spirit will enlighten you, and teach you all things. —The...
Breathe life into you, —**and teach**...
Glory to you, Source of all Being, Eternal Word, and Holy Spirit. —**The**...

CANTICLE OF MARY

Ant I have made known your name to those you gave me, that they may keep your word, alleluia.

INTERCESSIONS:

You will not leave us orphans but will return, and rejoice our hearts. We cry out in joy:

Alleluia, alleluia, alleluia!

O God, you send your Spirit to dwell with us always;
—make us conscious of your presence in our innermost being.
May all nations and peoples recognize the gifts of your Spirit,
—that our world might live in peace and harmony.
Through the gift of your Spirit, you enabled all to hear in their own tongue;
—give us a listening heart that we may hear the hearts of others and accept our differences.
Your Spirit, O God, comes in silence and thunder;
—open our hearts and the heart of the world that we may receive you in all your manifestations.

PRAYER: O God, you brood over our world and call us your sons and daughters. Send your Spirit and renew us that we may realize our eternal heritage with you. We ask this in the name of Jesus, our brother. Amen.

MORNING PRAYER

Ant 1 What was spoken in scripture by the Holy Spirit has come to be, alleluia.

Ant 2   The heavens proclaim the glory of the Most High; God's children rejoice in freedom, alleluia.

Ant 3   If we love one another, God lives within us, alleluia.

READING

RESPONSORY

You rose, O Christ, and are with us, that we might rise with you. —**You**...
Have mercy on us, your people, —**that we**...
Glory to you, Source of all Being, Eternal Word, and Holy Spirit. —**You**...

CANTICLE OF ZECHARIAH

Ant   For the sake of my followers, I consecrate myself, that they also may be consecrated in truth, alleluia.

INTERCESSIONS:

Mindful that you call us not servants, but friends, we confidently pray:
Remain with us always.

Christ Jesus, you ascended and now are our advocate;
—grant that all may experience your reign of justice and peace.
You prayed that all may be one;
—unite us in our loving acceptance of diversity.
Christ Jesus, you asked God that we might see your glory;
—open our eyes to see your wonders in our daily lives.
You are the Alpha and the Omega, the First and the Last, the Beginning and the End;
—born in time but made in your image, may we breathe our last in your loving embrace.

PRAYER: O God, you brood over our world and call us your sons and daughters. Send your Spirit and renew us that we may realize our eternal heritage with you. We ask this in the name of Jesus, our brother. Amen.

DAYTIME PRAYER

(Concluding prayer as in Morning Prayer)

EVENING PRAYER II

Ant 1   You, O God, are our ruler, the Most High over all the earth, alleluia.

Ant 2   The heavens opened, and Jesus, the Christ, appeared at the side of the throne of God, alleluia.

Ant 3   The Spirit and the Bride say: Come, Lord Jesus, alleluia!

READING

RESPONSORY

The Holy Spirit will enlighten you, and teach you all things. —**The**...
Breathe life into you, —**and teach**...
Glory to you, Source of all Being, Eternal Word, and Holy Spirit. —**The**...

CANTICLE OF MARY

Ant I live in you, and you live in my love, that your unity may be complete, alleluia.

INTERCESSIONS:

You bid us to drink of your life-giving water, and so we cry out:
We thirst for you, Christ Jesus.

Send forth your Spirit, O God,
—for the healing of the nations and the renewing of the earth.
Send forth your Spirit, O God,
—upon the despondent, the despairing and the living dead.
Send forth your Spirit, O God,
—into the hearts of those who call you by another name.
Send forth your Spirit, O God,
—to accompany those you call to yourself this night.

PRAYER: O God, you brood over our world and call us your sons and daughters. Send your Spirit and renew us that we may realize our eternal heritage with you. We ask this in the name of Jesus, our brother. Amen.

MONDAY

(Antiphons and psalms from the Psalter, Week III)

MORNING PRAYER

READING

RESPONSORY

Christ rose from the grave, alleluia, alleluia. —**Christ**...
Conquering sin and death, —**alleluia, alleluia**...
Glory to you, Source of all Being, Eternal Word, and Holy Spirit. —**Christ**...

CANTICLE OF ZECHARIAH

Ant Paul laid his hands on the believers and the Holy Spirit came upon them, alleluia.

INTERCESSIONS:

O God, you send your Spirit that we may be confirmed in our faith. Let us pray:
O God, we believe; help our unbelief.

Christ Jesus, you spoke plainly to us that we might believe;
—help us to communicate simply and honestly with one another.
Only in you can we find our peace;
—be present to us when our hearts are in turmoil.
You remind us that we will suffer in this world;
—give us courage and belief in your final victory.
In the gift of the Spirit, you give us freedom;
—help us to claim that freedom and free ourselves from all that pulls us toward darkness.

PRAYER: Christ Jesus, send the Spirit of wisdom into our hearts that we may live our lives discerning your way for us. We ask this in your name. Amen.

DAYTIME PRAYER

(Concluding prayer as in Morning Prayer)

EVENING PRAYER

READING

RESPONSORY

The Spirit of truth will come, alleluia, alleluia. —**The**...
And guide you into all truth, —**alleluia**...
Glory to you, Source of all Being, Eternal Word, and Holy Spirit. —**The**...

CANTICLE OF MARY

Ant   I have told you the truth that you may have peace. Rejoice, I have overcome the world, alleluia.

INTERCESSIONS:

God of Wisdom, we pray to you as we say:
         Send forth your Spirit upon us.
O God, give us the eyes of faith to see the world as you see it,
   —and hearts to love as you love.
You speak to us in dreams and visions;
   —give us insight to see and to understand your revelations.
Your wisdom appears to many as foolishness;
   —grant us the courage to follow your ways in spite of ridicule or rejection.
O God, you draw us to fullness of life;
   —free us from the superficial, and from dependence on the status quo.

PRAYER: Christ Jesus, send the Spirit of wisdom into our hearts that we may live our lives discerning your way for us. We ask this in your name. Amen.

TUESDAY

(Antiphons and psalms from the Psalter, Week III)

MORNING PRAYER

READING

RESPONSORY

Christ rose from the grave, alleluia, alleluia. —**Christ**...
Conquering sin and death, —**alleluia, alleluia**...
Glory to you, Source of all Being, Eternal Word, and Holy Spirit. —**Christ**...

CANTICLE OF ZECHARIAH

Ant   I have given glory to God on earth by finishing the work I was given to do, alleluia

INTERCESSIONS:

You ascended on high, Christ Jesus, but did not leave us orphans. With confident hope we pray:

Be with us all our days.

O God, united with Jesus, we are your sons and daughters;
  —grant that we may some day receive our eternal inheritance.
Give us your Spirit of Understanding;
  —that we may care for our earth and help to renew it in Christ's image.
You are a God of mercy and forgiveness;
  —help us live in harmony with our environment and all humankind.
You look upon our frailties with compassion;
  —ease the loneliness of the elderly and the alien, and comfort the dying.

PRAYER: O God, we stand before you with our weaknesses and limitations. Use them that your power may be manifested, and bring us all to the knowledge of our need for each other that we may grow in understanding and love. We ask this through Jesus who is our way. Amen.

DAYTIME PRAYER

(Concluding prayer as in Morning Prayer.)

EVENING PRAYER

READING

RESPONSORY

The Spirit of truth will come, alleluia, alleluia. —The...
And guide you into all truth, —alleluia...
Glory to you, Source of all Being, Eternal Word, and Holy Spirit. —The...

CANTICLE OF MARY

Ant   I entrust to you what God has entrusted to me, alleluia.

INTERCESSIONS:

Christ Jesus, you were raised from the dead as you promised. We sing your praises and pray:

Send us the Spirit of Understanding.

O God, we live in countries populated by people of diverse cultures;
  —may it lead us to understanding and not to dissension.
We espouse a common faith expressed through our various nationalities;
  —may each expression lead us to freedom and away from bondage.
We live in families and communities with our individual personalities;
  —help us to grow in appreciation of our differences.
We are a people who call you by many names and some by no name;
  —may our creeds lead us to love and not to violence.

PRAYER: O God, we stand before you with our weaknesses and limitations. Use them that your power may be manifested, and bring us all to the knowledge of our need for each other that we may grow in understanding and love. We ask this through Jesus who is our way. Amen

WEDNESDAY

(Antiphons and psalms from the Psalter, Week III)

MORNING PRAYER

READING

RESPONSORY

Christ rose from the grave, alleluia, alleluia. —Christ...
Conquering sin and death, —alleluia, alleluia...
Glory to you, Source of all Being, Eternal Word, and Holy Spirit. —Christ...

CANTICLE OF ZECHARIAH

Ant The word of God enlarges our hearts and expands our vision, alleluia

INTERCESSIONS:

Christ Jesus, you prayed that we may share your joy completely and so we ask you:
Make us one with you now and forever.

O God, you gift us with your Spirit;
 —help us serve each other with the talents and gifts you give us.
You give us the gift of time;
 —may we cherish the moments we spend with you and with others.
In Jesus you taught us that to love is to serve;
 —give us the willingness to put aside our plans, schedules and activities when others call upon us.
You chose the weak of the world in preference to the strong;
 —comfort the sick, the suffering and those who are mentally disturbed.

PRAYER: O God, be with us on our journey to fullness of life lived in you. Let us not be discouraged by our failures, but keep us resolute in our efforts to begin anew. This we ask in the name of Jesus. Amen.

DAYTIME PRAYER

(Concluding prayer as in Morning Prayer)

EVENING PRAYER

READING

RESPONSORY

The Spirit of truth will come, alleluia, alleluia. —The...
And guide you into all truth, —alleluia...
Glory to you, Source of all Being, Eternal Word, and Holy Spirit. —The...

CANTICLE OF MARY

Ant Loving God, keep those you have given me safe in your name, that they may be one, even as we are one, alleluia.

INTERCESSIONS:

We pray to you, Holy Mystery, and ask with earnest hearts:
Send us your gift of Knowledge.

O God, you created our universe and universes beyond our knowing;
—free us from ignorance and open our minds to your wonders.
You created diversity in vegetation, in animals and in people;
—free us from narrow-mindedness that we may enjoy the variety and the
differences.
You are the God that fills infinite space;
—help us expand the frontiers of our universe, not for national gain, but for
your glory.
Through scientists and scholars, new knowledge comes to light;
—may it further the quality of life for all people and all creatures on the
journey to wholeness.

PRAYER: O God, be with us on our journey to fullness of life lived in you.
Let us not be discouraged by our failures, but keep us resolute in
our efforts to begin anew. This we ask in the name of Jesus. Amen.

THURSDAY

(Antiphons and psalms from the Psalter, Week III)

MORNING PRAYER

READING

RESPONSORY

Christ rose from the grave, alleluia, alleluia. —**Christ**...
Conquering sin and death, —**alleluia, alleluia**...
Glory to you, Source of all Being, Eternal Word, and Holy Spirit. —**Christ**...

CANTICLE OF ZECHARIAH

Ant   May all those who were with me be one in us, that the world may believe
you sent me, alleluia.

INTERCESSIONS:

Strengthen us, O God, as we begin this day. We humbly ask you:
Give us your Spirit.

Open our hearts to receive all things as gift with a deep sense of gratitude,
—knowing that your love works all things to our good.
Teach us to love and care for our world and our universe,
—recognizing all as your gift to us to be cherished and protected.
Give us the unity Jesus prayed for;
—that together we can enhance the quality of life for all living beings.
Reveal the glory manifested in Jesus,
—to all who will die this day.

PRAYER: O God, we await your Spirit with eager hearts. Fill our longing with the fullness of your being that we may give witness to your love and concern for all that you made. We ask this through Jesus who lives with you and with the Holy Spirit for all ages. Amen.

DAYTIME PRAYER

(Concluding prayer as in Morning Prayer)

EVENING PRAYER

READING

RESPONSORY

The Spirit of truth will come, alleluia, alleluia. —The...
And guide you into all truth, —alleluia...
Glory to you, Source of all Being, Eternal Word, and Holy Spirit. —The...

CANTICLE OF MARY

Ant   I live in you, and you in me, that your joy may be complete, alleluia.

INTERCESSIONS:

Filled with anticipation for your coming, we call out to you;
Come, Spirit of God, with your gift of Counsel.
You call us to relationship;
—free us from the loneliness of personal decisions and enable us to see alternatives in difficult situations.
We continue our journey toward fullness of life in community and family;
—bless all who help us through direction or personal guidance.
You speak to us in the people and circumstances of our everyday lives;
—give us listening hearts and open minds that we may recognize your voice.
You promise to be with us all our days;
—bless all those new-born today and those who will be born to eternal life.

PRAYER: O God, we await your Spirit with eager hearts. Fill our longing with the fullness of your being that we may give witness to your love and concern for all that you made. We ask this through Jesus who lives with you and with the Holy Spirit for all ages. Amen.

FRIDAY

(Antiphons and psalms from the Psalter, Week III)

MORNING PRAYER

READING

RESPONSORY

Christ rose from the grave, alleluia, alleluia. —Christ...
Conquering sin and death, —alleluia, alleluia...
Glory to you, Source of all Being, Eternal Word, and Holy Spirit. —Christ...

CANTICLE OF ZECHARIAH

Ant   "Simon, do you love me?" "Yes, Lord, you know that I love you."

INTERCESSIONS:

You commissioned your church, Christ Jesus, to feed your lambs and so we pray:
> **Good Shepherd, teach us your ways of gentleness and compassion.**

Give wisdom to all ecclesiastical and religious leaders,
> —that they may guide their people with love and patience.

Give wisdom to confessors, counselors and directors,
> —that they may lift the burdens of those weighed down by legalism and fear.

May all who shepherd others be open to the Spirit,
> —who may lead them in ways they would not freely choose.

Call us back to you when we have strayed,
> —that we may again belong to your sheepfold.

PRAYER: O God, give us your Spirit that we may reverence you and all things that draw us to you. You know that we love you. Increase our desires that we may grow in this love and reverence. Through Jesus Christ who lives and reigns with you, Source of all life, and with the Holy Spirit. Amen.

DAYTIME PRAYER

(Concluding prayer as in Morning Prayer)

EVENING PRAYER

READING

RESPONSORY

The Spirit of truth will come, alleluia, alleluia. —**The**...
And guide you into all truth, —**alleluia**...
Glory to you, Source of all Being, Eternal Word, and Holy Spirit. —**The**...

CANTICLE OF MARY

Ant   "You know all things; you know that I love you," alleluia.

INTERCESSIONS:

We have received your Spirit in baptism and so we ask you:
> **Give us the gift of Fortitude.**

Help us to be steadfast,
> —in time of disappointment, discouragement and trial.

Strengthen us as a community of believers,
> —through the witness of those who choose life over death, light over darkness, hope over despair.

Give us moral courage,
> —when society or governments try to lead us toward destruction of self or others.

Keep us patient, persevering and open,
> —in committees, action groups, and other gatherings in which we work with others to achieve a common good.

PRAYER: O God, give us your Spirit that we may reverence you and all things that draw us to you. You know that we love you. Increase our desires that we may grow in this love and reverence. Through Jesus Christ who lives and reigns with you, Source of all life, and with your Holy Spirit. Amen.

SATURDAY

(Antiphons and psalms from the Psalter, Week III)

MORNING PRAYER

READING

RESPONSORY

Christ rose from the grave, alleluia, alleluia. —**Christ**. . .
Conquering sin and death, —**alleluia, alleluia**. . .
Glory to you, Source of all Being, Eternal Word, and Holy Spirit. —**Christ**. . .

CANTICLE OF ZECHARIAH

Ant   I will pour out upon you my Spirit of Truth, alleluia.

INTERCESSIONS:

O God, breathe within us the breath of your Spirit as we call out to you:
Give us the gift of Piety.
Pray in us when we are unable,
    —and free us from whatever inhibits us from taking the time to pray.
Open our eyes and our hearts,
    —that we may be sensitive to the symbols that put us into contact with you.
Teach us to see reality as holy,
    —that we may meet you both in the unexpected and the ordinary.
Detach us from our spiritual possessions,
    —that your grace may have sway in us.

PRAYER: Create in us a new heart and a new vision, O God, that the gifts of your Spirit may work in us and renew the face of the earth. May we be one with you so that our work is yours and your work is ours. We ask this in the name of Jesus, the Eternal Word, who lives with you and with the Holy Spirit, forever. Amen.

DAYTIME PRAYER

(Concluding prayer as in Morning Prayer)

PENTECOST

EVENING PRAYER I

Ant 1   O my people, says our God, I will put my Spirit within you, and you shall live, alleluia. (Psalm 113)

Ant 2   The Spirit helps us in our weakness, for we do not know how to pray; it is the Spirit who prays in us, alleluia. (Psalm 147:1–11)

Ant 3   Receive the Holy Spirit. If you forgive the sins of any, they are forgiven, alleluia. (Rev. 15:3–4)

READING
RESPONSORY

I give you my Spirit, alleluia, alleluia. —**I give**...
You will be my witnesses; —**alleluia**,...
Glory to you, Source of all Being, Eternal Word, and Holy Spirit. —**I give**...

CANTICLE OF MARY

Ant   God declares: In the last days it shall be that I will pour out my Spirit upon all flesh, and your sons and daughters shall prophesy, alleluia.

INTERCESSIONS:

On the day of Pentecost, the women and men gathered together were filled with the Holy Spirit and began to proclaim the works of God. Let us pray:
> **Come Holy Spirit, enkindle in us the fire of your love.**

Holy Spirit, father and mother of the poor,
—bring to birth in us the desire and means to deliver the poor from want.
Holy Spirit, strong and gentle comforter,
—tend the grief of those who mourn those missing or dead.
Holy Spirit, free spirit,
—liberate those bound by injustice or ignorance.
Holy Spirit, healing presence,
—bind our broken relationships and teach us to forgive one another.

PRAYER: O God, you have sent your Holy Spirit to hover over the abyss of our broken world. Help us to be open to the grace of your coming that you may create us anew. Banish our darkness with your wisdom; set us on the firm ground of counsel and fortitude. Bless our coming and going with your sevenfold gifts, that your reign may come upon the earth, that we may live with you for all eternity. Amen.

PENTECOST
MORNING PRAYER

(Psalms from Feasts and Solemnities)

Ant 1   They were all filled with the Holy Spirit and began to speak in many tongues, alleluia.

Ant 2   Seas and rivers, bless the Most High; praise and exalt God forever, alleluia.

Ant 3   When they had prayed, they were all filled with the Holy Spirit and boldly spoke the word of God, alleluia.

READING

RESPONSORY

Flames as of fire rested over the disciples, alleluia, alleluia. —Flames...
They spoke as the Spirit gave utterance, —alleluia...
Glory to you, Source of all Being, Eternal Word, and Holy Spirit. —Flames...

CANTICLE OF ZECHARIAH

Ant   Peace be with you. Receive the Holy Spirit, alleluia.

INTERCESSIONS:

The followers of Jesus began to speak in foreign tongues and all who heard them
understood. Let us pray:

Holy Spirit, Light of God, shine on our minds and confirm us in truth.

Jesus, you have sent your Holy Spirit to dwell in our hearts;
—teach us to live quietly, ever attentive to your voice.
Through the power of the Holy Spirit, you guide your people to salvation;
—bless our church and all nations with enlightened and upright leaders.
You send your Spirit to remind us of all that you have taught us;
—endow scripture scholars with a love and understanding of your word, and
with the means to enlighten us all.
Your Spirit of love can change our hearts;
—send that same Spirit to draw us to grow in our dedication and love for
you.

PRAYER: Jesus, our Lord and Savior, all that you do is for our good; you
give us your Spirit to guard and guide us. Help us to keep in mind
the meaning of your life, death, and resurrection, that we may be a
church alive with the message of your gospel. We ask this in your
holy name, for you are one with our Source and with the Spirit, for
all ages. Amen.

DAYTIME PRAYER

Ant 1   Jesus poured forth his Spirit into the hearts of his followers, alleluia.
(Psalm 120)

Ant 2   Lord Jesus, send us your Spirit of wisdom and love, alleluia. (Psalm 121)

Ant 3   It is the Spirit who gives life and light, alleluia. (Psalm 122)

(Prayer as in Morning Prayer)

EVENING PRAYER II

Ant 1   There are varieties of gifts, but the same Spirit who gives them, alleluia.
(Psalm 110:1-5, 7)

Ant 2   To each person is given the manifestation of the Spirit for the common
good, alleluia. (Psalm 114)

Ant 3   By one Spirit we were all baptized into one body, and all were made to
drink of the one Spirit, alleluia. (Rev. 19:1-7)

READING

RESPONSORY

Send forth your Spirit, O God, alleluia, alleluia. —**Send**...
Renew the face of the earth; —**alleluia**...
Glory to you, Source of all Being, Eternal Word, and Holy Spirit. —**Send**...

CANTICLE OF MARY

Ant   This day has God poured out the Spirit of Jesus on those gathered in Christ's name. The Holy Spirit inflamed the hearts of the believers who boldly went forth to proclaim God's word, alleluia, alleluia.

INTERCESSIONS:

The Holy Spirit descended with gifts of wisdom, fortitude, piety, and reverence for God. With longing hearts, we pray:

Spirit of God, rain down your gifts on our parched spirits.

O God, you create and recreate with the power of love;
—open our hearts to your indwelling Spirit that we may be one with you in all that we do.
You send your Spirit to banish our fears and to bring us peace;
—let our lives mirror your mercy and goodness and so reveal your love.
Our ways are known to you; you are always with us;
—bless all who are traveling, those who are lonely, and those who have no one to care for them.
You are faithful, O God, and your mercy lasts forever;
—send your Spirit to awaken in our hearts a readiness to praise you with loving confidence.

PRAYER: O God, you have sent your Holy Spirit to hover over the abyss of our broken world. Help us to be open to the grace of your coming that you may create us anew. Banish our darkness with your wisdom; set us on the firm ground of counsel and fortitude. Bless our coming and going with your sevenfold gifts, that your reign may come upon the earth, that we may live with you for all eternity. Amen.

TRINITY SUNDAY
SUNDAY AFTER PENTECOST

EVENING PRAYER I

Ant 1   We give glory to you: Creator, Redeemer, Spirit of Life, one God forever, alleluia. (Psalm 113)

Ant 2   I am your God, one and eternal; my presence will go with you and give you rest, alleluia. (Psalm 147:12–20)

Ant 3   We honor you, Holy Mystery: Source of all Being, Eternal Word and Holy Spirit; we worship you forever, alleluia. (Eph. 1:3–10)

READING

RESPONSORY

We give you glory, most Holy Trinity; Three in One. —**We**...
We sing your praises; —**Three**...
Glory to you, Source of all Being, Eternal Word, and Holy Spirit. —**We**...

CANTICLE OF MARY

Ant Honor and thanksgiving to you, O triune God, one and undivided, Source of life, grace and love; alleluia.

INTERCESSIONS:

To God, Source of all Being, Eternal Word, and Holy Spirit, be praise honor and glory forever. Let us pray:
> **Praise to you most Blessed Trinity!**

Creator God, saving Word, abiding Spirit, renew and enlighten your church and awaken the world to your presence;
 —give all who believe in you the grace to proclaim your glory.
Holy Trinity, one in unity, guide to the truth all who profess your name,
 —that the richness of your word may be magnified on the earth.
Blessed Trinity, eternal in unity, bless families and communities and all who bond together in your name;
 —let our relationships be loving, mature, loyal and just.
Jesus, Word of God, you prayed that we all might be one with you;
 —be for us the beginning and end of our life's journey.

PRAYER: O God, Trinity in Unity, our minds and hearts cannot understand the mystery of your being. We are your creatures; we believe your word; we know your guiding presence. We praise you for your love and mercy and ask for the grace to persevere in love and fidelity to you. Praise to you Source of all Being, Word and Spirit, now and forever. Amen.

MORNING PRAYER

(Psalms from Feasts and Solemnities)

Ant 1 Alleluia! Glory and praise to our God for all ages; alleluia, alleluia!

Ant 2 All nations worship you, Holy Mystery, Blessed Trinity, alleluia.

Ant 3 All glory and honor is yours, Creator God, through Jesus Christ, by the power of the Spirit, alleluia.

READING

RESPONSORY

From God and through God and to God are all things. —**From**...
To God be glory forever; —**to God**...
Glory to you, Source of all Being, Eternal Word, and Holy Spirit. —**From**...

CANTICLE OF ZECHARIAH

Ant   You alone are the Holy One, triune God, yet undivided; we praise you with joy; alleluia.

INTERCESSIONS:

What we believe of our Creator, we believe of the Word and of the Holy Spirit. God, our God, is One. In adoration we pray:

All glory and praise to you!

O God, holy and undivided Trinity, all your judgments are just and all your ways are true;
—grant wisdom and integrity to all who lead our church and the nations of the world.

O God, Trinity whom we adore, you alone are holy;
—bless our efforts to grow in the way of your commandments.

All the angels sing your praise, and you call us to union with you;
—make us worthy of the promises of Christ.

Holy and Blessed Trinity, God of beauty, truth and goodness,
—may we live and love in your image and likeness.

PRAYER: Holy God, Holy Mighty One, you have created all things and you continue to call us to new life. Teach us to reverence in one another the gift of life that we share. Give us a hunger for your Word, and let us walk in union with your Spirit all the days of our lives. Glory to you, Source of all Being, Eternal Word, and Holy Spirit, forever and ever. Amen.

DAYTIME PRAYER

(Psalms from Sunday, Week I)

Ant 1   Glory to you, holy triune God, now and for all ages, alleluia.

Ant 2   All nations shall come and worship you, for you alone are holy, alleluia.

Ant 3   Blessed, triune God, in faith and hope we pray to you, alleluia.

(Prayer as in Morning Prayer)

EVENING PRAYER II

Ant 1   Source of all Being, Eternal Word and Holy Spirit, you are one God and there is no other besides you, alleluia. (Psalm 110:1–5, 7)

Ant 2   Holy Trinity, come and live in us; renew your people and all creation, alleluia. (Psalm 114)

Ant 3   Holy are you, Holy Mystery; the earth proclaims your glory, alleluia. (Rev. 19:1–7)

READING

RESPONSORY

We give you glory, most Holy Trinity; Three in One. —**We...**
We sing your praises; —**Three...**
Glory to you, Source of all Being, Eternal Word, and Holy Spirit. —**We...**

CANTICLE OF MARY

Ant Blessing and glory, wisdom and thanksgiving, honor and power be to our God, forever and ever! Amen, alleluia!

INTERCESSIONS:

To God, Source of all Being, Eternal Word, and Holy Spirit, be praise honor and glory forever. Let us pray:

Praise to you most Blessed Trinity!

Creator God, saving Word, abiding Spirit, renew and enlighten your church and awaken the world to your presence;
—give all who believe in you the grace to proclaim your glory.
Holy Trinity, one in unity, guide to the truth all who profess your name,
—that the richness of your word may be magnified on the earth.
Blessed Trinity, eternal in unity, bless families and communities and all who bond together in your name;
—let our relationships be loving, mature, loyal and just.
Jesus, Word of God, you prayed that we all might be one with you;
—be for us the beginning and end of our life's journey.

PRAYER: O God, Trinity in Unity, our minds and hearts cannot understand the mystery of your being. We are your creatures; we believe your word; we know your guiding presence. We praise you for your love and mercy and ask for the grace to persevere in love and fidelity to you. Praise to you Source of all Being, Word and Spirit, now and forever. Amen.

SUNDAY AFTER TRINITY SUNDAY
THE FEAST OF THE BODY AND BLOOD OF CHRIST

EVENING PRAYER I

Ant 1 We thank you, O God, for you provide food for those who love you and are ever mindful of your covenant, alleluia. (Psalm 111)

Ant 2 In the sharing of the bread, we are made one people of God, alleluia. (Psalm 147:12–20)

Ant 3 The bread that comes from God gives life to the world, alleluia. (Rev. 11:17–18; 12:10b–12a)

READING

RESPONSORY

You, O Christ, are the bread of eternal life, alleluia, alleluia. —**You**...
We live in you forever; —**alleluia**...
Glory to you, Source of all Being, Eternal Word, and Holy Spirit. —**You**...

CANTICLE OF MARY

Ant I will lift up the cup of salvation, O God; I will give thanks to you for all your goodness to us. Alleluia!

INTERCESSIONS:

Those who eat your flesh and drink your blood will have eternal life, and you will raise them up on the last day. In faith, we proclaim:
    This is the bread that came down from heaven.

Jesus, you longed to eat the paschal meal with your disciples before you gave your life for us;
 —teach us to walk your way of total self-giving.
On the night of your Last Supper, you washed the feet of your disciples;
 —help us to realize that the bread of life you give us is the bread of service and reverence.
Jesus, the new Moses, you give a new law and a new manna;
 —release us from all that is dead in our past and make us eager to receive your word and bread of life.
Jesus, Good Shepherd and guardian of your church,
 —open the way for all people to share and serve at your table.

PRAYER: Christ Jesus, our Living Bread, we praise your mercy in the memorial of your love. As we keep in mind your life, death, and resurrection, let our eucharistic banquet enable us to share with one another the goodness and love you have showered upon us. We ask this in your name. Amen.

MORNING PRAYER

(Psalms from Feasts and Solemnities)

Ant 1 I will give you the food which endures to eternal life; alleluia.

Ant 2 Your holy people offer you thanks with gifts of bread and wine; alleluia.

Ant 3 I am the living bread which came down from heaven. They who eat of this bread will live forever, alleluia.

READING

RESPONSORY

You sustain us with bread and wine unto life everlasting. —**You**...
You, yourself, are life for us; —**unto**...
Glory to you, Source of all Being, Eternal Word, and Holy Spirit. —**You**...

CANTICLE OF ZECHARIAH

Ant The bread I give you is my life for the salvation of the world; alleluia.

INTERCESSIONS:

The bread that I shall give is my flesh for the life of the world. In gratitude, we exclaim:
    You have prepared a banquet for your people.

Christ Jesus, priest of the new covenant, you invite all to your banquet table;
 —let our lives lead others to know and love you.
Christ Jesus, Living Bread, you refresh those who are burdened and weary;
 —help us to bear one another's burdens and so share the bread of your mercy.

Christ Jesus, you broke bread with those who would deny and betray you;
— may the sharing of the eucharistic meal bring a spirit of reconciliation to the world.
Christ Jesus, every time we share the eucharistic meal, we proclaim your death until you come;
— may this same sharing make of our lives a proclamation of your goodness and love.

PRAYER: Christ Jesus, through your life, death, and resurrection, you have brought new life to the world. Through the Holy Eucharist, the sacrament of unity, you nourish that life and give us hope. Strengthened by this bread, may we walk in your truth and learn to love one another as you have loved us. We ask this in your name. Amen.

DAYTIME PRAYER

(Psalms from Sunday, Week I)

Ant 1 When his hour had come, Jesus sat at table with his disciples; alleluia.

Ant 2 Jesus took bread, gave thanks, broke the bread and gave it to them; alleluia.

Ant 3 This is my body given for you. This is the cup of the new covenant, my blood poured out for you; alleluia.

(Prayer as in Morning Prayer)

EVENING PRAYER II

Ant 1 Jesus, you are the bread of life, given up for us; alleluia.
(Psalm 110:1–5, 7)

Ant 2 The cup poured out for us is the cup of the covenant; alleluia.
(Psalm 116:10–19)

Ant 3 Jesus was revealed in the breaking of the bread; alleluia. (Rev. 19:1–7)

READING

RESPONSORY

You, O Christ, are the bread that we share; we live forever in you. —**You**. . .
Yours is the cup of eternal salvation; —**we live**. . .
Glory to you, Source of all Being, Eternal Word, and Holy Spirit. —**You**. . .

CANTICLE OF MARY

Ant We praise you, O Christ, bread of heaven and pledge of eternal life; we proclaim you among us in the bread and wine of the new covenant, alleluia!

INTERCESSIONS:

Those who eat your flesh and drink your blood will have eternal life, and you will raise them up on the last day. In faith, we proclaim:
This is the bread that came down from heaven.

Jesus, you longed to eat the paschal meal with your disciples before you gave your life for us;
  —teach us to walk your way of total self-giving.
On the night of your Last Supper, you washed the feet of your disciples;
  —help us to realize that the bread of life you give us is the bread of service and reverence.
Jesus, the new Moses, you give a new law and a new manna;
  —release us from all that is dead in our past and make us eager to receive your word and bread of life.
Jesus, Good Shepherd and guardian of your church,
  —open the way for all people to share and serve at your table.

PRAYER: Christ Jesus, our Living Bread, we praise your mercy in the memorial of your love. As we keep in mind your life, death, and resurrection, let our eucharistic banquet enable us to share with one another the goodness and love you have showered upon us. We ask this in your name. Amen.

FRIDAY AFTER THE SECOND SUNDAY AFTER PENTECOST
SACRED HEART
EVENING PRAYER I

Ant 1   No greater love can I have, than to lay down my life for you.

Ant 2   You shall love your God with all your heart, with all your soul, and with all your might.

Ant 3   You are faithful, O God; you keep your covenant with your people.

READING

RESPONSORY

Your compassion, O God, is eternal, your love is everlasting. —**Your**. . .
Your faithfulness is renewed each day; —**your love**. . .
Glory to you, Source of all Being, Eternal Word, and Holy Spirit. —**Your**. . .

CANTICLE OF MARY

Ant   Let us love one another, for love is of God.

INTERCESSIONS:

Jesus said to the disciples: I have come to cast fire on the earth and would that it were already enkindled! We pray with zealous hearts:
  Send forth your Spirit, O God, and enkindle in us the fire of your love.

Jesus, you were moved to pity and you healed the widow's son;
  —teach us how to bring comfort and hope to those who mourn.
You wept over Jerusalem and longed to gather the people to your heart;
  —increase our zeal for the development and safety of all people.
You cried out in pain at the death of your friend, Lazarus;
  —teach us and our children the value of loyal and faithful relationships.
You grieved for the women who wept at your cross;
  —give us large hearts and teach us selfless love.

PRAYER: O God, you have revealed your love for us through the compassionate heart of Jesus. Let his forgiving love call us all to a change of heart. Strengthen in us the desire to live for one another and for the glory of your name. Amen.

MORNING PRAYER

(Psalms from Feasts and Solemnities)

Ant 1   Out of love for us, God has made with us a covenant of peace.

Ant 2   If God so loves us, we also must love one another.

Ant 3   I drew you to myself with bonds of compassion and love, says our God.

READING

RESPONSORY

Christ died for us, that we might live forever. —**Christ**...
Pouring forth the Spirit into our hearts; —**that**...
Glory to you, Source of all Being, Eternal Word, and Holy Spirit. —**Christ**...

CANTICLE OF ZECHARIAH

Ant   Learn from me, for I am gentle and lowly in heart, and you will find rest.

INTERCESSIONS:

Let us recall the prayer of the Suffering Servant: Insults have broken my heart. I looked for comforters, but I found none. Let us pray in loving response:
By your wounds, we are healed.

Jesus, you forgave those who crucified you;
  —give us the grace to put no limits on our forgiveness of others.
You loved sinners and helped them to change their lives;
  —give us patience and understanding when we strive to help those who harm themselves and others.
Your love is everlasting; you never cease to call us to salvation;
  —give us the wisdom and generosity to follow you and to draw others to your heart.
A soldier pierced your heart with a lance;
  —open our hearts to the wonders of your love and to the challenge of your gospel.

PRAYER: Christ Jesus, you draw us to salvation with the loving heart of a friend. Teach us to find rest for our spirits in your way of humility and meekness. Set our hearts ablaze with zeal for the coming of your reign, fullness of life, both now and for all eternity. Amen.

DAYTIME PRAYER

(See current week of the psalter for psalms)

Ant 1   May Christ dwell in our hearts by faith.

Ant 2   Let us know your love, O Christ, which surpasses all knowledge.

Ant 3   The heart of Christ was pierced, and blood and water flowed out.

(Prayer as in Morning Prayer)

EVENING PRAYER II

Ant 1 The love of God has been poured into our hearts by the Holy Spirit. (Psalm 110:1–5, 7)

Ant 2 While we were yet sinners, Christ died for us. (Psalm 111)

Ant 3 Rejoice with me; I have found the one who was lost. (Phil. 2:6–11)

READING

RESPONSORY

Your compassion, O God, is eternal; your love is everlasting. —**Your**...
Your faithfulness is renewed every morning; —**your**...
Glory to you, Source of all Being, Eternal Word, and Holy Spirit. —**Your**...

CANTICLE OF MARY

Ant All will know you are my followers if you have love for one another.

INTERCESSIONS:

Jesus said to the disciples: I have come to cast fire on the earth and would that it were already enkindled! We pray with zealous hearts:

Send forth your Spirit, O God, and enkindle in us the fire of your love.

Jesus, you were moved to pity and you healed the widow's son;
—teach us how to bring comfort and hope to those who mourn.
You wept over Jerusalem and longed to gather the people to your heart;
—increase our zeal for the development and safety of all people.
You cried out in pain at the death of your friend, Lazarus;
—teach us and our children the value of loyal and faithful relationships.
You grieved for the women who wept at your cross;
—give us large hearts and teach us selfless love.

PRAYER: O God, you have revealed your love for us through the compassionate heart of Jesus. Let his forgiving love call us all to a change of heart. Strengthen in us the desire to live for one another and for the glory of your name. Amen.

CALENDAR OF FEASTS AND COMMEMORATIONS

January

2   Mary Ward
4   St. Elizabeth Ann Bayley Seton
5   Blessed John Neumann
20   Martin Luther King, Anwar Sadat,
      Mahatma Ghandi
24   St. Francis de Sales, (patron of authors)
27   St. Angela Merici

February

1   St Bridget
10   St. Scholastica
20   Frederick Douglass

March

3   Katherine Drexel
15   St. Louise de Marillac
17   St. Patrick
19   St. Joseph
24   Oscar Romero
25   Feast of the Annunciation

April

7   St. Julie Billiart
10   Teilhard de Chardin
17   Anna Dengel
29   St. Catherine of Siena

May

1   St. Joseph the Worker (See Mar. 19)
23   Bl. Brother André
25   St. Madeleine Sophie Barat

June

1   Helen Keller
3   Pope John XXIII

July

11   St. Benedict
14   Bl. Kateri Tekawitha
31   St. Ignatius of Loyola

August

4	St. John Mary Vianney
6	Feast of the Transfiguration
8	St. Dominic
9	Bl. Edith Stein
	Etty Hillesum
11	St. Clare of Assisi
15	Feast of the Assumption
24	Simone Weil

September

17	St. Hildegarde of Bingen,
	Julian of Norwich, Meister Eckhart
27	St. Vincent de Paul

October

1	St. Thérèse of Lisieux
4	St. Francis of Assisi
6	Jean Pierre Médaille, SJ
15	St. Teresa of Avila
21	Janet Erskine Stuart

November

1	Feast of All Saints
2	Feast of All Souls
11	Catherine McAuley
13	St. Frances Zavier Cabrini
17	Bl. Philippine Duchesne
22	Jeanne Fontbonne (Mother St. John)
26	Sojourner Truth
29	Dorothy Day
Last Thursday	Thanksgiving

December

2	Maura Clarke, Jean Donovan
	Ita Ford, Dorothy Kazel
3	St. Francis Xavier
8	Feast of the Immaculate Conception
10	Thomas Merton
14	St. John of the Cross
26	St. Stephen
27	St. John
28	Holy Innocents

January 2

MARY WARD

MORNING / EVENING PRAYER*

(Psalms from the current week in the Psalter.)

Ant 1   Blessed are you when people revile you and say all manner of evil against you; your reward shall be great.

Ant 2   My God, cast us not away from your face, and take not your Spirit from us.

Ant 3   You have broken my bonds; I will sacrifice to you a sacrifice of praise.

READING

RESPONSORY

Suffering without sin is no burden; into your hands I commend my spirit.
    —**Suffering**...
Show me your mercy and grant me your salvation; —**into your**...
Glory to you, Source of all Being, Eternal Word, and Holy Spirit.
    —**Suffering**...

CANTICLE

Ant   God will assist and help you, it is no matter the who but the what; and when God shall enable me to return, I will serve you.

INTERCESSIONS:

Christ Jesus, you were rejected by your own but your love never failed. In hope we pray:
                    Shelter us in the shadow of your wings.

O God, your daughter, Mary, was labeled as "heretic, schismatic, rebel to Holy Church" and her congregation was suppressed;
    —grant courage to those misunderstood or misjudged by ecclesiastical or civil authorities.
O God, in spite of failure and exile, Mary accepted all with patience and a sense of humor;
    —grant us hearts that are humble and help us not take ourselves too seriously.
Imprisoned, Mary was refused the sacraments even when she was thought to be dying;
    —comfort all who are unjustly imprisoned and give them hope.
O God, you gifted Mary with vision and courage;
    —support all those whose vision and gifts further the work of bringing this world to fullness of life especially in their times of trial.

PRAYER: O God, purify our hearts and give us courage to work for the coming of your reign in our hearts. Knowing that the work we do is yours to accomplish, let us not be discouraged by lack of results. We thank you for all those who have faithfully persevered in spite of adversity and ask them to intercede for us. Grant this through Jesus who is our Way, our Truth and our Life. Amen.

*Responsory and canticle based on her writings.

January 4
ST. ELIZABETH ANN BAYLEY SETON

MORNING PRAYER

(Psalms from the current week in the Psalter.)

Ant 1   God has done great things for me; may God be forever praised, alleluia.

Ant 2   The valiant woman is a pearl of great price—all generations will call her blessed, alleluia.

Ant 3   What you have done for the least of my sisters and brothers, you have done for me, alleluia.

READING

RESPONSORY

Those who sow in tears shall reap with shouts of joy. —**Those**...
She who goes forth weeping —**shall**...
Glory to you, Source of all Being, Eternal Word, and Holy Spirit. —**Those**...

CANTICLE

Ant   Many waters cannot quench love, neither can floods drown it.

INTERCESSIONS:

O God, you raised up Elizabeth Seton to be an inspiration for many. In thanksgiving for the gift of her life we pray:
Blessed be God forever!

Elizabeth Seton was widowed at an early age,
  —may all who sorrow and are lonely be comforted.
She was the mother of five children,
  —empower those entrusted with the rearing of children to guide them with values that will lead to their fulfillment and lasting happiness.
Through the intercession of Elizabeth Seton, a convert to Catholicism,
  —may we come to more understanding of and appreciation for our differences in our efforts to live the gospel.
You inspired her to found the Sisters of Charity,
  —help us to be faithful to our religious commitment that we may be transformed into Christ.
You filled her with zeal for the education of youth,
  —guide all teachers and educators to enable students to grow in knowledge and to become good citizens of the earth and
heirs of heaven.

PRAYER: O God, we give you thanks for the life of Elizabeth Seton. May the values she cherished be realized in our lives that all may enjoy a better quality of life. May the holiness of her life inspire us to serve you and work only for your glory. Bless all the Sisters of Charity, that they may faithfully continue the work she began. We ask this in the name of Jesus. Amen.

January 5

BLESSED JOHN NEUMANN

MORNING / EVENING PRAYER

(Psalms from the current week in the Psalter.)

Ant 1 I will give you shepherds after my own heart; they will nourish you with knowledge and sound teaching.

Ant 2 I shall feed my flock; I shall search for the lost and lead back those who have strayed.

Ant 3 My life is at the service of the Gospel; God has given me this grace.

READING

RESPONSORY

May God answer you in the day of trouble. —**May**...
May God grant you your heart's desire, —**in the**...
Glory to you, Source of all Being, Eternal Word, and Holy Spirit. —**May**...

CANTICLE

Ant Our gospel came to you not only in word, but also in power and in the Holy Spirit and with full conviction.

INTERCESSIONS:

O God, you selected some to be leaders of your people—to teach, strengthen and support them. We lift our hearts and pray:
> **Send down your Spirit on those you have chosen.**

O God, your Church has given us John Neumann as an example of priestly holiness;
— may he be an inspiration for all in positions of authority.
Through the intercession of Blessed John Neumann,
— may the work of Christian educators be fruitful.
As bishop of Philadelphia, he served the many immigrants in his diocese;
— help all bishops in their efforts to serve the alienated and the poor.
Christ, you washed the feet of your followers;
— may our bishops be strengthened by your example as they carry out their mission of service to the people of God.
The blessed live with you in glory;
— may all who die share eternal happiness with you.

PRAYER: O God, you lived among us as one who served. Teach us how to empty ourselves of pride, selfishness and vainglory that we may be filled with your fullness. May all in authority be clothed in Christ's Spirit so that once again the lame will walk, the blind will see, and the poor will have the gospel preached to them. We ask this through Jesus who is our way, our truth and our life. Amen.

January 20

IN MEMORY OF MARTIN LUTHER KING, JR., ANWAR SADAT AND MAHATMA GHANDI

MORNING / EVENING PRAYER

(Psalms from the current week in the Psalter.)

Ant 1　These are they who surrendered their bodies in witness to the gospel; they have washed their robes in the blood of the Lamb.

Ant 2　They who lose their life because of me will find it forever.

Ant 3　I saw the souls of those put to death for the word of God and for their faithful witness.

READING

RESPONSORY

O God, you will hear the desire of the meek, you will strengthen their heart.
　—**O God**...
You will incline your ear, —**you will**...
Glory to you, Source of all Being, Eternal Word, and Holy Spirit. —**O God**...

CANTICLE

Ant　Jesus taught them, saying: Blessed are those who hunger and thirst, for they shall be satisfied. Blessed are the peacemakers, for they shall be called children of God.

INTERCESSIONS:

Lord Jesus, you promised the peacemakers on this earth that they will share eternity with you. We give you thanks for them as we pray:
　　Glory to God on high and peace to all people on earth.

Through the reconciliation of Esau and Jacob,
　—may we be reconciled to each other that we may know peace in our families and in the family of all humankind.
Through the love Ruth bore Naomi,
　—may those from different cultures learn to appreciate the goodness and the dignity of the other.
You chose to be known as a Galilean—a man of Nazareth,
　—teach us to respect minorities, the outcast, the unprotected and uneducated, and know them as your own.
Through your holy death which won redemption for all people,
　—may we come to know God as Mother and Father of all, uniting us in one family as sisters and brothers.
Through your glorious resurrection, the final victory over death,
　—may we be not discouraged by our failures.

PRAYER:　O God, you inspire in our hearts a dream for a better world where we can live in love and freedom. We give you thanks for those who keep the vision alive and ask you to help us keep our eyes on Jesus who is our way to accomplishing the task you have given us. We ask this in the name of Jesus and all who have died for the sake of justice. Amen.

January 24

St Francis de Sales, Patron of Authors

COMMEMORATING GEORGE HERBERT, GERARD MANLEY HOPKINS, CARYLL HOUSELANDER, FLANNERY O'CONNOR, RABINDRANATH TAGORE, FRANCIS THOMPSON, MASIE WARD, AND OTHER INSPIRATIONAL WRITERS

MORNING / EVENING PRAYER

(Psalms from the current week in the Psalter.)

Ant 1 The world is charged with the grandeur of God.
It will flame out, like shining from shook foil. *(Hopkins)*

Ant 2 Ah! must, Designer Infinite!
Ah! must Thou char the wood ere Thou canst limn with it? *(Thompson)*

Ant 3 My heart did heave, and there came forth, 'O God!'
By that I knew that Thou wast in the grief. *(Herbert)*

READING

RESPONSORY *(Houselander)*

In each comes Christ; in each Christ comes to birth. —**In each**...
In every cot, Mary has laid her Child; —**in each**...
Glory to you, Source of all Being, Eternal Word, and Holy Spirit. —**In each**...

CANTICLE

Ant All that I am, that I have, that I hope, and all my love have ever flowed
toward thee in depth of secrecy.
One final glance from thine eyes, and my life will be thine own. *(Tagore)*

INTERCESSIONS:

For all this, nature is never spent; there lives the dearest freshness deep down things;* and so we pray:

Open our eyes that we may see.

Your beauty, O God, is revealed in all creation;
—bless all those who enable us to see it through their eyes and their words.
Grant us to speak and to express thoughts worthy of the gifts you give us;
—that your glory may be revealed in us.
You give us vision, O God, that we may speak of your glory,
—enable us to see and to hear your gentle stirrings in the depths of our being.
Through the eyes of your poets, O God, you transform darkness into light,
despair into hope, and death into life;
—may we transform the ordinariness of our lives into the awareness of your life lived in each moment of ours.

PRAYER: O God, we thank you for those special gifts that enable men and women to stir our hearts and desires through their words. May we continue to recognize you in the works of creation, that we may ever give you thanks and glory. This we ask of you through Jesus, your Incarnate Word, who dwells among us. Amen.

(Hopkins)

January 27

ST. ANGELA MERICI

MORNING / EVENING PRAYER*

(Psalms from the current week in the Psalter.)

Ant 1   Have hope and firm faith that God will help you in all things.

Ant 2   Blessed are those who sincerely take up the work of serving God's people.

Ant 3   Let your first refuge always be to turn to Jesus Christ.

READING

RESPONSORY

Angela joyfully served others for the glory of God alone. —**Angela**...
She lived in wisdom and holiness; —**for the**...
Glory to you, Source of all Being, Eternal Word, and Holy Spirit. —**Angela**...

CANTICLE

Ant   Cling together with the bonds of love, esteeming, helping and supporting one another in Christ Jesus.

INTERCESSIONS:

O God, through your daughter, Angela, you promised to provide for all our needs. In confidence we turn to you and say:

Hear our prayer and help us.

Angela told us that the more united we are, the more God is among us;
   —teach us to overcome the obstacles of prejudice, selfishness, and fear, and to enable all people to know that you are present to them.
Angela worked to live and teach your gospel;
   —help all missionaries and teachers to spread your reign by word and action.
You blessed Angela with the gift of understanding the Scriptures,
   —grant us the grace to know and live your word.
Many and varied are the ways you are served by those who claim Angela as their foundress;
   —give the church unity in its diversity and in its trust in the presence of your Spirit.

PRAYER: Loving God, in St. Angela you give us an example of prayerful and dedicated service for your people. May her prayers for us help us to live your gospel as witnesses to your presence in the world. We ask this through her intercession and all her faithful followers who now live with you. Amen.

*Antiphons, responsory and canticle based on her writings.

February 1 / March 17
ST. BRIDGET – ST. PATRICK

MORNING / EVENING PRAYER

(Psalms from the current week in the Psalter.)

Ant 1   My soul clings fast to you; your hand holds me.

Ant 2   Sing praises to our God on the lyre and harp.

Ant 3   Let the mountains, the sea and all that lives give glory to our God.

READING

RESPONSORY

Go to all the nations; sharing the good news of Christ Jesus. —**Go to**...
Announce liberty to the captives; —**sharing**...
Glory to you, Source of all Being, Eternal Word, and Holy Spirit. —**Go to**...

CANTICLE

Ant   We give thanks to God for you always, remembering before our God
       your work of faith and labor of love.

INTERCESSIONS:

O God, you call us to arise each day in the light of your sun and in the radiance of
your moon. In faith we pray:
                       Christ be with me!

Christ within us,
   —breathe into our hearts a renewed faith that seeks peace and justice for all
       peoples.
Christ beside us,
   —give us the confidence that you are with us in all we do.
Christ in danger,
   —sustain us and let the light of your passion bring meaning to our difficulties.
Christ in quiet,
   —enkindle our hearts as we seek you in prayer.
Christ to comfort and restore us
   —be with us at the hour of our death.

PRAYER: O God, we celebrate in Bridget and Patrick your gifts of holiness,
             service and leadership. May they continually call us to a deeper
             faith and to pray for the country of Ireland which they loved with
             the mind and heart of Christ. We ask this through the same Jesus
             Christ who lives with you and the Holy Spirit forever. Amen.

February 10 / July 11

ST. SCHOLASTICA – ST. BENEDICT
MORNING / EVENING PRAYER

(Psalms from the current week in the Psalter.)

Ant 1 God has made him the father of many nations.

Ant 2 She opens her mouth with wisdom, and the teaching of kindness is on her tongue.

Ant 3 Listen my child, to the precepts of your master and incline the ear of your heart.

READING
RESPONSORY

Seek and you shall find; knock and it shall be opened. —**Seek**...
Ask and you shall receive; —**knock**...
Glory to you, Source of all Being, Eternal Word, and Holy Spirit. —**Seek**...

CANTICLE

Ant They shall grow as tall as palms, like cedars they shall stand, planted firmly in their God.

INTERCESSIONS:

To those who are pure of heart you manifest yourself, O God. In joyful expectation we pray:

Prepare our minds and our lips to praise your holy name.

Through the intercession of Scholastica teach us to pray and to trust in your care for us;
—teach us to live by the law of love.

Through the intercession of Benedict endow our religious leaders with wisdom and courage;
—that all their precepts will guide and draw us to you.

We praise you, O God, in the remarkable hospitality taught by Benedict and Scholastica;
—let all who travel, all in distress, find care and solace through christians everywhere.

Your servants lauded the value of prayer and work;
—give us the grace always to make time for prayer and to do our work with reverence and creativity.

Bless all who derive their rule of life from Benedict and Scholastica;
—keep them faithful to their calling and let them also bear fruit in abundant life for the church.

PRAYER: O God, you have endowed your servants, Benedict and Scholastica, with the gifts of prayer and universal charity. Their lives, like the good tree planted near living water, have born fruit in countless women and men who have embraced their way of life. In your mercy, raise up in our day those who are so dedicated to you, that they, too, will guide and nourish all who seek you in spirit and truth. This we ask in Jesus' name. Amen.

February 20 / November 26

FREDERICK DOUGLASS – SOJOURNER TRUTH

MORNING / EVENING PRAYER

(Psalms from the current week in the Psalter.)

Ant 1   Nobody knows the trouble I've seen; nobody knows my sorrows.

Ant 2   When I cried out with my mother's grief, none but Jesus heard me!

Ant 3   I have been forty years a slave and forty years free, and would be here forty years more to have equal rights for all.

READING

RESPONSORY

There are no more distinctions, male or female, slave or free, we are one in Christ. —**There**...
Children of God, a priestly people, —**we are**...
Glory to you, Source of all Being, Eternal Word, and Holy Spirit. —**There**...

CANTICLE

Ant   Thou art my last master, and thy name is Truth; and Truth shall be my abiding name till I die!

INTERCESSIONS:

O God, you created us all and we are equal in your sight. We cry out in hope:
Free at last! Free at last! Thank God Almighty, we're free at last!

O God, through Moses, you led your people out of slavery;
—raise up men and women who will free those still held in bondage.

O God, through Daniel, you confounded the treachery of the judges;
—give us the courage to speak the truth and confront evil.

O God, through Esther, you saved your people from destruction;
—bring all prejudice to light that genocide may be no more.

O God, through Sojourner Truth, you again call us to freedom;
—open our ears and our hearts that we may hear the prophets of our day.

PRAYER: O God, you speak to us in every age through men and women of every race and creed, yet we fail to recognize your voice. Free us from our limitations, our prejudices and blindness that we may respect the dignity of every person on this earth. Especially today we pray for all women that they may know their freedom and use it for the good of all. We ask this in Jesus' name. Amen.

*Antiphons and canticle based on the writings of Sojourner Truth.

March 3 / April 17

KATHERINE DREXEL – ANNA DENGEL

MORNING / EVENING PRAYER*

(Psalms from the current week in the Psalter.)

Ant 1   We must go forward with great optimism founded and grounded on faith to glorify God and let our light shine.

Ant 2   Blessed are those who serve the poor, the neglected, the unjustly treated.

Ant 3   Love is inventive, interested and long-suffering; it is accommodating, tireless and selfless.

READING

RESPONSORY

You do for me, what you do for those thought to be least; they are the living temples of God's divinity. —**You do**...
All are made in your likeness, —**living**...
Glory to you, Source of all Being, Eternal Word, and Holy Spirit. —**You**...

CANTICLE

Ant   With clearness and truth, in justice and charity, let us resolve to press on toward the restoration of all things in Christ.

INTERCESSIONS:

We give you thanks, O God, for the inspiration of Anna Dengel and Katherine Drexel, who served you in the poor of this world, and enabled others to continue this mission through the orders they founded. With grateful hearts we pray:

Blessed are those who follow your way.

O God, in Katherine, you served the outcast, the forgotten, those oppressed;
—give us her vision to recognize those in our society who are being denied their rights and their dignity.

O God, through Anna, you enabled religious women to practice medicine that they may serve you in the poor of the world;
—grant that the gifts of women may be fully utilized in the church and in society.

O God, Katherine gave her fortune and herself to serve you in your people;
—may those who are wealthy and prosperous recognize their responsibility to share their resources with those in need.

O God, you gave Anna the vision and the call to serve you both in christians and non-christians alike;
—may we recognize your face and presence in all people of this world and know them as our sisters and brothers.

O God, Katherine founded a congregation dedicated to the education of Blacks and Native Americans; Anna founded a congregation dedicated to medical mission work for the poor of the world wherever they may be;
—bless all those who follow their inspiration and continue to serve the poor in the Orders they each founded.

*Antiphons. responsory and canticle based on their writings

PRAYER: O God, continue to give our world women like Katherine Drexel and Anna Dengel that the deaf may hear, the blind may see, the sick may be healed, and the poor may hear the good news. Give us the faith to believe that "the impossible of today is the work of tomorrow" and the courage to live it. We ask this in Jesus' name. Amen.

March 15 / September 27

ST. LOUISE de MARILLAC – ST. VINCENT de PAUL

MORNING / EVENING PRAYER*

(Psalms from the current week in the Psalter.)

Ant 1 After having seen the beauty of virtue, we must proceed to resolve to practice it; otherwise prayer is not well made.

Ant 2 The virtue of cordiality should not stand alone for it is in need of another virtue, which is respect.

Ant 3 Prayer and mortification are two sisters who are so closely united together that one will never be found without the other.

READING

RESPONSORY

You have given us an example of love and service; help us to be faithful.
    —You...
Walk in humility and confidence; —**help**...
Glory to you, Source of all Being, Eternal Word, and Holy Spirit. —**You**...

CANTICLE

Ant It is into hearts who seek God alone that God is pleased to pour forth the most excellent lights and greatest graces.

INTERCESSIONS:

O God, through Vincent and Louise, you taught us a deeper love and respect for the poor and so we entreat you:
    Help us to serve them, respecting their dignity.

Christ Jesus, you inspired the sons of Vincent and the Sisters of Charity to be men and women of compassion and empathy in their service to humankind;
    —help us to grow in compassion and understanding.
Loving Creator, we thank you for the example of untiring collaboration shown us in your son, Vincent, and in your daughter, Louise;
    —may we follow their example in our service to the church.
O God, send laborers into your harvest to mirror the gospel values of justice and love of Christ;
    —may our lives give you glory and praise.

*Antiphons, responsory and canticle based on their writings.

Christ Jesus, the seed planted in France by Vincent and Louise and nourished
    by you has grown into a world wide community;
    —may you continue to guide them in their works of justice and charity.

PRAYER: O God, you inspired Vincent and Louise with the spirit of charity
    for the poor. In response to your call, they envisioned a new way of
    living the vows. Their daughters' cloister would be the streets of the
    city or the wards of hospitals, their cell a hired room, and their
    grill, obedience. Grant us the grace to serve those whose lives we
    touch with the same spirit of love, and may the family of Vincent
    and Louise continue to grow and multiply throughout the world.
    Amen.

March 17

ST. PATRICK – ST. BRIDGET

(See February 1)

March 19

SAINT JOSEPH

EVENING PRAYER I

Ant 1   Joseph, the husband of Mary, was a just man (alleluia). (Psalm 113)

Ant 2   Do not fear to take Mary as your wife, for that which is conceived in
    her is of the Holy Spirit, (alleluia). (Psalm 146)

Ant 3   Joseph did as God told him and took Mary as his wife, (alleluia).
    (Eph. 1:3–10)

READING

RESPONSORY

You spoke your word to Joseph, O God, and he fulfilled your will. —**You**...
You blessed him with holiness; —**and he**...
Glory to you, Source of all Being, Eternal Word, and Holy Spirit. —**You**...

CANTICLE OF MARY

Ant   Praise to you, O God, who chose Joseph to be the faithful protector and
    provider of Jesus, the Word made flesh (alleluia).

INTERCESSIONS:

Let us give praise for Joseph the just man, who was called the father of Jesus, the
Christ:

Blessed are those whom you choose, O God.

O God, you chose Joseph to be the guide and teacher of the child, Jesus;
    —direct our minds and hearts as we strive to instruct children in your ways.

Through the intercession of Joseph, spouse of Mary,
   —give husbands and wives the grace to relate to each other with reverence
   and mutual respect.
Joseph supported his family with the work of his hands;
   —grant meaningful employment and an adequate wage to all.
Joseph knew the joys and sorrows of parenthood;
   —bless all parents with the courage and patience to care for their children
   with love and compassion.

PRAYER: O God, you gave Joseph the ineffable joy of joining Mary in
           caring for the child, Jesus. Through his intercession, grant us the
           grace to nurture the life of Christ in our lives. Help us to guide and
           support one another in truth and in love, and so build up the body
           of your church. We ask this in the name of Jesus who lives with
           you, Source of all Being and with the Holy Spirit, forever. Amen.

MORNING PRAYER

(Psalms from Feasts and Solemnities)

Ant 1   In a dream Joseph was told to take the child and his mother into Egypt
        (alleluia).

Ant 2   Joseph rose and took Mary and Jesus at night into Egypt (alleluia).

Ant 3   An angel appeared to Joseph in a dream telling him to return to Israel
        (alleluia).

READING

RESPONSORY

O God, you spoke your word to Joseph, and he fulfilled your will. —**O God**...
You blessed him with holiness; —**and he**...
Glory to you, Source of all Being, Eternal Word, and Holy Spirit. —**O God**...

CANTICLE OF ZECHARIAH

Ant   They said of Jesus: isn't this the son of Joseph, the carpenter?

INTERCESSIONS:

O God, you direct the life of the church through the guidance of the Holy Spirit.
We have named Joseph its guardian and protector, and so we pray:
              Help us to walk the ways of your holy ones.
In praise of Joseph we recall his humility and goodness;
   —deliver us from harmful ambition and self-seeking.
Joseph entered into the mysteries of the life of Jesus;
   —grant us the faith to recognize and follow the call of your Spirit in our lives.
Joseph cared for his family in an occupied land;
   —be merciful to those who are in bondage and grant them freedom and peace.
Joseph died knowing the love of Jesus and Mary;
   —give us the grace to die at peace with our families and with confidence in
   your mercy.

PRAYER: O God, you gave Joseph the ineffable joy of joining Mary in
caring for the child, Jesus. Through his intercession, grant us the
grace to nurture the life of Christ in our lives. Help us to guide and
support one another in truth and in love, and so build up the body
of your church. We ask this in the name of Jesus who lives with
you, Source of all Being and with the Holy Spirit, forever. Amen.

DAYTIME PRAYER

(Psalms from the current weekday in the Psalter)

Ant 1   Through Joseph and his spouse, Mary, God fulfilled the covenant
promised to Abraham and Sarah, (alleluia).

Ant 2   In the hills of Nazareth, you fulfilled your plan for us in silent and
hidden ways (alleluia).

Ant 3   Joseph grew strong in faith, giving glory to God (alleluia).

(Prayer as in Morning Prayer)

EVENING PRAYER II

Ant 1   Jesus and his parents went to Jerusalem every year at the feast of
Passover (alleluia). (Psalm 15)

Ant 2   As they returned to Jerusalem, Jesus remained behind, and they searched
three days for him (alleluia). (Psalm 112)

Ant 3   The parents of Jesus found him among the teachers, listening to them
and asking them questions (alleluia). (Rev. 15:3–4)

READING

RESPONSORY

O God, you spoke your word to Joseph, and he fulfilled your will. —**O God**. . .
You blessed him with holiness; —**and he**. . .
Glory to you, Source of all Being, Eternal Word, and Holy Spirit. —**O God**. . .

CANTICLE OF MARY

Ant   Jesus returned to Nazareth with his parents and was obedient to them
(alleluia).

INTERCESSIONS:

Let us give praise for Joseph the just man, who was called the father of Jesus, the
Christ:
    Blessed are those whom you choose, O God.
O God, you chose Joseph to be the guide and teacher of the child, Jesus;
    —direct our minds and hearts as we strive to instruct children in your
    ways.
Through the intercession of Joseph, spouse of Mary,
    —give husbands and wives the grace to relate to each other with
    reverence and mutual respect.

Joseph supported his family with the work of his hands;
  —grant meaningful employment and an adequate wage to all.
Joseph knew the joys and sorrows of parenthood;
    —bless all parents with the courage and patience to care for their
    children with love and compassion.

PRAYER: O God, you gave Joseph the ineffable joy of joining Mary in
caring for the child, Jesus. Through his intercession, grant us the
grace to nurture the life of Christ in our lives. Help us to guide and
support one another in truth and in love, and so build up the body
of your church. We ask this in the name of Jesus who lives with
you, Source of all Being and with the Holy Spirit, forever. Amen.

March 24

COMMEMORATION OF OSCAR ROMERO

MORNING / EVENING PRAYER

(Psalms from the current week in the Psalter.)

Ant 1   Unless a grain of wheat falls into the ground and dies, it remains just a
single grain; but if it dies, it will bear much fruit.

Ant 2   His faith was founded on solid rock; he feared no wicked threats.

Ant 3   Whatever you have done for the least of my people you have done for
me.

READING

RESPONSORY

You have lifted me up from the gates of death, that I may give you praise.
    —**You**...
Be gracious to me, O God, —**that**...
Glory to you, Source of all Being, Eternal Word, and Holy Spirit. —**You**...

CANTICLE

Ant   When the days drew near for Jesus to be taken up to heaven, he set his
face to go to Jerusalem.

INTERCESSIONS:

O Christ, you gave us the example that one can have no greater love than to lay
down one's life for one's friends, and so we pray:
      Teach us to love one another as you have loved us.
Christ Jesus, you inspired your servant, Oscar Romero, to speak fearlessly your
    gospel of love;
    —give us the grace to stand up for our convictions in the face of adversity.
You enabled Archbishop Romero to become attentive to the cries of the poor;
    —keep our hearts open that we may hear your voice and follow it.

You promised your followers a peace that the world cannot give;
— may nations learn that peace cannot be achieved through war or acts of violence.

You have told us that the meek will inherit the earth;
— may there be true land reform in countries where ownership is controlled by the rich and powerful.

Grant all those who have been killed by acts of violence,
— eternal peace and joy in your presence.

PRAYER: O God, you have given us women and men who, like Jesus, have preached the gospel with their lives. May their example spur us on to be more committed to the cause of justice and peace. Help us so live your gospel in our lives that its effects will influence the political and economic decisions that affect the quality of life for all peoples on this earth. We ask this through the intercession of those who have died for the sake of justice and now live with you for all eternity. Amen.

March 25

ANNUNCIATION

EVENING PRAYER I

Ant 1   A virgin shall conceive and bear a child and the child shall be called Emmanuel (alleluia). (Psalm 113)

Ant 2   Sacrifice and offerings you have not desired, but a body you have prepared for me. (alleluia). (Psalm 147:12–20)

Ant 3   As the rain falls from heaven and does not return until it has given growth to the seed, so shall my word accomplish my purpose (alleluia). (Phil. 2:6–11)

READING

RESPONSORY

You are the honor of our race, you are the joy of our people. —**You**...
The promise has been fulfilled; —**you are the joy**...
Glory to you, Source of all Being, Eternal Word, and Holy Spirit. —**You**...

CANTICLE OF MARY

Ant   The angel of God declared unto Mary, and she conceived by the Holy Spirit (alleluia).

INTERCESSIONS:

Mary, full of grace, is called to be the mother of Jesus. We rejoice in you, O God, as we say:

       You are the honor of your people, O blessed virgin Mary.

Mary is blessed among women with the joy all ages have awaited;
— through her intercession free all women who are in bondage and who lead lives less than human.

Mary chose freely to become the mother of the savior;
—grant to all people the freedom to choose their way of life.
Mary rejoiced at the mystery of her motherhood;
—grant your grace and guidance to mothers who do not want their children.
Mary went in haste to support and to share the mystery of new life with her
cousin, Elizabeth;
—teach us how to share with others, the fruit of your Spirit in our lives.

PRAYER: O God, in the fullness of time, you called the virgin, Mary, to be the
mother of Jesus. As we celebrate this mystery of the annunciation,
of Mary's entrance into the mystery of redemption, grant us the
grace of opening our lives to all that you would call us to be. Give
us the mind and heart of Mary that we too may bear Christ to the
world. We ask this through Jesus Christ, the Incarnate Word, one
with you, Source of all life, and with the Holy Spirit. Amen.

MORNING PRAYER

(Psalms from Feasts and Solemnities)

Ant 1 The angel Gabriel said to Mary: Hail, full of grace, the Most High is
with you (alleluia).

Ant 2 Favored daughter of Israel, you have found favor with God (alleluia).

Ant 3 You will give birth to Jesus who will save his people from their sins
(alleluia).

READING

RESPONSORY

Mother of our savior, mother pierced with a lance, pray for us who trust in you.
—**Mother**...
You are the cause of our joy; —**pray**...
Glory to you, Source of all Being, Eternal Word, and Holy Spirit. —**Mother**...

CANTICLE OF ZECHARIAH

Ant I am God's handmaid, be it done to me according to your word (alleluia).

INTERCESSIONS:

The mercies of God endure from age to age, working marvels for the people. With
grateful hearts we pray:
O God, holy is your name.
You blessed the holiness of Mary with the joy of your call;
—give us the grace to persevere in faith and in prayer when our efforts seem
fruitless.
Mary's fiat brings salvation to the world;
—let all of our choices promote life and give you praise and glory.
Mary heard the word of God and entered the mystery of redemption;
—give us the grace to follow the lure of your call to growth.
Mary's "yes" to God brought motherhood and martyrdom of heart;
—bless all parents who must bear deep suffering in their children; be their
refuge and strength.

PRAYER: O God, in the fullness of time, you called the virgin, Mary, to be the mother of Jesus. As we celebrate this mystery of the annunciation, of Mary's entrance into the mystery of redemption, grant us the grace of opening our lives to all that you would call us to be. Give us the mind and heart of Mary that we too may bear Christ to the world. We ask this through Jesus Christ, the Incarnate Word, one with you, Source of all life, and with the Holy Spirit. Amen.

DAYTIME PRAYER

(Psalms from the current weekday in the Psalter)

Ant 1 I delight to do your will, O God; your law is within my heart (alleluia).

Ant 2 All generations shall call me blessed; most holy is your name (alleluia).

Ant 3 You have favored the lowliness of your handmaid and have lifted up the powerless (alleluia).

(Prayer as in Morning Prayer)

EVENING PRAYER II

Ant 1 Blessed is she who believed that God's word in her would be fulfilled (alleluia). (Psalm 110:1–5, 7)

Ant 2 The power of the Most High overshadowed Mary, and the Spirit came upon her (alleluia). (Psalm 130)

Ant 3 The Holy One born of you shall be called the Son of God (alleluia). (Col. 1:12–20)

READING

RESPONSORY

Blessed are you among women and blessed is the fruit of your womb.
  —**Blessed**...
Hail, ark of the covenant, —**blessed is**...
Glory to you, Source of all Being, Eternal Word, and Holy Spirit. —**Blessed**...

CANTICLE OF MARY

Ant My spirit rejoices in God, my savior (alleluia).

INTERCESSIONS:

Mary, full of grace, is called to be the mother of Jesus. We rejoice in you, O God, as we say:

You are the honor of your people, O blessed virgin Mary.

Mary is blessed among women with the joy all ages have awaited;
  —through her intercession free all women who are in bondage and who lead lives less than human.
Mary chose freely to become the mother of the savior;
  —grant to all people the freedom to choose their way of life.
Mary rejoiced at the mystery of her motherhood;
  —grant your grace and guidance to mothers who do not want their children.

Mary went in haste to support and to share the mystery of new life with her
  cousin, Elizabeth;
  —teach us how to share with others, the fruit of your Spirit in our lives.

PRAYER: O God, in the fullness of time, you called the virgin, Mary, to be the
          mother of Jesus. As we celebrate this mystery of the annunciation,
          of Mary's entrance into the mystery of redemption, grant us the
          grace of opening our lives to all that you would call us to be. Give
          us the mind and heart of Mary that we too may bear Christ to the
          world. We ask this through Jesus Christ, the Incarnate Word, one
          with you, Source of all life, and with the Holy Spirit. Amen.

April 7

ST. JULIE BILLIART

MORNING / EVENING PRAYER*

(Psalms from the current week in the Psalter.)

Ant 1   If you would follow me, take up your cross.

Ant 2   Let the little children come to me.

Ant 3   In you, O God, we trust and have our being.

READING

RESPONSORY

Do not be frightened, God will never fail you. —**Do not**...
In joy or adversity, —**God**...
Glory to you, Source of all Being, Eternal Word, and Holy Spirit. —**Do not**...

CANTICLE

Ant   As gold in the furnace God proved her.

INTERCESSIONS:

You use the weak ones of the earth to accomplish your works, O God, and so we
pray:
          Blessed are they who suffer persecution for your sake.
O God, through the intercession of Julie Billiart;
  —may all threatened by revolutions and political unrest know the peace the
    world cannot give.
O God, through the intercession of your daughter, Julie;
  —give courage to those who are injured and physically disabled.
O God, through the intercession of your daughter, Julie;
  —bless all those who follow her inspiration in the Congregation she founded.
O God, through the intercession of your daughter, Julie;
  —comfort all who suffer misunderstanding as they follow the guidance of the
    Spirit.

*Responsory and canticle based on her writings.

PRAYER: O God, you blessed your daughter, Julie, with humility and wisdom in the midst of struggle and misunderstanding. Through her many came to know your love and concern. Bless her followers, the Sisters of Notre Dame, that they may continue the work you began in her. We ask this in the names of Jesus and his mother, Mary. Amen.

April 10

IN MEMORY OF TEILHARD DE CHARDIN
MORNING / EVENING PRAYER*

(Psalms from the current week in the Psalter.)

Ant 1 O God, blessed is the one whom you instruct.

Ant 2 The universe reflects your glory, O God. You reveal its secrets to the wise and simple.

Ant 3 All creation sings your glory—even the stones shout for joy.

READING

RESPONSORY

I will give thanks to God with my whole heart. —**I will**...
I will tell of all your wonders; —**with**...
Glory to you, Source of all Being, Eternal Word, and Holy Spirit. —**I will**...

CANTICLE

Ant Nothing in the world is more intensely alive and active than purity and prayer, which hang like an unmoving light between the universe and God.

INTERCESSIONS:

Let us give thanks to God who has created this wondrous universe. With heartfelt joy we pray:

May all creation give you glory!

O Cosmic Christ, you are present in the heart of the world;
— may we reverence you in all your works.
Unifying Center of the world, you draw all things to yourself;
— bring all creation to the fullness of being.
Redeemer of the world,
— help us to protect our environment for future generations.
God of the heavens,
— may our ventures into space be for the good of all humankind and in accord with gospel values.
Christ, the Alpha and the Omega,
— may all who have died enjoy the glory of resurrection and aid us on our way.

PRAYER: We give you thanks, Creator God, for your servant, Teilhard, and all those who help us to see your universe. May creation be continually transformed that all may share in the life, death and resurrection of God become human, our Lord Jesus Christ. Amen.

*Antiphons and canticle based on his writings.

April 17

ANNA DENGEL – KATHERINE DREXEL

(See March 3)

April 29 / August 8

ST. CATHERINE OF SIENA – ST. DOMINIC

MORNING / EVENING PRAYER*

(Psalms from the current week in the Psalter.)

Ant 1 The seed will moulder if it is hoarded up, it will fructify if it is sown.

Ant 2 Jesus is the way that is the bridge leading to the very height of heaven.

Ant 3 It is the book of charity which teaches us all things.

READING

RESPONSORY

O eternal Trinity, when I consider myself in you, I see that I am your image.
  —O eternal...
You are in love with the beauty of what you have made; —I see...
Glory to you, Source of all Being, Eternal Word, and Holy Spirit. —O
  eternal...

CANTICLE

Ant Remake the vessels you created and formed in your image and likeness;
reform them to grace in the mercy and blood of Christ Jesus.

INTERCESSIONS:

You favor us, O God, through the witness of your saints. We joyfully proclaim:
  We praise you; we glorify you; we give you thanks.

Dominic was sensitive to the Word spoken in the heart of every man and
  woman, especially those who were enslaved in misery and need;
  —free those enslaved by their addictions or by economic and political
  oppression.
Through Catherine, you called the laity and the clergy to work together as the
  people of God;
  —further the work of dialogue and ministry that each person's gifts may be
  used.
Through the Order of Preachers, the Church has been blessed with many
  teachers and theologians;
  —endow all scholars with wisdom and knowledge that they may further the
  understanding of the mysteries of God and creation.
Dominic was at the heart of the church in the service of the world;
  —enable all who share in that charism and his prophetic vision to proclaim
  the Word that the Spirit puts into their hearts.

*Antiphons, responsory and canticle based on their writings.

O God, you have spread the Dominican Order to many nations;
—bless each of its members and keep them true to their charism.

PRAYER: O God, you continue to bless us with men and women who enable
us to further our understanding of your revelation in Jesus. May we
profit from their wisdom that we may better serve you. Grant this
in the name of Jesus and through the intercession of all the saints of
this Order. Amen.

May 1

ST. JOSEPH THE WORKER

(See March 19)

May 23

BL. BROTHER ANDRÉ BESSETTE

MORNING / EVENING PRAYER

(Psalms from the current week in the Psalter.)

Ant 1   Come to me all who are weary and I will give you rest.

Ant 2   These signs will accompany those who believe; in my name they will
cure the sick.

Ant 3   Those who exalt themselves shall be humbled; and those who humble
themselves shall be exalted. . . .

READING

RESPONSORY

Ask and you shall receive; God gives all that we need. —**Ask**. . .
Seek and you will find; —**God**. . .
Glory to you, Source of all Being, Eternal Word, and Holy Spirit. —**Ask**. . .

CANTICLE

Ant   What you have hidden from the wise and the learned, you have revealed
to the merest children.

INTERCESSIONS:

Most gentle God, you continue to reveal your love for us through your faithful
friends. In confidence we implore you:
Heal us and anoint us in your love.
Through the intercession of Brother André, increase our faith in you;
—that we may be vessels of your healing and reconciling love.
You inspired Brother André to cure the sick in the name of St. Joseph;
—enable us to serve the sick and the oppressed in humility and with grateful
hearts.

You call some men to minister among us as brothers;
—may they experience your presence in their ministries and be signs of faith in our world.
You remind us that in you all things are possible;
—assist all who work in apparent difficulty to find equitable and just solutions through discerning faith in you.

PRAYER: Most gracious God, help us to reveal your love in our work place this day. Fill us with the zeal and understanding that whatever we do for the least among us is done unto you. We ask for this grace in the name of Jesus. Amen.

May 25

ST. MADELEINE SOPHIE BARAT

MORNING / EVENING PRAYER*

(Psalms from the current week in the Psalter.)

Ant 1   It is the interior spirit that gives life and fruitfulness to everything.

Ant 2   The proof of true love is forgetfulness of self and one's own interests.

Ant 3   What difference does it make how you pray, provided your heart is seeking the One whom you love?

READING

RESPONSORY

O God, let us drink with joy from your life-giving waters. —O God...
Cleanse our hearts and our minds, —with joy...
Glory to you, Source of all Being, Eternal Word, and Holy Spirit. —O God...

CANTICLE

Ant   Let us have no memory but to remember, no heart but to bless, no strength but to serve.

INTERCESSIONS:

O God, we pray to you as we commemorate this holy woman:
May you be glorified in your saints.
Christ Jesus, you invited the little children to come to you;
—may all children know your love and concern by the respect given to them.
Through the intercession of Madeleine Sophie,
—bless all those responsible for the education of children.
O God, in Madeleine Sophie, you gave us a model of leadership;
—may all administrators be given the gift of wisdom and moderation.
O God, you gave Madeleine Sophie a great love of humility;
—let all recognize you as the source and giver of all that we are and possess.

*Antiphons, responsory and canticle based on her writings.

PRAYER: O God, we bless you for the life of Madeleine Sophie. We thank you for all that you accomplished through her. Bless all those who follow and are guided by her inspiration as they continue your work in this world. May they be faithful to her spirit and counsels. This we ask in the name of Jesus. Amen.

June 1

HELEN KELLER

MORNING / EVENING PRAYER

(Psalms from the current week in the Psalter.)

Ant 1   Out of the depths I cry to you, O God; hear the sound of my pleading.

Ant 2   The water that I shall give them will become in them a spring of living water welling up to eternal life.

Ant 3   Blessed are those who have not seen and have believed.

READING

RESPONSORY

Seek and you shall find; knock and it shall be opened. —**Seek**...
Ask and you shall receive; —**knock**...
Glory to you, Source of all Being, Eternal Word, and Holy Spirit. —**Seek**...

CANTICLE

Ant   Eye has not seen nor ear heard nor has it entered into the heart of anyone what you have prepared for those who love you.

INTERCESSIONS:

God has done wonderful things through men and women of all ages. Let us give praise for the marvelous life of Helen Keller:

Wonderful are your works, O God.

O God, you have created us in your image; you have created us free;
   —through the manifestation of vibrant life in Helen Keller, give us a reverence for our own and all life, and keep us grateful to you.

O God, our lives are replete with the mysteries of joy and suffering;
   —help us to see your loving care and call in both and to remain faithful to you to the end.

O God, in the face of a living "death," Helen Keller was able to choose life;
   —give us the grace to cherish every aspect of our lives and to let hope in you be our guide through adversity.

O God, Helen Keller found new life through the patient care of others;
   —remembering your mercy to us, let us bear with one another in our journey to wholeness.

O God, your servant, Helen Keller, transformed her cross into a gift for the world;
   —bless us, too, with the insight and creativity to bring life to ourselves and others out of the things that afflict us.

PRAYER: O God, we thank you for making known to the world the valiant life of Helen Keller. Let her love for life give courage to those who live in the shadow of death. Let her courage in the face of deprivation spur us on to engage the challenges of our lives with hope and creativity. Teach us how to help one another, and give us the faith to embrace and revere the mystery of creation. Through it all may you be praised forever, Source of Life, Savior and Sanctifier of the world. Amen.

June 3

IN MEMORY OF POPE JOHN XXIII,
Angelo Gieuseppe Roncalli

MORNING / EVENING PRAYER

(Psalms from the current week in the Psalter.)

Ant 1 You are the chosen vessel of God; you preached the truth throughout the whole world.

Ant 2 God's grace in me has not been without fruit; it is always at work in me.

Ant 3 You are the shepherd of the flock, you must strengthen the faith of your sisters and brothers.

READING

RESPONSORY

Commit your work to God, your plans will be established. **—Commit...**
God has made everything for its purpose, **—your...**
Glory to you, Source of all Being, Eternal Word, and Holy Spirit.
  —Commit...

CANTICLE

Ant A patient man will endure until the right moment, and then joy will burst forth for him. He will hide his words until the right moment, and many will tell of his good sense.

INTERCESSIONS:

O God, you send your Spirit to renew the Church, the people of God, and call them to holiness in the world. We give you thanks and pray:
  Grant to us, Christ Jesus, a heart renewed.

O God, you inspired Pope John to open the windows to the breath of the Spirit;
  —keep our hearts and attitudes open to you in the signs of our times.
You called your servant, Pope John, to work for Christian Unity;
  —may we continue to work for the unity that respects differences.
Through his leadership, Pope John convened Vatican Council II;
  —may it continue to call us forth and seed renewal for the future.
Pope John honored St. Joseph by including his commemoration in the eucharistic banquet;
  —may St. Joseph intercede for all the people of God.

Through his warmth and humor, Pope John witnessed your loving concern for all humankind;
  —help us to learn the wisdom of simplicity and the power of weakness.

PRAYER: O God, you graced your Church under the leadership of Pope John to be a witness to the world. Bless all who are in positions of church leadership. Make them holy and true witnesses of the gospel you gave us. May all come to know their calling to be a priestly people, that the church will be seen by the world as God's holy people. We ask this in the name of Jesus who founded the church on Peter. Amen.

July 11

ST. BENEDICT – ST. SCHOLASTICA

(See February 10)

July 14

IN MEMORY OF BL. KATERI TEKAWITHA, AND ALL NATIVE AND ABORIGINAL PEOPLES

MORNING / EVENING PRAYER

(Psalms from the current week in the Psalter.)

Ant 1   From the mouths of the innocent you have perfected praise.

Ant 2   You have come to your people to set them free.

Ant 3   Earth's peoples and all living creatures sing your praise.

READING

RESPONSORY

Incline our hearts to justice, O God, that justice may be given to all.
    —Incline...
Give us eyes to see and ears to hear; —that...
Glory to you, Source of all Being, Eternal Word, and Holy Spirit. —Incline...

CANTICLE

Ant   Earth our mother, eagle our cousin. Tree, he is pumping our blood. Grass is growing. And water. And we are all one.*

INTERCESSIONS:

Rock stays, earth stays. I die and put my bones in cave or earth. Soon my bones become earth—all the same. My spirit has gone back to my country—my mother.* With all created beings we pray:
          In you we move, and live and have our being.

*Big Bill Neidjie of the Gagudju (Australia).

God of the universe, you created the land, the seas and the heavens;
—give us the wisdom to respect and care for our natural resources as do our native people.

God of the living, you created the birds, the fish and all the animals;
—enable us to protect their environment and to preserve the rights of every species that share our planet with us.

God of the holy, you reveal yourself in every time and age;
—we give you thanks for all primitive peoples who recognized the holy in beasts, rocks, plants and in all the elements of our earth.

God of our ancestors, you revealed yourself in dreamers, seers and prophets;
—help us to recognize and hear the prophets who speak to us today.

God of all peoples, your loving providence extends to every race and nation;
—give us your vision and love that we may respect the rights of all peoples, especially those indigenous to our lands.

PRAYER: O God, we have sinned against you in the oppression of our native peoples. Forgive the blindness of our past and enable us to atone for our guilt by restoring the rights of all people to live on their land in peace and with dignity. May all native peoples experience your love and providence through us. We ask this for the sake of all our native peoples who died because of our greed, and in the name of Jesus who brought us your forgiveness. Amen.

July 31

ST. IGNATIUS OF LOYOLA

MORNING / EVENING PRAYER*

(Psalms from the current week in the Psalter.)

Ant 1 All for the greater honor and glory of God.

Ant 2 As you have sent me into the world, so I have sent them.

Ant 3 Here I am, O God, I come to do your will.

READING

RESPONSORY

You, O God, are my inheritance; your goodness is with me always. —You...
You show me the path to life; —your...
Glory to you, Source of all Being, Eternal Word, and Holy Spirit. —You...

CANTICLE

Ant It is not ourselves that we preach, but Christ Jesus, our redeemer.

*Antiphon, canticle and prayer based on his writings.

INTERCESSIONS:

In the cross of Christ is our salvation; in confidence, let us pray:
Forever I will sing your praises!

You gave Ignatius the wisdom to be a spiritual guide for others;
—may you continue to encourage spiritual directors to rely on your wisdom and to share their gifts.

You call us all to be your companions and to journey together in freedom and love;
—help us to be generous, supportive and challenging in our relationships with one another.

You invite us to let go of all things in order to possess you;
—enable us to recognize that attachment to you is commensurate with our attachment to all our sisters and brothers.

You give us life in abundance and we return it to you;
—assist us to nurse the sick with gentleness, to teach our youth with kindness, and to comfort the oppressed with compassion.

PRAYER: Take, O God, receive all my liberty, my memory, my understanding, my entire will. You have given all to me, now I return it. All I have is yours. Dispose of it, wholly according to your will. Give me only your love and your grace, with these I am rich enough. I desire no more. Amen.

August 4

ST. JOHN MARY VIANNEY

MORNING / EVENING PRAYER

(Psalms from the current week in the Psalter.)

Ant 1 Learn from me, for I am gentle and lowly in heart, and you will find rest for your souls.

Ant 2 Behold my servant whom I have chosen. He will not break a bruised reed or quench a smoldering wick.

Ant 3 You are a priest forever, according to the order of Melchizedek.

READING

RESPONSORY

Come to me, all who labor and are heavy laden, and I will give you rest.
—Come...
Take my yoke upon you, —and...
Glory to you, Source of all Being, Eternal Word, and Holy Spirit. —Come...

CANTICLE

Ant God of heaven and earth, you have hidden these things from the wise and prudent and revealed them to little ones.

INTERCESSIONS:

God endowed John Vianney with special gifts of discernment and a love for penance and so we pray:

Teach us the ways of holiness.

O God, you have given us John Vianney as patron of priests;
  —inspire all priests with love and gratitude for their calling.
You gave John Vianney the grace to overcome his limitations;
  —encourage and enlighten seminarians in times of difficulty and doubt.
You inspired John Vianney to enrich his apostolate through penance and mortification;
  —give our priests the wisdom to entrust their lives and labor into your hands.
You blessed John Vianney with a special gift for healing souls in the sacrament of reconciliation;
  —fill our hearts with patience, understanding, and compassion for one another.

PRAYER: O God, you inspired John Mary Vianney with the desire to fill up in his flesh what was wanting in the sufferings of Christ. His love for you and for the church drew multitudes to your table of forgiveness and unity. Through his intercession, bless our priests and all who aspire to this calling. Let them know your love and the support of those whom they serve, that together we may praise you who live and reign with Jesus and your Holy Spirit, now and forever. Amen.

August 6

TRANSFIGURATION

EVENING PRAYER I

Ant 1 The skies opened and I saw the Holy One receive from God dominion, glory, and power. (Psalm 113)

Ant 2 The reign of Christ is everlasting; it shall never pass away. (Psalm 117)

Ant 3 The heavens proclaim the goodness of God; all peoples behold God's glory. (Rev. 19:1–7)

READING

RESPONSORY

You are covered with glory, O Christ; we bow down and adore you. —You...
In brilliant light you stand before us; —we...
Glory to you, Source of all Being, Eternal Word, and Holy Spirit. —You...

CANTICLE OF MARY

Ant As Jesus stood transformed before them, the disciples were overcome with awe.

INTERCESSIONS:

Jesus was transfigured before his disciples and Elijah and Moses appeared with him. In God's presence we proclaim:

It is good for us to be here.

Jesus, beloved of God, fulfillment of prophecy,
  —help us to listen to your word spoken through the prophets of our day.
You appeared in the splendor of a vision to your apostles;
  —strengthen with the gift of prayer all who labor in your vineyard.
You shone in glory on Mt. Tabor and descended the mount to take up your cross;
  —keep us faithful to you as we carry our own daily cross.
On Tabor you shone with a radiant light;
  —let your presence in our lives be light for others as they seek to follow you.
Your transfiguration foretold your resurrection in glory;
  —comfort the dying with the hope of eternal life.

PRAYER: O Christ, you gave comfort and strength to your apostles through the vision of your transfiguration. Have mercy on us, and show yourself to all who face suffering and death for the cause of truth. Bless us all with the hope of resurrection. This we ask through the power of your name. Amen.

MORNING PRAYER

(Psalms from Feasts and Solemnities)

Ant 1 Jesus received glory and praise from the Most High.

Ant 2 Jesus was transfigured in the sight of the disciples.

Ant 3 Moses and Elijah appeared with Jesus, the fulfillment of the law and the prophets.

READING

RESPONSORY

Christ Jesus was clothed in brilliance, and we saw his glory. —**Christ**...
Sovereign over all creation; —**and we**...
Glory to you, Source of all Being, Eternal Word, and Holy Spirit. —**Christ**...

CANTICLE OF ZECHARIAH

Ant Light dawns for the upright, and joy for the pure of heart.

INTERCESSIONS:

On the mountain Jesus was transfigured in glory and his apostles were overcome with awe. With holy reverence, we proclaim:
Jesus, you are the Chosen One of God!
Jesus, you took your faithful friends to the mountain to pray;
  —bless us with relationships that keep us faithful to you.
On the mountain you prepared for your suffering and death;
  —let all that we do make us more and more open to whatever life may ask of us.
On the mountain you spoke with prophets from the past and with apostles of the future;
  —open our minds and hearts to the magnitude of God's ways.
Yours are the heavens and yours is the earth;
  —bless our civic and religious leaders with the gift of wisdom.

On the mountain you were bathed in light, your garments white as snow;
—dispel from our world all that blinds us to you; make us a forgiving and
thankful people.

PRAYER: O Christ, coming down the mountain, the disciples saw "only
Jesus!" Enable us to recognize the presence of the transcendent in
the ordinary and the mundane, knowing that you are with us in all
the circumstances of our lives. We ask this that we might give you
glory in all that we do. Amen.

DAYTIME PRAYER

(Psalms from the current weekday in the Psalter)

Ant 1   As Jesus was praying, the appearance of his face changed and his
clothing became dazzling white.

Ant 2   Moses and Elijah appeared with Jesus and they spoke of his death in
Jerusalem.

Ant 3   Peter, James and John saw the glory of God on the Mount of Tabor.

(Prayer as in Morning Prayer)

EVENING PRAYER II

Ant 1   Jesus took with him Peter, James and John, and went up on the
mountain to pray. (Psalm 110:1–5, 7)

Ant 2   As Jesus prayed, his appearance changed, and Moses and Elijah stood
with him. (Psalm 121)

Ant 3   This is my Beloved, my Chosen One!

Canticle   1 Timothy 3:16

Praise our Savior, all you nations.
Christ manifested in the flesh,
Christ justified by the Spirit.

Praise our Savior, all you nations.
Christ seen by the angels,
Christ proclaimed to unbelievers.

Praise our Savior, all you nations.
Christ believed in by the world,
Christ taken up in glory.

Praise our Savior, all you nations.
Glory...

READING

RESPONSORY

Praise to you, transformed in glory; we bow down before you. —**Praise**...
Your sun has risen, O Christ, your holiness is revealed; —**we**...
Glory to you, Source of all Being, Eternal Word, and Holy Spirit. —**Praise**...

CANTICLE OF MARY

Ant   Jesus touched the disciples and said: Arise, have no fear. When they
looked up, they saw no one but Jesus.

INTERCESSIONS:

Jesus was transfigured before his disciples and Elijah and Moses appeared with him. In God's presence we proclaim:

It is good for us to be here.

Jesus, beloved of God, fulfillment of prophecy,
—help us to listen to your word spoken through the prophets of our day.
You appeared in the splendor of a vision to your apostles;
—strengthen with the gift of prayer all who labor in your vineyard.
You shone in glory on Mt. Tabor and descended the mount to take up your cross;
—keep us faithful to you as we carry our own daily cross.
On Tabor you shone with a radiant light;
—let your presence in our lives be light for others as they seek to follow you.
Your transfiguration foretold your resurrection in glory;
—comfort the dying with the hope of eternal life.

PRAYER: O Christ, you gave comfort and strength to your apostles through the vision of your transfiguration. Have mercy on us, and show yourself to all who face suffering and death for the cause of truth. Bless us all with the hope of resurrection. This we ask through the power of your name. Amen.

August 8

ST. DOMINIC – ST. CATHERINE OF SIENA

(See April 29)

August 9

IN MEMORY OF BL. EDITH STEIN, ETTY HILLESUM, AND OTHER VICTIMS OF THE HOLOCAUST

MORNING / EVENING PRAYER*

(Psalms from the current week in the Psalter.)

Ant 1 O God, redress the wronged, hear the orphan's plea, defend your people.

Ant 2 The earth will reveal the blood upon it, and no longer conceal its slain.

Ant 3 Though our sins be as scarlet, they may become white as snow.

READING

RESPONSORY

I offer myself for the sake of peace; it is already the twelfth hour —I offer...
More will be called to the same sacrifice in these days; —it is...
Glory to you, Source of all Being, One God Almighty, Holy Mystery.
—I offer...

CANTICLE

Ant We praise the Almighty even at the grave of our loved ones.

*Responsory and canticle based on their writings.

INTERCESSIONS:

Oh God, you called Abraham and Sarah to form a nation in covenant with you. Recalling your promise to them, we pray:

Remember your people you called to be your own.

God of Abraham and Sarah,
  —bless their inheritance and descendants forever.
God of Isaac and Rebecca,
  —bring peace to the land made holy by their presence.
God of Jacob, Leah and Rachel,
  —protect the Jewish people from prejudicial laws and governments.
God who forgave David,
  —forgive all who have done violence to your chosen people.
God who calls all to repentance,
  —may the ashes of Auschwitz, Dachau and other places of terror burn our memories and hearts that humankind will never again be guilty of genocide.

PRAYER: O God, full of tenderness and mercy, look with compassion on us for we have sinned. May the memory of those who perished in the holocaust be engraved on our hearts that we may learn compassion and avoid the evil of prejudice. We ask forgiveness of all victims of violence who now enjoy peace with you and beg them to pray for us on our behalf that we may learn your ways. Amen.

August 11 / October 4

ST. CLARE OF ASSISI – ST. FRANCIS OF ASSISI
MORNING / EVENING PRAYER*

(Psalms from the current week in the Psalter.)

Ant 1   The Highest One revealed to me that I should live in accordance with the holy gospel.

Ant 2   Go forward securely, joyfully and swiftly on the path of prudent happiness.

Ant 3   Praised be you with all your creatures: Brother Sun and Sister Moon, Brother Wind and Sister Water.

READING

RESPONSORY

Yours are the praises, the glory, the honor and all benediction; my God and my All. —**Yours**...
To you alone, Most High, do they belong; —**my**...
Glory to you, Source of all Being, Eternal Word, and Holy Spirit. —**Yours**...

CANTICLE

Ant   In following in the footprints of the poor and humble Jesus Christ, I can rejoice truly and no one can rob me of this joy.

*Antiphons, responsory and canticle based on their writings.

INTERCESSIONS:

O God, through Francis and Clare you taught us the values of community and downward mobility, and so we ask you:

               Grant us simplicity of heart.

Loving Creator, your son, Francis, and your daughter, Clare, praised you in all your creatures;

     —strengthen all who labor to preserve our endangered species and ravaged land; let them see the rewards of their labors.

Christ Jesus, you came to preach the gospel to the poor;

     —may the poor of our world hear the gospel in the way we serve them.

Through Francis and Clare you taught us love and care for the sick and the dying;

     —grant that we may follow their example of service.

From the hills of Umbria, you raised up an Order that encircles the globe;

     —bless all the followers of Francis and Clare and keep them true to the spirit of their founders.

PRAYER: O loving God, you renewed the marks of the suffering of Jesus in the body of Francis and the heart of Clare. Inflame our hearts with the fire of your love. Through their intercession and all the saints of the Franciscan Order, may we learn the joy of humility and simplicity, and live in love as sisters and brothers. We ask this through Jesus, our brother. Amen.

August 15

ASSUMPTION

EVENING PRAYER I

Ant 1   Arise, O God, go to your resting place, you and the ark of your covenant; alleluia. (Psalm 113)

Ant 2   Thanks be to God, who gives us victory over death through Jesus Christ, alleluia. (Psalm 147:12–20)

Ant 3   Blessed is the one who hears the word of God and keeps it, alleluia. (Phil. 2:6–11)

READING

RESPONSORY

Mother of our redeemer, pray for us. —**Mother**. . .
You reign with Christ forever; —**pray**. . .
Glory to you, Source of all Being, Eternal Word, and Holy Spirit. —**Mother**. . .

CANTICLE OF MARY

Ant   You have shown might and mercy; you have exalted the lowly, alleluia.

INTERCESSIONS:

O God, you are blessed in your angels and saints. Most blessed are you in your daughter, Mary. In joy we proclaim:

               You have lifted up the lowly.

O God, you chose Mary to be the mother of Jesus and the mother of the church;
—bless all who follow her example and bring Christ to the world.
Mary lived the mystery of Jesus and followed him to the cross;
—give us the faith to follow you all the days of our lives.
Mary's glory is her union with your will;
—through her intercession may we always do what is pleasing to you.
You called Mary to be the new Eve, the gate of heaven;
—as we ponder your word, enkindle our hearts with love for your will, that we too may attain eternal life.

PRAYER: O God, you called Mary to be the mother of Jesus and the mother of our salvation. Let the example of her fidelity inspire us to open ourselves to the fullness of your grace, that we, too, may bear your Christ to the world. Grant this in the name of the same Jesus Christ who lives with you and the Holy Spirit forever. Amen.

MORNING PRAYER

(Psalms from Feasts and Solemnities)

Ant 1 A great sign appeared in heaven; a woman clothed with the sun.

Ant 2 Rejoice, O Heaven, and you that dwell therein!

Ant 3 O Mary, full of grace, you dwell with God forever.

READING

RESPONSORY

Blessed are you, O Mary, for your faith in the word of God. —**Blessed**...
The Most High exalts you forever, —**for your**...
Glory to you, Source of all Being, Eternal Word, and Holy Spirit. —**Blessed**...

CANTICLE OF ZECHARIAH

Ant May your servants be clothed in holiness, O God; may they sing for joy, alleluia.

INTERCESSIONS:

Mary enters heaven to the joy of all the angels and saints, and so we pray:
You are the glory of your people.

O God, through the intercession of Mary,
—number us among your saints in glory.
Jesus, through your mother, Mary, you learned to pray;
—teach us to pray and to be open to your Spirit.
You changed water into wine at the request of your mother;
—increase our faith in your care for our needs.
Your mother was your first disciple;
—as we meditate on the words of your gospel, may it bear fruit in our lives.

PRAYER: Glory to you, O God, in the entrance to eternal life of the ever Blessed Virgin Mary. Through her intercession, may we live the gospel of Jesus with constancy and love. As we celebrate her joy, may we imitate her fidelity. We ask this in the name of Jesus, the Eternal Word, who lives with you and with the Holy Spirit, forever. Amen.

DAYTIME PRAYER

Ant 1   Blessed is Mary who believed that what was spoken to her by God would be fulfilled. (Psalm 120)

Ant 2   Hail, full of grace; God is with you forever. (Psalm 129)

Ant 3   Through all generations, your name will be blessed. (Psalm 131)

(Prayer as in Morning Prayer)

EVENING PRAYER II

Ant 1   Mary is glorified with Christ; she dwells with the Trinity in heaven forever. (Psalm 122)

Ant 2   Your consent, O Mary, enabled God to take on our human nature and live among us. (Psalm 127)

Ant 3   God has given good things to the hungry, and has shown compassion to the lowly. (Eph. 1:3–10)

READING

RESPONSORY

The Savior dwelt within you, Holy Mother of God. —**The**...
Now you dwell with Christ forever, —**Holy**...
Glory to you, Source of all Being, Eternal Word, and Holy Spirit. —**The**...

CANTICLE OF MARY

Ant   God is glorified in Mary, who is taken into heaven and intercedes for us in her loving kindness.

INTERCESSIONS:

O God, you are blessed in your angels and saints. Most blessed are you in your daughter, Mary. In joy we proclaim:
> **You have lifted up the lowly.**

O God, you chose Mary to be the mother of Jesus and the mother of the church;
  —bless all who follow her example and bring Christ to the world.
Mary lived the mystery of Jesus and followed him to the cross;
  —give us the faith to follow you all the days of our lives.
Mary's glory is her union with your will;
  —through her intercession may we always do what is pleasing to you.
You called Mary to be the new Eve, the gate of heaven;
  —as we ponder your word, enkindle our hearts with love for your will, that we too may attain eternal life.

PRAYER: O God, you called Mary to be the mother of Jesus and the mother of our salvation. Let the example of her fidelity inspire us to open ourselves to the fullness of your grace, that we, too, may bear your Christ to the world. Grant this in the name of the same Jesus Chrsit who lives with you and the Holy Spirit forever. Amen.

HYMN

Ave, Regina caelorum,	Gaude, Virgo gloriosa
ave, Domina angelorum,	super omnes speciosa;
salve, radix, salve, porta,	vale, o valde decora,
ex qua mundo lux est orta.	et pro nobis Christum exora.

August 24

COMMEMORATION OF SIMONE WEIL

MORNING / EVENING PRAYER

(Psalms from the current week in the Psalter.)

Ant 1 Blessed are those who hunger and thirst for justice.

Ant 2 There is no greater love than to lay down one's life for one's friends.

Ant 3 Serving the least of my people, you give service to me.

READING

RESPONSORY

My only desire is to do your will, O God. —**My only**...
To love you and to serve you; —**to do**...
Glory to you, Source of all Being, Eternal Word, and Holy Spirit.
     —**My only**...

CANTICLE

Ant I bear the marks of your passion in my body and my spirit.

INTERCESSIONS:

O God of compassion, you will the good and happiness of all your people. We cry out to you:
     Give bread to the poor, and ease the burden of those in need.
Creator of all, your love is all-inclusive;
     —help us to open our hearts to every race and every need.
Christ Jesus, you sent the Samaritan woman to spread the good news;
     —raise up apostles in every age that we may worship in spirit and in truth.
Christ Jesus, you lauded the faith of the Canaanite woman;
     —may we recognize your Spirit that transcends our assumptions.
Christ Jesus, your love was poured out as you hung on the cross;
     —may all who give themselves for others know the peace the world cannot give.

PRAYER: O God, we thank you for the men and women like Simone Weil who live the good news of Jesus by their lives of selfless love and compassion. Teach us compassion that we too may be bearers of your gospel that all people may know you are with us, that they may enjoy fullness of life, and someday live with you for all eternity. Amen.

September 14
TRIUMPH OF THE CROSS
EVENING PRAYER I

Ant 1   The cross of Christ is the power and wisdom of God to those who believe, alleluia. (Psalm 147:1–11)

Ant 2   Jesus humbled himself and became obedient unto death, even death on a cross, alleluia. (Psalm 147:12–20)

Ant 3   God has exalted Christ above every other creature, alleluia. (Phil. 2:6–11)

READING

RESPONSORY

By the cross of Christ, we have been redeemed. —**By the**...
Through Jesus' death and resurrection, —**we have**...
Glory to you, Source of all Being, Eternal Word, and Holy Spirit. —**By the**...

CANTICLE OF MARY

Ant   I must be lifted up so that all who believe in me may have life eternal.

INTERCESSIONS:

Faithful cross, tree like no other, on you Christ triumphed over death. Let us pray:
Praise to you, Lord Jesus Christ!

Jesus, through your ignominious death on the cross,
   —give comfort and hope to those who suffer torture or imprisonment.
Jesus, pierced with a lance,
   —open our hearts in an outpouring of love and care for the poor.
Jesus, raised on high on the cross,
   —help us to rise above our petty desires and complaints.
Jesus, reviled and rejected on the cross,
   —deliver us from all forms of pride and human respect that would separate us from you.

PRAYER: O God, you love the world so much that you sent your Word Incarnate to save us and to bring us new life. Give us the grace to follow Jesus in humility, obedience, and persevering love. Let the glory of his cross enable us to bear the cost of discipleship and to remain true to you till the end. We commend our spirits to you this day and at the hour of our death. Amen.

MORNING PRAYER

(Psalms from Feasts and Solemnities)

Ant 1   I have been crucified with Christ; I live now, not I, but Christ lives in me.

Ant 2   If we are crucified with Christ, we will live with Christ forever.

Ant 3   By the power of the cross we have been redeemed; death no longer has dominion over us.

READING

RESPONSORY

Christ is triumphant over sin and death. —Christ...
By his cross, Jesus won victory, —over...
Glory to you, Source of all Being, Eternal Word, and Holy Spirit. —Christ...

CANTICLE OF ZECHARIAH

Ant   Jesus came into the world, not to condemn us, but to reconcile us to God.

INTERCESSIONS:

As the serpent was lifted up in the desert, Jesus was lifted up on the cross. In exaltation, we proclaim:

Indeed this is the Holy One of God!

Jesus, you died on the cross betrayed by your friends;
—give us the grace to be faithful to you till death.
Jesus, crucified for us, your love reaches to the ends of the earth;
—teach us how to proclaim your word to the world.
You forgave those who crucified you and prayed for us all;
—sign us with the cross of reconciliation and mercy.
Obedient to death on a cross, you are the source of our salvation;
—keep us faithful to your teaching and make us worthy of the healing power of your cross.

PRAYER: O God, you love the world so much that you sent your Word Incarnate to save us and to bring us new life. Give us the grace to follow Jesus in humility, obedience, and persevering love. Let the glory of his cross enable us to bear the cost of discipleship and to remain true to you till the end. We commend our spirits to you this day and at the hour of our death. Amen.

DAYTIME PRAYER

(Psalms from the current weekday in the Psalter)

Ant 1   If you wish to be my disciple, take up your cross and follow me.

Ant 2   Come to me, you who are burdened, and I will give you rest.

Ant 3   If you wish to save your life, you must lose it for my sake.

(Prayer as in Morning Prayer)

EVENING PRAYER II

Ant 1   We who were once dead because of sin, are now alive in God because of Christ's death on the cross. (Psalm 110:1–5, 7)

Ant 2   Christ endured the cross and was raised in glory. (Psalm 116:10–19)

Ant 3   We praise you, O Christ, who for our sake opened your arms on the cross. (Rev. 4:11; 5:9, 10, 12)

READING

RESPONSORY

Jesus, Lamb of God, have mercy on us. —**Jesus**...
You take away our sins by your holy cross, —**have**...
Glory to you, Source of all Being, Eternal Word, and Holy Spirit. —**Jesus**...

CANTICLE OF MARY

Ant Worthy is the Lamb who was slain to receive power and wealth, wisdom and honor.

INTERCESSIONS:

Faithful cross, tree like no other, on you Christ triumphed over death. Let us pray:
Praise to you, Lord Jesus Christ!

Jesus, through your ignominious death on the cross,
  —give comfort and hope to those who suffer torture or imprisonment.
Jesus, pierced with a lance,
  —open our hearts in an outpouring of love and care for the poor.
Jesus, raised on high on the cross,
  —help us to rise above our petty desires and complaints.
Jesus, reviled and rejected on the cross,
  —deliver us from all forms of pride and human respect that would separate us from you.

PRAYER: O God, you love the world so much that you sent your Word Incarnate to save us and to bring us new life. Give us the grace to follow Jesus in humility, obedience, and persevering love. Let the glory of his cross enable us to bear the cost of discipleship and to remain true to you till the end. We commend our spirits to you this day and at the hour of our death. Amen.

September 17

IN MEMORY OF DAME JULIAN OF NORWICH, MEISTER ECKHART, HILDEGARDE OF BINGEN, AND MYSTICS OF ALL AGES
MORNING / EVENING PRAYER*

(Psalms from the current week in the Psalter.)

Ant 1 They who live in the goodness of their nature live in God's love; and love has no why.

Ant 2 She is with all and in all and of beauty so great in her mystery that none could comprehend how sweetly she bears with us.

Ant 3 God did not say, "You shall not be troubled, you shall not be diseased; but you shall not be overcome."

READING

RESPONSORY

The almighty truth of the Trinity is our Father; the deep wisdom of the Trinity is our Mother. —**The almighty**...

*Antiphons, responsory and canticle based on their writings.

The high goodness of the Trinity is our Lord; —the deep...
Glory to you, Source of all Being, Eternal Word, and Holy Spirit. —The
 almighty...

CANTICLE

Ant   This has ever been a comfort to me; that I chose Jesus for my Heaven.

INTERCESSIONS:

We praise you, O God, for all the ways you reveal yourself to us, and so we say:
 Show us your face and we shall be saved.

O God, Julian recognized you as Father and as Mother;
 —may we appreciate the fullness of your reality and the depth of your
  mystery.
O God, Hildegarde praised you in poetry and song;
 —bless all those who enrich our worship with their gifts.
O God, through your servant Meister Eckhart, you revealed the depths of your
 indwelling presence;
 —sharpen our awareness of your presence that we may know you are all
  in all.
As Julian contemplated the hazel nut, she experienced you in all of creation;
 —may we know you as God-with-us and so proclaim, "All shall be well"!
O God, in Hildegarde you give us a model of a woman who theologized from
 the depths of her experience;
 —may our theology today reflect your interaction in our lives.
Meister Eckhart named you as the God of compassion;
 —deepen our compassion and may it extend to people, the animals, and the
  elements that sustain us.

PRAYER: O God, your voice echoes through the centuries in the writings of
            those who were your intimate friends. May we grow ever closer to
            you that those who follow us may know your revelation in this our
            time. We ask this in the name of Jesus who lives with you and the
            Holy Spirit, now and forever. Amen.

September 27

ST. VINCENT de PAUL – ST. LOUISE de MARILLAC

(See March 15)

October 1 / December 3

ST. THÉRÈSE OF LISIEUX – ST. FRANCIS XAVIER

MORNING / EVENING PRAYER*

(Psalms from the current week in the Psalter.)

Ant 1   What touches me alone, touches me not at all; but what touches God,
        touches me to the quick.

*Antiphons, responsory and canticle based on their writings.

Ant 2   We can never have too much confidence in the good God. As we hope, so shall we receive; God is so mighty, so merciful.

Ant 3   In your dealings with all, be pleasant and cheerful.

READING

RESPONSORY

We are the body of Christ; in the heart of the church I will be love.
    —We...
We are the people of God; **—in the...**
Glory to you, Source of all Being, Eternal Word, and Holy Spirit. **—We...**

CANTICLE

Ant   We must become as little children to learn the language of God's business; and grant that we may imitate the little ones in simplicity and purity of soul.

INTERCESSIONS:

O God, you have inspired your church to name Francis and Thérèse as special patrons of the missions and so we pray:
                May their desires enkindle our own.

O God, you sent Francis to preach the good news to the nations of the Indies;
    —may we, by our example, preach the good news in our own spheres of influence that others may be drawn to you.
Enclosed in a monastery, Thérèse spanned the earth through prayer;
    —deepen the longings of our hearts and strengthen our determination to take the time to pray.
Francis touched others by his cheerfulness and happy disposition in spite of the burdens and sufferings he bore;
    —may we hold our burdens lightly so that we can ease the sufferings of others and give them comfort.
Thérèse, saint of the ordinary, soared like an eagle in her desire to bring all to Christ;
    —help us, O God, to let every moment of our day enrich the life of your church.

PRAYER: O God, grant us the grace to understand that you can use each and every lifestyle to bring our world to fullness of life. Whether we circle the globe or remain where we are, help us to touch the lives of others in selflessness and compassion. Grant this through Jesus who is our way, our truth and our life. Amen.

October 4

ST. FRANCIS OF ASSISI – ST. CLARE OF ASSISI

(See August 11)

October 6 / November 22

JEAN-PIERRE MÉDAILLE, SJ – JEANNE FONTBONNE
(Mother St. John)

MORNING / EVENING PRAYER*

(Psalms from the current week in the Psalter.)

Ant 1 That all may be one, as you are in me, and I in you.

Ant 2 Love one another as I have loved you.

Ant 2 Put aside your old self so that you may emerge anew.

READING

RESPONSORY

Love your neighbors as yourself; love them as Christ Jesus loves you. —**Love**...
In living your life, —**love them**...
Glory to you, Source of all Being, Eternal Word, and Holy Spirit. —**Love**...

CANTICLE

Ant In life have only one desire: to be and to become the person God wills
in nature and in grace.

INTERCESSIONS:

Most gracious God, we place our trust in you. In confidence we pray:
That all may be one.

Jesus, you inspired Jean-Pierre Médaille to found a congregation animated by
great love, the Congregation of the Sisters of St. Joseph;
—may all women and men dedicated to serving others experience the gift
of your love in their ministry.
You call us by name to be one with you and with one another;
—help all teachers and ministers of your word to be living signs of your love.
You raised up Jeanne Fontbonne to reorganize the Sisters of St. Joseph in France
and to extend their services throughout the global community;
—may all missionaries be graced to walk humbly, to listen sensitively, and
to serve justly.
You invite us to build our future in fidelity to your gospel message;
—enable all members of faith communities to work for justice and peace, and
to alleviate the causes of oppression.
You share life with us in you banquet of love;
—may we be faithful to our commitments, respectful of our differences, and
one in our desire to love God.

PRAYER: God of love, you are rich in mercy and compassion. May we be so
united with you that we join your vision to our eyes; your words to
our tongues; your meekness to our gentleness; and your self-
emptying to our humility. Remove from us all self-seeking and root
us in loving and joyous service. Grant this in the mystery of your
triune life enfolding us forever. Amen.

*Antiphons, canticle and prayer based on his writings.

October 15 / December 14

ST. TERESA OF AVILA – ST. JOHN OF THE CROSS

MORNING / EVENING PRAYER

(Psalms from the current week in the Psalter.)

Ant 1　Wisdom is radiant and unfading and she is easily discerned by those who love her.

Ant 2　To fix one's thoughts on wisdom is perfect understanding. The one who is vigilant on her account will soon be free from care.

Ant 3　I will tell you what wisdom is and how she came to be and I will hide no secrets from you.

READING

RESPONSORY

I prayed and understanding was given to me. —**I prayed**...
I called upon God and the spirit of wisdom came to me; —**and understanding**...
Glory to you, Source of all Being, Eternal Word, and Holy Spirit.
　　—**I prayed**...

CANTICLE

Ant　Whoever drinks of the water that I shall give will never thirst. The water that I shall give will become an inner spring welling up to eternal life.

INTERCESSIONS:

O God of abundant life, you gave to Teresa and John the gift of lighting up the contemplative journey. Aware of our deepest desires we ask:
　　　　　　　　　Give us living water.

They went to Jesus as to a rich mine;
　—give us a spirit of wisdom and revelation in the knowledge of Jesus Christ.
They knew that prayer strengthens us for service;
　—help us to value prayer, to be able to do less to be more effective.
They found you in light and in darkness;
　—may times of difficulty strengthen our trust.
They experienced you at the center of their being;
　—may all that we do lead us to gratitude and adoration.
They reformed the order of Carmel;
　—may all Carmelites be faithful to their spirit and teachings.

PRAYER:　Most loving God, you have given us John and Teresa to reveal your desire to love and be loved by us, and to show us the way to the fullness of our contemplative gifts. Through their intercession and guidance, may we come to know you at our center and to be energized by your divine compassion for the world and all its peoples. Amen.

October 21 / November 17

JANET ERSKINE STUART – BL. PHILIPPINE DUCHESNE

MORNING / EVENING PRAYER*

(Psalms from the current week in the Psalter.)

Ant 1 Life only demands from us the strength we possess. Only one feat is possible: not to run away.

Ant 2 If we love well and much, we shall need no other preparation for death.

Ant 3 God will teach you without your knowing how, and you will hardly know what until afterwards.

READING

RESPONSORY

Increase our longings for you, O God, we thirst for your presence. —**Increase**...
In darkness and in light, —**we**...
Glory to you, Source of all Being, Eternal Word, and Holy Spirit. —**Increase**...

CANTICLE

Ant We must bear our burden of years along with the suffering that comes from unhappy events whether in public affairs or in our personal lives.

INTERCESSIONS:

O God, through the intercession of Philippine Duchesne and Janet Erskine Stuart, we pray for leaders of religious women, as we say:
Spirit of Wisdom, be with us.

O God, your Word became incarnate to show us the way,
   —may we grow in the mind, heart and attitudes of Jesus.
As Philippine braved new frontiers to serve those in need,
   —bless all missionaries and those they serve.
In Janet Erskine Stuart, you gave us a model of enabling leadership,
   —help all administrators empower those entrusted to their care.
O God, you used Philippine and Janet as spiritual guides for many who knew them,
   —enlighten all who act as spiritual companions to others.

PRAYER: Most gracious God, hear our prayers through the intercession of Philippine and Janet, who served you by serving others. Enkindle in us the zeal kindled in them that we, too, may participate in bringing this world to wholeness. This we ask through their intercession and in the name of Jesus whom they loved and served. Amen.

*Antiphons, responsory and canticle based on their writings.

November 1

ALL SAINTS

EVENING PRAYER I

Ant 1 Blessed are you, O God, in all your saints. (Psalm 113)

Ant 2 A multitude that no one could count stood before the Lamb, praising God. (Psalm 147:12–20)

Ant 3 Salvation belongs to God who sits upon the throne, and to the Lamb! (Rev. 19:1–7)

READING

RESPONSORY

These are the people that praise you, O God, and glorify your name. —**These**...
They dwell with you forever, —**and glorify**...
Glory to you, Source of all Being, Eternal Word, and Holy Spirit. —**These**...

CANTICLE OF MARY

Ant Blessed are the poor in spirit, the reign of God is theirs.

INTERCESSIONS:

God is blessed forever in the angels and in the saints. With them we pray:

Glory and praise to you, O God!

O Christ, like good earth the saints received the seed of your word and bore fruit a hundredfold;
—help us to draw courage and inspiration from their lives.
The saving gift of your cross enabled the martyrs to offer life for life;
—have mercy on those who are called to suffer for you; be their strength and courage.
You gave the gift of holiness to the simple and the great, to celibates and to those who are married;
—may we recognize your grace in the calling we now follow.
Women and men of every time and place have longed to see your face and to serve you unreservedly;
—each generation tells of your goodness and love.

PRAYER: O God, we praise you as we celebrate the company of martyrs and saints whose faithful witness reveals your steadfast love. May the hope that they give us nourish our longing to love and serve you more. Without you we can do nothing; remember your love, and make us worthy of the company of the blessed. This we ask in the name of Jesus, and in the names of all our loved ones who have joined the multitude singing your praise forever. Amen.

MORNING PRAYER

(Psalms from Feasts and Solemnities)

Ant 1 The saints have found eternal peace in God's presence.

Ant 2 All the saints praise you, O God, and proclaim your goodness to your people.

Ant 3 Your saints, O God, are a light to the nations.

READING

RESPONSORY

We glorify you, O God, in your saints who intercede on our behalf. —We...
We delight in the goodness of those, —who...
Glory to you, Source of all Being, Eternal Word, and Holy Spirit. —We...

CANTICLE OF ZECHARIAH

Ant　Blessed are the pure in heart, for they shall see God.

INTERCESSIONS:

Women and men of every age rejoice with the angels in eternal glory. In joy let us pray:

Blessed be God forever!

O God, Source of all life, the saints heard your creative voice in the depths of
their hearts;
　—help us to silence the distractions in our lives; complete the work in us that
　you have begun.
You inspire people of every age to walk steadfastly in the way of the gospel;
　—raise up saints in our day that your love for us may be revealed in their lives.
You bless the singlehearted and reveal yourself to them;
　—through the intercession of the saints, help us to see the truth and live it
　with courage.
Through the lives of your saints, you continue the mission of salvation;
　—give us the grace to embrace your call with generosity and perseverance.

PRAYER:　O God, we praise you as we celebrate the company of martyrs and
　　　　　saints whose faithful witness reveals your steadfast love. May the
　　　　　hope that they give us nourish our longing to love and serve you
　　　　　more. Without you we can do nothing; remember your love, and
　　　　　make us worthy of the company of the blessed. This we ask in the
　　　　　name of Jesus, and in the names of all our loved ones who have
　　　　　joined the multitude singing your praise forever. Amen.

DAYTIME PRAYER

Ant 1　The saints are those who have run the race and won the everlasting
　　　　crown. (Psalm 120)
Ant 2　The followers of the living God rejoice in light forever. (Psalm 121)
Ant 3　Those who were faithful to the end have received blessing and reward
　　　　from God, their savior. (Psalm 122)

(Prayer as in Morning Prayer)

EVENING PRAYER II

Ant 1 See what love God has bestowed upon us, that we should be called children of God. (Psalm 110:1–5, 7)

Ant 2 We have been chosen by God to follow the Lamb that was slain and now reigns in glory. (Psalm 116:10–19)

Ant 3 Jesus said to his followers: I have chosen you to bear much fruit and to glorify the One who sent me. (Rev. 4:11; 5:9, 10, 12)

READING

RESPONSORY

We praise you, O God, and rejoice with those who love you. —**We**...
May we live with you forever, —**and**...
Glory to you, Source of all Being, Eternal Word, and Holy Spirit. —**We**...

CANTICLE OF MARY

Ant Blessed are you who hunger and thirst for holiness, you shall be satisfied.

INTERCESSIONS:

God is blessed forever in the angels and in the saints. With them we pray:
Glory and praise to you, O God!

O Christ, like good earth the saints received the seed of your word and bore fruit a hundredfold;
  —help us to draw courage and inspiration from their lives.
The saving gift of your cross enabled the martyrs to offer life for life;
  —have mercy on those who are called to suffer for you; be their strength and courage.
You gave the gift of holiness to the simple and the great, to celibates and to those who are married;
  —may we recognize your grace in the calling we now follow.
Women and men of every time and place have longed to see your face and to serve you unreservedly;
  —each generation tells of your goodness and love.

PRAYER: O God, we praise you as we celebrate the company of martyrs and saints whose faithful witness reveals your steadfast love. May the hope that they give us nourish our longing to love and serve you more. Without you we can do nothing; remember your love, and make us worthy of the company of the blessed. This we ask in the name of Jesus, and in the names of all our loved ones who have joined the multitude singing your praise forever. Amen.

November 2
ALL SOULS DAY
MORNING PRAYER

Ant 1 From the earth you formed me, with flesh you clothed me; Christ, my Redeemer, raise me up on the last day. (Psalm 51)

Ant 2 May it please you to rescue me; look upon me and help me. (Isaiah 38:10–14, 17b–20)

Ant 3 My soul is thirsting for you, the living God; when shall I see you face to face? (Psalm 146)

READING

RESPONSORY

I know that my Redeemer lives and on the last day I shall rise again. —**I**...
My own eyes will gaze on God; —**on the**...
Glory to you, Source of all Being, Eternal Word, and Holy Spirit. —**I**...

CANTICLE OF ZECHARIAH

Ant I am the Resurrection and the Life. Those who live and believe in me I will raise up on the last day.

INTERCESSIONS:

Let us pray for an increase of faith in Jesus, the Resurrection and the Life:
O God, hear us.

In death, O Christ, life is changed, not taken away;
 —make us open in this life to your call to growth.
You wept for Lazarus and comforted his sisters;
 —show yourself to the dying and comfort those who mourn.
You bled in agony the night before you died;
 —give courage and strength to those who fear death.
Time passes swiftly; we do not know the day of death;
 —help us to cherish the lifetime given to us and to make each moment a preparation for our last.
You promised eternal life to all who follow your way;
 —raise up all who have died, particularly those we have loved and those who have loved us; grant that we may share eternal glory with them.

PRAYER: O God, our birth is the fruit of your love; our redemption, the fruit of your mercy. Help us to remember your goodness and make our lives a worthy revelation of your care. Let the hour of death be a longed-for reunion with you, our Creator, Savior, and Sanctifier. Amen.

DAYTIME PRAYER

Ant 1 You will hear me and rescue me when I call to you. (Psalm 70)

Ant 2 Look on the faith of your servants, and save those who hope in you. (Psalm 85)

Ant 3 Do not hold our sins against us; remember your saving love. (Psalm 86)

(Prayer as in Morning Prayer)

EVENING PRAYER

Ant 1   You are my savior; all my hope is in you. (Psalm 121)

Ant 2   I wait in hope for you, O my God; I trust in your word. (Psalm 130)

Ant 3   Jesus died for us that we might know eternal life. (Phil. 2:6–11)

READING

RESPONSORY

Praise to you, Christ Jesus, our redeemer; you conquered death for us.
   —**Praise**...
We will see your glory; —**you**...
Glory to you, Source of all Being, Eternal Word, and Holy Spirit. —**Praise**...

CANTICLE OF MARY

Ant   If the grain of wheat falls to the ground and dies, it produces an abundant harvest.

INTERCESSIONS:

Eye has not seen, nor ear heard, what you have prepared for those who love you, and so we pray:
   O God, all our hope is in your promise.
O God, we long to see your face and to praise you forever;
   —let this time of "not-seeing" strengthen our faith and hope in you.
For those who fear death, for those who see you as an exacting judge,
   —let our lives of trust and love be a comfort and a guide.
You sent your Christ not to judge, but that we might have eternal life;
   —teach us to look forward to our death as we do the birth of a child: to new life in your presence.
O Christ, many have lived without the consolation of your gospel; many die alone and afraid;
   —Heart of Jesus, once in agony, have pity on the dying.

PRAYER: O God, our birth is the fruit of your love; our redemption, the fruit of your mercy. Help us to remember your goodness and make our lives a worthy revelation of your care. Let the hour of death be a longed for reunion with you, our Creator, Savior, and Sanctifier. Amen.

November 11

CATHERINE McAULEY

MORNING / EVENING PRAYER*

(Psalms from the current week in the Psalter.)

Ant 1   Blessed are the merciful for they shall obtain mercy.

Ant 2   Teach me goodness, discipline and knowledge.

Ant 3   However painful the cross may be which you have prepared for me, I await it through your grace with entire submission.

*Antiphons and responsory based on her writings.

READING

RESPONSORY

I desire only to do your will, my God. —I desire...
To serve you in your people, —and to do...
Glory to you, Source of all Being, Eternal Word, and Holy Spirit. —I desire...

CANTICLE

Ant Whatever you do to the least of my people you do to me.

INTERCESSIONS:

O God, you chose Catherine McAuley to found an order dedicated to works of
mercy. With grateful hearts we pray:

> **We praise you; we thank you; we glorify you.**

Reared in a family with different religious persuasions, Catherine experienced
  love and returned love;
  —grant that the differences among us may enable us to grow in respect and
    appreciation for one another.
You call us to mercy rather than to sacrifice;
  —give us a spirit of moderation in all that we do.
Like Mary beneath the cross, Catherine suffered the loss of many she dearly
  loved;
  —strengthen those who attend and serve loved ones who are dying.
In your wisdom you led Catherine to found the Sisters of Mercy,
  —grant them the graces they need to carry on your work in this world.

PRAYER: O God, the poor and the needy are with us always. Grant that we
may recognize them in our families, our communities, as well as in
our cities, or in places far away. May they know your care and
concern in those who minister to them. This we ask of you through
the mercy of Jesus who died that we may live. Amen.

November 13

ST. FRANCES XAVIER CABRINI

MORNING / EVENING PRAYER

(Psalms from the current week in the Psalter.)

Ant 1   How blessed the woman whose heart goes out to the poor; those who
trust in God delight in showing mercy.

Ant 2   Go out to all nations and spread the word of the gospel.

Ant 3   You are the light of the world; a city set on a hill cannot be hidden.

READING

RESPONSORY

My heart is glad and my soul rejoices. —**My**...
You have shown me the path to life, —**and my**...
Glory to you, Source of all Being, Eternal Word, and Holy Spirit. —**My**...

CANTICLE

Ant Jesus went about all the cities and villages, teaching in their synagogues, preaching the gospel and healing every disease and infirmity.

INTERCESSIONS:

O Christ, you commissioned your early disciples to preach your gospel to all the nations. Down through the centuries, men and women have left their native lands to spread the good news to other nations and peoples and so we pray:

Praise to you, Lord Jesus Christ!

Christ our Redeemer, your Church has named Mother Cabrini the patron of emigrants;
—may they receive welcome and hospitality in their adopted homelands.
You came to serve the lowly and the poor;
—may the cause of justice triumph over personal or national greed.
As a child you fled to Egypt for safety;
—protect all refugees seeking asylum from unjust oppression.
You inspired Mother Cabrini to become a citizen of her new land;
—may all exercise their citizenship responsibly according to gospel values.
Mother Cabrini served you in the sick and the poor;
—may her work continue that they may know your love and your healing.

PRAYER: O God, we thank you for all the good you accomplished through the life of Mother Cabrini, and through those who have followed her example. May our country be blessed with a greater desire to embrace those seeking freedom or refuge. We ask this through Jesus Christ who lives with you, Source of all Being, and with the Holy Spirit, forever. Amen.

November 17

BL. PHILIPPINE DUCHESNE – JANET ERSKINE STUART

(See October 21

November 22

JEANNE FONTBONNE – JEAN-PIERRE MÉDAILLE, SJ
(Mother St. John)

(See October 6)

November 26

SOJOURNER TRUTH – FREDERICK DOUGLASS

(See February 20)

November 29

IN MEMORY OF DOROTHY DAY
MORNING PRAYER

(Psalms from the current week in the Psalter.)

Ant 1   When did we see you hungry and give you to eat? When did we see you thirsty and give you to drink?

Ant 2   Blessed are those who suffer persecution for justice sake, for God is their reward.

Ant 3   If you would be perfect, give all to the poor and come follow me.

READING

RESPONSORY

She opens her heart to the poor, and reaches out her hand to the needy.
  —**She**...
She opens her mouth with wisdom —**and reaches**...
Glory to you, Source of all Being, Eternal Word, and Holy Spirit. —**She**...

CANTICLE

Ant   God is in the midst of her, she shall not be moved.

INTERCESSIONS:

O God, you gave us Jesus to teach us that you hear the cry of the poor and the needy. Give us hearts of flesh that we may respond with compassion as we pray:
Have mercy on us.

O Christ, you reached out to the lepers and healed them,
  —help us to embrace the outcasts of our society.
You socialized with the tax collectors and sinners,
  —show us how to break down the barriers that divide us.
You talked with the Samaritan woman and healed the child of the
  Canaanite woman,
  —may we learn how to cross the thresholds of prejudice.
You fed the hungry by giving them bread of wheat and the bread of
  your body,
  —teach us how to feed each other.
You had compassion on the poor and the suffering,
  —may we see you in the street people, the destitute and the hopeless.

PRAYER: O God, look with tender mercy on the needs of the poor and the alienated, and teach us to hear and answer their cries. We praise you for those who have given their lives to serve you in the poor. May they know your support and love as they follow the way of Jesus. Bless especially all who serve the poor in the Catholic Worker movement. We ask this in the name of Jesus. Amen.

The Last Thursday in November
THANKSGIVING DAY

MORNING PRAYER

(Psalms from the current week in the Psalter.)

Ant 1   It is right to give you thanks and praise.

Ant 2   We praise you for the gift of your harvest.

Ant 3   You have blessed our land with your bounty; we lift our hearts in thanksgiving.

READING

RESPONSORY

Come, let us sing to God and shout for joy. —**Come**...
Let us approach with praise and thanksgiving, —**and shout**...
Glory to you, Source of all Being, Eternal Word, and Holy Spirit. —**Come**...

CANTICLE

Ant   How can we repay you, O God, for your goodness to us.

INTERCESSIONS:

O God, you have blessed our country with an abundance of your gifts and so we say:

We give you thanks, O God.

Most gracious God, you have blessed our land with more than we need,
  —increase our spirit of generosity that we may share with other lands.
You have saved our country from the ravages of war,
  —may we never cause destruction to other nations.
You have graced our country with great natural beauty,
  —grant that we may never exploit it, but endeavor to protect it.
O God, our forebears sat at table with our native Americans giving thanks for your bounty,
  —help us in our endeavors to restore the rights and dignity of those who inhabited this land before us.
You continually call us forward,
  —may we step into the future ever conscious of our responsibility to all humankind.

PRAYER: God, most bounteous, we are mindful that you gift us at each moment. Help us to receive all as gift and give you thanks that you are our God. Continue to grant us your favors and help us, as a government and as a people, to share your gifts with all in need. This we ask through Jesus, who lives with you and the Holy Spirit forever and ever. Amen.

December 2

COMMEMORATION OF MAURA CLARKE, ITA FORD, DOROTHY KAZEL AND JEAN DONOVAN

MORNING / EVENING PRAYER

(Psalms from the current week in the Psalter.)

Ant 1   Our lips will praise you, for sweeter than life is your merciful love.

Ant 2   They girded themselves with your strength. The light they have kindled will never go out.

Ant 3   Give them the reward of their deeds, for they served you in the poor.

READING

RESPONSORY

Our God is a stronghold for the oppressed, a stronghold in times of trouble.
   —**Our**...
Those who know your name put their trust in you, —**a stronghold**...
Glory to you, Source of all Being, Eternal Word, and Holy Spirit. —**Our**...

CANTICLE

Ant   You shall love your God with all your heart, and with all your soul and with all your mind, and your neighbor as yourself. Do this and you will live.

INTERCESSIONS:

O God, you have inspired men and women to follow Jesus, your Incarnate Word, who gave his life that we may have life. We lift our voices and say:
   Blessed are they who suffer persecution for the sake of the gospel.

Through the witness of Maura Clarke, Ita Ford, Dorothy Kazel and
   Jean Donovan,
   —may more people be inspired to serve the homeless and the oppressed.
May all who have died in Latin America for the sake of justice,
   —be seeds of liberty for all the oppressed.
God of freedom, protect the poor and the helpless,
   —from the greed of large corporations and those seeking personal profit.
Jesus, you lived in a land held captive by imperial Rome,
   —grant all peoples the right of self-determination that they may forge their
   own destinies.
God of the Americas, Christ of the Andes, Our Lady of Guadalupe,
   —look with love and compassion on the peoples of Central and South
   America, and grant them freedom from all oppression.

PRAYER: O God, lover of the poor and oppressed, in our remembrance of these four courageous women may we honor all the nameless men, women and children whose lives were forfeited by violence and hatred. May they now know your peace and the joy of seeing you face to face. We ask this through the intercession of all these victims who now stand before the Lamb singing your praises. Amen.

December 3

ST. FRANCIS XAVIER – ST. THÉRÈSE OF LISIEUX

(See October 1)

December 8

IMMACULATE CONCEPTION

EVENING PRAYER I

Ant 1 God has done marvelous deeds, let us sing a new song to the Most High. (Psalm 113)

Ant 2 You have called me, O God, to serve you in holiness. (Psalm 147:12–20)

Ant 3 Mother of mercy and holy hope, be near to those who pray to you. (Eph. 1:3–10)

READING

RESPONSORY

O Mary, Mother of the Christ, intercede for us. —**O Mary**...

God preserved you from sin; —**intercede**...

Glory to you, Source of all Being, Eternal Word, and Holy Spirit. —**O Mary**...

CANTICLE OF MARY

Ant You who are mighty have made me great; holy be your name.

INTERCESSIONS:

Let us praise God who has given us Mary as a model of holiness. We pray to her:
Mother of Christ, teach us to hear the word of God.

O Christ, be praised in Mary, comforter of the afflicted;
—teach us to be a healing presence in the lives of others.

Be praised in Mary, queen of martyrs;
—let all who bear the cross for your name's sake know her help and protection.

Be praised in Mary, queen of confessors;
—let all who confess your name in word or deed find justice and encouragement in the church.

Be praised in Mary, queen of peace;
—give us forgiving hearts and bless our world with the peace that only you can give.

PRAYER: O God, you have given us Mary, the mother of Jesus, to encourage and guide us on the way to union with you. Let her life of loving obedience and humble prayer be a beacon of light and courage for us as we seek to follow your Christ. This we ask in the name of that same Jesus Christ, the Eternal Word, who lives with you and with the Holy Spirit, forever. Amen.

MORNING PRAYER

(Psalms from Feasts and Solemnities)

Ant 1   Mother of the Word Incarnate, through you we received the Bread of Life. (Psalm 113)

Ant 2   Mother of the Word Incarnate, your holy womb was the chalice of our salvation. (Psalm 147:12–20)

Ant 3   Mother of the Word Incarnate, you gave us the body and blood of Jesus, the Christ, the Holy One of God. (Eph. 1:3–10)

READING

RESPONSORY

You have made me a vessel of salvation; a font of living water. —**You**...
Within my womb springs forth, —**a font**...
Glory to you, Source of all Being, Eternal Word, and Holy Spirit. —**You**...

CANTICLE OF ZECHARIAH

Ant   O Mary, you are the Dawn; through you all creation will see the Light of the World.

INTERCESSIONS:

Let us praise the Holy Spirit who throughout the centuries has inspired the faithful to call upon God through the intercession of Mary:
Lead us in the way of truth.

O God, be praised through Mary, help of christians;
   —help us all to proclaim the gospel with our lives.
Be praised through Mary, refuge of sinners;
   —teach us to support one another in our efforts to follow your will.
Be praised in Mary, ark of the covenant;
   —let our lives bear witness to your abiding presence in us.
Be praised in Mary, mother of good counsel;
   —form us to be discerning people.

PRAYER: O God, you have given us Mary, the mother of Jesus, to encourage and guide us on the way to union with you. Let her life of loving obedience and humble prayer be a beacon of light and courage for us as we seek to follow your Christ. This we ask in the name of that same Jesus Christ, the Eternal Word, who lives with you and with the Holy Spirit, forever. Amen.

DAYTIME PRAYER

Ant 1   Blessed are you, O Mary, for in you God's promise was fulfilled. (Psalm 120)

Ant 2   Rejoice, O highly favored daughter; the Holy Spirit has overshadowed you. (Psalm 129)

Ant 3   Blessed are you above all God's people; in you the Word became flesh. (Psalm 131)

(Prayer as in Morning Prayer)

EVENING PRAYER II

Ant 1   God has raised up the lowly and filled the hungry with good things. (Psalm 122)

Ant 2   Blessed are you among women, and blessed is the fruit of your womb. (Psalm 127)

Ant 3   You are the new Eve, the beginning of a new creation. (Eph. 1:3–10)

READING

RESPONSORY

You are the mother of holy hope, the glory of Jerusalem. —**You**...
The fairest daughter of Israel, —**the glory**...
Glory to you, Source of all Being, Eternal Word, and Holy Spirit. —**You are**...

CANTICLE OF MARY

Ant   In you all women have been blessed; in you all creation has found hope.

INTERCESSIONS:

Let us praise God who has given us Mary as a model of holiness. We pray to her:
   Mother of Christ, teach us to hear the word of God.

O Christ, be praised in Mary, comforter of the afflicted;
   —teach us to be a healing presence in the lives of others.
Be praised in Mary, queen of martyrs;
   —let all who bear the cross for your name's sake know her help and
   protection.
Be praised in Mary, queen of confessors;
   —let all who confess your name in word or deed find justice and
   encouragement in the church.
Be praised in Mary, queen of peace;
   —give us forgiving hearts and bless our world with the peace that only you
   can give.

PRAYER: O God, you have given us Mary, the mother of Jesus, to encourage and guide us on the way to union with you. Let her life of loving obedience and humble prayer be a beacon of light and courage for us as we seek to follow your Christ. This we ask in the name of that same Jesus Christ, the Eternal Word, who lives with you and with the Holy Spirit, forever. Amen.

December 10

IN MEMORY OF THOMAS MERTON

MORNING / EVENING PRAYER

(Psalms from the current week in the Psalter.)

Ant 1 Blessed are the peacemakers for they shall be called children of God.

Ant 2 You made us for yourself, O God; our hearts are restless until they rest in you.

Ant 3 I lift up my eyes to your holy mountain.

READING

RESPONSORY

I have trusted in your steadfast love. —**I have**...
My heart shall rejoice in your salvation, —**in your**...
Glory to you, Source of all Being, Eternal Word, and Holy Spirit. —**I have**...

CANTICLE

Ant Wisdom is radiant and unfading, easily discerned by those who love her, and found by those who seek her.

INTERCESSIONS:

O God, you call us to holiness of life; we cry out with great earnestness:
We long to see your face.

Strengthen those whose unique service to humanity is a life of contemplation,
—that others may be encouraged to seek intimacy with God in their way.
Encourage us to go beyond clear and comfortable ideas of God,
—to a deeper trust, purer love and more complete surrender to One beyond our understanding.
Lead us through contemplation to spiritual understanding, freedom and a new capacity to love,
—that our action in and for the world may spring from you.
Help us to value prayer and solitude,
—that we may live in your presence and always walk in truth.

PRAYER: O God, enable us to live in the love that invites us to union with you and all creation. May we be enriched by the depths that contemplative love unfolds for us in our world and have the courage to surrender in total freedom to the God of our life. Amen.

December 14

ST. JOHN OF THE CROSS – ST. TERESA OF AVILA

(see October 15)

CANTICLE OF ZECHARIAH

Blessed are you, God of Israel
for you have visited and redeemed your people,
and have raised up a horn of salvation for us
in the house of your servant.

As you spoke through the mouths
of your holy prophets from of old,
that we should be saved from our enemies,
and from the hand of all who oppress us;

to perform the mercy promised to our ancestors,
and to remember your holy covenant,

the oath you swore to Abraham and Sarah,
to grant us deliverance from evil,
that we might serve you without fear,
in holiness and righteousness
all the days of our lives.

And you, child,
will be called the prophet of the Most High,
for you will go before the Holy One
to prepare God's ways,

to give knowledge of salvation to God's people
in the forgiveness of their sins,

through the tender mercy of our God
when the day shall dawn upon us from on high

to give light to those who sit in darkness
and in the shadow of death,
to guide our feet
into the way of peace.   Glory* . . .